D0926477

Stephen Olford is one of my favorite preachers! God always speaks to me when I hear God's truth's expounded by him.

Kay Arthur, Founder, Precept Ministries

Some books on preaching contain much useful information. Other reflect wide experience. Still others have passion. But this new book on passionate expository preaching by Stephen and David Olford has all three, and I commend it to preachers everywhere.

James Montgomery Boice, Minister,
Tenth Presbyterian Church, Philadelphia

Stephen Olford's preaching and personal example of industry, integrity, and intensity have served as a point of reference for me in my ministry. With his gifted son, David, he has given us a rich resource that I trust all preachers will read to their profit and their congregations' blessing.

Stuart Briscoe, Senior Pastor, Elmbrook Church

The great strength of this book is that, within its heritage, it powerfully melds together the character of the preacher, the nature of expository preaching, and a passionate concern to preserve and promulgate the good news that must be preached.

Don Carson, Research Professor of New Testament,
Trinity Evangelical Divinity School

Teaching scores of preachers each year to refine their preaching skills at the Stephen Olford Center of Biblical Preaching has well prepared both of these Doctors of preaching to prescribe for all of us what is practical, spiritual, and unapologetically biblical for preachers committed to proclaiming the healing power of the gospel.

Bryan Chapell, President
Covenant Theological Seminary

A tremendous treatise on Spirit-anointed proclamation of the word of God! Giving their counsel the ring of authenticity is the authors' own exemplary practice of what they teach.

Robert E. Coleman, Director
of School of World Mission & Evangelism,
Trinity Evangelical Divinity School

I wholeheartedly recommend this landmark book to every serious-minded man of God who truly desires to preach the Word of God through the Spirit of God for the sole purpose of exalting the Son of God.

> James O. Davis, National Evangelists Representative,
> The General Council of the Assemblies of God

This work promises to become one of the standard texts on preaching for many years to come. This is must reading for every pulpiteer.

> Tony Evans, Senior Pastor,
> Oak Cliff Bible Fellowship

This is an excellent guide and resource for developing an expository preaching ministry that the church so desperately needs.

> Lewis A. Drummond,
> Billy Graham Professor of Evangelism and Church Growth,
> Beeson Divinity School

If we used the term as we once did, we would say Stephen Olford is a "prince of the pulpit." He is known as one of the world's most outstanding expository preachers. With his son David, he has given us the essence of his rich experience and unequaled expertise. Every preacher—regardless of age and experience—will profit from this volume."

> Maxie D. Dunnam, President
> Asbury Theological Seminary

Drs. Stephen and David Olford's work is required reading for the preacher who desires an exemplary Christian walk worthy of his calling and who aspires to more effectively proclaim the truths of God's Word.

> James Flanagan, President,
> Luther Rice Seminary

I welcome this book with enthusiasm and pray that God will use it mightily to bring about a thoroughgoing Reformation based on the faithful and fervent proclamation of God's Holy Word. *Soli Deo Gloria!*

> Timothy George, Dean,
> Beeson Divinity School, Samford University

Every serious preacher has been waiting for this most excellent book. It is a textbook, a devotional book, a book of instruction, and a book that will cause a paradigm shift for the minister who desires to grow in his skill as a preacher.

Wayde I. Goodall, National Coordinator, Ministerial Enrichment
The General Council of the Assemblies of God

Throughout our generation Stephen Olford has championed expository preaching in a memory-assisting, three-point formula that climaxes in a plea for a Spirit-filled life.

Carl F. H. Henry,
Evangelical author and religion correspondent

Anointed Expository Preaching provides teachers with unique biblical and theological insights about the Purpose, Person, and Power of Expository Preaching. It also furnishes preachers with the practical skills necessary to enhance the walk they must purpose, enrich the work they must perform, and empower the Word they must proclaim.

Edward E. Hogg, President,
Trinity College and Seminary

The emphasis on holiness of life is timely, telling, and thrilling. You feel as though the very Word of God is exposing you to its double-edged blade, but then leading you to an appropriate response to get right with God.

John C. James, Senior Minister,
Tabernacle Baptist Church, Penarth, South Wales

Anointed Expository Preaching is a veritable treasure chest of information, practical advice and sound spiritual guidance for the preaching mission of the Church. Students and pastors alike will be encouraged, strengthened, and challenged to excel in one of the most important areas of ministry that is floundering so badly in our day. I wholeheartedly recommend this volume to all who seek to do a better job at ending the famine of the hearing and doing of the Word of God in our day.

Walter C. Kaiser Jr., President,
Gordon-Conwell Theological Seminary

One of the best ways to study preaching is to latch on to a great preacher and learn all you can, up close and personal. Pastors looking for spiritual refreshment and a booster shot for their preaching need look no further. Stephen Olford's enthusiasm for biblical preaching and his ability to encourage others in its practice is unexcelled.

Duane Litfin, President,
Wheaton College

I believe this volume is the comprehensive, cornerstone work on the mission, mandate, and message of the preacher for our time and for future generations of proclaimers. It will not only help you, it will infuse passion into your pulpit!

Crawford W. Loritts, Jr., Preacher, Author,
Campus Crusade for Christ

Dr. Olford has given us a landmark book—the fruit of a lifetime of devotion to biblical preaching. His passion for the clear proclamation of God's Word comes through in a readable, engaging style that is sure to ignite a similar passion in the hearts of readers.

John MacArthur, Pastor-teacher,
Grace Community Church,
President, The Master's College and Seminary

This is the book many have been waiting for—the complete Olford! The thousands of pastors who look to Stephen Olford as their model and mentor in expository preaching will find here a compendium of the best of Olford on the preacher and his trade— pulpit proclamation with power. And those thousands of non-preachers who have met God in a life-transforming way under the ministry of Olford will not be disappointed either. The message of victory in Christ is here. Straight from the Bible text!

J. Robertson McQuilkin, President Emeritus,
Columbia International University

Dr. Stephen F. Olford and Dr. David L. Olford offer an encyclopedia and energetic defense of expository preaching. Their approach is at once both theologically grounded and practically applied. This book will be of great usefulness and encouragement to any preacher serious about the exposition of the Word of God. Through this book, we should pray that a generation of preachers will truly be anointed to the task of biblical exposition.

R. Albert Mohler, President,
Southern Baptist Theological Seminary

Dr. Stephen and David Olford have captured the *pathos, ethos,* and *logos* of years of monumental preaching and the teaching of preaching and placed it in one priceless volume. If you are serious about preaching, study the masters in *Anointed Expository Preaching.*

Paige Patterson, President,
Southeastern Baptist Theological Seminary

Stephen and David Olford bring different skills to bear upon the preacher and his preaching. Stephen Olford is the exegetical artist; David is the scientist. Stephen Olford can move you to tears. David makes you think. Stephen Olford is the triumphant orator, David is the trained scholar. The two men in this father-son partnership are wholly different in their personalities, gifts, and calling, David will make you cross your *t*'s and dot you *i*'s. Stephen will make you spread your wings and soar. Together they make an impressive team.

John Phillips, author of *Only One Life*

I predict that out of all of the significant contributions that have come from the pen of Dr. Olford, *Anointed Expository Preaching* will surely be his magnum opus.

Earl D. Radmacher, President Emeritus,
Western Seminary

With balance and blessing the Olfords lead the student of preaching—and who of us does not need such help?—into paths of discipline, devotion, and dynamic that will result in better preachers and better preaching.

Ted S. Rendall, Chancellor,
Prairie Bible Institute

Stephen Olford's summa compresses years of his key roles as pastor, preacher, and professor of pastoring and preaching into a comprehensive pastoral instruction book.

Ramesh Richard, President, RREACH International

This book is a veritable encyclopedia for preachers and their preaching. It is filled with practical, pointed, and pertinent guidelines that are clothed in seasoned counsel and concern for restoring expository preaching to the place it ought to occupy in ministry.

Charles C. Ryrie, Professor Emeritus,
Dallas Theological Seminary

It's about time! Now the definitive word on expository preaching by the master himself and his capable son. This book will need to be in every preacher's library. I recommend it without reservation.

Jerry Vines, Pastor,
First Baptist Church, Jacksonville, Florida

When any of us in Christian leadership thinks of expository preaching, our minds immediately flash to Mr. Expositor himself, Dr. Stephen F. Olford. His personal life, practical training, and expository preaching and the secrets of "anointed proclamation" of God's word have influenced the entire body of Christ. Those of us who have been called to preach rejoice that the distilled essence of the secrets behind the legendary preaching of Dr. Olford are finally shared with all of us in *Anointed Expository Preaching*.

Bruce Wilkinson, President,
Walk Thru the Bible Ministries

ANOINTED

EXPOSITORY

PREACHING

© 1998
by Stephen F. Olford and David L. Olford
All rights reserved
Printed in the United States of America

0-8054-6085-3

Published by Broadman & Holman Publishers, Nashville, Tennessee
Page Design: James E. Taulman

Dewey Decimal Classification: 251
Subject Heading: PREACHING
Library of Congress Card Catalog Number: 97-31305

Unless otherwise stated all Scripture citation is from the New King James Version,
copyright © 1979, 1980, 1982, Thomas Nelson, Inc., Publishers. Other versions cited
are NASB, the New American Standard Bible, © the Lockman Foundation, 1960,
1962, 1963, 1968, 1971, 1972, 1973, 1975, 1977; used by permission; NIV, the Holy
Bible, New International Version, copyright © 1973, 1978, 1984 by International
Bible Society; RSV, Revised Standard Version of the Bible, copyrighted 1946, 1952,
© 1971, 1973; Phillips, reprinted with permission of Macmillan Publishing Co., Inc.
from J. B. Phillips: *The New Testament in Modern English,* revised edition, © J. B.
Phillips 1958, 1960, 1972; REB, *The Revised English Bible,* copyright © Oxford
University Press and Cambridge University Press, 1989; *Williams New Testament: The
New Testament in the Language of the People,* by Charles B. Williams, copyright ©
1937, 1966, 1986 by Broadman Bible Publishers.

Library of Congress Cataloging-in-Publication Data
Olford, Stephen F.
    [Anointed expository preaching]
    Anointed expository preaching / Stephen F. Olford, David L. Olford
        p. cm.
    Includes bibliographical references.
    ISBN 0-8054-6085-3
    1. Preaching. 2. Clergy—Office. 3. Clergy—Religious Life. 4. Bible—
Inspiration. I. Olford, David L. (David Lindsay). II. Title.
BV4211.2.O57 1998
251—dc21

                       97-31305
                       CIP

1 2 3 4 5 02 01 00 99 98

ANOINTED
EXPOSITORY
PREACHING

Stephen F. Olford
with David L. Olford

Foreword by Dr. Adrian Rogers

BROADMAN
& HOLMAN
PUBLISHERS

Nashville, Tennessee

Dedicated to those who faithfully

"preach the Word"

—2 Timothy 4:2

CONTENTS

93497

FOREWORD

Preaching has always been central in God's plan to communicate His purposes and will to mankind. In the dawn of civilization, Enoch was a prophet. Noah preached with the ring of hammers behind him and the wrath of God before him. Moses was called to preach in spite of his stammering tongue. The prophets of Israel were anointed to declare "Thus saith the Lord." The apostles were preachers touched with Pentecostal fire.

But above and beyond all of these was the Master Preacher. "Jesus came . . . preaching" (Mark 1:14). We must always remember that our Lord was a preacher sent from heaven.

I am convinced that much in America and in the world could be changed radically, dramatically, and quickly for God and for good if we had a generation of preachers who would preach as preaching is delineated in this strategic volume.

We need God-called men who will take the Book of God and preach the Son of God with the anointing of the Spirit of God. We need men with warm hearts, wet eyes, clear heads, and tongues aflame.

Is the ability to preach an art, a science, or a spiritual gift? The truth is—it is all three of these.

Stephen and David Olford are a wonderful team, who individually and together display the art, the science, and the gift of preaching.

It has been my joy to know, fellowship with, and observe these men in action. They are incarnational examples of the content of this helpful volume.

This volume is so crafted as to touch both the mind and heart. It is deeply spiritual and yet intensely practical.

Much that I know about preaching I have learned from the Olfords, and I have yet much to learn. I am convinced that every preacher will be enriched by this book.

Adrian Rogers
Senior Pastor
Bellevue Baptist Church
Memphis, Tennessee

ACKNOWLEDGMENTS

Our sincere thanks:

To the "Prince of Preachers," even our Lord Jesus Christ.

To the untold number of preachers whose lives, prayers, and recommendations impacted the writing of this book.

To our dear friend Adrian Rogers for writing the foreword with the passion and precision of a pastor and preacher.

To our beloved wives, Heather and Ellen, whose patience, encouragement, and sacrifice inspired the writing of *Anointed Expository Preaching*.

To the secretarial staff who typed and prepared the manuscripts for publication. In particular, we mention Anita Bosley, Ellen Dickson, Victoria Kuhl, Anne Pritchard, and Jennifer Balmer.

To Leonard Goss and John Landers and the editors of Broadman & Holman Publishers for their invaluable assistance in making our original dream of a book on preaching a reality!

INTRODUCTION

The Old Testament preacher warned: "Of making many books there is no end, and much study is wearisome to the flesh" (Eccles. 12:12). This cautionary word addresses the vast amount of literature in every age that wastes our time to read. On the other hand, as J. Stafford Wright observes: "This verse is certainly not intended to discourage Christian writers. . . . [who] write constructively and expound in modern terms those truths of life that are in the Scriptures."[1]

So, in quiet confidence, we, the authors, introduce to our readers yet another book on preaching! In doing so we want to make our reasons clear for launching this literary endeavor.

First, this is a *commissioned* book. Preachers from all over the world have requested repeatedly that we write a book on preaching that would incorporate much of the material that appears in these chapters. The story behind this is simple. In 1986 we established what is now called "The Stephen Olford Center for Biblical Preaching" in Memphis, Tennessee. Once again, this was a response to preachers/pastors at home and abroad who implored us to provide spiritual teaching and practical training in the specific discipline of expository preaching. In defining our strategy we settled on a statement of purpose which reads: "The Institute for Biblical Preaching is to equip and encourage pastors and lay

leaders in expository preaching and exemplary living, to the end
that the church will be revived and the world will be reached with
the saving Word of Christ." We believe that true "heaven-sent"
revival and aggressive evangelism will only come when there is a
return to the preaching and obeying of God's inerrant Word.

The chapters that follow are, in essence, the lectures and lessons
that have been prayerfully prepared and offered in answer to "the
felt needs" of men from every spectrum and status of evangelical
churchmanship. We are not a Bible college, seminary, or school, as
such, but we are a renewal and research center where hungry and
harassed preachers can come to share their burdens and seek God's
blessings. In our interaction and question-and-answer periods, no
holds are barred, and no issues avoided in seeking God's answers
through His holy Word and the leading of the Holy Spirit; our book
mirrors all this and more.

Another reason for this book was dictated by the gracious invitation from Broadman & Holman Publishers to write such a book. After
prayerful considerations and negotiations, a contract was signed.

Secondly, this is a *constricted* book. The word *constricted* means
"to narrow—especially at one place." Preaching is an enormous
field of study. Endless volumes, ancient and modern, have been
written on the subject, and we are well aware of the literature that
is available. But our purpose in writing this book is to reflect not
only the felt needs of the preachers we have worked with, but also
to reveal the real needs in the ministry today.

What does *the Bible* say about preaching? That is the crucial
question. In an age of communication that boggles the mind, little
can be added to what is being taught and learned about the techniques of imparting knowledge. But at the same time scant attention has been given to the *nature* of preaching and the *stature* of
the preacher. Paul, the apostle, "reflects this peculiar and remarkable identification of the preacher and the message when he says,
'What we preach is not ourselves, but Jesus Christ as Lord, [and]
ourselves as your servants' (2 Cor. 4:5). Paul did not preach himself or his own religious experiences, but Christ; and in preaching
Christ he knew that *he himself was part of the content of his message* [emphasis ours]. This is quite different from sharing one's faith
and religious experiences in order to bring people to Christ."[2]

The inextricable union between the preacher and his message
is strikingly revealed in the mysterious words of Jesus to His commissioned "seventy" when He said, "He who hears *you* hears *Me*"
(Luke 10:16, emphasis ours).

As James Daane observes: "The mystery of an event in which a human being speaks God's words and God thereby speaks his Word through human words cannot be explained in human language without recourse to paradox. It is clear, [however], that both *what* Jesus says and *how* he says it point to the awesome mystery of the nature of [Christian] proclamation."[3] No wonder Paul came to Corinth saying, "I . . . [declare] to you the [mystery] of God" (1 Cor. 2:1).

With this awesome understanding of the incarnational nature of preaching, we have majored on the man in the first section of the book. If a preacher is to be used of God, there is *the walk that he must pursue.* Each of the chapters in part 1 is an *exposition*[4] of an appropriate Scripture passage relating to the preacher's life. The *method* is discussed in the second section. This is likewise *based* on scriptural principles and represents *the work that the preacher must perform.* Paul's word to Timothy was: "Be diligent to present yourself approved to God, a worker who does not need to be ashamed, rightly dividing the word of truth" (2 Tim. 2:15). Finally, the *message* is discussed in the last section of the book. This is *the Word that the preacher must proclaim.* Here, once more, are expositions that deal with the essential aspects of proclamation, with all the associated implications and ramifications.

The Scriptures and practical experience have taught us that God is more concerned with *what we are* than with *what we do.* If what we are does not satisfy His holy demands, then what we do is virtually worthless. To quote Dr. Daane again:

> Preaching has fallen on evil days because the sermon is regarded as just another form of human speech, rather than a special genre. The preacher is just another Christian without any special authority; the pulpit (whether within the church or on those frontiers where the church addresses the world) is just another platform or lectern—sometimes (even worse) it is a private stage. And when preachers believe this way, they lack the courage to speak with authority and to bless. Since they do not see themselves as speaking with authority, they easily conclude that they have no special responsibility or calling. Eventually, they begin to wonder why they are in the pulpit at all. Hence the exodus of capable ministers from the pulpit, and the readiness of so many qualified seminary students to avoid the pulpit to serve the cause of Christ in some other ministry.
>
> For this low view of proclamation not only undermines the ministry of the pulpit, but also the minister. Someone has aptly defined preaching as "the communication of truth through personality." For that reason the individual in the pulpit who does not understand the nature of the Word and its proclamation will experience a personal

crisis of self-identity, uncertain of what a preacher is and does. What a preacher is and what a preacher's function is, are interrelated, and both derive from the nature of the Word preached. In a code word: the preacher is part of what is preached.[5]

Thirdly, this is a *committed* book Throughout our years together at the Stephen Olford Center for Biblical Preaching, and in the writing of this book, we have been committed to three ingredients in the very nature of preaching that are non-negotiable:

1. We are committed to *biblical revelation*. We believe in the dictum of St. Augustine, that "when the Scriptures speak, God speaks." In His inscrutable wisdom God has chosen to reveal Himself in time, space, and language through His Son in a book called the Bible. "Our faith response to God's Word, and acts recorded and interpreted by the prophets and apostles, calls for us to embrace with humble teachableness, without finding fault, whatever . . . is taught in Holy Scripture."[6]

2. We are committed to *biblical exposition*. If "the preaching of the Word of God *is* the word of God"[7] (emphasis ours), as the Reformers contended, then a sermon is the proclamation of the Word of God only if the text of the Word is accurately expounded and preached. So, in the strictest sense of the term, *authentic* preaching is expository preaching.

Few men have modeled expository preaching like John R. W. Stott. In his book *Between Two Worlds,* he writes: "It is my contention that all true Christian preaching is expository preaching." By that he means what is not expository is not Christian. He goes on to say:

> If by an "expository" sermon is meant a verse-by-verse explanation of a lengthy passage of Scripture, then indeed it is only one possible way of preaching, but this would be a misuse of the word. Properly speaking, "exposition" has a much broader meaning. It refers to the content of the sermon (biblical truth) rather than its style (a running commentary). To expound Scripture is to bring out of the text what is there and expose it to view. The expositor [pries] open what appears to be closed, makes plain what is obscure, unravels what is knotted and unfolds what is tightly packed. The opposite of exposition is "imposition," which is to impose on the text what is not there. . . . The "text" in question could be a verse, . . . a sentence, or even a single word. It could equally be a paragraph, or a chapter, or a whole book. The size of the text is immaterial, so long as it is biblical. What matters is what we do with it. Whether it is long or short, our responsibility as expositors is to open it up in such a way that it speaks its message clearly,

plainly, accurately, relevantly, without addition, subtraction or falsification. In expository preaching the biblical text is neither a conventional introduction to a sermon on a largely different theme, nor a convenient peg on which to hang a ragbag of miscellaneous thoughts, but a master which dictates and controls what is said.[8]

A detailed discussion of the hermeneutics and homiletics involved in expository preaching are the main thrust of part 2 of this book.

3. We are committed to *biblical proclamation*. In some circles today, the very terms "preach" and "preaching" have fallen into disrepute. But we believe that, till the end of time, "preaching" will prevail. As someone has put it, "There is only one thing that will take the place of great preaching and that is greater preaching!" It is the divine will that this should be so (1 Cor. 1:21). "Wherever in the New Testament the *call* to preach is spoken of, preaching is the point made emphatic"[9] (emphasis ours). Therefore its importance to the life of the church and the lostness of the world can never be exaggerated.

United Methodist Bishop Carl J. Sanders of Alabama, writing on the need to improve the quality and priority of preaching, sums it up perfectly:

> In the multiple roles of a pastor, his identity as a "preacher" may be lost; the quality of his preaching may decline as he fills other functions and neglects the disciplines required for effectual preaching; and confidence in the superior efficacy of preaching may fade as other ministries appear to be more redemptive. . . . History proves, however, that the church can exist without buildings, without liturgies, without choirs, without Sunday Schools, without professional clergymen, without creeds, without even women's societies. But the church cannot possibly exist without preaching the Word. Preaching has power like nothing else the church has or does. Moreover, preaching reaches more people than anything else the preacher can do, whether it is teaching, visiting, administrating, or counseling. . . . The time has come to restore preaching to its rightful place, its primary position in the work of the ministry. In preaching there is power! The power of the Spirit is the power of the Word. As the Word is proclaimed, the Spirit is busy working in the mind and heart of the hearer.[10]

We send forth this book with the fervent prayer and earnest hope that God will use these chapters to elevate the art of preaching and motivate the heart of every preacher to "preach the word!" (2 Tim. 4:2).

Stephen F. Olford
David L. Olford

PART ONE
THE WALK TO PURSUE

CHAPTER ONE

THE PREACHER AND THE CALL OF GOD

It pleased God, who separated me from my mother's womb and called me through His grace, to reveal His Son in me, that I might preach Him among the Gentiles.

—Galatians 1:15–16a

Study Text: Galatians 1:1–17

All Christians are "called ones." This basic "call" is to Christ as Lord and Savior (Eph. 1:18; 4:1; 2 Tim. l:9; Heb. 3:1; 2 Pet. 1:10). But God also calls with a view to "good works, which God prepared in advance for us to do" (Eph. 2:10 NIV). Included in the "good works" is the call to preach. The call of Moses (Exod. 3:4–22), of Samuel (1 Sam. 3:4), of Jeremiah (Jer. 1:4–10), and in

7

the New Testament, the call of the disciples (Mark 3:13–19), of Paul (Rom. 1:1; 1 Cor. 1:1; Gal. 1:15), and of Barnabas (Acts 13:2) are all good examples.

The call to preach must not be confused with the desire to serve as an elder or deacon (see 1 Tim. 3:1), even though the very desire (if noble) is "inspired by God's Spirit."[1] The call to preach must not be conditioned by the need for the gospel, even though we are commanded to "go into all the world and preach the gospel to every creature" (Mark 16:15). "This goes against the grain of much modern thinking. But in our Lord's day none of the twelve volunteered to follow Christ. They made no application, they completed no forms. On the contrary, it was the magnetic authority of the Lord which compelled them. . . . For the disciples, the call was the verbal command of the Lord."[2] The call to preach must not be controlled by the church, even though the elders of a local church are expected to confirm the call (1 Tim. 4:14; 2 Tim. 1:6). In the final analysis, the call to preach is the sovereign initiative of God in the life and experience of the one who is predestinated to fulfill that role.

When Paul writes of his conversion experience, he refers to it "as a pattern [a prototype] to those who are going to believe on [Jesus Christ] for everlasting life" (1 Tim. 1:16). Two important points are expressed in this "public display of [God's] grace to a notable sinner."[3] The first is the mercy of God shown to Paul. The word mercy is in the verbal form. Literally it reads, "I was mercied." The second is the call of God. Paul states categorically: "[God] considered me faithful, appointing me to his service" (1 Tim. 1:12 NIV). A quote from Augustine is appropriate here: "God does not choose a person who is worthy, but by the act of choosing him he makes him worthy [translation mine]."[4]

In his Galatian epistle, Paul amplifies the story of his conversion experience to include his call to preach the gospel to the Gentiles. We do well, therefore, to examine the apostle's testimony and lift from his words the universal principles that define and delineate the call of God.

Looking back upon his initial encounter with Jesus Christ he could say, "It pleased God, who separated me from my mother's womb and called me through His grace, to reveal His Son in me, that I might preach Him among the Gentiles" (vv. 15–16). Three important aspects of Paul's testimony call for attention: the nature, the knowledge, and the purpose of God's call to preach.

THE NATURE OF GOD'S CALL TO PREACH

"It pleased God, who separated me from my mother's womb and called me through His grace" (v. 15). The verb separated means "to mark off by bounds." In this context, the word denotes "the divine action in setting man apart for the work of the gospel" (W. E. Vine). In the preceding verses, Paul has been recounting his past life. With heavy heart he has confessed his fanaticism for the Law. In fact, it was because of his unenlightened zeal for the Law that he had become such an archpersecutor of the church. He had destroyed the local assemblies. But in spite of all this, it pleased God to call him into the service of the gospel. Paul could never get over this. It was such unmerited favor and unspeakable grace! Paul could put forth only two explanations for this divine activity.

God's Eternal Call of Grace

"It pleased God, who separated me from my mother's womb" (v. 15). To the apostle, the call of God was no unpremeditated event. Before time was determined, Paul was in the mind of God. This is the significance of the phrase "separated . . . from my mother's womb." Before Paul could think, speak, or act, God had marked him out as a chosen vessel to preach the gospel to the Gentiles (see John 15:16).

Centuries before, God "separated" Jeremiah to be a preacher. "The word of the Lord came to [Jeremiah], saying: 'Before I formed you in the womb I knew you; before you were born I sanctified you; . . . I ordained you a prophet to the nations'" (Jer. 1:4–5). This was the eternal call of grace to Jeremiah. Warren W. Wiersbe sums it up this way: addressing His prophet, God said, "'You will be what I want you to be, go where I want you to go, and say what I want you to say. I supervised your conception, I consecrated you, and now I am ordaining you.'" Then Wiersbe adds: "If God calls you, believe what He says and obey Him. You may not feel up to it, but your adequacy comes from God, not from yourself"[5] (see Jer. 1:6–9). The call of Jeremiah refutes the idea that the work of God's servants was always provincial (cf. Jer. 25:15–29; 46–51). God is the Lord of the nations, and when He calls, our answer must be: "Anywhere, anytime, any place, I am ready, Lord; send me."

A. J. Gossip tells how Alexander Whyte faced his ordination in his first church. In his message to his people, Whyte declared that "all through time and eternity God had been preparing [him] for this congregation, and this congregation for [him] and, prompt to the minute, He had brought them together."[6] This is a mind-boggling concept—one that we need to recall every time we are tempted to speak glibly about the call of God!

God's Effectual Call of Grace

"God . . . called me through His grace" (v. 15). What was eternal became effectual in Paul's experience when he initially encountered the living Christ. Three times in the Acts of the Apostles (9:4; 22:7; 26:14) Luke describes in vivid detail the nature of this spiritual crisis and call. In chapter 9 he tells us that it all started when Paul saw a face—"As he journeyed he came near Damascus, and suddenly a light shone around him from heaven" (Acts 9:3). Later Paul interpreted this light as "the heavenly vision" in which "He was seen by me" (Acts 26:19; 1 Cor. 15:8). That appearance was none other than the face of the risen Christ (2 Cor. 4:6).

Then Saul heard a voice—"Saul, Saul, why are you persecuting Me?" (Acts 9:4). What a shock these words must have been to Saul! How could he be persecuting the One who was in heaven? And yet, in that moment of destiny, he learned one of the greatest truths of the New Testament: that the Church is the Body, of which Christ is the Head. Later he could write: "Christ is head of the church; and He is the Savior of the body" (Eph. 5:23). The revelation of the saviorhood of Christ broke in upon Saul's soul as he knelt in the dust of that Damascan road.

Following this Saul made a choice. He pleaded, "Lord, what do You want me to do?" (Acts 9:6). He owned Jesus as Lord and surrendered spirit, soul and body to the sovereignty of Christ. With that response Saul of Tarsus was converted and called by the grace of God. The eternal call had now become the effectual call. From then on Saul knew himself to be a chosen vessel. He did not consider himself chosen for honor, but for service; not for ease, but for battle; not for life, but for death, in the cause of worldwide evangelization (see Acts 26:16–18).

This is what God has been doing throughout the centuries. Have you heard the call? If so, do not be "disobedient to the heavenly vision" (Acts 26:19). When Jeremiah tried to refrain from preaching, he tells us, "I was weary of holding it back, and I could not" (Jer. 20:9). That should be the experience of every true preacher. "Such an one will have 'a divine commission behind him, a divine summons before him, and a divine conviction within him,' and what more can anyone have or need?"[7]

THE KNOWLEDGE OF GOD'S CALL TO PREACH

The second thing that Paul tells us in this amazing testimony concerns the knowledge of God's call to preach. "God . . . called me through His grace, to reveal His Son in me" (vv. 15,16). Now we come to the heart of things. Those words "His Son in me" are dynamite! They correspond to "Christ lives in me" (Gal. 2:20) and "God . . . sent . . . the Spirit of His Son into [our] hearts" (Gal. 4:6).

The Revelation of the Indwelling Son

"His Son in me" (v. 16). The conscious knowledge of the indwelling Son of God is the indispensable "inner witness" of God's call to preach. It is true, of course, that every Christian can say, "Christ lives in me," and that the outliving of the indwelling Christ is the normal Christian life. But for the preacher, those words "His Son in Me" have far-reaching implications. Preaching is essentially incarnational. If we would be followers of the Prince of Preachers, then all our preaching should be a "fleshing out" of the pattern that Jesus left for us. John records this pattern in the prologue to his gospel: "The Word became flesh and dwelt among us, and we beheld His glory, the glory as of the only begotten of the Father, full of grace and truth. . . . No one has seen God at any time. The only begotten Son, who is in the bosom of the Father, He has declared [exegeted] Him" (John 1:14, 18). Jesus was an incarnational Exegete of the Father. By the power of the Holy Spirit, He revealed the God "no one has seen at any time," in terms that "common people" could see and hear.

In a similar way, we must preach the gospel. All the fullness of the gospel is totalized in Jesus, and Jesus lives in us. As we exegete the Word, in the power of the Holy Spirit, Christ must come through with "grace and truth." This is exactly what Paul says in our text, "His Son in me, that I might preach Him" (v. 16, emphasis ours). He could have written "that I might preach the gospel"; but for Paul the gospel was Christ. So the knowledge of the call of God is inextricably related to the mystery and ministry of the indwelling Son of God.[8]

The Revelation of the Impelling Son

"His Son in me" (v. 16). As Richard N. Longenecker observes: "The Christological title 'Son of God,' 'his [God's] Son,' or simply 'the Son' appears in Paul's writings fifteen times ('Son of God': Rom. 1:4; 2 Cor. 1:19; Gal. 2:20; 'his Son' or 'the Son': Rom. 1:3, 9; 5:10; 8:3, 29, 32; 1 Cor. 1:9; 15:28; Gal. 1:16; 4:4, 6; 1 Thess. 1:10)."[9] As we study each reference in context, it becomes clear that the title conveys the ideas of power and action. Writing to the church at Rome, Paul refers to "Jesus Christ our Lord . . . declared to be the Son of God with power" (Rom. 1:3, 4). It was as the Son of God, authenticated by the resurrection, that He could say to His disciples: "As the Father has sent Me [the Son], I also send you" (John 20:21). Throughout His life the Lord Jesus had a strong sense of being commissioned and sent. It is a study in and of itself to count the number of times the two main verbs send or sent are found in the Gospel of John alone.[10] The mission of God was an inescapable imperative to Him. He was forever using the word must. This impersonal verb signifies necessity, obligation, and commitment. It is found most frequently in the Gospels, the Acts, and the Book of Revelation. As the Son, the Lord Jesus could say, "I must be about My Father's business" (Luke 2:49); as the Savior, He could say, "As Moses lifted up the serpent in the wilderness, even so must the Son of Man be lifted up" (John 3:14); as the Servant, He declared, "I must work the works of Him who sent Me while it is day; the night is coming when no one can work" (John 9:4). Finally, at the end of His life He could exclaim, "I have finished the work which You have given Me to do" (John 17:4). In the light of such a life of dedicated service, He could charge, "As the Father has sent Me, I also send you" (John 20:21). This power and action of the Son of God were inwardly revealed to the apostle Paul. He was a man indwelt and impelled by the Son of God. That is why he could make such statements as "I am a debtor both to Greeks and to barbarians, both to wise and to unwise. So, as much as is in me, I am ready to preach the gospel to you who are in Rome also. . . . for necessity is laid upon me; yes, woe is me if I do not preach the gospel!" (Rom. 1:14–15; 1 Cor. 9:16). When we read words like these we are bound to ask ourselves whether we know the power of the impelling Son of God in our lives.

Preachers often ask us to explain the call of God in terms of assurance or conviction. The answer is not an easy one. We are all different in talents, training and temperament; yet one thing is certain: if a man is indwelt and impelled by the living Son of God, there can be no doubt about the call! Dr. Martyn Lloyd-Jones affirms:

> The preacher is a man who is possessed and he is *aware* of this [emphasis ours]. I do not hesitate to make this assertion. I would say that I only begin to know something about preaching on those occasions when, as it were, I am looking on. I am speaking, but I am really a spectator. I am amazed at what is happening. I am listening, I am looking on in utter astonishment, for I am not doing it. It is true preaching when I am conscious that I am being used; in a sense, I am as much a spectator as the people who are listening to me. There is this consciousness that it is outside me, and yet I am involved in it; I am merely the instrument and the vehicle and the channel of all this.[11]

If that is the spiritual "sense" of the call, what are the biblical "tests" of the call? There are at least five of them that must be carefully and prayerfully considered. Ask yourself these questions:

> 1. *Do I meet the qualifications of a preacher, as set forth in the Word of God?* When God called Paul to be a preacher, He clearly delineated what was involved and required (see Acts 9:15–16, 20; 22:14–15; 26:16–18). You cannot study these divine instructions without discerning both the qualifications and responsibilities of a preacher.
>
> 2. *Have I the witness of the Spirit in my heart that God has called me?* The same Holy Spirit who witnesses with my spirit that I have been born of God also witnesses with my spirit that I have been called of God to be a preacher (Rom. 8:14; Gal. 1:15–16; 2 Tim. 1:8–11). As you pray earnestly about the matter, "the sense of call" will either come alive or die altogether. When Paul prayed "Lord, what do You want me to do?" he received the answer.
>
> 3. *Has the gift of the preacher become evident in my life and service?* First Corinthians 12:7 declares that "the manifestation of the Spirit is given to each one for the profit of all." The Revised English Bible renders this "In each of us the Spirit is seen to be at work for some useful purpose." This "manifestation" is not human ability alone, but rather the indwelling and directing power of the Holy Spirit. Sometimes the "sense of call" comes through "inferential" means. A set of circumstances will be ordered providentially to bring about a growing conviction that God has called you to be a preacher. This will explain why men who initially followed other professions

subsequently become preachers. Peter, Andrew, James, and John were fishermen when Jesus called them (Mark 1:16–20)!

4. *Has my church recognized and confirmed my preaching gift?* First Timothy 4:14 and 2 Timothy 1:6–7 give a significant object lesson in the divine/human recognition and confirmation of a person's gift and ministry in the early church (see also Acts 13:1–4).

5. *Has God used my preaching gift to the salvation of souls and the edification of saints?* Writing to the Corinthians, Paul could affirm with confidence, "You are the seal of my apostleship in the Lord" (1 Cor. 9:2). Can you point to converts or disciples and say the same thing?[12]

THE PURPOSE OF GOD'S CALL TO PREACH

"God . . . called me through His grace, to reveal His Son in me, that I might preach Him among the Gentiles" (vv. 15, 16). The purpose is simple and specific. We are called to preach Christ. Anything and everything else is either irrelevant or merely secondary. To help us understand this important facet of the call of God, Paul employs definitive language. He insists that to fulfill the purpose of the call of God;

We Must Preach the Gospel

"God . . . called me . . . that I might preach Him," who is the gospel (vv. 15, 16). Paul's gospel was a direct revelation from heaven. He declares, "I make known to you, brethren, that the gospel which was preached by me is not according to man. For I neither received it from man, nor was I taught it, but it came through the revelation of Jesus Christ" (vv. 11–12). While Paul's experience was unique in this respect, he also was affirming a fundamental fact for all time. That fact is that the gospel is wholly apart from man's philosophical ideas, scientific methods, or religious efforts (see 1 Cor. 1 and 2; Gal. 2:15–16; 6:12–15). The gospel of salvation is by grace alone, in Christ alone, through faith alone. This calls for faithful, fearless, and fervent preaching. Look carefully at the context:

We Must Be Faithful in Our Preaching. "I marvel that you are turning away so soon from Him who called you in the grace of Christ, to a different gospel, which is not another. . . . But even if we, or an angel. . . . preaches any other gospel to you than what you have received, let him be accursed" (vv. 6–9). Paul uses a special word to describe those who had so soon changed their position on the fundamentals of the gospel. He calls them "turn-coats" because, under pressure of the Judaizers and perverters of the gospel, these Galatians had espoused "a different gospel." With a play on words, Paul scolds them for substituting the real for the false, the orthodox for the heterodox.

Two things must be noted about faithful preaching. The first is that the truth of God always exposes the characteristics of heresy—"I marvel that you are turning away so soon from Him who called you in the grace of Christ, to a different gospel, which is not another; but there are some who trouble you and want to pervert the gospel of Christ" (vv. 6–7). Commenting on this verse, C. I. Scofield notes: "The test of the Gospel is grace. If the message excludes grace, or mingles law with grace as the means of either justification or sanctification (Gal. 2:21; 3:1–3), or denies the fact or guilt of sin which alone gives grace its . . . opportunity [to function in our lives], it is 'another' gospel, and the preacher . . . is under the anathema of God (vs. 8–9)."[13] The second thing is that the truth of God always discloses the consequences of heresy—"But even if we, or an angel from heaven, preach any other gospel to you than what we have preached to you, let him be accursed" (v. 8). To preach or propagate heresy has serious consequences. Without contrived diplomacy, the apostle bluntly says, "Let him be accursed [or damned]" (vv. 8, 9). The word anathema was used both in the Old and New Testaments to denote that which is devoted to destruction because of its hate-fulness to God. So Paul sums up his condemnation of heresy by saying, "If we, or an angel from heaven, preach any other gospel to you than what we have preached to you, let him be accursed" (v. 8).

We Must Be Fearless in Our Preaching. "For do I now persuade men, or God? Or do I seek to please men? For if I still pleased men, I would not be a bondservant of Christ" (v. 10). In the light of these solemn words that Paul boldly asserts, the matter of fear-less preaching becomes a "must" to the authentic preacher.

We live in an hour when peer pressure—leave alone satanic opposition—tempts us to compromise. Popularity, power, and position are often prized higher than the quality of integrity. If we are called of God, we must face the challenge once and for all. Like the saintly martyrs of the past and the sovereign Master of the present, we must draw a line in the sand and declare with the holy courage of Martin Luther, "Here I stand; I can do no other."

The ancient King Redwald of East Anglia once built a unique sanctuary. At one end was an altar for the worship of the true God, while at the other end was an altar for the worship of false gods.[14] Tragically, the church today is making similar compromises.

We Must Be Fervent in Our Preaching. The Christians of Paul's day were saying, "'He who formerly persecuted us now preaches the faith which he once tried to destroy.' And they glorified God" (Gal. 1:23–24). If we want to find out how he persecuted the church, we have only to look back at verse 13: "For you have heard of my former conduct in Judaism, how I persecuted the church of God beyond measure and tried to destroy it." The two words persecuted and destroyed are in the imperfect tense, which denotes continuous action. It describes the fervency and fury with which Saul, "the zealot," devastated the church of Christ. Paul describes these activities to highlight the radical change that had taken place in his life. Now with "sanctified fervency" he was preaching the gospel with such unction that believers who heard him glorified God (see Acts 9:20–29; 1 Cor. 9:16; Gal. 1:23–24)!

There is no other way to preach the gospel if we are going to beat the devil at his own game. We have to pursue him with–in the words of G. Campbell Morgan–"truth, clarity and passion." The old masters called it "logos, ethos and pathos."

Yet the call of God goes even further beyond preaching the gospel.

We Must Reach the People

"God . . . called me . . . that I might preach Him among the Gentiles" (vv. 15, 16). It is possible to preach the gospel without reaching the people. This is one of the greatest problems in our evangelical witness today. We have our church services, our radio broadcasts, and our literature programs, but we are not reaching the people.

For Paul, reaching the people was getting beyond religious circles. It is true that he invariably visited the synagogues first, but he was never satisfied with mere religious discussion; his burden was for a lost world. Therefore, he went all out for the Gentiles. Paul makes this clear in the closing paragraphs of his epistle to the Romans. Having solicited the prayers of his readers, he goes on to state, "I have made it my aim to preach the gospel, not where

Christ was named, lest I should build on another man's foundation" (Rom. 15:20).

A preacher who is satisfied with feeding overstuffed saints, while a pagan world goes to hell, has never understood the call of God to preach the gospel "to every creature" (Mark 16:15). In making that statement, we are not unmindful of the pastor/teacher's responsibility to "feed [the] sheep" (John 21:17; Acts 20:28; 1 Pet. 5:2–4). Paul's imperative to "preach the word" embraces "teaching" (2 Tim. 4:2–3), but it does not end there. He concludes with another imperative: "Do the work of an evangelist" (2 Tim. 4:5). Unlike Philip the evangelist (Acts 21:8), Timothy was primarily a teacher (1 Tim. 4:13, 15–16); but with this gifting he was commanded to "do the work of an evangelist." Certainly we must edify the saved, but we must also evangelize the lost. Preaching includes both aspects of proclamation. So whether we are in a city pulpit or a city park, we are to "preach the word! Be ready in season and out of season. [We are to] convince, rebuke, exhort, with all longsuffering and teaching. . . . [We are to] do the work of an evangelist" (2 Tim. 4:2, 5, emphasis ours).

It must be clear then that the call of God to preach is not just an evangelical cliché: it is an evangelical charge—with redemptive significance. The nature of the call is intrinsically bound up with the eternal and effectual grace of God. The knowledge of that call can only be appreciated when the indwelling and impelling Son of God becomes a message we have to deliver. The purpose of this call of God is to preach the gospel and to reach the people. Are you fulfilling that divine call or are you missing God's plan for your life? It is sobering to realize that a person can disobey the call and enter heaven "saved, yet so as through fire" (1 Cor. 3:15). Oh, the wastage! Oh, the regrets! Oh, the loss of reward! Face it, preacher, if you are saved at all, then you are saved to serve. The call of God is binding upon you. Make sure that when you stand before the judgment seat of Christ you can look into your Master's face and say, "I have fought the good fight, I have finished the race, I have kept the faith" (2 Tim. 4:7).

Jeremiah Whitaker (1539–1654) was educated at Cambridge where, because of his scholastic attainments and Christian virtues, he was held in high esteem. He loved to preach the gospel and had an undying passion for the souls of the people. But the heart of his testimony was, "I had much rather be a minister of the gospel than [be] an emperor."[15]

Likewise, Samuel Chadwick, the noted Methodist preacher, stated: "I would rather preach than do anything else in the world. I would rather preach than eat my dinner or have a holiday. I would rather pay to preach than be paid not to preach. It has its price in agony and sweat and tears, and no calling has such joys and heartbreaks, but it is a calling an archangel might covet. Is there any joy like that of saving a soul? Any thrill like that of opening blind eyes? Any reward like the love of children to the second and third generation? Any treasure like the grateful love of hearts healed and comforted?"[16]

Two thousand years ago, Paul's response to the call of God was capsulized in those passionate words in 1 Corinthians 9:16: "If I preach the gospel, I can claim no credit for it; I cannot help myself; it would be an agony for me not to preach" (REB).

Preacher! What is your response? Oh, to be able to say and sing with Charles Wesley:

A charge to keep I have, a God to glorify,
A never-dying soul to save, and fit it for the sky.

To serve the present age, my calling to fulfill;
O may it all my pow'rs engage, to do my Master's will!

Arm me with jealous care, as in Thy sight to live;
And O Thy servant, Lord, prepare a strict account to give!

Help me to watch and pray, and on Thyself rely,
And let me ne'er my trust betray, but press to realms on high.

CHAPTER TWO

THE PREACHER AND THE WORD OF GOD

All Scripture is given by inspiration of God, and is profitable for doctrine, for reproof, for correction, for instruction in righteousness, that the man of God may be complete, thoroughly equipped for every good work.
—2 Timothy 3:16–17

Study Text: 2 Timothy 3:10–4:5

If a man is truly called of God to be a preacher, then he is committed to declare "the whole counsel of God" (Acts 20:27). He must believe that the Bible, as sovereignly preserved by God throughout the centuries, is inerrant and "(1) infallibly achieves its [intended purpose], (2) gives us reliable testimony to the saving revelation and redemption of God in Christ, (3) provides us with

[the] authoritative norm of faith and conduct, and (4) speaks [today] through the infallible Spirit of God by whom it [was inspired]."[1]

Even though limited to the Old Testament Scriptures, Paul could write: "All Scripture is given by inspiration of God, and is profitable for doctrine, for reproof, for correction, for instruction in righteousness, that the man of God may be complete, thoroughly equipped for every good work" (2 Tim. 3:16–17); and then with an imperatival ring, he adds "Preach the word" (2 Tim. 4:2).

Commenting on this verse, James S. Stewart asserts that "Paul as a Jew, and later as a Christian, held the high view that 'every word' of the Old Testament was the 'authentic voice of God.'"[2] We hold that what is true of the Old Testament is equally true of the New Testament. While the Old Testament is God's prophetic record, the New Testament is God's apostolic record. Jesus said to his apostles, "When He [the Holy Spirit] has come, He will guide you into all truth" (John 16:13). "The fulfillment of that prophecy is in the New Testament. The major ministry of the Holy Spirit [was] to lead the apostles into all the truth and to give us in the New Testament this wonderful body of truth that remains our authority. [This] does not mean that the ministry of the Holy Spirit has ceased. It means that the role of the Holy Spirit has changed from the revelation of new truth to giving us a profounder perception and application of old truth."[3]

So we come to the text that we have selected for this chapter. Read it again. "All Scripture is given by inspiration of God, and is profitable for doctrine, for reproof, for correction, for instruction in righteousness, that the man of God may be complete, thoroughly equipped for every good work" (2 Tim. 3:16–17).

A serious understanding of this apostolic statement demands a threefold response from those of us who are called to expound the Word of God.

THE PREACHER MUST BE DEVOTED TO THE SCRIPTURES

Ponder again the words of Paul to Timothy: "*Continue* in the things which you have learned and been assured of, knowing from whom you have learned them" (v. 14, emphasis ours).

From childhood Timothy had sat under the teaching of the Old Testament prophets, the great apostle Paul and godly women like Lois and Eunice (2 Tim. 1:5). Paul urges him to continue in the things he had learned and had been assured of.

Whether young or old, *continuance and obedience* require discipline.

The Preacher Must Read the Word of God Privately

"Give attention to reading" (1 Tim. 4:13). This is one of the most neglected areas in the minister's life. The devil sees to this! He knows that if he can distract or divert us from this daily tryst with our Lord, the consequences will be defeat, despair, and disaster.

After years of Christian experience, the saintly George Müller confessed: "I saw more clearly than ever that the first great and primary business to which I ought to attend every day was to have my soul happy in the Lord. The first thing to be concerned about was not how much I might serve the Lord, . . . but how I might get my soul into a happy state, and how my inner [life] might be nourished."[4] Mr. Müller came to see that his business, day by day, was to meditate upon the Word of God, searching as it were, into every verse for the sake of obtaining food for his soul. He knew what the Lord Jesus meant when He declared, "Man shall not live by bread alone, but by every word that proceeds from the mouth of God" (Matt. 4:4).

Without this heavenly nourishment, it is impossible for the preacher to serve victoriously in a demonically dominated world. Indeed, this was the apostle's concern for Timothy. Paul reminds his colleague that "all who desire to live godly in Christ Jesus will suffer persecution" and that "evil men and impostors will grow worse and worse, deceiving and being deceived" (vv. 12–13).

The private and devotional reading of God's Word must be celebrated at a time and place that distinguishes it from the disciplines of study habits and sermon preparation. The personal attitude and spiritual appetite should accord with the psalmist's heart-cry: "My soul thirsts for God, for the living God" (Ps. 42:2).

The following procedural movements may be found helpful for some:

Wait—Samuel Chadwick warned that "hurry is the death of prayer," and so it is. A few minutes in quiet waiting upon God will yield far more profit than a longer period with an eye on the clock. Wait on God—to sense His presence, to seek His purpose, and to see His power in your life.

Read—At this juncture, reverently open the Bible and read the portion for the day—and we mean the entire portion for the day. System and sequence must be observed. The value of reading the Word of God is often lost with the "lucky dip" method! Therefore, plan your reading passage by passage, or chapter by chapter. Remember that a short portion well read is better than a chapter or more skimmed.

Think—Having read the portion through several times—generally, carefully, then meditatively—ask these personal questions: Is there a promise to claim; a lesson to learn; a blessing to enjoy; a command to obey; a sin to avoid; a new revelation of God in Christ, or the Holy Spirit; a new thought about the devil? *What is today's thought?* Such prayerful reflection under the control of the Holy Spirit will never fail to reveal a word from the Lord.

Write—Psychologists say that there is no impression without expression; and, conversely, no expression without impression. It is profitable, therefore, to test and confirm God-given impressions on paper. Such a practice must never develop into sermon preparation or essay writing! That would rob the meditation of its true purpose and challenge. What we suggest is that you record *briefly* the thoughts gleaned, in a devotional form, for personal appropriation and practical application.

Pray—Now turn the meditation into prayer and pray it back to God until your will has been adjusted to His will in terms of all that the Holy Spirit has newly revealed to you. At this point you will have opened heaven *to every dimension of prayer,* for Jesus said, "If you abide in Me, and *My words abide in you*, you will ask what you desire, and it shall be done for you" (John 15:7, emphasis ours).

The apostle Paul spells out the dimensions of prayer when he lists four of the seven different Greek words for prayer found in the New Testament: "supplications, prayers, intercessions, and giving of thanks" (1 Tim. 2:1). *Confessional prayer* or "supplications" carries the idea of desire or needs. In prayer we confess to God our desires and our needs. Then there is *consecrational prayer.* "Prayers" is the most general word for prayer, but is exclusively used of our address to God; therefore, it emphasizes the sacredness of prayer and the need for reverence and worship in our devotions. Next is *conversational prayer*—"intercessions." While this is translated "petition" (prayer, 1 Tim. 4:5), its basic meaning is "to meet with in order to converse" (W. E. Vine). How often do we take time to "converse" with our heavenly Father?

Finally, there is *celebrational prayer*—"giving of thanks." This is a dimension of prayer that should never be absent in our dealings with God. Thanksgiving should not merely conclude a "selfish prayer." Thanksgiving should be the normal activity of a grateful and adoring heart. Archbishop Trench reminds us that this is one aspect of prayer that will continue throughout eternity, where it will be "longer, deeper, fuller than here."[5] As did Elijah of old, we must prove, day by day, that "the effective fervent prayer of a righteous man avails much" (James 5:16). Preacher, remember the words of Jesus, "Men always ought to pray and not lose heart" (Luke 18:1). If you are not praying, you are fainting.

Share—As you leave the place of prayer determine to share the good of your quiet time with somebody during the day. This may be done in a variety of ways: through conversation with God's people, through personal evangelism, through writing, and so on. Not to use what the Lord has given you is merely to acquire knowledge that puffs up (1 Cor. 8:1). As was seen in the wilderness, the Israelites who *hoarded* the manna found that it bred worms (Exod. 16:20).

So we have seen that growing into "the measure of the stature of the fullness of Christ" (Eph. 4:13) is a devotional and daily discipline. Therefore, like Jehovah's Servant (the Lord Jesus Himself), we must be able to say, "The Lord God has given Me the tongue of the learned, that I should know how to speak a word in season to him who is weary. He awakens Me morning by morning, He awakens My ear to hear as the learned. The Lord God has opened My ear; and I was not rebellious, nor did I turn away" (Isa. 50:4–5; see also Mark 1:35). Jesus *never* missed His quiet time. Dare we do anything less? It is estimated that the average pastor spends less than ten minutes per day in this devotional discipline.[6] God have mercy on us!

Paul's call for *continuance* in the Word must be matched, with *obedience* to the Word of God. Paul stresses that "the Holy Scriptures . . . are able to make [us] wise for salvation through faith which is in Christ Jesus" (v. 15). Scripture only affects the life when it is coupled with the obedience of faith. The writer to the Hebrews speaks of those who never entered fully into the covenant blessing of God because the Word was not "mixed with faith" (Heb. 4:2). There is no substitute for faith-obedience. Jesus made this abundantly clear when He stated, "If anyone wills to do His will, he shall know concerning the doctrine, whether it is from

God, or whether I speak on My own authority (John 7:17). And the apostle James bluntly commands, "Be doers of the word, and not hearers only, deceiving yourselves. For if anyone is a hearer of the word and not a doer, he is like a man observing his natural face in a mirror; for he observes himself, goes away, and immediately forgets what kind of man he was. But he who looks into the perfect law of liberty and continues in it, and is not a forgetful hearer but a doer of the work, this one will be blessed in what he does" (James 1:22–25). You will observe that blessing follows obedience. How true are the words of John Sammis:

> Trust and obey, for there's no other way
> To be happy in Jesus, but to trust and obey.

The Preacher Must Read the Word of God Publicly

When the apostle exhorts, "Give attention to reading" (1 Tim. 4:13), he has in mind more than Timothy's devotional life; he also visualizes the gathered assembly of believers listening to the public reading of the Holy Scriptures. In Paul's day, the public reading of God's Word was crucial. For those gathered for worship, this was the only chance they had to "hear" God's voice. Few, if any, possessed their own scrolls or parchments.

We submit that the public reading of God's Word is equally crucial in our day. Augustine stated it perfectly when he declared, "When the Bible speaks, God speaks!" That means that the reading of Scripture is *the most important* part of public worship. Even the sermon must come under the sentence of the Word!

When Ezra and his assistants stood on the platform of wood at the convocation called by Nehemiah, it is recorded: "They read *distinctly* from the book, in the Law of God, and they gave the sense, and helped them to understand the reading" (Neh. 8:8, emphasis ours).

To practice and perfect the public reading of Scripture should constitute a regular discipline in your preparation for preaching. As a preacher you should read aloud, at pulpit speed, a chapter of the Bible every day. It is preferable that this be done standing, with a mental picture of your congregation. The reading should be recorded and listened to for self-criticism. *Great care should be given to articulation, pronunciation, and enunciation.* These three words are similar, but not synonymous. They come from the world of phonetics and are part and parcel of the preacher's arsenal. *Articulation = speech.* The word means "speech sounds" and emphasizes the need for clarity in communication.

Pronunciation = *sense*. The etymology indicates "the pronunciation of [a word] with phonetic symbols." It is speaking a word in the required or standard manner. For example, one could say, "He could not *pronounce* my name." *Enunciation* = *sound*. The meaning, from two Latin words, signifies "to speak out." In fact, *nuntius* can be translated "messenger" or "herald." Put all this together and you have speech, sense, and sound! When you read or preach the Word of God there should be clarity of articulation, purity of pronunciation, and energy of enunciation. Paul said it first: "Devote yourself to the public reading of the Scriptures" (1 Tim. 4:13 REB). (For further treatment see chap. 13, "The Preacher and Proclamation.")

THE PREACHER MUST BE DIRECTED BY THE SCRIPTURES

Paul also insists that we rely upon the Scriptures for direction. "All Scripture is given by inspiration of God, and is profitable for doctrine, for reproof, for correction, for instruction in righteousness" (v. 16). In making this statement, the apostle was not stressing the inspiration of Scripture, for this was a doctrine generally assumed by all devout Jews. On the contrary, he was reminding Timothy that the basis of Scripture's profitableness lay in its inspired character.

We need to bear this in mind in a day when Christian standards are being questioned by leaders and laymen alike. The Battle for the Bible is on, but however hot the debate, we must stand on the authority of the Scriptures. Once we are clear on this, we will have no problem in making the Bible the final and only   rule of faith and practice. It is sufficient for all our needs.

The Bible Is Sufficient for Revelation

"All Scripture is . . . profitable for doctrine" (v. 16). The Bible is the only book in the world that imparts knowledge concerning God's revelation in Christ. This is why Paul emphasizes that "the Holy Scriptures . . . are able to make you wise for salvation through faith which is in Christ Jesus" (v.15). No other source contains this wisdom. And the wonderful thing about it is that the more we read it, the more we understand the nature and scope of God's "so great salvation" (Heb. 2:3).

If there were no other incentive for the daily and disciplined reading of the Word of God, "so great salvation" in Christ should be enough! Who does not long to be more like Jesus? Yet this conformity to Christ can never take place without reading and obeying Scripture. This is why we are exhorted to behold "as in a mirror the glory of the Lord" and so be "transformed into [Christ's] image from glory to glory, . . . by the Spirit of the Lord" (2 Cor. 3:18).

The Bible Is Sufficient for Refutation

"All Scripture is . . . profitable for . . . reproof" (v. 16). No one can aspire to be a man of God without encountering false teaching and wrong living. Concerning the first, we are told to hold "fast the faithful word as [we have] been taught, that [we] may be able, by sound doctrine, both to exhort and convict those who contradict" (Titus 1:9).

As the coming of the Lord draws near, evil men and seducers are going to increase, both in number and influence. So the preacher, especially, must know how to "contend earnestly for the faith which was once for all delivered to the saints" (Jude 3).

As to wrong living, Paul is just as strong. He exhorts, "Have no fellowship with the unfruitful works of darkness, but rather expose them" (Eph. 5:11). And in another place he commands, "Those who are sinning *rebuke* in the presence of all, that the rest also may fear" (1 Tim. 5:20, emphasis ours). This approach to what is evil is a far cry from the compromise of our day! The man of God must ever remember that while times change, *truth never changes.*

The Bible Is Sufficient for Restoration

"All Scripture is . . . profitable . . . for correction" (v. 16). If reproof underscores the negative aspect, "correction" accents the positive. Like the previous word, this one is only found here in the New Testament. This suggests that Paul is being very specific with his choice of language. Correction means "to set up straight" or "to restore to the original position."

The message is clear. The delinquents must not only be rebuked, they must be restored. To those who need the restoring word, Jesus declares: "You are already clean because of the word which I have spoken to you" (John 15:3). How reassuring to know that God's people can be cleansed by the Word! (Ps. 119:9; John 17:17).

The Bible Is Sufficient for Regulation

"All Scripture is . . . profitable . . . for instruction in righteous-ness" (v. 16). The man of God must be "regulated" if he is to pros-per in the sphere where God's will is considered normative. And to this end "the grace of God that brings salvation has appeared to all men, teaching [or discipling] us that, denying ungodliness and worldly lusts, we should live soberly, righteously, and godly in the present age" (Titus 2:11–12).

In a time when indulgence and indiscipline abound on every hand, we need to learn afresh what is meant by "instruction in righteousness" (v. 16). In essence, it is the life of discipleship. To all of us Jesus says, "If you abide in My word, you are My disci-ples indeed. And you shall know the truth, and the truth shall make you free" (John 8:31–32). It is evident, therefore, that if we are to be men of God, we must be directed by the Scriptures in every area of our lives.

THE PREACHER MUST BE DEPENDENT ON THE SCRIPTURES

Lastly, Paul instructed Timothy that a preacher must be dependent on the Word of God: "That the man of God may be complete, thoroughly equipped for every good work" (v. 17). The title "the man of God" appears to apply specifically to Christian teachers and preachers, rather than to believers generally (see 1 Tim. 6:11). Be that as it may, one thing is clear: if the preacher is to fulfill his functions in the home, in the church, and in the world, he must be dependent upon the Word of God. Only then will he be equipped by the Spirit of God to engage in the service of God. This is so vital that we need to look at it more closely.

Depend upon the Word of God for Spiritual Maturity

"That [we might] be complete" (v. 17). We cannot lead others into spiritual maturity if we are still babes! This is what the writer to the Hebrews means when he asserts, "For though by this time you ought to be teachers, you need someone to teach you[7] again the first principles of the oracles of God; and you have come to need milk and not solid food. For everyone who partakes only of milk is unskilled in the word of righteousness; for he is a babe. But solid food belongs to those who are of full age [mature], that is, those who by reason of use have their senses exercised to discern both good and evil" (Heb. 5:12–14). That phrase, "the word of righteousness," is the key to our understanding of this strong and searching passage. Christian maturity is the spiritual ability to cope with relationships of life—Godward, manward, and selfward. *Righteousness* here means "the right conduct God expects believers to follow."[8] The man who cannot cope with Christian conduct is a babe. He is still on milk, instead of solid food. Because of failure to use the Word of God skillfully, he has no sense to discern between good and evil in any given situation. Therefore he divides the church of God like the immature Corinthians (1 Cor. 3). There is no shortcut to maturity. We must depend upon the Word of God day by day.

Depend upon the Word of God for Spiritual Activity

"Thoroughly equipped for every good work" (v. 17). The phrase "every good work" includes our call to the ministry. The apostle makes this clear when he tells us that "we are [God's] workmanship, created in Christ Jesus for good works, which God prepared beforehand that we should walk in them" (Eph. 2:10).

One of the greatest discoveries we can ever make is to learn that before the universe was brought into existence, and before we were physically or spiritually born, God had a plan for each of our lives. The thrill of Christian service is to find, follow, and finish that plan to the glory of His name.

What a challenge this brings to those of us in the Christian ministry! It is easy to go on day after day in the religious "rat race" without the smile of God's favor. We can organize programs and manipulate results, but the fact remains that, in the light of the judgment seat of Christ, nothing of any value will appear or remain!

When Moses built the tabernacle, he had to follow meticulously the *pattern* shown him "on the mountain" (Heb. 8:5). God still has a pattern for service here on earth, and that pattern is revealed in the Holy Scriptures. That is why we must be devoted to, directed by, and dependent on the Word of God. For the preacher, it must be *all* the Word of God for *all* the work of God.

CHAPTER THREE

THE PREACHER AND THE LIFE OF GOD

Walk in the Spirit, and you shall not fulfill the lust of the flesh. . . . If we live in the Spirit, let us also walk in the Spirit.

—Galatians 5:16, 25

Study Text: Galatians 5:13–6:5.

T he renowned Puritan preacher, John Owen (1616–83), wrote prolifically on the person and work of the Holy Spirit. In his discourse *On the Holy Spirit* (1674) there occurs a remarkable passage in which he states: "The sin of despising [the person of the Holy Spirit] and rejecting His work *now* is the same nature with idolatry of old, and with the Jews' rejection of the person of the Son" (emphasis ours).[1] In plain terms, John Owen tells us that if the sin of Old Testament times was the rejection of God the Father, and the sin of New Testament times was the rejection of God the Son, then the sin of our times is the rejection of God the Holy Spirit. This message is both profound and poignant—especially as we think of our contemporary religious scene. Someone might say, "How can you talk about the rejection of the Holy Spirit when His person, work,—and especially His gifts—are the 'buzz words' in both Protestant and Catholic circles of discussion and debate?"

There is no simple answer to that question; but there is a serious one. With all the talk about the Holy Spirit, there is a rejection of Him in two respects—and both are sins. There is the sin of "escapism." Some preachers will not even mention the Holy Spirit for fear of being "labeled." For this reason their pulpits are silent on the subject. At the other end of the spectrum is the sin of "extremism." The shallow ministry, subtle manipulations, and senseless manifestations that are so prevalent today do not square with the Word of God or, indeed, the glory of God. Both these sins—escapism and extremism—are, in fact, a rejection of the Holy Spirit in all the glory of His person, work, and gifts. What we need is *biblical balance!*

One thing is certain: No preacher can fulfill his ministry, in terms of his life and work, without the lordship and leading of the Holy Spirit. This chapter is about the life of God in the Spirit. While the text we have chosen does not *specifically* address the preacher/pastor, the truth it reveals concerns both members and leaders in the church of Jesus Christ. The life of the preacher matters! God is far more interested in what we are as preachers, than in what we do. The preacher must exemplify the life of God.

The verses assigned for reading unfold to us the evidences of this "walk" or life in the Spirit. Nothing is more important for the preacher in his personal, relational, and vocational life than to "walk [or live] in the Spirit" (v. 16). The verb *walk* (Gk. *stoicho*) is an exhortation to keep step with one another in submission of heart to the Holy Spirit, and therefore keeping step with Christ who is our life.[2] It behooves us to ponder prayerfully the essential lessons that emerge from this passage.

LIFE IN THE SPIRIT DEMANDS SPIRITUAL FREEDOM

Paul begins chapter 5 of Galatians with a command—a command to keep on doing an action as one's general habit or lifestyle.

He urges us to "stand fast . . . in the liberty by which Christ has made us free, and do not be entangled again with a yoke of bondage. . . . For you, brethren, have been called to liberty; only do not use liberty as an opportunity for the flesh, but through love serve one another" (vv. 1, 13). The believers in Galatia were threatened by a twofold yoke of bondage. On the one hand, there was the bondage of religious legalities (see vv. 1–15), and on the other, the yoke of rebellious carnalities (see vv. 16–21). With this situation in mind Paul exclaims, "Stand fast therefore in the liberty by which Christ has made us free." We, as preachers, must follow this command and serve in the liberty of the Spirit.

We Must Know Freedom from Religious Legalities

"Stand fast therefore in the liberty by which Christ has made us free, and do not be entangled again with a yoke of bondage" (v. 1). When Paul wrote these words, Judaizers had invaded the Galatian church and were attempting to bring the believers under the bondage of the law from which Christ had set them free through sovereign grace. Their religious legalities covered a whole range of regulations and limitations.

What was true then is also true now. We all know about personal legalism, denominational legalism, traditional legalism, ecclesiastical legalism, racial legalism, and even theological legalism ("boxing" God into self-serving theological concepts that have no biblical basis or balance).

Yet, we must remember that Christ came to set us free by the power of His cross and by the power of His Spirit. In a similar context, Paul affirms that "where the Spirit of the Lord is, there is liberty" (2 Cor. 3:17). This liberty is not license, nor limitation, but rather the power to do what we ought in the light of God's Word and the power of God's Spirit.

Are you free or are you bound? Read again the liberating words of the apostle: "It was for freedom that Christ set us free; therefore keep standing firm and do not be subject again to a yoke of slavery" (Gal. 5:1 NASB).

We Must Know Freedom from Rebellious Carnalities

"Walk [or live] in the Spirit, and you shall not fulfill the lust of the flesh. . . . Now the works of the flesh are evident" (vv. 16, 19), and Paul lists a grim catalog of them! Even though we are born again, we still possess the old nature. Until that old nature is brought under the mortifying power of the cross, through the applied ministry of the Holy Spirit, we can be plagued and fettered by rebellious carnalities. Paul details these carnalities under three categories: sexual sins, spiritual sins, and social sins.

Sexual Sins. "Adultery, fornication, uncleanness, lewdness" (v. 19). It is significant that the first sins to head the list have to do with sexual relations. This is not because sexual sins are intrinsically more evil than others, rather it is because sexual sins reveal more graphically the self-centeredness and rebellion of those who dare to prostitute God's holy norms for human relationships. Alas, as preachers, we can be involved in these sexual sins—unless we know the liberating power of the Spirit.

Charles Colson in his book *The Body* observes that "the divorce rate among clergy is increasing faster than in any other profession. Numbers show that one in ten have had an affair with a member of their congregation, and 25 percent have had illicit sexual contact."[3] These are serious statistics that we need to *face* without fear or favor, and then *fight* in the power of the Spirit. God has called us to a life of victory and purity—and we must not relent (1 Pet. 1:15, 16; 1 Cor. 15:33–34, 57).

Spiritual Sins. "Idolatry, sorcery" (v. 20). Idolatry means anything or anyone who comes between God and ourselves, thereby becoming the center of our worship and attention. God has forever condemned idolatry, and the apostle John warns, "Little children, keep yourselves from idols" (1 John 5:21). How many of us are guilty of worshiping idols! What about TVs, computers, F16s, and other inventions of our modern age? *Sorcery* can refer to the "use of drugs"—as we see all around us today. Indeed, drug taking has invaded the church of Jesus Christ. What Aldous Huxley and others predicted has come to pass. Even some pastors seek religious experiences through the "kicks" of substance abuse. The brainwashing of the New Age movement and other satanic activities has encouraged these subtle forms of addiction.

Social Sins "Envy, . . . drunkenness, revelries" (v. 21). These sins can be found in our hearts—unless we know what it is to be protected by the blood of Christ and the power of the Spirit. Paul is not talking about the act of sin so much as the *habit* of sin. While it is true that the believer is not under the law, but under grace, that is no excuse for sin (Rom. 6:15). If anything, it is a challenge to live in victory! Paul states in our text that we have been "called to liberty," but he also reminds us: "Do not use liberty as an opportunity for the flesh, but through love *serve one another*" (v. 13, emphasis ours).

So we return to our theme: Walking or living in the Spirit. To do so demands spiritual freedom; and, thank God, "Where the Spirit of the Lord is, there is liberty" (2 Cor. 3:17).

LIFE IN THE SPIRIT DISPLAYS SPIRITUAL FRUIT

"The fruit of the Spirit is love, joy, peace, longsuffering, kindness, goodness, faithfulness, gentleness, self-control. Against such there is no law" (vv. 22–23). As we crucify "the flesh with its passions and desires" (v. 24) by the power of the Spirit (Rom. 8:13), and as we yield to the control of the Spirit, spiritual fruit appears in our lives. There is no better portrayal of this spiritual fruitage than what is described in verses 22–23, and it is nothing less than a ninefold configuration of the life of Christ. John Stott describes this cluster of nine Christian graces as "[the believer's] attitude to God, to other people, and to himself."[4]

The Believer's Attitude to God
"Love, joy, peace" (v. 22). Love for God, joy in God, and peace with God are aspects of the God-centered life. In other words, we are describing unconditional love, unbelievable joy, and unperturbable peace. Can others see these characteristics in our lives as we stand behind our pulpits, walk the wards of the hospital, or enter the homes of our parishioners?

The Believer's Attitude to Other People
"Longsuffering, kindness, goodness" (v. 22). Our social lives will display the *longsuffering* of courageous endurance without quitting; the *kindness* of Christian servanthood in a selfish world; and the *goodness* of agape love fleshed out in generosity and hospitality.

The Believer's Attitude to Himself
"Faithfulness, gentleness, self-control" (vv. 22–23). In our personal lives we will manifest the fruit of faithfulness in dependability and in accountability in our service to God and man. We will manifest the fruit of gentleness in Christlike behavior in every situation of life. We will manifest the fruit of self-control in the God-given ability to harness natural passions for redemptive purposes.

Now while it is possible for the old nature to counterfeit some of the fruit of the Spirit, it can never produce the full-orbed character of Christ in us. When the Spirit produces fruit, God gets the glory and the Christian is not conscious of his spirituality. On the other hand, when the flesh is at work, the person is inwardly proud of himself and is pleased when others compliment him. Any preacher who says he does not enjoy a compliment is lying! But to whom do we ascribe the glory? The work of the Spirit is to make us more like Christ *for His glory* and not for the praise of men (note Luke 6:26a).

If the question be asked, "How can I know the fruit of the Spirit in my life?" the answer is clear. We must "be filled with the Spirit" (Eph. 5:18). This calls for a moment-by-moment openness to the Lord. We must "walk in the light as He is in the light" (1 John 1:7). We must not "grieve the Holy Spirit" (Eph. 4:30) by any known sin or "quench the Spirit" (1 Thess. 5:19) by giving place to self. This openness is an essential condition for a Spirit-filled life.

Along with the daily openness there must also be a daily obedience to the Lord. We are told that God has given the Holy Spirit "to those who obey him" (Acts 5:32). There is no substitute for *total* obedience to the Word of God. In practical terms, this means a disciplined quiet time on a regular basis (see chap. 2). It also calls for prayer that *asks.* Jesus promised, "If you then, being evil, know how to give good gifts to your children, how much more will your heavenly Father give the Holy Spirit to those who ask Him!" (Luke 11:13).

Our Lord confirmed these conditions for fruitful Christian living in that exquisite allegory in John 15 where He speaks of the vine and the branches. He taught: "Abide in Me, and I in you. As the branch cannot bear fruit of itself, unless it abides in the vine, neither can you, unless you abide in Me" (v. 4). The whole concept of abiding is that of openness and obedience to the Lord. Indeed, Jesus said, "If you keep My commandments, you will abide in My love" (John 15:10). Then He added, "If you love Me, keep My commandments. And I will pray the Father, and He will give you another Helper [the Holy Spirit], that He may abide with you forever" (John 14:15–16; 15:10).

It is also important to understand that when Paul issued his command to be filled with the Spirit he employed the passive voice. His words were: "Let the Spirit fill you." Quite clearly, he implied yieldedness and submission to the control of the Holy Spirit in dependence and obedience.

LIFE IN THE SPIRIT DIRECTS SPIRITUAL FOCUS

"Brethren, if a man is overtaken in any trespass, you who are spiritual restore such a one in a spirit of gentleness, considering yourself lest you also be tempted" (6:1). If we know the freedom of the Spirit and the fruit of the Spirit in our lives, then there is a focus of the Spirit that emerges in our daily ministry. Paul expounds this spiritual focus in these opening verses of the sixth chapter of Galatians. The more we examine these words, the more comprehensive becomes our ministry.

We Are to Restore the Fallen

"Brethren, if a man is overtaken in any trespass, you who are spiritual restore such a one in a spirit of gentleness, considering yourself lest you also be tempted" (6:1). Two of the ugliest sins of the church today are judgmentalism and unforgivingness. This is why there is so much bitterness in the Body. This is "why revival tarries." If we walk in the Spirit there is a focus of ministry to be performed in and through us. In the first instance, it is to restore the fallen. Paul gives us an example of a man who had been over-taken in a sin. What are we to do if we are truly filled with the Spirit? The answer is precisely given: we are to restore such a person in the spirit of meekness, realizing that we also could be tempted to fall.

The verb *restore* is in the present active imperative. The term is used in Matthew 4:21 for mending nets and comes from a Greek root for "equipping thoroughly." This does not mean that sin is to be compromised in any shape or form. Indeed, our pastoral duty is to rebuke sin (especially when committed by leaders) "in the presence of all, that the rest also may fear" (1 Tim. 5:20). But having applied the principles of discipline, the purpose of restoration is to bring a person back into fellowship and wholeness.

We Are to Release the Fettered

"Bear one another's burdens, and so fulfill the law of Christ" (6:2). The legalist is not interested in lifting burdens. Instead, he *adds* to the burdens of others (Acts 15:10). This was one of the sins that the Master severely condemned: "They [the Pharisees] bind heavy burdens, hard to bear, and lay them on men's shoulders; but they themselves will not move them with one of their fingers" (Matt. 23:4).

Paul uses the word *burdens* to show the subtlety and cruelty of legalism. In fact, legalists exacerbate the problems of those who are already weighed down.

By way of contrast, he who is Spirit-filled has a releasing ministry. In love he wants to see his brother set free for service (5:13)!

All around us are people who are fettered. They may not have fallen, but they are fettered. What a ministry to set such people free with the word of liberating authority through Jesus Christ our Lord! Jesus declared, "If the Son makes you free, you shall be free indeed" (John 8:36).

We Are to Rebuke the Foolish

Not only are we to restore the fallen and release the fettered, we also are to rebuke the foolish. "If anyone thinks himself to be something, when he is nothing, he deceives himself. But let each one examine his own work, and then he will have rejoicing in himself alone, and not in another. For each one shall bear his own load" (6:3–5). In this passage there are three corrective principles we must face if we would focus on the Spirit's ministry in and through us.

We Must Get Right with Ourselves. "If anyone thinks himself to be something, when he is nothing, he deceives himself." Pride issues in self-deception (Jer. 49:16) and leads to divine resistance (James 4:6).

Sure, we must accept who and what we are, as redeemed people in Christ, and rejoice in what grace has done; but to think ourselves to be something when actually we are nothing is to deceive ourselves in arrogant overevaluation. Jesus warned, *"Without Me you can do nothing"* (John 15:5, emphasis ours). To get right and stay right with ourselves we must constantly live in a spirit of repentance. And the first step in repentance is the correct appraisal of ourselves in the sight of God.

We Must Get Right with Our Service. "Let each one examine his own work, and then he will have rejoicing in himself alone, and not in another" (v. 4). God has given each of us a special task to perform. The apostle reminds us that "we are His workmanship, created in Christ Jesus for good works, which God prepared beforehand that we should walk in them" (Eph. 2:10). Our responsibility is not to be concerned with our brother's business, but rather to find, follow, and finish what each of us has been called to do. You will remember that after his restoration Peter wanted to know what John was going to do. Jesus told him that it was none of his business; his task was to follow Jesus to the very end (John 21:21–23). The temptation to compare ourselves with others is another roadblock in our ministry, and it often leads to jealousy, strife, and division in the church of Jesus Christ.

We Must Get Right with Our Savior. "For each one shall bear his own load [or his 'own pack']" (v. 5). The reference here is to the final day of reckoning. Paul offers here what he expresses a little differently in Romans 14:12: "Each of us shall give account of himself to God." Ultimately, it is what the Savior thinks or says that matters. No one can answer for his brother. Each one of us has to bear his own load of responsibility and accountability and answer for it at the judgment seat of Christ (1 Cor. 3:9–15).

So this is the sequence: we must get right with ourselves; we must get right with our service; and we must get right with our Savior. Very simply, the focus of the Holy Spirit in a yielded preacher is to restore the fallen, release the fettered, and rebuke the foolish—and that includes ourselves as preachers!

We must ask ourselves: Are we living in the Spirit? If we are, the clear evidence will be spiritual freedom, spiritual fruit, and spiritual focus in our lives, hour by hour and day by day.

One more thing needs to be added, and it is crucial. If we live in the Spirit, we must be *led* by the Spirit (vv. 16, 18). This leadership implies lordship, and "where the Spirit of the Lord is there is liberty?" (2 Cor. 3:17). It is the Spirit who makes the lordship of Christ a reality in our lives. What God the Father has planned, and God the Son has purchased, can never be experiential until God the Holy Spirit *personalizes* that redemptive work in us as we yield "moment by moment" to His lordship.

> Holy Spirit, reign in me,
> With your own authority—
> That my life, with constancy,
> May "flesh out" your liberty.

—Stephen F. Olford

CHAPTER FOUR

THE PREACHER AND THE MAN OF GOD

You, O man of God, flee these things and pursue righteousness, godliness, faith, love, patience, gentleness.

—1 Timothy 6:11

Study Text: 1 Timothy 6:12–16

In this chapter we are going to discover that the preacher must be a man of God. This is how Paul addresses Timothy: "You, O man of God." The designation recalls the words of ordination that were employed when Timothy was appointed to the ministry.

In Old Testament times, this appellation was assigned to a person who had been entrusted with a divine office. Moses was called "the man of God" (Deut. 33:1); David was called "the man of God" (2 Chron. 8:14); Elijah was called "man of God" (2 Kings 1:9); the prophets were called men of God (1 Sam. 2:27).

Today, every believer is constituted a man of God by virtue of the anointing of the Holy One (1 John 2:20; 1 Pet. 2:9). In the above text, however, the apostle has in mind young Timothy, who had been called to be the preacher and pastor of the church(es) in the city of Ephesus and its environs. Therefore the object of Paul's address is both instructional and inspirational. As his father in the faith, he wants Timothy to rise to the challenge of his noble task.

With this in mind, let us analyze the verses before us and learn what is expected of the preacher as a "man of God."

THE MAN OF GOD MUST FLEE ALL VICES IN HIS MINISTRY

"O man of God, flee these things" (v. 11). The immediate context is divided into two main parts: the first has to do with false teachers, while the second has to do with wrong values. As Paul reflects upon what he has written on these two matters he pleads, "O man of God, flee these things." There are two vices that are to be shunned.

The Vice of Liberalism

"If anyone teaches otherwise and does not consent to wholesome words, even the words of our Lord Jesus Christ, and to the doctrine which accords with godliness, . . . from such withdraw yourself" (1 Tim. 6:3–5). In Paul's day, there were liberal teachers and preachers, just as we have them in our time, and Paul was most concerned that young Timothy not be caught up in the "battle of words" which characterized their brand of indoctrination.

William Barclay informs us that: "The circumstances of life, in the ancient world, presented the false teacher with an opportunity which he was not slow to take. On the Christian side, the church was full of wandering prophets whose very way of life gave them a certain prestige. Christian [worship] was much more informal than it is now. Anyone who felt he had a message was free to give it; and the door was wide open to men who were out to propagate a false and misleading message."[1]

It is a sad fact of life that when a preacher rejects the sound or healthy words of the gospel, he succumbs to a spiritual malaise that manifests itself in a subversive liberalism. Were it not for the keeping power of the grace of God, this should scare us to death! And the reason for this is clearly spelled out. Four things happen when liberalism affects our preaching.

The Message Becomes Corrupted. We no longer "consent to wholesome words . . . of our Lord Jesus Christ" (1 Tim. 6:3). The verb *consent* suggests the act of one who accepts another's offer. The liberal refuses to accept the simple words of the gospel and settles for "a different gospel" (Gal. 1:6, 9). Instead of being determined, like the apostle Paul, to know nothing but "Jesus Christ and Him crucified" (1 Cor. 2:2), the liberal tends to focus on national politics, social concerns, liberation theology and other attractive subjects. We all know men who were once flaming prophets of the gospel but are now so sidetracked with their own agendas that the message of the gospel no longer comes through with searching clarity and saving power. We are not suggesting that some of the above-mentioned issues should not be addressed in our contemporary times; but when they take precedence over the centrality of Christ and the simplicity of the gospel, the divine power of preaching is neutralized and the glory departs. Paul warns, "If we, or an angel from heaven, preach any other gospel to you than what we have preached, . . . let him be accursed" (Gal. 1:8).

The Mindset Becomes Conceited. "If anyone teaches otherwise . . . he is proud, knowing nothing" (vv. 3–4). In pronouncing this verdict, Paul uses strong language. He tells us that a preacher like this is blinded by conceit. The Williams translation renders it, "He is a conceited ignoramus." It is impossible to reason with anyone thus minded.

Unnumbered hours have been spent trying to straighten out men who are too proud to listen to words of caution or counsel. Such preachers attract gullible followers because of their natural charisma and seductive oratory; but they do more harm than can be estimated this side of eternity (see 2 Tim. 4:3–4).

The Manner Becomes Contentious. "If anyone teaches otherwise . . . . he is . . . obsessed with disputes and arguments over words, from which come envy, strife, reviling, evil suspicions, useless wranglings of men of corrupt minds and destitute of the truth (1 Tim. 6:3–5). Paul enumerates five social consequences that flow from this self-deceptive condition (vv. 4–5). Worse still, is the spiritual character of the men who are occupied with such teaching. They are described as "men of corrupt minds and destitute of the truth" (v. 5).

The Motive Becomes Commercial. "Men . . . who suppose that godliness is a means of gain" (v. 5). When a man of God departs from the truth, he soon finds himself involved in materialism. He makes himself believe that a show of godliness is a profitable investment, a lucrative business, advancing one's worldly interests. We shall return to this matter of covetousness in a moment; but suffice it to say here that the love of gain is a deadly vice when it grips a preacher! We should shun it like the plague.

Even though the text of the United Bible Societies omits the words at the end of verse 5, the warning is still valid; for with the vice of liberalism in mind, we need to "withdraw" ourselves from any compromise with biblical *truth.* It is popular today to be liberal in doctrine and, consequently, loose in behavior. With eroding standards in the pulpit and in the pew, many preachers are thought to be naive and outdated when they conform to the "wholesome words, even the words of our Lord Jesus Christ" (v. 3). May God make us *all* faithful to the gospel—cost what it may!

The Vice of Mammonism

"Those who desire to be rich fall into temptation and a snare, and into many foolish and harmful lusts which drown men in destruction and perdition. For the love of money is a root of all kinds of evil, for which some have strayed from the faith in their greediness, and pierced themselves through with many sorrows" (1Tim. 6:9–10). Jesus warned that we "cannot serve God and mammon" (Matt. 6:24). Mammon is the worship of wealth or riches. The problem is not the money in and of itself; it is the *love* of money that poses the danger. In verse 10 the apostle quotes a secular proverb which reads, "The love of money is the metropolis [or world] of every evil."[2] While there is some difference of opinion as to whether or not the verse should read *"a* root" or *"the* root of all kinds of evil," it is immaterial. There are other roots or sources of evil beside the love of money, such as bitterness (see Heb. 12:15), desire (James 1:15), and unforgivingness (see Eph. 4:30–32), but the love of money is indeed "a root of all kinds of evil" (v. 10).

You will remember that in Nathan's parable the love of money caused the man with many flocks and herds to steal the poor man's lamb (see 2 Sam. 12:1–7). It also caused the handsome young ruler to turn away from Christ (see Luke 18:23) and it caused the rich fool to deceive himself into thinking all was well when, in point of fact, he was on the brink of hell (see Luke 12:16–20). And perhaps saddest of all, it caused Ananias and

Sapphira to lie to the Holy Spirit and bring great distress upon the early church at Jerusalem (see Acts 5:1–11). The desire for money has been the cause of innumerable frauds, dollar-sign marriages, shameful divorces, and ruined ministries.[3]

If preachers do not go astray theologically or morally, they often wreck their ministries on the rocks of material gain. It is sad to have to state it—and yet it is unquestionably true—that our religious world is infiltrated with preachers and evangelists who are nothing more than financial rapists. Whether permanent or itinerant in their ministries, they are forever after money and are not only destroying the work of the Lord, but also dishonoring His name.

It is important to notice how this vice of mammonism develops.

Mammonism Starts with a Lure. "Those who desire to be rich fall into temptation and a snare" (v. 9). There is something very attractive about being rich, and men of the cloth are not immune. In fact, many of them preach a "health and wealth gospel" for this very reason.

We were once in the Philippines for a series of meetings. After visiting some of the poverty-stricken areas of one of the islands, we were taken to a hotel to stay. We felt embarrassed to be in the relative comfort of a room that had a television set. We were even more shocked when we turned on the TV and heard an evangelist from the United States telling his viewers of the Cadillacs he possessed, and how the Lord had provided them all. There he was, in his psychedelic suit, shiny shoes, and a red flower attached to his lapel, telling people that if they would only trust God they could be as rich as he. Later that day we were interviewed by the press. The first question asked was whether we preached the "health and wealth gospel." Our reply was a resounding no! We affirmed that we followed a Christ who was born in a stable, had nowhere to lay His head during His itinerant ministry, was nailed to a cross, and was laid to rest in a borrowed tomb—a Christ who challenged His followers to *deny themselves,* take up the cross, and follow Him. Beware of the lure of mammon!

Mammonism Leads to a Lust. The Word says, "Those who desire to be rich fall into . . . many foolish and harmful lusts" (1 Tim. 6:9). That word *lusts* suggests the insatiable passion that stops at nothing. It affects not only individuals but also religious organizations.

Jeffrey K. Hadden, a University of Virginia sociologist, notes that churches, synagogues and their charities take in $25 billion a year—more than the sales of all but eleven of the largest U.S. corporations. "It's a serious matter," he says, "when donors can no longer be sure that their money is being spent honestly and well.

Many church historians relate the surge in financial scandals to the growth of ministries operating outside the financial control of major denominations."[4]

Mammonism Ends with a Lostness. "Those who desire to be rich fall into . . . harmful lusts which drown men in destruction and perdition" (v. 9). The term *destruction* relates to the ruin of body and soul, while *perdition* warns of the loss of the soul for all eternity. Indeed, Paul employs the word *drowned* to depict a man sinking in the turbulent waves of a materialistic world. This whole matter of mammonism raises the question of our responsibility and accountability as men who handle money in the cause of the gospel. It is true that "those who preach the gospel should live from the gospel" (1 Cor. 9:14), and that "the laborer is worthy of his wages" (Luke 10:7). Still we need to watch with prayerful vigilance, lest we be caught up in the lure, lust, and lostness of mammonism. Indeed, as men of God we must flee the vices of liberalism and mammonism. We must maintain a margin of safety by walking in the light and trusting in "the blood of Jesus Christ [God's] Son [which goes on cleansing and protecting] us from all sin" (1 John 1:7).

THE MAN OF GOD MUST FOLLOW ALL VIRTUES IN HIS MINISTRY

"O man of God, . . . pursue righteousness, godliness, faith, love, patience, gentleness" (v. 11). Paul chose these words carefully to represent important virtues of the man of God.

A Holy Man of God

"Pursue righteousness [and] godliness" (v. 11). There is a sense in which righteousness and godliness are the two sides of the coin of holiness. *Righteousness* is our relation to God, whereas *godliness* is our reflection of God. The righteousness called for here demands *maturity in the Word of God.* We are reminded that "everyone who partakes only of milk is unskilled in the word of righteousness, for he is a babe" (Heb. 5:13). What a challenge this brings! Are we men of the Word? What about our devotional life? Is it disciplined and consistent? We are only as tall in the pulpit as we are on our knees in the study. Donald Grey Barnhouse used to say, "The man who is to thunder in the court of Pharaoh with an imperious 'Thus saith the Lord' must first stand barefooted before the burning bush."[5]

Righteousness also demands *conformity to the will of God*— "Everyone who practices righteousness is born of Him" (1 John 2:29). Holiness of life is not an option; it is the obligation of a man who is born of God (1 Pet. 1:14–16).

After the death of the saintly Robert Murray McCheyne, a letter addressed to him, which he had never shown to anyone, was found locked in his desk. The anonymous writer testified that McCheyne had been the means of leading him to Christ, and concluded, "It was nothing you said that made me wish to be a Christian; it was rather the beauty of holiness which I saw in your face!"[6] Can the same be said of us?

Righteousness further demands *activity in the work of God*. John speaks of "the righteous acts of the saints" (Rev. 19:8). All we say and do should be characterized by moral rectitude and ministerial integrity, which result from a right relationship to God. Our preaching, like our living, should be a righteous activity.

A. W. Tozer once said,

> I've heard all kinds of preachers. I've heard the dull, dry ones; I've heard the eloquent ones; but the ones who have helped me the most were the ones who were awestruck in the presence of the God about whom spoke. They might have a sense of humor, they might be jovial; but when they talked about God another tone came into their voice altogether; this was something else, something wonderful. I believe we ought to have again the old biblical concept of God which makes God awful and makes men lie face down and cry, 'Holy, Holy, Holy, Lord God Almighty.' That would do more for the church than . . . anything else."[7]

But then there is "godliness," which is a reflection of God.[8] As we think of this aspect of holiness, we are reminded of the Shunamite woman who entertained Elisha in her home. After some days she said to her husband, "I know that this is a holy man of God, who passes by us regularly" (2 Kings 4:9). As people observe preachers in the home, over the meal table, on the golf course, or in the pulpit, they must be able to say: "This is a holy man of God." After all, this is what really matters!

Alexander Maclaren once told a group of ministers: "The first, second and third requisite for our work is personal godliness; without that, though [we] have tongues of men and angels, [we are] harsh and discordant as sounding brass, monstrous and unmusical as tinkling cymbals. . . . It takes a crucified man to preach a crucified Savior."[9]

As men of God, we must be holy, even as God is holy (see 1 Pet. 1:16). Holiness must permeate every area of our lives (see Heb. 12:14).

A Happy Man of God

"Pursue . . . faith [and] love" (v. 11). Paul's favorite words are *faith, hope* and *love* (see 1 Cor. 13:13). They have been described as "the summation of Christian doctrine and duty" (W. Griffith Thomas). But in verse 11 the apostle employs just the two—"faith" and "love." In this context they "reflect trust in God and benevolence and goodwill toward others (see 2 Thess. 1:3; Titus 2:2)."[10] In practical terms, the two words describe the happiness of a man "whose transgression is forgiven, whose sin is covered. . . . and in whose spirit there is no deceit" (Ps. 32:1–2)

Happiness Is a Life of Faith. "Pursue . . . faith" (v. 11). We "live by faith" (Rom. 1:17), we pray by faith (see Matt. 21:22), we fight by faith (see Eph. 6:16), we win by faith (see 1 John 5:4), and we die by faith (see Heb. 11:13). Little wonder the Bible says, "Whoever trusts in the Lord, happy is he" (Prov. 16:20). There is no greater ambition in life than to please God; and we know that "without faith it is impossible to please Him" (Heb. 11:6). This faith grows and glows as we look off to "Jesus, the author and finisher of . . . faith" (Heb. 12:2). Faith grows and glows as we live in the Word of God, for "faith comes by hearing, and hearing by the word of God" (Rom. 10:17). Faith grows and glows as we lean on the Spirit, for "the fruit of the Spirit is . . . [faith]" (Gal. 5:22). Faith is:

> Simply trusting every day,
> Trusting through a stormy way;
> Even when my faith is small,
> Trusting Jesus, that is all.
>
> Edgar P. Stiles

Happy is the man of God whose trust is in the Lord!

Happiness Is a Life of Love. "Pursue . . . love" (v. 11). The Bible teaches that "the fruit of the Spirit is love" (Gal. 5:22); and "the love of God [is] poured out . . . by the Holy Spirit who was given to us" (Rom. 5:5). From heaven's standpoint, love on earth is three-dimensional: it is spiritual, social, and personal.

If we would know spiritual happiness, we must love the Lord our God with all our heart, soul, mind, and strength (see Mark 12:30). The missionary motto of the Moravian Brethren was a picture representing an ox in the foreground standing between a plow on one side and an altar on the other. Underneath the picture, which spoke for itself, were the words "Ready for either!"[11] That spirit typifies true Christianity: ready for service or sacrifice—whatever the Lord may require. Having been bought with a great price, even the precious blood of our Lord Jesus Christ, we belong to Him—spirit, soul, and body. Therefore, out of love, it is our reasonable service to dedicate our *all* to Him.

If we would know *social happiness*, we must love our neighbor as ourselves (Mark 12:31); we must "love the brotherhood" (1 Pet. 2:17); and we must love our enemies (see Matt. 5:44). Supremely, this includes and involves a passion for souls (Rom. 9:1–5). We shall never be happy here, or at the judgment seat of Christ, if we have not "shed tears" for lost souls.

If we would know *personal happiness,* we must love our wives as our own bodies, for "he who loves his wife loves himself" (Eph. 5:28). In these challenging days in which we live, this is an area where there is unprecedented breakdown in the lives of preachers. God's Word teaches that if a pastor/preacher does not know how to rule his own house well and have his children in submission with all reverence, he virtually disqualifies himself from taking care of the church of God (see 1 Tim. 3:4–5).

As husbands, we should love our wives with a *sacrificial* love, just as Christ loved the church and gave Himself for her. We should go back to Calvary repeatedly and watch the Savior's blood flow to the last drop—and tell Him, and then our wives, how much we love them! (Eph. 5:25). We should love our wives with a *spiritual* love that sanctifies and cleanses "with the washing of water by the word" (Eph. 5:26).[12] As leaders in the home, we should live and teach the Word with such loving authority that our wives and families are influenced for good and the glory of God. We should love our wives with a sympathetic love, even as we love our own bodies and take care of them in every respect (see Eph. 5:28). Only then shall we know personal happiness and freedom in our ministry.

A Humble Man of God

"Pursue . . . patience [and] gentleness" (v. 11). Humility is both a discipline and a devotion, and no man can be used by God who does not seek and show humility. "God resists the proud, but gives grace to the humble" (James 4:6).

Humility Is a Christ-Ordered Discipline. "Pursue . . . patience" (v. 11). Humility is implied in this word *patience.* The term means "an abiding under" (*hupo,* "under"; *meno,* "to abide" [W. E. Vine]). This calls for strong discipline *under* the lordship of Christ.

One of the greatest sins in the ministry today is indiscipline—in our quiet time, in our family prayers, at meal times, in physical exercise, in listening to others, in planning time with the wife and family, and on and on we could go. Only godly discipline produces the humility that Andrew Murray calls "the beauty of holiness."

Humility Is a Christ-Offered Disposition. "Pursue . . . gentleness" (v. 11). The word *gentleness* could be interpreted as "Christlikeness." After all, it was the Lord Jesus who said, "Learn from Me, for I am gentle and lowly in heart, and you will find rest for your souls" (Matt. 11:29). This holy "mind-set" took the Lord Jesus to the death of the cross and to the glory of the throne. It was the virtue that set the Savior above men. Like David of old, He could say, "Gentleness [Hebrew=humility, meekness] has made me great" (Ps. 18:35).

THE MAN OF GOD MUST FIGHT ALL VARIABLES IN HIS MINISTRY

"Fight the good fight of faith, lay hold on eternal life, to which you were also called and have confessed the good confession in the presence of many witnesses. I urge you in the sight of God who gives life to all things, and before Christ Jesus who witnessed the good confession before Pontius Pilate, that you keep this commandment without spot, blameless until our Lord Jesus Christ's appearing" (vv. 12–14).

Paul always had a healthy fear about the possibility of not finishing the course God had mapped out for him: "Therefore I run . . . not with uncertainty. Thus I fight; not as one who beats the air. But I discipline my body and bring it into subjection, lest, when I have preached to others, I myself should become disqualified" (1 Cor. 9:26–27). As Paul handed over the torch of responsibility to Timothy, he exhorted him to fight compromise in the ministry. As we weigh these words, there are two variables that should challenge every preacher.

The Temptation to Vary Our Christian Confession

"Fight the good fight of faith" (v. 12). The verb is in the present tense. Literally it reads, "Go on agonizing or contesting for the faith." The word implies a disciplined struggle (see Col. 1:29). The question is, What faith is Paul referring to here? The answer, of course, is personal faith in the Lord Jesus Christ, based upon the *body of faith* which is objective truth. Indeed, the text goes on to read, "Lay hold on eternal life, to which you were also called and have confessed the good confession in the presence of many witnesses" (v. 12). In effect, Paul tells Timothy, "Just as you first trusted Christ and declared your faith at your baptism and ordination, so fight to the very end."

Now sad and strange as it may appear, this Christian confession is what constitutes one of the variables of our Christian ministry. We all know men who had a radiant testimony when they were converted, and even when they entered the ministry, but now they have lost the glow and glory of it all. Paul was so concerned about this that he encouraged his son in the faith to recall the stand that Jesus took when He witnessed a good confession before Pontius Pilate (see v. 13). To Timothy, this conjured up those tragic, yet triumphant, hours before the crucifixion when Christ, in His humanity, stood before Pilate, under every conceivable pressure, and *never varied* His confession of faith. As the Son of man, He was hungry, He was bleeding, He was exhausted; but notwithstanding all this, He affirmed, "You say rightly that I am a king. For this cause I was born, and for this cause I have come into the world, that I should bear witness to the truth. Everyone who is of the truth hears My voice" (John 18:37).

Oh, that God would enable us to live out this "unflinching steadfastness" of our blessed Savior, by the power of the indwelling Spirit! It is one thing to start the race, and even to continue it, but quite another story to be able to say at the end, "I have fought the good fight, I have finished the race, I have kept the faith. Finally, there is laid up for me the crown of righteousness, which the Lord, the righteous Judge, will give to me on that Day, and not to me only but also to all who have loved His appearing" (2 Tim. 4:7–8).

While the temptation to vary our Christian confession can be hazardous, the second variable is just as perilous.

The Temptation to Vary Our Christian Commission

"I urge you in the sight of God . . . that you keep this commandment without spot, blameless until our Lord Jesus Christ's appearing" (vv. 13, 14). William Hendriksen, in his commentary, points out that the preacher's mandate is to keep the commission of the ministry without spot, so that here on earth—or later at the judgment seat of Christ—he might be able to present his certificate of ordination without a stain.[13]

With regret we admit that there are pastors/preachers who have not only varied in their Christian confession but have varied in their Christian commission. When Jesus challenged His disciples to serve Him to the end, He said, "No one, having put his hand to the plow, and looking back, is fit for the kingdom of God" (Luke 9:62). Our religious world is littered with those who have wavered either in their confession to trust Christ or their commission to serve Christ. This explains the tragedy of the vacated pulpits of men who have made shipwreck of their ministries.

We see, then, that this issue of being a man of God is intensely serious. It is one thing to be ordained to the ministry, but quite another matter to serve faithfully to the very end. Thus, the apostle's words come to us afresh: "O man of God, flee these things and pursue righteousness, godliness, faith, love, patience, gentleness. Fight the good fight of faith, lay hold on eternal life, to which you were also called and have confessed the good confession in the presence of many witnesses" (vv. 11–12). What a call to flee the vices of the ministry, to follow the virtues of the ministry, and to fight the variables of the ministry! Only as we respond can we join in the doxology with which the apostle concludes this paragraph, and exclaim, "He . . . is the blessed and only Potentate, the King of kings and Lord of lords, who alone has immortality, dwelling in unapproachable light, whom no man has seen or can see, to whom be honor and everlasting power. Amen" (vv. 15, 16). Quite obviously, the secret of our ministry and the solution to our mistakes is *the daily surrender of our lives to Jesus Christ as King of kings and Lord of lords*. With every step along the pathway of progressive sanctification, we must declare Jesus Christ as Lord of *all,* or else He is not Lord at all. Let us see to it that all areas of both our personal lives and public service are under His sway. With the hymnwriter let us sing and mean:

> Have Thine own way, Lord!
> Have Thine own way!
> Hold o'er my being Absolute sway!
> Fill with Thy Spirit Till all shall see
> Christ only, always, Living in me.

> —Adelaide A. Pollard

CHAPTER FIVE

THE PREACHER AND THE WORK OF GOD

Be diligent to present yourself approved to God, a worker who does not need to be ashamed, rightly dividing the word of truth.
—2 Timothy 2:15

Study Text: *2 Timothy 2:1–14*

The Bible opens with a picture of God as a "worker." Later Jesus said, "My Father has been working until now, and I have been working" (John 5:17). To be created in God's image implies, in part, that man has a capacity to work. The idea that work resulted from Adam's fall does not reflect biblical truth. A sinless human was placed in the Garden to cultivate and dominate the flora and fauna. The concept of labor was part of God's original commission to mankind.

In ministerial terms, this lays upon the preacher a solemn responsibility to be a "worker who does not need to be ashamed, rightly dividing the word of truth" (2 Tim. 2:15).

Earlier in Paul's instruction to Timothy, the apostle employs three word pictures of disciplined endeavor to illustrate the various aspects of the preacher's responsibility (2 Tim. 2:4–6).

First, the preacher is challenged to develop *the disciplined endurance of a soldier*: "Endure hardship as a good soldier of Jesus Christ" (2:3). As preachers, we must be ready for *suffering*: "Endure hardship" or more accurately, "take your share of suffering." No preacher can get very far in the ministry without encountering intense spiritual warfare (see Eph. 6:1–20), as well as a fair share of ill treatment—even from unexpected sources. He must also be ready for *sacrifice*: "No one engaged in warfare entangles himself with the affairs of this life" (2:4). A soldier "on service" cannot afford to be preoccupied with the things of this life. Failure to observe this call to sacrifice can lead to "entanglement." This word envisages a soldier's weapon trammeled in his long-flowing "civilian" cloak, while he sits "at ease in Zion" (Amos 6:1). There is nothing intrinsically wrong with "the affairs of this life" (2:4); but if they entangle, they must be resolutely cast aside. It is a sad commentary on shallow preaching when the reason given for lack of biblical substance or spiritual power is that the preacher is too busy for God! All week he has been engaged in "the affairs of this life" (2:3) and, therefore, has had no time to pray or prepare (Acts 6:4). Once again, he must be ready for *service*. A soldier must "please him who enlisted him as a soldier" (2:4). He can only please the commander in chief when he fulfills the purpose for which he has been chosen. The apostle already reminded his colleague Timothy that, as a man of God, he must "fight the good fight of faith" (1 Tim. 6:12). In a day of compromise and political correctness, all preachers need to remember this solemn imperative. We may lose human applause, but we gain heaven's approval.

The second challenge the preacher must face is to develop *the disciplined obedience of the athlete:* "If anyone competes in athletics, he is not crowned unless he competes according to the rules" (2:5). The key word in this example is *nominos,* which must be interpreted in light of the Olympic games. These rules extended not only to the race itself but also to the prescribed training. Indeed, one authority cites the fact that athletes had to state, on oath, that they had fulfilled ten months of training before they were eligible to enter the contests. The three objectives of an athlete were energy, honesty, and victory. First, there was *energy.* The whole point of disciplined training was to develop stamina, speed, and style. Even more important was the matter of *honesty.* Severe penalties were imposed on anyone who infringed the rules. Such honesty is also demanded in our day when it comes to competing in sporting events. The delightful and brilliant professional golfer Paul Azinger tells in his autobiography of an occasion when he was well on the way to winning a tournament when he inadvertently infringed a rule. The penalty for this was not one stroke or two strokes, but the entire tournament![1] What would happen to men in the ministry if the same standard of honesty were strictly applied. The apostle Paul took the athlete's type of discipline so seriously that he wrote, "I discipline my body and bring it into subjection, lest, when I have preached to others, I myself should become disqualified" (1 Cor. 9:27). He carried this holy fear right through to his final days on earth: "I have fought the good fight, I have finished the race, I have kept the faith" (2 Tim. 4:7). A preacher needs both physical and spiritual energy; and for this, he has to work out on his feet *and* on his knees! Finally, of course, there is the *victory:* "He is . . . crowned" (v. 5). Donald Guthrie points out that "the apostle is here exhorting Timothy to keep strictly to the 'rules' fixed by the life and teaching of Christ." Then he adds, "There is one important difference between the metaphor and its application; only one athlete may gain the crown, but every Christian will be crowned who strives loyally in the contest."[2]

The third challenge the preacher must face is to develop *the disciplined dependence of a farmer:* "The hard-working farmer must be first to partake of the crops" (2:6). This illustration significantly places the emphasis on *toil*—"the hard-working farmer" (2:6). The point that Paul makes is that the farmer who labors with diligent toil has rights that a lazy man forfeits. Yet along with the toil there must be *trust.* A farmer can prepare the soil, sow the seed, and water the ground, but, ultimately, he has to trust his Creator-God to bring the seed to life. This, too, is one of the great challenges of the preaching ministry. As men of God, we can prepare our sermons, and deliver our souls in proclamation, but, ultimately, we have to trust God to bring to life those who are "dead in trespasses and sins" (Eph. 2:1). Peter reminds his readers that they were "born again, not of corruptible seed but incorruptible, through the word of God which lives and abides forever." Then he adds, "This is the word which by the gospel was preached to you" (1 Pet. 1:23, 25).

With this descriptive triad of metaphors—the soldier, the athlete, and the farmer—the apostle applies the explicit threefold challenge with these words, "Consider what I say, and may the Lord give you understanding in all things" (2:7). What he has stressed in these vignettes is *hard work,* which involves disciplined endurance, disciplined obedience, and disciplined dependence. It is a tough lesson for many of us to learn, but without a wholehearted follow-through, we can never present ourselves "approved to God," *workers* who do "not need to be ashamed, rightly dividing the word of truth" (2:15).

Following the National Congress on Biblical Exposition in Anaheim, California (March 3–6, 1986), questionnaires filled in by preachers revealed that the main hindrance in their prayer life, serious Bible study, and expository preaching was "laziness"! Preachers were not prepared to pay the price of *hard work.* It is little wonder that the apostle Paul stresses this aspect of the pastor/preacher's responsibility before God. We do well, therefore, to examine two aspects of the work of God that must concern every man in the ministry.

THE WORK OF GOD IN THE PERSONAL LIFE

"Be diligent to present *yourself* approved to God" (v. 15, emphasis ours). As a young preacher, Timothy was exhorted to exert every effort to present himself to God as one *approved.* That term comes from the world of industry and coinage; it has to do with the testing of metals. Only that which is fully up to standard is marked *dokimos* or approved. The apostle Peter uses it when he writes of the genuineness of faith "being much more precious than gold that perishes, though it is *tested* by fire" (1 Pet. 1:7, emphasis ours).

In terms of practical experience, the work of God in the personal life covers at least four areas: the moral, the mental, the marital, and the manual or physical.

The Moral Life
"Awake to righteousness, and do not sin" (1 Cor 15:34). This calls for *hard work!* When Paul exhorts Timothy to "take heed to yourself and to the doctrine" (1 Tim. 4:16), he is affirming that "moral and spiritual rectitude is an indispensable preliminary to

doctrinal orthodoxy."[3] Therefore the apostle warns, "Take heed," which literally means "fasten your attention on." For Timothy, and every preacher since, this is no light matter. Paul sums up our moral responsibility in two powerful words: flee and follow. "Flee . . . youthful lusts; but [follow] pursue righteousness" (2 Tim. 2:22). The RSV renders this: "Shun youthful passions and aim at righteousness." Timothy was a young man, probably in his thirties, and so the older apostle tells him to *flee* the evil desires of youth. At no age, however, are we free from temptation; therefore, we are to "flee" (present continuous action). We are to "make no provision for the flesh to fulfill its lusts" (Rom. 13:14). "This present evil world" (Gal. 1:4 KJV) is ever with us inciting our "flesh," inviting our "eyes" and inflating our "pride" (1 John 2:15–17). We must, therefore, face every temptation with the power of the mortifying Spirit (Rom. 8:13 KJV). When certain programs on TV proved to be seductive to one young preacher, he put a card on top of the set reading, "Be ye holy!" (1 Pet. 1:15–16 KJV). But the second verb Paul uses is just as important: "*Follow* righteousness" (2 Tim. 2:22 KJV). The verb is in the present imperative and carries the thought of "pursuing" or "running after" that which is holy and good. There is the "word of righteousness" (Heb. 5:13) which we must study and master, lest we become "unskilled" in handling it; but there is also the "way of righteousness" (2 Pet. 2:21) which calls for total obedience to God's "holy commandment." The bottom line is that morality matters in a preacher's life (read again chap. 4).

The Mental Life

"Whatsoever things are true, whatsoever things are honest, whatsoever things are just, whatsoever things are pure, whatsoever things are lovely, whatsoever things are of good report; if there be any virtue, and if there be any praise, *think on these things*" (Phil. 4:8 KJV, emphasis ours). A great danger in the ministry is to become stale, stunted, or stilted in our mental life. We must avoid this at all costs. The only positive and practical way to ensure the freshness and fullness of mental health is to "devour" good books, appreciate great music and art, and interact with people of intellectual ability as well as spiritual maturity. Concomitant with this is listening to anointed expository preaching and attending institutes and seminars where such preaching is taught and modeled. These mental exercises will not come fortuitously; they must be carefully planned and pursued.

The Marital Life

"If a man does not know how to rule his own house, how will he take care of the church of God?" (1 Tim. 3:5). Your ministry is only as strong as your relationship with your wife and children. Alas, this is where unbelievable breakdown is prevalent today. As a pastor/preacher, you must see to it that you devote sufficient time in your daily schedule to your wife and family.

Make it your practice to take one day off a week with your wife. The average pastor/preacher spends many more hours with other women than with his own wife. This is simply due to the proportion of women in any given church, and their natural disposition to seek the counsel of their pastor. For this reason the wife deserves one full day a week for recreation, fellowship, prayer, communication, and mutual enjoyment with her husband. This also is an opportunity for you to plan together for the week ahead, so that you are both aware of what is taking place in your respective busy schedules. Think of it this way: if Sunday is "King's Day"—then Monday (or any other selected day) is "Queen's Day!"

The children, likewise, should be given attention at specific periods throughout the week. For example, give them Saturday mornings. You will discover that what really matters is not the length of time you spend with your kids but the intensity of interest you show in all their affairs when you *make* time. From their earliest years, inculcate the three As—accessibility, availability, and adaptability. You must always be *accessible,* even when you have to say no to the "high and mighty." Your boy or girl must *never* have to say: "I could never get near my father." But watch out; you can be accessible without being *available.* In fact, you can be in the same room without being available. If your head is in a book or the daily paper, or your eyes are "glued to the tube," you are not available! Finally, you must be *adaptable.* Perhaps this is even more applicable to a preacher than to the average father. So often the pulpit and study have very little in common with a healthy and lively home. For some pastors/preachers, it is a funeral home! Be flexible and adaptable. Plan your time creatively with the children—and even more so as they reach the critical teenage years.

When the children understand the meaning of the three As, there will be no problem with insecurity, on the one hand, or possessiveness, on the other. Needless to say, family life can never enjoy true spiritual reality or stability without the *meaningful* reading of the Bible and family prayers. The husband must be prophet, priest, and king in his own home and exercise his authority as the spiritual leader of the household. If a preacher does not do this, how can he preach about the Christian home to his congregation?

The Manual Life

"Bodily exercise profits a little" (1 Tim. 4:8). The NIV reads, "Physical training is of some value." According to *The Expositor's Bible Commentary,* "Physical training . . . rather clearly refers to athletic discipline. Some think that in view of the earlier verses (1–5) *ascetic* discipline may . . . be included (emphasis ours). But would the apostle assign any worth to it? [He says quite clearly— it 'profits a little'!] The Greek word for 'training' is *gymnasia,* from which we get 'gymnasium.'"[4] Paul deeply believed in the doctrine of a healthy physical body. In his epistles he teaches that the body is to be *dedicated* (Rom. 12:1), *preserved* (1 Thess. 5:23), *exercised* (1 Tim. 4:8), and *disciplined* (1 Cor. 9:24–27). He recognized also that we have to use spiritual weapons to control the body (2 Cor. 10:4–6). After all, the body is "the temple of the Holy Spirit" in which, and through which, we are to "glorify God" (1 Cor. 6:19–20). For this reason, every preacher should have some "disciplined" diversion. For some, this will mean sports such as golf, tennis, basketball, fishing, and so on. For others, it may be carpentry, gardening, painting, or even needlepoint!

Walter Wilson, a medical doctor and pastor/teacher in Kansas City, worked hard and wrote much to help preachers on this subject. In a series of lectures that he delivered in Chicago many years ago, he astonished the group by stating that one hour of *abandoned preaching* was equal to eight hours at the executive desk and twelve to fourteen hours of manual labor. As a doctor, he substantiated these statistics with tests that he conducted on preachers of all ages and sizes. His text for that series of lectures was taken from those words in the Gospels, where Jesus declared, "I perceive that *virtue is gone out of me*" (Luke 8:46, KJV, emphasis ours).

Many of us are unaware of the intellectual, spiritual, emotional, and physical energy we expend in the course of our ministry. The fact is, there is hardly any other occupation on earth more demanding on the total personality than anointed preaching. For this reason alone, there should be time not only for *spiritual restoration* and *mental relaxation* but also for *physical recreation.*

We have dealt with spiritual restoration (see chap. 2, "The Preacher and the Word of God"). Our Lord, in His perfect humanity, *never* missed His quiet time; nor must we (see Isa. 50:4–9; Mark 1:35).

Mental relaxation is another story! How often do we see a preacher *really* relaxed? And yet this "détente" (a lessening of tension) is essential to mental and emotional well-being. For some, it takes light reading, listening to music, or enjoying a day of fishing; for others, it requires more sophisticated therapy. But relax we must!

> There is a famous story told of the aged apostle John, who was once enjoying some relaxation, playing with his favorite doves. A hunter returning from the fields espied him, and approaching him expressed genuine surprise that one so holy and absorbed with higher interests should be thus occupied. The wise Apostle (not without a twinkle in his eye, we suspect), pointing to the hunter's bow, asked why it was that the string was not taut. Quickly the reply came that hunting-time was over and it was necessary for the string to be loosed, if the bow were to preserve its elasticity and strength. "Well spoken," said the apostle John, "and I too must loose the string of my bow after the toil of the day: hence this favorite pastime of mine."[5]

Along with the mental relaxation, we must *work hard* on physical recreation. Sitting at our study desks, at board gatherings, at committee meetings, at counseling sessions, and other sedentary commitments means that we *must* find time to engage in exercise. As we have observed already, our bodies are the "temple of the Holy Spirit" (1 Cor. 6:19–20) and we are honor bound to keep them in tip-top form. Workout options are legion and you must make your choice; but most authorities agree that heel-to-toe rhythmic walking is hard to beat. We must "glorify God in [our bodies] and in [our spirits], which are God's" (1 Cor. 6:20).

THE WORK OF GOD IN THE PASTORAL LIFE

"Be diligent to present yourself approved to God, a *worker* who does not need to be ashamed, rightly dividing the word of truth" (2 Tim. 2:15, emphasis ours). Our discussion now shifts from the personal aspect of our work to the pastoral demands of people, programs, and pulpit. Let us look carefully at this threefold division of pastoral work.

The People of the Church

"Take heed . . . to all the flock . . . of God" (Acts 20:28). The pastor/preacher must be identified with the grassroots issues with which his people are grappling. Failure to observe this basic principle will create all manner of problems in the study as well as in the pulpit. Few men have addressed these problems with such perception and distinction as John R. W. Stott in his excellent book for preachers, *I Believe in Preaching* (British edition of *Between Two Worlds*). He states: "The task of preaching today is *extremely exacting* as we seek *to build bridges* between the Word and the world" (emphasis ours).[6] To do our work pastorally and properly, we must have on our regular agenda three important tasks: shepherding, counseling, and visiting.

Shepherding. Jesus not only said, "Feed My lambs," He also stressed, "Tend My sheep" (John 21:15–17). Both of these verbs are present active imperatives. As ministers, we are responsible for our people now, and accountable for them in a day to come (see Heb. 13:17). "The good shepherd gives His life for the sheep" (John 10:11).

Counseling. "And let us consider one another in order to stir up love and good works, not forsaking the assembling of ourselves together, as is the manner of some, but exhorting one another, and so much the more as you see the Day approaching" (Heb. 10:24–25). While counseling comes under the rubric of shepherding, it is more specific and demands great discernment and discipline.

Counseling is a biblical term, even though it has assumed a more technical connotation in our day and age. The basic definition of a counselor is one who analyzes a situation and gives advices for responsible decision making. In Old Testament times, counselors were employed on a regular basis (see 2 Sam. 16:23; 1 Kings 12:6–14; Isa. 1:26; 3:3; Mic. 4:9). God is often regarded as a Counselor (Ps. 16:7; 32:8; 73:24); the Messiah likewise (Prov. 8:14–16; Isa. 9:6; 11:2), and the Holy Spirit is our indwelling counselor (John 14:16, 26; 15:26; 16:7). As preachers we must learn how to "rightly divide the word of truth" and submit to the leading of the Holy Spirit; only then can we be used in counseling.

In the more technical sense, however, counseling must be categorized as practical, pastoral, or professional. *Practical counseling* comprehends soul-winning, discipling, and the encouragement of one another in love and truth. Anyone engaged in such work *should be trained under pastoral super-vision.* Courses should be taught regularly to equip potential counselors.

Pastoral counseling is more complex and confidential. For this reason, all pastors/preachers should submit to some professional training in counseling. Without this underpinning and experience, serious problems can arise. Seventy-five percent of moral break-down in pastoral ministry can be traced to emotional involve-ments arising out of counseling sessions. The average pastor does not have the professional objectivity and clinical training to han-dle the relational tangles and tragedies of modern times. No pas-tor should have more than four "in-depth" sessions with any one person—especially with a woman—before deferring to a profes-sional counselor.[7] Another piece of advice is that women should counsel women, for the most part. This will generally eliminate many who don't mean business with God or with themselves.

Professional counseling, with a Christian perspective, is a must in most churches today; the burden of responsibility is too heavy for a conscientious pastor to bear alone. Having made that point, however, it must be added that a good deal of counseling should be done from the pulpit! It was Martyn Lloyd-Jones who observed that "excessive counseling in the pew was a reflection of poor preaching from the pulpit."[8] Obviously he was referring to the spir-itual and practical problems, rather than to the complicated areas of pathology.

So counseling is *hard work,* but it must be done if we, as preachers, are to be "approved to God."

Visiting. Paul calls this showing "mercy, with cheerfulness" (Rom. 12:8). Arthur S. Way renders it, "If you come with sympa-thy to sorrow, bring God's sunlight on your face." For this aspect of pastoral preparation, we need to implement the teaching of Ephesians 4:7–12 and 1 Timothy 3:1–7.

A perusal of these passages makes it abundantly clear that no pastor/preacher is able to visit or care for every member of his church at one and the same time—especially if he has a large membership. With pastoral honesty he must make a distinction between *perception* and *reality.* He must give the perception that he is genuinely interested in everyone in his church, but, in real-ity, he can only cope with one person at a time. In any case, God never intended *one* pastor to do all the work. As preacher, teacher, and pastor, his duty is to equip "the *saints* for the work of min-istry" (Eph. 4:12, emphasis ours). As a result of such instruction, "gifting" will emerge in the church to cover the needs of the Body. Among the gifts will be those with the *pastoral burden*. Call them what you will—elders, lay pastors, shepherds, deacons, or whatever—but such men should be honored and harnessed to "take heed . . . to all the flock" (Acts 20:28). Remember, these words were addressed to elders who were left in charge of the Ephesian church *after* their pastor (Paul) had departed for good. No one in your church need be neglected if these true biblical principles are taught and obeyed. Of course, you will do your share of shepherding, counseling, and visiting, *but you cannot do it all!* And what is more, God never intended you to do so. Your supreme responsibility, as we shall see in a moment, is to give yourself "continually to prayer and to the ministry of the word" (Acts 6:4).

The Programs of the Church

The apostles called this aspect of pastoral care "serving tables" and "business" (see Acts 6:2, 3). Acts 6:1–7 is a passage every pastor/preacher should study with great care and creativity. It describes what goes on in every church in regard to "business" matters. Read between the lines and you will see that money, management, and "murmuring" were part of the problem! It would have been the natural thing for the pastors to put "down their tools" and address the situation. But God said no. Led by the Holy Spirit, they informed the church that "it [was] not desirable that [the pastors] should leave the word of God and serve tables" (Acts 6:2). This does not mean that the pastor/preacher should *not* be interested in the programs of the church; on the contrary, the action taken by these early pastors shows that they were deeply concerned. Therefore, they directed measures to address the situation in question. It is their God-inspired methodology that is important to observe. First, the pastors *appointed deacons* or a "task force" (Acts 6: 3, 5–6).[9] These men were Hellenists dealing with a Hellenistic problem. More importantly, they had *spiritual* as well as practical credentials to cope with the crisis that faced the church. Secondly, the pastors *assigned duties* (vs. 3–4), and they were specific. The appointed ones were to resolve the problems in the church and also to relieve the pastors. Then, with unflinching determination, the pastors announced: "We will give ourselves continually [exclusively] to prayer and to the ministry of the word" (Acts 6:4)

The eminent scholar and brilliant expositor Richard N. Longenecker has a fine comment here: "While Christian ministers wish such qualities were more characteristic of their own board and councils, it is only fair to say that boards and councils often wish their ministers were given to more prayer and the ministry of the word! A pattern is set here for both lay leaders and clergy, and God's work would move ahead more efficiently, were it followed more carefully."[10]

Pulpit Preparation

"Be diligent to present yourself approved to God, a worker who does not need to be ashamed, rightly dividing the word of truth" (v. 15).

We now come to the ultimate responsibility of a preacher's high calling. Since we are primarily committed to the ministry of the Word, the study of Scripture is one of our foremost duties. John R. W. Stott reminds us of what the bishop of the Church of England says to a candidate at his ordination. In the words of the Ordinal of 1662, he charges:

> Seeing that you cannot by any other means compass the doing of so weighty a work, pertaining to the salvation of man, but with doctrine and exhortation taken out of the holy Scriptures, and with a life agreeable to the same, consider how studious ye ought to be in reading and learning the Scriptures. . . . We have good hope that you have well weighed and pondered these things with yourselves long before this time; and that you have clearly determined, by God's grace, to give yourselves wholly to this Office, whereunto it hath pleased God to call you: so that, as much as lieth in you, you will apply yourselves wholly to this one thing, and draw all your cares and studies this way; and that you will continually pray to God the Father, by the mediation of our only Savior Jesus Christ, for the heavenly assistance of the Holy Ghost; that, by daily reading and weighing of the Scriptures, ye may wax riper and stronger in your ministry.[11]

From these weighty words we deduce that the pulpit demands from every pastor/preacher (a) time to prepare and (b) truth to proclaim. Let us examine these two demands.

Time to Prepare. "A [toiler] who does not need to be ashamed" (v. 15). No question is asked more often in our Institute for Biblical Preaching than the one concerning *time*. For most pastor/preachers, time is a rare commodity. Paul's conception of time is that it is a fragment of eternity, given by God to man as a solemn stewardship. So he exhorts us to "[redeem] the time, because the days are evil" (Eph. 5:16). Many believe that these words were borrowed from Daniel 2:8. You will recall that Nebuchadnezzar used this language to rebuke his astrologers for investing time in vain delays. The apostle, however, employs the same phrase in the *good* sense of *redeeming time* by foregoing the solicitations of indolence and self-indulgence. How often—and before we are aware of it—we become absorbed in the distracting cares and interests of everyday experience, only to find later that we have been turned aside from the priorities of life. For us, those priorities are *"prayer and . . . the ministry of the word"* (Acts 6:4).

In order to make time for disciplined sermon preparation, we suggest a procedure that works! Simply stated, it is as follows. At the beginning of every week—preferably on a Monday—take a sheet of paper (or better still, a loose-leaf notebook), and with your dairy before you, work out an entire program for the upcoming week. Write out the following.

The General Assignments. These, of course, involve the duties of each day throughout the week. The main point of listing assignments is to first determine what to *include* in the duties of the ministry. Having in mind Acts 6:1–5, determine personally, as well as officially, what areas and responsibilities need to be covered in the week ahead of you. Second, determine what to *exclude* in the duties of the ministry. These duties have to be relegated or delegated to paid staff, trusted members of the board, or able members of the church. As pastor/preacher, you must remember that your task, as leader in the church, is to train others to assume the duties and details that would otherwise rob you of time for study, prayer, and other disciplines of your pastoral ministry. This principle is clearly taught in Ephesians 4:7–12.

The Special Appointments. With days and duties in mind, carefully allocate time—in other words, make appointments—for the following:
- Study appointments
- Prayer
- Correspondence
- Counseling
- Visitation
- Extra reading
- Serious writing
- Relaxation
- Family
- Preaching

The purpose of such close planning should be obvious. It has been well said: "If you aim at nothing, you are sure to hit it!"

Such assignments and appointments discipline one's use of time. You know only too well that when you go out to shop, you invariably forget the items you did not list. The same is true in business and the ministry: plan carefully and write it down!

The Crucial Adjustments. In every pastor/preacher's life there are the unexpected events and emergencies that change the program of any day. These must be carefully and prayerfully weighed before God and then handled as follows:

Take Care of the Emergency at Hand. This may be a matter of life and death or some unusual call of duty that cannot be delegated or ignored. In such cases your responsibility is clear.

Take Note of the Expenditure of Time. It is possible to be called away from your desk and study books and, because of the change of pace, waste time unnecessarily. This is especially true when you are tired. With courtesy and firmness you must excuse yourself when the duty is done. This applies particularly to so-called "emergency long distance calls"! It also applies to the unannounced appearance of friends or relatives.

W. E. Sangster, of Westminster Central Hall in London and author of *The Craft of the Sermon: Its Construction and Illustration*, had an ingenious way of handling interruptions in the middle of sermon preparation. He made such occasions an opportunity for trying out his sermon. After the initial introductions and pleasantries, Dr. Sangster would say something like this: "My dear friends, I am so excited about Sunday's sermon that I must share some of the thoughts and blessings that God has given to me." And with that opening statement he would launch right into a full discourse! Three benefits inevitably followed: (1) it profited his visitors—and perhaps sent them going before they intended; (2) it clarified and deepened his own thinking; and (3) perhaps most important, it redeemed the time!

The Personal Assessments. Knowing that unexpected interruptions or crises can occur in anyone's life, it is important to have time for daily and weekly assessments. There must be time to review progress, revise plans, and resolve problems. Without taking time for evaluation of this kind, it will not be long before there is confusion and frustration in your pastoral ministry. Personal assessment must include three vital questions if you are to be approved of God:

1. How have I expended God's week?
   - Has the week been wasteful?
   - Has the week been useful?

2. How have I extended God's work?
   • Has there been advancement?
   • Has there been retardment?
3. How have I expounded God's Word?
   • Have I rightly divided the Word of truth?
   • Have I poorly divided the Word of truth?

Where necessary, revise plans and resolve problems.

You cannot follow these simple procedures day after day and week after week without developing both discipline and dedication in your ministry.

Truth to Proclaim. "Rightly dividing the word of truth" (v. 15). The pulpit demands that we have *something to say* to our congregations—whether it be in the setting of a local church, or the wider circles of the Christian ministry. In this book, *Anointed Expository Preaching,* we are committed to the view that *what we have to say, is what God has to say!* In plain language—this involves *the exposition of the Word of God in the power of the Holy Spirit.*

To help you understand what we mean by expository preaching, we draw on the perceptive insights of the president and Distinguished Professor of Old Testament at Gordon-Conwell Theological Seminary in South Hamilton, Massachusetts, Walter C. Kaiser Jr. In a magazine article entitled "The Crisis in Expository Preaching Today," he writes:

> Expository preaching is that method of proclaiming the Scriptures that takes as a minimum one paragraph of Biblical text (in prose narrative or its equivalent in other literary genre) and derives from that text both the shape (i.e., the main points and subpoints of the sermon) and the content (i.e., the substance, ideas, and principles) of the message itself. . . . What such a tactic rules out are the following: (1) bumper sticker slogan preaching, derived either from Scripture or elsewhere that becomes little more than psychological boosters; and (2) preaching from market-driven forces that dictate what will and what will not 'go over' with certain age groups, clienteles, or classes of listeners. *The Scriptures must be given priority in setting the agenda and the diet for our spiritual welfare* (emphasis ours).[12]

With Dr. Kaiser's definition of expository preaching as our frame of reference, we must be "diligent to present [ourselves] to God, [workmen] who do not need to be ashamed, rightly dividing the word of truth" (v. 15). We must distinguish between imposition and exposition; eisegesis and exegesis. With the text before us, we must ask: What does the Scripture say? What does the

Scripture mean? And only then, What does the Scripture say to me and my congregation? Whatever hermeneutical or homiletical principles we employ must not obscure the *definitive* meaning of the text of God's Word. This will call for the highest level of integrity and efficiency from those of us who preach the Word.

To summarize: every expository sermon must be historically definitive, contextually definitive, linguistically definitive, grammatically definitive, and doctrinally definitive. With the selected text before us we must:

1. Crystallize the subject
2. Analyze the structure
3. Organize the substance
4. Finalize the sermon

For the full treatment of sermon preparation, we now move on to part 2 of our book. As we proceed from the preacher and the walk he must pursue, to the preacher and the work he must perform, let us determine to be vessels for "honor, sanctified and useful for the Master, prepared for every good work" (2 Tim. 2:21).

PART TWO

The Work to Perform

CHAPTER SIX

THE PREACHER AND EXPOSITION

I charge you therefore before God and the Lord Jesus Christ, who will judge the living and the dead at His appearing and His kingdom: Preach the word! Be ready in season and out of season. Convince, rebuke, exhort with all longsuffering and teaching. For the time will come when they will not endure sound doctrine, but according to their own desires, because they have itching ears, they will heap up for themselves teachers; and they will turn their ears away from the truth, and be turned aside to fables. But you be watchful in all things, endure afflictions, do the work of an evangelist, fulfill your ministry.

—2 Timothy 4:1–5

Study Text: 2 Timothy 4:1–5

I n our introduction to this book we stated that we are committed to biblical exposition. What we mean by this, and how to
set about it, is the subject and substance of this second section of *Anointed Expository Preaching.*

Even as we address this task, however, we are well aware of the
aversion to expository preaching that some preachers and congregations evince. But this is nothing new. The apostle Paul faced similar
opposition. Having exhorted Timothy to "preach the word!" (v. 2), he
warned that the time would come when people would not endure
sound doctrine; they would "turn their ears away from the truth"
(vv. 3–4). Christian history is replete with examples of "the deliberate refusal" of men and women "to hear" the Word of the Lord
expounded.But this must not deter us. The imperative "Preach the
word!" must be obeyed. When John R. W. Stott was asked if he
had "changed his mind" about the indispensability of biblical
preaching, he retorted:

> To the contrary! I still believe that preaching is the key to the
> renewal of the church. I am an impenitent believer in the power of
> preaching. I know all the arguments against it—that the television age
> has rendered preaching useless, that we are a spectator generation,
> that people are bored with the spoken word, disenchanted with any
> communication by spoken words alone. All these things are said these
> days.
>
> Nevertheless, when a man of God stands before the people of God
> with the Word of God in his hand and the Spirit of God in his heart,
> you have a unique opportunity for communication. I fully agree with
> Martyn Lloyd-Jones that the decadent periods in the history of the
> church have always been those periods marked by preaching in
> decline. That is a negative statement. The positive counterpart is that
> churches grow to maturity when the Word of God is faithfully and sen-
> sitively expounded to them.
>
> If it is true that a human being cannot live by bread only, but by
> every word which proceeds out of the mouth of God, then it is also
> true of churches. Churches live, grow, and thrive in response to the
> Word of God. I have seen congregations come alive by the faithful and
> systematic unfolding of the Word of God.[1]

We share Stott's conviction, and call upon every preacher who
reads this book to remember that we preach the Word "before
God and the Lord Jesus Christ, who will judge the living and the
dead at His appearing and His kingdom" (v. 1).

What, then, is this awesome task of "expository preaching"? Let
us start with three definitions.

1. *The Westminster Directory* (1645) states that "the true idea of [expository] preaching is that the preacher should become a mouthpiece for his text, opening it up and applying it as a word from God to his hearers, . . . in order that the text may speak . . . and be heard, making each point from his text in such a manner 'that [his audience] may discern [the voice of God].'"[2]

2. Our own definition reads: Expository preaching is the Spirit-empowered explanation and proclamation of the text of God's Word with due regard to the histo rical, contextual, grammatical, and doctrinal significance of the given passage, with the specific object of invoking a Christ-transforming response.

3. Paul exhorts: "Be diligent to present yourself approved to God, a worker who does not need to be ashamed, rightly dividing the word of truth" (2 Tim. 2:15).

With these terms of reference before us, let us proceed to consider two main aspects of expository preaching: biblical authority and practical artistry.

THE BIBLICAL AUTHORITY FOR EXPOSITORY PREACHING

"Preach the word!" (v. 2). When Paul gave expression to this solemn exhortation he was speaking with all the authority of heaven. He knew that the life, growth, health, and strength of the church depend on expository preaching. What is more, as a Jewish scholar, the apostle would have been familiar with this approach to the Holy Scriptures.[3] The final word on this matter, however, is that expository preaching is supported by *biblical authority*.

The Old Testament Evidence

"So they read distinctly from the book, in the Law of God; and they gave the sense, and helped them to understand the reading" (Neh. 8:8). The context of this remarkable verse records a time of revival in the history of God's ancient people. Nehemiah had called the nation to face up to the Law of God. Ezra was the evangelist. He built a pulpit of wood and, with thirteen Levites (as assistants), read and expounded the Law of God to a most attentive audience. While the whole passage can (and should) be studied to see what an impact God's Word had upon the people, for our purposes now, we want to point out the three aspects of expository preaching that were employed.

The Reading of the Text of God's Word. "So they read⁴ distinctly from the book, in the Law of God" (Neh. 8:8). Underscore that word *distinctly*. They read "making clear . . ." How seldom is the Word of God read clearly in our day and generation! Too often preachers stumble and mumble in the public reading of God's Holy Word. The reverence and expertise with which we undertake this holy exercise can never be overestimated. In some cultures, the way the Bible is opened and its pages turned conveys a solemn significance.

To practice and perfect the reading of Scripture should constitute a strict discipline in the quiet of our studies. As often as possible, every preacher should stand and read aloud, at pulpit speed, the passage on which he will be preaching, while mentally visualizing an audience before him.⁵ It would be good to record the reading and then listen to it for self-criticism. The purpose of this exercise is to read distinctly—especially when it comes to complicated passages and difficult names, words, and punctuation. It is helpful to interpret the word *distinctly* in terms that have similar meaning but are, at the same time, quite distinct. To be precise, pulpit reading must be performed with *composed articulation*—the emphasis here is on *speech; controlled pronunciation*—the emphasis here is on *sound;* and *convinced enunciation*—the emphasis here is on *sense.*

On October 7, 1857, C. H. Spurgeon preached to his largest audience ever: 23,654 assembled in the mammoth Crystal Palace for a national day of fasting and prayer. "A few days previously he went to the hall to test the acoustics. Standing on the platform, he lifted up his voice like a silver trumpet and cried, 'Behold, the Lamb of God that taketh away the sin of the world.' A workman, busy painting high up in one of the galleries, heard the words which seemed to come to him from heaven. In deep conviction of sin he went home and did not rest until he was able to rejoice that Christ was his Savior."⁶ Something about Spurgeon's reverent tone and resonant voice, when quoting that text, arrested the attention of that man. Would to God that were true of all preachers!

The Revealing of the Truth of God's Word. "So . . . they gave the sense" (Neh. 8:8). Ezra's congregation was no longer familiar with the Old Testament Scriptures. They needed expositors. These people were "returnees" from captivity and had forgotten the idioms of the holy scrolls. The Law was not only read but explained, to ensure that the people grasped the meaning. These may also have been translations from Hebrew to Aramaic. The doctrine of the perspicuity (clarity) of Scripture is that the things necessary for salvation can be understood from the Bible without special techniques or higher education. This truth does not eliminate the need for faithful exposition of the Scriptures by persons trained for this." So our task, as preachers of the Word of God, is to unfold the truth in language people can understand, "in demonstration of the Spirit and of power" (1 Cor. 2:4).

The Relating of the Thrust of God's Word. "They . . . helped them . . . understand the reading" (Neh. 8:8). To understand the reading, there must be application of doctrine to duty and of principle to practice. Preaching does not accomplish its objective if it fails to change character and conduct! Preaching must have as its goal not only the impartation of truth, but also the transformation of life.

This, then, is biblical exposition as seen in the Old Testament.

The New Testament Evidence

On that first resurrection day, Jesus *"expounded* to [the two disciples] in all the Scriptures the things concerning Himself" (Luke 24:27, emphasis ours). As the Prince of all expositors, He expounded the truth and illustrated His points. With consummate authority, He adopted the customary method of reading and exegeting the Scriptures (John 1:18). Whether in the synagogue, in the home, on the hillside, or from an anchored boat, Jesus consistently expounded the Word of God to hungry hearts (see Mark 1:22; 2:1–2; 4:34; Luke 4:16–22, etc.).

Peter did the same on the Day of Pentecost (Acts 2:14–36). Analyze that sermon carefully and you will discover that Peter birthed his message in the prophecy of Joel (2:28–32) and then supported his dominating theme from two psalms (16:8–11; 110:1).

Stephen's sermon, as recorded in Acts 7, was an expository treatment of the historic portions of Genesis and Exodus, and Philip followed the same procedure in dealing with the Ethiopian eunuch (see Acts 8:26–35; Isa. 53).

Second only to our Lord Himself was that great expositor, the apostle Paul. He knew no other method than that of expository preaching. So when he writes to Timothy he exhorts, "Give constant attention to the public reading of the Scriptures, to public appeals, to *exposition*" (1 Tim. 4:13 Way). Again he says, "Be diligent to present yourself approved to God, a worker who does not need to be ashamed, rightly dividing the word of truth" (2 Tim. 2:15). That closing statement, "rightly dividing the word of truth," perfectly defines expository preaching. While difficult to translate into English, it essentially means "handling aright the word of truth; declaring the word of truth without distortion; rightly administering the word of truth; holding a straight course in the truth; giving the truth a right of way." This renders the verb as "the skillful application of parts or aspects of truth adapted to affect persons specially in need of instruction."

So we have both Old and New Testament evidence of *the biblical authority* for expository preaching. Now let's discuss how to put it into practice.

THE PRACTICAL ARTISTRY FOR EXPOSITORY PREACHING

"Preach the word!" (v. 2). When Paul dictated these words he added, "Convince, rebuke, exhort, with all longsuffering and teaching" (v. 2). In employing this language, Paul had in mind what today we would term the hermeneutical and homiletical presentation of truth.

The question then arises as to how this kind of preaching can become a practical reality in our busy ministries. The answer involves hard work—*and we mean hard work!* Our experience, whether we are dealing with a single text, a whole paragraph, or a complete book, is that expository preaching demands "blood, sweat, and tears." To help us understand the art in simple terms, let us first set forth our approach to expository preaching.

There Must Be the Study of the Text

When Paul talks about "rightly [or accurately] dividing the word of truth" (2 Tim. 2:15), he implies an approach to Holy Scripture that calls for accurate interpretation.

We Must Be Historically Accurate. We must look at the setting or the historical background of the passage under consideration. We must ask questions like Who? Why? When? Where? and What? What was the occasion of this writing? What are the historical factors that make these verses come alive? This historical examination must include the country, the customs, the culture, and sometimes even the climate behind the text. By *climate* we mean the ethos, the underlying and distinctive character or spirit of the people addressed and not just the geographical environment (although that should be studied if it has relevance to the text under consideration). Never come to a passage without studying its historical setting.

We Must Be Contextually Accurate. This principle is extremely important. No verse should be interpreted in isolation from its context. It has been said that "a text out of context is a pretext." Both the immediate context and the inclusive context must be carefully examined. The Bible is *one book*, so we should make sure that we understand the *total* context, including the Old and New Testaments, as the text may demand.

One reason so many cults exist today is because the proponents have deviated from traditional truth by taking texts out of context. For instance, by taking verses out of context, we could prove that you should commit suicide immediately! Matthew 27:5 says that Judas "went and hanged himself." By linking that verse with Luke 10:37, we could challenge you to "go and do likewise"; and by turning to John 13:27 we could urgently add, "What you do, do quickly."

Now we have deliberately exaggerated the treatment of the above unrelated verses to make the point that we must be historically and contextually accurate if we are going to "[rightly handle] the word of truth" (v. 15). We must *never* take a verse out of context. Often in informal and inductive Bible studies we take a single verse and try to explain it without regard to its larger context. This is also easy to do in *topical preaching*. We quote a particular verse and try to support it with other isolated texts to make our point, simply because there is a recurring word that has to do with the topic before us; when examined *in context,* the verses may not really prove what we are seeking to communicate.

So strong is Walter C. Kaiser's aversion to topical messages that he has advised his students "for some years now to preach a topical sermon only once every *five* years—and then immediately to repent and ask God's forgiveness!"[7] To soften those words, Dr. Kaiser acknowledges a measure of hyperbole in the statement, but quickly adds, "The serious note that lies behind this playfulness is a loud call for preaching that is totally biblical in that it is guided by God's Word in its origins, production, and proclamation."[8] That's expository preaching!

We Must Be Grammatically Accurate. Every effort should be made to discover precisely what the original author meant. The Lord Jesus was very specific about this when He said, "For assuredly, I say to you, till heaven and earth pass away, one jot or one tittle will by no means pass from the law till all is fulfilled" (Matt. 5:18). Commenting on that one statement, John Walvoord, former president of Dallas Theological Seminary, contended that "Jesus upheld the inerrancy of Scripture in its *entirety,* not simply in its moral sense" (emphasis ours). Not one word for Him was irrelevant.

Grammar matters when it comes to understanding what is written. It requires the study of the forms and structures of words known as *morphology.* Furthermore, it means the study of the arrangement of phrases and sentences—or what is called *syntax.* Know your subjects, know your objects, know your predicates, know your verbs, and know the tenses of those verbs. Know your prepositions; many a doctrine swings on a simple preposition. Once again, that preposition may be exactly the same as you find it in another place, yet it may carry a different connotation altogether because of the context.

We must also give attention to the study of word meanings or the science of *semantics.* Scholars have compiled studies of the history of words in their settings so that we can select any word in the Bible, define its meaning, and observe why and how it was used.

In summation, grammar is the analysis of sentences, phrases, words, including verbs, prepositions, conjunctions, personal and proper pronouns, and more. If you have a difficulty in this area, take a refresher course in grammar. If you are studying Hebrew or Greek, we encourage you to continue your study of biblical languages because it is so valuable. For those who don't know Hebrew or Greek, don't let that become a barrier to understanding the Word of God. There are numerous reference books[9] available to help us understand the particular version of the Bible that we are using. We must do all we can to be grammatically accurate in our biblical interpretation.

We Must Be Doctrinally Accurate. Never leave a passage without asking, What is the theological message of this passage? What are the principles that transcend centuries, cultures, countries, and other barriers that may be derived from the passage? Some preachers say, "I will preach the Bible, but I will not bother about doctrine." That is absolutely contrary to Paul's exhortation. He commanded, "Preach the word! Be ready in season and out of season. Convince, rebuke, exhort, with all longsuffering and teaching *[doctrine]*" (v. 2). Every sermon must have theological content.

There Must Be the Subject of the Text

To craft an expository sermon we must first crystallize the *theme* of the text or unit of Scripture under consideration. Only when this is determined can we really decide on the subject of the sermon. Even structure and sequence cannot be developed until the subject becomes clear. We must always keep in mind that "the secret of communication is not saying seven things, but saying one thing seven times" (F. B. Meyer). We must capsulize the subject in one word, phrase, or sentence—"the big idea," the core of the message, the sermon in a nutshell. It is what the "lead" is to the journalist. Good journalism calls for a pithy, catchy, condensed headline, and we contend that the construction of a good sermon requires the same.

There Must Be the Structure of the Text

We have now come to an interesting and exciting aspect of expository preparation. Studied exegesis and analysis should disclose what are the main points of the text under consideration. These *must not be forced,* but should naturally arise out of the immediate context. Once they emerge, they should be structured to reveal two essential components.

First, there must be *homiletical distinctiveness.* The language employed should literally point up the natural structure in the text. To achieve this, there are questions that need to be asked of every passage under consideration:[10]

1. *What is the dominating theme?* Almost every passage of Scripture has more than one theme; however, since you can only preach one at a time, you must select the dominating theme that serves your immediate sermonic purpose.

2. *What are the integrating thoughts?* Every theme is made up of thoughts that are extracted from the literary unit with exegetical accuracy and spiritual sensitivity. These thoughts become the structure of the expository sermon. Here you must distinguish between *exposition* and *imposition.* The textual, thematic sermon *must* say what God says, and *not* what you want it to say!

As you seek to develop these integrating thoughts, there are four essential ingredients that must be included. First, each point must be biblical. Remember, you are expounding a given passage and you must let the Word of God speak for itself. As we have stated above, we must shun eisegesis and strive for exegesis. Even a subheading must be a corroborative part of your text. Second, each point must be logical. Whether or not members of the congregation have studied logic does not imply that they are not logical. The listener is waiting for you to move from 1 to 2, and from 2 to 3, etc., and so the text must be handled in this fashion. *The line of discovery may not always be the line of delivery.* Third, each point must be practical. Exposition must never be divorced from application and illustration. You must not leave the relationship of doctrine to duty until the end of the sermon; the message must be practical. Fourth, each point must be critical. No expository sermon should ever be preached without *purpose.* To achieve that purpose demands critical preaching. A crisis of decision must be precipitated.

3. *What is the motivating thrust?* With the *unity* (theme) and *movement* (thoughts) of a sermon there must be the *purpose* (thrust). Before standing in the pulpit you must decide what the sermon is to achieve. What is the bottom line? What is the motivating thrust? When this work has been carefully done, you can set your points out in some memorable form. As well as being biblical, logical, practical, and critical, it is good to be *memorable.* This is where alliteration (using words with a similar sound) can be most helpful. Whether or not such artistry is used, the headings should still be homiletically distinctive. Abuses can occur at both extremes. Either clever alliteration can be carried to the point of absurdity, or clumsy delineation can be carried to the point of obscurity. Both are wrong.

The second essential in the structure is *harmonious relatedness.* Continuity of thought is the primary purpose of an outline; therefore, it is imperative to make every point line up with the subject of the sermon. This cannot be overemphasized. Without this structural and sequential treatment of the text, there will be confusion in the pulpit as well as in the pew. Think of this harmonious relatedness in terms of the human body: the head linked to the neck, the neck to the torso, the torso to the arms and legs, so that symmetry and continuity characterize the entire body. Let this be a pattern for your outline!

There Must Be the Substance of the Text

This is the essence of the sermon. A well-prepared sermon must have three substantial parts: the introduction, the exposition, and the peroration.

The introduction should be carefully thought out and concisely stated. It should contain contextual information that leads the audience without delay into the *background* and *burden* of the sermon.

The exposition is the substance of all preaching. Great care should be taken to interrelate the three component parts of an expository sermon: the explanation, the application, and the illustration. The *explanation* is the exposition of the passage, and it will demand all the disciplines we have already considered. The *application* must be an integral part of the sermon from beginning to end. Unwillingness to obey truth nullifies the impact of preaching. The expositor must be careful to present truth in such a way that its relation to character and conduct is both indisputable and irresistible. In his epistle to the Romans, Paul reminds his readers that they "obeyed from the heart that form of doctrine to which [they] were delivered" (Rom. 6:17). Applied truth should always be personal, practical, and pertinent. The third component, the *illustration,* is also an important part of the sermon. The aim of an illustration is to illustrate! If it does not do that, it is worse than useless; indeed, it distracts. Just as a window lets in the light, an illustration shows in living color the thought or idea that is being conveyed. As C. H. Spurgeon once warned, "Illustrate by all means, but do not let the sermon be all illustrations. . . . We are not sent into the world to build a Crystal Palace."[11] To tell a story or an anecdote just for the sake of humor or theatrical effect is unpardonable for the consecrated and conscientious preacher.

One law of biblical interpretation applies here: *the law of illustrative mention.* This law teaches that every main doctrine in Scripture has an illustrative counterpart. For example, we have the illustration of the Passover for teaching on redemption (Exod. 12–14); we have the illustration of the life of Job for teaching on disciplinary trial; we have the illustration of Miriam for teaching on jealousy (Num. 12); we have the illustration of Ananias and Sapphira for teaching on deceitfulness (Acts 5), and so on.

The peroration is the concluding part of a discourse. There are vital elements in the peroration that should form the climax of the sermon. One is *condensation*-crystallizing the truth. A few words of summation help to focus on the motivating thrust. Another element is *exhortation*-personalizing the truth. We move from the general to the personal. Even though we have applied truth throughout the sermon, we must now put a special emphasis on the listener. Finally, there is *invitation*-actualizing the truth. Even before calling for a public confession of faith there should be a Spirit-anointed challenge to the mind, the heart, and the will of the listener to respond to God's truth as it is being expounded. Still, we should never leave the pulpit without calling for a verdict. In one sense the peroration (or conclusion) is even more important than the introduction. More sermons are ruined by a poor conclusion than for any other reason. Therefore, a conclusion should really conclude the message. It should leave the audience with the distinct impression that, having said the last word, nothing more needs to be added. God has spoken.

Once all the material has been read, researched, and recorded, then comes the task of writing out the sermon in full. The value of this exercise is that it serves as a "form" of preaching, helping to impress the material upon your mind. It also encourages a free flow of contemporary English, rather than the language of the books you have been studying. Another value in this exercise is the opportunity it affords to eliminate the unnecessary and extraneous material that is not immediately pertinent to the main flow and thrust of the message. (Such redundant information can be filed for future sermons.) The importance of writing out the sermon in longhand cannot be overemphasized.

With the manuscript before you, there are three disciplines that you must follow, if the sermon is to be incarnational and redemptive by the enabling of the Holy Spirit.

Prayerfully Review the Sermon. You cannot do this unless the manuscript is before you. In reviewing your sermon, look for "ugly bulges" that destroy the symmetry and the artistry of the sermon. Although it may mean eliminating quite a lot, you don't have to destroy this material. Catalog it and put it in your files for future reference and development. As you reread your sermon, watch for recurring sentences or places where you've used the same word repeatedly. Perhaps you have included theological terms that may not be clear to your congregation. Change them. Correct split infinitives and bad grammar. Ensure that you have smooth-flowing sentences throughout. All this is involved in reviewing the sermon and making it a work of art—"unashamed workmanship."

Prayerfully Relate the Sermon. This step involves thinking through the sermon in relation to yourself, in terms of your personal obedience to what you've written down on paper. Be intensely personal and ask: Have I a right to preach to my congregation any truth that I have not obeyed myself? As you reflect on the sermon in this way, an incarnational miracle takes place. Just as the Eternal Seed was planted in the womb of Mary, so the sermon, as the Word of God, is planted in your own heart. The Word thus becomes flesh, and at "full term" you are able to deliver Jesus! That's incarnational preaching.[12] The message is alive to you. *Now* you can tell other people what God has said to you.

A. W. Tozer, that wonderful preacher of the Christian and Missionary Alliance, used to say that when he got to this point in his preparation he would lie prostrate on the study floor with just a tissue under his nose so that he would not inhale the carpet dust. That's the way he wanted to be in the presence of his Lord. You must determine your own mind-set and posture before Almighty God.

Prayerfully Rehearse the Sermon. Beginning with the subject, the introduction, and the exposition and right through to the conclusion, *seek the Lord's appro v a l*-point by point, subheading by subheading. As you work your way through the sermon, there will be moments when you experience a check in your spirit. You will "hear" an "inner voice" telling you to change an illustration because of exaggerated details. The fact is, the story is a lie, and before you can stand "approved to God" in the pulpit, you must seek forgiveness and correct the illustration or delete it altogether. Once you have earned His smile of satisfaction, you will be liberated in your spirit and you will be ready to preach! This gives a sense of authority and "quiet confidence" as you represent your Lord before your congregation. This is what is meant by "anointed expository preaching"!

Having presented this "overview" of the preacher and exposition, we now invite you to "dig deeper" into what Paul describes as "rightly dividing the word of truth" (2 Tim. 2:15). Only as we do this with the "unction from the Holy One" (1 John 2:20 KJV) will we be workers who do not need to be ashamed when we "preach the word" (2 Tim. 4:2). That charge is just as obligatory today as when Paul first uttered the words, and we fail in our holy task if we do not preach with the same sense of responsibility and accountability. So we repeat: Preach the Word! Preach the Word! Preach the Word!

CHAPTER SEVEN

THE PREACHER AND PREPARATION: SELECTION

You know . . . how I kept back nothing that was helpful, but proclaimed it to you, . . . Therefore I testify to you this day that I am innocent of the blood of all men. For I have not shunned to declare to you the whole counsel of God.
—Acts 20:18, 20, 26–27

Study Text: Acts 20:17–38

How do you know that you have the right text for a sermon? What comes first, the text or the topic? Should you plan a preaching ministry, and if so, for how long? Is there a standard length of text you should use for an expository message? How do the needs of people, specific occasions, crises, etc., impact the selection of the topic and text?

The above questions, along with many others, have to do with *what* to preach and, more specifically, *what to preach on a given occasion.* How we choose what to preach—how we select texts and topics—is critical for each message preached, as well as the whole character and content of a preaching ministry.

What begins as a simple question, What do I preach next Sunday? (for instance), actually forces the preacher to consider what preaching itself is supposed to be and do, what the content of preaching needs to be on any given occasion, how the Holy Spirit works, and how God sovereignly plans and orchestrates situations. Let it be said that ultimately there is a majestic mystery intrinsic to this whole process. Although we will seek to bring biblical truth to bear on these matters, that in no way means that the question above can be answered simply, unless you say, "Preach what God has told you to preach."

To provide a basis and framework for practical comments and suggestions concerning text and topic selection, we will consider an instructive biblical passage, Acts 20:17–38. These verses clearly have much more to offer than principles for text and topic selection, and we will seek to be fair to the broader themes presented. But, within these broader themes, the nature and content of a preaching ministry will be addressed.

After three missionary journeys (that we know of) the apostle Paul headed for Jerusalem, wanting to be there by Pentecost. His haste did not allow him to spend time in Ephesus or Asia, so from the coastal town of Miletus, he sent for the elders of the church in Ephesus, where he had ministered for some three years. The elders came. Acts 20:17–38 is a marvelous account of an emotional real-life farewell. Paul told the leaders that they would never see him again, which caused great grief as they prayed, wept, embraced, kissed, and then went to the departing ship. Paul also used the occasion to speak of his ministry while in Ephesus. He informed the leaders of his immediate plans and exhorted them to shepherd the church, entrusting them to God for that purpose.

There is an apologetic thrust to much of Paul's words as he defends his manner and message in Ephesus. He likewise defends his plans to go to Jerusalem, despite the warnings of suffering ahead. This text is a powerful apostolic statement and defense of ministry and an exhortation to appointed leaders to be faithful to their charge (Acts 20:28–30).

It is instructive to view this text in light of Paul's departure and to examine the subjects that attracted his focus and attention in his

solemn parting words. What was important to Paul at such a time.
And what has Luke given us of that occasion and of those parting words? We see at least three main ministerial matters that
Paul addresses in this "speech." They point out the lasting legacies of Paul's ministry in Ephesus and, indeed, can be a model
for those of us who would follow in Paul's steps. The legacies
were and are: (1) a personal example, (2) a preached Word,
and (3) a prepared leadership. Paul describes and defends his
manner of living and ministry, speaking of such things as his
personal humility (v. 19), pastoral intensity (v. 31), and practical integrity (vv. 34–35). Paul points to his personal example in
these matters without regret.

Paul also emphasizes his preached Word at Ephesus and,
indeed, defends it. He clearly preached evangelistic messages
(vv. 21, 24–25). He sought also to present edifying messages,
evidently on different topics (v. 20). Furthermore, Paul's statement "I have not shunned to declare to you the whole counsel
of God" (v. 27) indicates that Paul believed that he had delivered
faithfully and comprehensively the message God had given him.
This is why he was innocent of men's blood—he had faithfully
served his charge, and declared the truth he was obligated to
communicate. The exact content of the whole counsel of God is
not given, although we can assume it included "repentance
toward God and faith toward our Lord Jesus Christ" (v. 21), "the
gospel of the grace of God" (v. 24), and "the kingdom of God"
(v. 25). Also, at the broadest level it included both evangelistic
and edifying proclamation and instruction (v. 20). What is especially important to us as preachers is that Paul testifies to faithfulness. He was not negligent or selective with the truth he had
to declare. At Ephesus he left behind a comprehensive message
and instruction that would enable further growth of the church
in the future (v. 32).

In this account, Paul specifically defends his ministerial manner
(a personal example) and message (a preached Word). He also
exhorts his prepared leadership (the third legacy). It is evident
from the text that these leaders were appointed (v. 28), instructed
(vv. 28–31), exhorted (v. 31), and entrusted (v. 32) with the shepherding of the church. Much more could be said about the importance of entrusting a local church to a prepared leadership, but the
focus of our chapter brings us back to the second legacy: a
preached Word.

At the heart of the matter of texts and topics is the issue, What do you want to leave behind? What lasting legacy do you want to entrust to those who remain when you depart?

From this text we would conclude that *we must be faithful to the message God has entrusted to us and we must seek to proclaim it comprehensively so that it can become the source of strength for the future growth of the church*. The preached Word must be measured against Paul's statement: "I have not shunned to declare to you the whole counsel of God" (v. 27). There is a need for faithfulness, thoroughness, and commitment to the "whole counsel of God." The preacher's priority is to communicate a God-given message—revealed truth. Paul testifies to faithfulness in this task over a three-year period. He is not speaking about an individual message, but the comprehensive cumulative content of his preaching. Paul sensed an *accountability* to divine truth that dictated his preaching ministry. He was accountable to an "objective content" in the sense of God-revealed truths. For the evangelical preacher, that truth is contained within the completed canon of Scripture, the Word of God bearing witness to "the counsel of God." We make this distinction between the written Scriptures (Old and New Testament) and "the whole counsel of God" because Paul did not have the completed canon, nor was he referring to it explicitly when he made this statement.

This word *counsel (boule)*, common in Lucan literature, can mean *"purpose, counsel, resolution, decision . . ."*[1] Significant other uses to compare are found in Acts 2:23, 13:36, and then in Ephesians 1:11. I. H. Marshall, speaking of Paul's declaration of innocence in Acts 20:26 says, "Paul's assurance was derived from his confidence that he had faithfully preached the gospel in every particular; he had dealt with the whole of God's plan of salvation."[2]

Faithfulness and thoroughness to an entrusted "message" is what Paul asserts. Certainly at the core of Paul's preaching and teaching, according to Luke, was the gospel of the grace of God calling for repentance toward God and faith towards our Lord Jesus Christ. The other key phrase used in this passage is "the kingdom of God," which indicates continuity with the preaching of Jesus and the early apostolic gospel. We also need to note Paul's references to not holding back or shunning to declare things "profitable" (v. 20 KJV) and the "whole [purpose, counsel] of God" (v. 27). Here we see evidence for a breadth and depth of ministry, an accountability to the divine revelation, and sensitivity to the need for edification that the local church presented.

THE PRINCIPLES OF SELECTION

What principle or principles can be gleaned fairly from the particulars of this account of Paul's farewell address? We offer the following for those who would seek a starting place for text and topic selection: Our purpose in text/topic selection is to proclaim faithfully on a given occasion that aspect of God's revelation "necessary," keeping in mind the broad responsibility of proclaiming the whole counsel of God (see Acts 20:20, 27). We bring together the two statements that speak of things Paul did not fail or shun to do. We observe that Paul's great concern was to edify the people through his preaching and teaching (Acts 20:20), and his ultimate accountability was to the whole counsel of God (Acts 20:27). Paul's preaching program, if you will allow that phrase, was driven by the responsibility to preach all that God had revealed to him of "His counsel." At the same time, within the diversity of opportunities and the realities of ministering to people, Paul speaks passionately of his faithful attempt to declare anything and everything that would build up the people.

Responsibility and faithfulness to the truth of God (which ultimately edifies) does not negate the need to speak appropriately at any given time, to proclaim that aspect of God's truth that is "necessary" for the hearers. We need to affirm here, though, that the preacher's conviction and confidence to preach a "necessary" word should come from a correct appreciation of the nature and power of God's revelation (the Scriptures) and the work of the Holy Spirit.[4] Paul, later, in his instructions to Timothy, presents the ability of the God-breathed Scriptures to lead people to salvation through faith in Christ Jesus, and to edify believers towards maturity and proper activity (2 Tim. 3:14–17). These strong statements concerning the efficacy of the Scriptures come right before Paul's charge to Timothy to "preach the word" (2 Tim. 4:2). So, when we speak of sensitivity to people's situations and needs, we are stating also that the God-breathed Scriptures address these situations and needs ultimately and sufficiently. The preacher does not—and must not—frantically seek for some way to speak to people that hinders the power of the Word of God which is itself joined with the work of the Holy Spirit. That which is "necessary" is to be viewed in the light of the sufficient truth of God and the necessary work of the Holy Spirit as you face a specific audience and preaching context.

It may appear that we have made "heavy weather" of a rather obvious point. However, the place to begin when considering what to preach on any given occasion is to have a principle based on biblical evidence that acts as an objective standard for assessing the preaching/teaching pattern and program.

Now let's consider this principle within a contemporary framework, in the light of the canon of Scripture. The preacher must be concerned to communicate biblical truth (the balance of Scripture), preaching the gospel and the whole counsel of God! The preacher must seek the Lord as to how to accomplish this within any given situation. The preacher seeks to have the right message— that is based on the written Word—for his hearers on any given occasion. Living "in" the Word, seeking the leading of God in prayer, and seeking God's direction for every occasion or set of occasions is a necessary practice and discipline. Sometimes a need, crisis, topic, or doctrinal issue will drive the preacher to the Word. At the same time the preacher needs to have that sense of responsibility to communicate biblical truth (indeed the balance of Scripture) from core to circumference. The Scriptures give us the parameters for the truth we speak, and the balance of the preaching ministry needs to be guided, generally, by the balance of Scripture. We say "generally" because we believe that God does call and allow preachers to exercise special ministries with particular emphases. One of the problems in addressing this issue is that we must allow for diversity of callings, giftings, emphases, and related ministries. Even so, every preacher should consider how a particular ministry lines up with the balance of Scripture, whether the preaching is primarily evangelistic or for the edification of the saints.

THE PROCEDURES FOR SELECTION

If one allows for an objective standard for preaching, with which the Spirit of God concurs, then the preacher has the double blessing of an outward and inward witness to the authentic and appropriate nature of his preaching. The preacher has a double responsibility as he seeks to be faithful to the leading of the Holy Scriptures and the Holy Spirit. Given that the preacher must know the truth and be sensitive to the Holy Spirit's leading, can certain procedures be suggested for selecting texts and topics? While we say yes, we must also add that this does not mean preprogramming and planned execution that are devoid of openness to the Spirit or to the realities of life. D. Martyn Lloyd-Jones voiced his concern about such an approach in the book *Preaching and Preachers.* He did this by noting a difference of approach to preaching on the part of the Puritans and C. H. Spurgeon.

One of the greatest preachers of the last century, if not the greatest of all, Charles Haddon Spurgeon, took a very strong line on this. He did not believe in preaching a series of sermons; indeed he opposed doing so very strongly. He said that there was a sense in which it was impertinent for a man to decide to preach a series of sermons. He held that the texts should be given to the preacher, that he should seek the Lord in this matter and ask for guidance. He held that the preacher should not decide but pray for the guidance and the leading of the Holy Spirit, and then submit himself to this. He will thus be led to particular texts and statements which he will then expound in sermonic form. That was the view held by Spurgeon and by many others. I myself was brought up in a tradition which adhered to that view. We never heard a series of sermons based on a book, or part of a book, of the Bible or on a theme. But over and against that you have the position of the Puritans who were clearly great believers in preaching series of sermons. It is interesting to note, in passing, that though Spurgeon was such a great reader of the Puritans, and such a great admirer of them, at this point he disagreed with them entirely.

What, then does one say about this? All I can say is that it seems to me to be quite wrong to be rigid in this matter, and to lay down any hard and fast rule. I cannot see why the Spirit would not guide a man to preach a series of sermons on a passage or book of the Bible as well as lead him to one text only. Why not? What is important—and here I am with Spurgeon whole-heartedly—is that we must preserve and safeguard "the freedom of the Spirit." We must not be in control in this matter; we must not decide in cold blood, as it were, what we are going to do, and map out a programme, and so on. I am sure that that is wrong. I have known men who have done that. I have known men who, at the beginning of a season after a vacation, would actually hand out a list of their texts for many months ahead and would indicate what was going to be preached every particular Sunday during that period of time. I reprobate that entirely and completely. I am not saying, I dare not presume to say, that this is impossible: under the freedom of the Spirit it is not impossible, because "the wind bloweth where it listeth." We must not say that the Spirit will always, and must always, work in one particular way. But, speaking generally, I feel that to plan and publish such a programme is surely to put certain limits upon the sovereignty and the leading of the Spirit in this matter. So, having asserted that we are subject to the Spirit, and that we must be careful to make sure that we really are subject to Him, I argue that He may lead us at one time to preach on odd texts and at another time to preach a series of sermons. I would humbly claim that I have known this many times in my experience.[5]

Having sounded this note of caution, we now offer some practical steps to consider. We will state them in very specific terms which can be used, altered, or ignored as the preacher chooses.

Prayerfully Establish Priorities

In the light of the Scriptures, the preacher must affirm the truths that need to be declared. These truths appear in Scripture in ever-widening concentric circles.

Establish Biblical Priorities. Take out a sheet of paper, a set of three-by-five-inch cards, or create a file on the computer, etc. New Testament preachers must articulate the central message to be preached: "Jesus Christ and Him crucified" (1 Cor. 2:2), "Him we preach" (Col. 1:28), "God was in Christ" (2 Cor. 5:19), "the gospel" (Rom. 1:16), etc. It is possible to preach messages based on biblical texts and still miss the central message. We can preach particulars without a sense of how they relate to Christ. We *must not* miss the central message. For simplicity and comprehensiveness we define the central message as our first circle:

The second "circle" of preaching material consists of *central doctrines* (the faith). Paul was a man who taught tolerance on matters of opinion, but if you touched "the truth of the gospel" you were in trouble, as Peter found out (Gal. 2:11–19). This truth of the gospel seemed to include certain truths and ramifications that were directly connected to the very essence of the gospel. Jude switches direction in his letter writing and calls for the earnest contending "for the faith which was once for all delivered to the saints" (Jude 3). Here the reference seems to be to a belief, a set of truths to which assent and affirmation had been established. As one assesses a preaching ministry or plans a preaching

ministry, the central truths that surround that core message must be preached.

You can develop a list of critical truths from the personal reading of Scripture. At the same time, reference to biblical and systematic theologies will provide headings and Christian witness to those major doctrines that surround and support faith in Christ Jesus.

Then we would see a third level of content that includes "the whole counsel of God" and "all things profitable." At this point the preacher must recognize a responsibility to the diversity and depth of Scripture. The apostle Paul instructs Timothy concerning the edifying role of "all Scripture," and we can affirm that truth for both Old and New Testaments.

Within this "circle" of priority we stress the valid concern to expose people to the Scriptures as a whole—to teach the Bible. Although Paul did not mean "the Old and New Testaments" in his use of the phrase "the whole counsel of God," *we* have the completed canon. We believe it would be within the "spirit" of

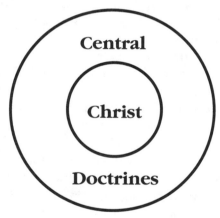

Paul's statements in Acts 20:20 and 20:27 to seek to cover the "balance" of Scripture in a preaching ministry fairly and thoroughly. Text selection is not just a subjective response to what one feels ought to be preached without concern for what God has given to us to preach. We must "preach the Word" from center to circumference—Christ, the faith, the Scriptures.

Establish Ministry Priorities. The preacher must also consider priorities in the light of the "realities" of the ministry God has called him to exercise. Here we face the issue of the starting point for preaching. You may have three years or three days. Where do you begin? As a preacher, you must take the biblical priorities established above and prayerfully consider them in the light of the "specifics" of ministry.

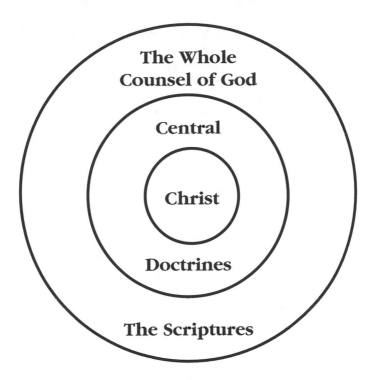

No two preachers are the same. No two ministries are the same. No two preaching opportunities or events are exactly the same. The preacher has to apply the biblical priorities and patterns to the details, the specifics, and the realities of the ministry "at hand." A lot depends on gifting and the ministry to which you have been called. A pastor of a well-established church may need to tackle his actual preaching responsibilities differently than a pioneer missionary or a youth group leader. Some are called to unique ministries that demand special emphases in their preaching. This is understood, but it still is helpful for all preachers to sense how their message fits into the concentric circles we have presented. God may call someone to have a prophetic or revivalist thrust in their preaching ministry. God may give a preacher a "particular message" for a given period of time. The Bible and history are filled with examples of this rich variety. How your message relates to Christ, the central truths of the faith and the whole counsel of God is significant. An emphasis can be God-given; error isn't. Keeping biblical perspective is critical.

The preacher must, therefore, come to grips with God's gift, ministry, and the message given to him. At the same time, the specific people being ministered to will impact the way the preacher seeks to faithfully proclaim God's Word. Two missionaries we know, evangelizing people who did not have a concept of a personal, sovereign, creating God, began their "gospel" with Genesis 1. Not everyone beginning a ministry will sense the need to start at Genesis 1. But we will need Spirit-led sensitivity to proclaim the message and the Scriptures carefully and understandably within given contexts. "Where must I begin to preach faithfully to my people over a given time?" "How must I proceed?" These questions must be answered as the balance of Scripture is applied by the Spirit-led preacher.

Then, within the framework of the ministry given, and the people God has given to address, the preacher considers opportunities to preach. He will need to make and to take opportunities to present God's message. Assessing the nature of each potential preaching event is a wise exercise. God is sovereign and He orchestrates these events, which will lend themselves to different emphases, lengths of message, etc. The synagogue is a different setting from the Areopagus. The business breakfast with twenty-five executives is different from a Sunday morning worship service. The ministry calls for a marvelous blend of spirituality and practicality.

In the light of these practical variables mentioned above, the preacher must establish priorities, priorities that are subject to the Word of God, the witness of the Spirit, and practical wisdom. These priorities should then lead to a *plan* for ministry that we will now consider.

Prayerfully Plan an Expository Ministry Submitted to God's Sovereignty and His Spirit's Leading

As we discuss this matter of planning, we are speaking of planning that is submitted to the sovereign leading of God's Spirit. Whether a person preaches message by message, series by series, doctrinally, liturgically, calendrically, annually, thematically, etc., all of these can ignore God's leading completely. On the other hand, if God can lead a preacher to preach an individual message, why not a series as Lloyd-Jones has pointed out? The plan, though, needs to be Word and Spirit led.

Planning can help in balancing a biblical ministry over a period of time. People will be exposed *intentionally* to a breadth of biblical truth that will enable them to live balanced Christian lives. Planning, also, helps the preacher in preparation, specifically in the use of study and preparation time. Knowing the direction of your preaching will help the preacher maximize study times and gain more insight and material for preaching. In addition, planning can help in the maturing of messages, series, and the preacher's theology as one seeks to approach the Scriptures carefully and thoroughly over a given period of time.

At the end of one's ministry in any given place, the preacher should be able to say: that he did not shun, he never "hesitated" to proclaim the *whole* counsel of God; that Christ-centered, biblical agenda was evident throughout his preaching ministry; that preaching was not deceptively selective, nor was there negligence in this matter; and from center to circumference, the truths of the Word of God were declared. This should be the concern that "drives" any preaching plan, not petty or personal agendas. Creativity is certainly called for in the preaching ministry, but the preacher's agenda should not be controlled by concern about what's "hot," what will work, what's new, etc., etc. Plan to preach Christ, to guard "the faith," and to lead people into the "deep things of God."

How? Message by message? Series by series? Quarterly? Doctrinally? Annually? The answer is: all of the above! The Word of God is to be handled carefully and accurately, not only within individual messages, but also as the preaching ministry continues over a period of time. John Stott has pointed out various factors that may influence the specific messages preached on any given occasion: he includes "liturgical," "external," "pastoral," and "personal" factors.[6]

Before we suggest a few considerations for the preaching program, may we exhort the preacher to take time for this important matter. Whether it is a day every two months, two mini- retreats a year, or some other plan, it is wise to detach yourself from the routines of ministry and focus on the preaching agenda.

As you consider future preaching responsibilities, ask questions on different levels. Sinclair Ferguson offers the following questions to help the preacher assess where to go from here: "Am I covering the whole range of biblical teaching—Old and New Testament, historical and theological, poetic and prose, exhortatory and denunciatory? Am I covering the whole range of biblical doctrines—God and man, Christ and Spirit, sin and grace, heaven and hell? Am I dealing with all the applications of the gospel message—to individual, home and family, business and pleasure, man and woman, church and society, personal and civil? The expositor will be a man who engages in this kind of analysis of his own ministry, so that one element in his choice will always be that he is operating within the total framework of biblical revelation and doctrine."[7]

Questions can be asked prayerfully to draw attention to what might be profitable in the near future: What has been the recent preaching/teaching thrust in the life of the church? What has God been saying and doing in the church? How would I describe my people right now doctrinally, practically, spiritually, and actually? Is there a particular aspect of God's revelation needed at this time to give biblical strength, growth, and balance to my people? Has God laid a "burden" of truth upon my heart that must be shared? Has God been dealing with me on some issues that He now wants me to preach/teach my people? Are there issues or events that demand biblical and pastoral response in the near future? How can I best use the regular preaching opportunities ahead to preach the whole counsel of God? Even if the preacher has a regular practice of preaching through the Bible, many of the above questions are still worth asking.

Wait on God

Time used to focus on future ministry, specifically preaching, is a worthwhile use of time. Such a time will call for silence before God, putting self aside, putting the questions aside, and being open to God Himself in prayer and through the Word. Ultimately, waiting on God is what is needed. The servant-preacher waits on His Lord for a sense of immediate direction, which may mean a message, a series, twenty series, etc.

Well, what can or should be added to such a discussion if this matter of a "preaching plan" is ultimately a matter between the preacher and God? We share some practical suggestions and observations. These suggestions amount to *options* and *factors* in light of the amount of preparation needed for preaching faithfully and often.

Consider the Values of Preaching through Biblical Books. Such preaching follows the text as written, so the preacher not only expounds individual messages, he also teaches through that part of the Bible. Certainly we live in a day when greater knowledge of the Scriptures is needed, and such knowledge can be gained through book series. Then, continuous series through biblical books provide a consistent context for congregational understanding of each message within the series.[8] In other words, those attending consistently throughout the series will have a sense of the context of the message before the preacher even starts. This can help understanding. Also, key theological truths will be seen *clearly and in full as presented within that biblical book.* Such preaching can help the preacher, since the focus for study is known, and recent study (for the same series) will be directly relevant to the next message. This fact helps to maximize the use of study hours.

Somewhere within the program or plan of ministry, preaching through biblical books can be a valuable aspect of the preaching ministry. It is our experience that such series are enriching to the preacher and congregation alike. One can start with Genesis and press on. At the same time, book series can be approached differently, with an attempt to have variety and balance: Old Testament, New Testament, a movement between Gospels and Epistles, Law and History, Psalms and Wisdom, Literature, Prophecy, and Apocalyptic Books, etc. Book series can be presented thematically or even within a doctrinal or theological framework. In suggesting that the preacher is going to do expository series through biblical books, a number of options remain open.

Usually when expository series through biblical books is referred to, the assumed practice is to go verse by verse, paragraph by paragraph, or literary unit by literary unit through that book. Some other variations and options for preaching through biblical books are worthy of mention. Representative key texts from a biblical book can be selected for briefer series. A survey of the book can tie these texts together, or contextual information for each key text can help to put the whole book in perspective. Certainly selecting key psalms or proverbs can be a good way to expose the essence of these genres of biblical literature. Also, key texts within any biblical book can be a necklace of pearls that can be strung together with beauty and balance. Another idea is to go through a biblical book section by section in an overview fashion. Still another option is to prepare overview messages of whole biblical books; this is not a continuous series within biblical books, but a continuous series of biblical books! Such messages help to give regular hearers a rounded picture of the Scriptures. The primary goal is still to present the truth of God on each preaching occasion. At the same time, we must save our people from an atomistic view of the Bible. Fragments of the Word of God are heard and possibly understood, but an appreciation of biblical theology and literature as a whole can be lacking. This type of preaching through biblical books can address this need.

Consider the Values of Freedom and Variety in Text Selection. Encouraging book studies as an essential part of the preaching plan does not mean that the preacher is limited to such continuous studies. Certainly God lays individual messages on the preacher's heart. Crises may call for adjustment in schedule and the seeking of God's truth to address the immediate need. People live their lives calendrically and seasonally, and practical wisdom would suggest remembering this. Seasonal messages often present opportunities to address fundamental biblical truths that need to be proclaimed.

Variety can include doctrinal series. This could follow a systematic framework; or key doctrines could be lined up with appropriate book studies. It certainly is worthwhile to reaffirm the essentials of the gospel and the central truths of the faith on a regular basis. Great gospel texts could be used for the one (the essentials of the gospel), and representative book studies could be used for the other (central truths of the faith). The preacher may want to consider a definite time within the church calendar to affirm and reaffirm the essential doctrines of the faith with a special call to covenant commitment.

Freedom and variety allow for balance. They keep the preacher fresh, provide material for other preaching opportunities. Possibilities abound, such as biographical studies, thematic studies, social issues, and Christian growth and discipleship series.

All the above must not be viewed as a capitulation to the "tickling ear" syndrome. On the contrary, such ministry appropriately reflects the diversity within the biblical literature itself. Other categories could be used, such as devotional, prophetic, didactic, apocalyptic, evangelistic, etc. God's servant needs to remember that the Word itself bears witness to the variety and creativity of truth that should impact all preaching.

Consider Personal Gifting and the Total Preaching/Teaching Ministry. The preacher, even if itinerant, should not be preaching in a vacuum. An awareness of the bigger picture of ministry available to the people being addressed is vital. For the pastor or preacher/teacher within a regular context, such knowledge is crucial. Regular preaching needs to be viewed within the context of the total church ministry. Other teaching or preaching gifts may be exercised within the church. The pastor/preacher is not the only one communicating the Word of God. Within such contexts, preachers must assess their roles, gifts, and opportunities to max-imize their preaching ministries. Preaching the whole counsel of God includes the awareness of what is being taught or preached by others within the local church, and making sure that aspects of God's truth are not being neglected. If the preacher is more gift-ed as a teacher than an evangelist, then it would be wise to make sure that quality evangelistic preaching takes place through appro-priate ministry from outside. It could also mean that an evangelist is invited to come and complement the regular ministry. Other staff people or members of the church may be able to use evan-gelistic gifts so that this aspect of preaching and ministry is not lacking. Be aware always of the gifting needed for a balanced ministry.

Consider Relevant Practical Factors. The preacher has a lot of demands on his time. Within the routines of ministry there can be a balancing of: (1) new messages prepared from scratch, (2) messages prepared from unfinished notes, outlines, etc., as well as (3) the preaching of messages that have been prepared and preached previously. As we shall observe later, every message needs to be fresh, but the wise preacher saves study notes, outlines, and complete manuscripts.

Let's say the preacher has three regular preaching responsi-bilities in a week. On top of that, there may be a briefer devo-tional needed, an outside opportunity, special preparation for heavy ministry responsibilities ahead, many other commitments: radio, television, print, even computer networking.

Careful preparation of completely new messages from scratch will need to be supplemented with messages that take less time to prepare. This does not mean that some sermons need to be subpar, with apologies to the congregation! No! Previous work can be the basis for less study time. Thinking specifically of a preaching plan, the preacher needs to be real-istic concerning the study time available for the opportunities available. We certainly want to encourage as much original research and preparation as possible; but one's own files and materials, alongside of trusted materials from others, can be a source of substantial help. An honest assessment of study time available will impact decisions made concerning various mes-sages to be preached.

There may be certain sermons that are so fundamental and complete within the context of the preacher's ministry that an annual repeat of the same text and theme may be significant to

the life of the church. Repetition of certain messages is important for clarity and emphasis, and repetition of basic truths over
time serves the same function. The obvious point we are making is that the preacher must think about the practical realities
of his schedule and ministry to maintain time for personal
preparation and to maintain accuracy and quality in the preaching ministry. It may be more worthwhile, on occasions, to adjust
and pray through an old message than to force oneself to tackle a difficult text for the first time when the hours are just not
there!

Are there guidelines? The preacher needs to stay fresh and keep
studying. Make it your goal to prepare *new* sermons regularly, and
use old material in a supplemental way.

There will be a certain rhythm to the preacher's life due to
personal, family, church, and even community responsibilities.
Obviously, if the preacher knows that certain weeks are not
going to offer as much quality time—think ahead, plan ahead,
study ahead. Special events will impact the schedule and must
be prepared for if at all possible. The vicissitudes of life are reason enough why the preacher must guard *quality study time* on
a routine basis. The wise preacher will not only guard quality
study time, but will recognize that certain messages and series
will call for intense extra study. The preacher will have to divide
up his study time to make sure that the messages are "approved
workmanship."

In all these practical matters, the preacher must recognize his
unique ministry before the Lord. Specific guidelines are helpful for
some, but for others they may, in fact, be "Saul's armor." What is
critical is the awareness of all the factors that impact a God-given
and God-led ministry. Accountability ultimately is not to the
church, or our own goals and priorities, but to God. That accountability, moreover, is not just a subjective sense of doing the right
thing at the right time, but rather the recognition of the *objective
content* that must be preached, and preached within the spiritual
and practical dynamics that make up the preacher's life.

In other words, the preacher must be:
- biblical
- spiritual
- practical

God Himself is the Enabler and upon Him we must depend to
plan, prepare, and preach the Word.

Prayerfully Select the Specific Text and Topic for the Specific Occasion

Let's say that the preacher has thought through a basic plan or pattern for preaching. There is still the need to ask: What does God want me to preach for this specific occasion? On what aspect of God's revelation am I to focus? What message is needed for "such a time as this"? When there is a clear answer to the above questions, the preacher can proceed to study the text and develop the specific message within that planned series.

If the message or series is one that is driven doctrinally, thematically, or topically, then the preacher needs to consider the primary text for study. We suggest that the preacher consider a "full-mention" text related to the doctrine or theme that needs to be preached. By a full-mention text, we mean a biblical text that presents the doctrine or theme in question as fully as can be found within the canon of Scripture. There may be a number of full-mention texts on a given theme, but the selection process has begun and the preacher can think and pray through which text will be the right text for the occasion. This approach will narrow the focus and save precious time.[9]

When selecting texts, the preacher needs to appreciate the true boundaries of that text. To gain a sense of the text's boundaries, the literary genre needs to be taken into account. For instance, a narrative text may cover a whole chapter or more. The preacher will need to study this whole text, even if the ultimate focus of the exposition is narrower. Therefore, the preacher needs to be aware of the literary genre and to know what the divisions are within the literature. It is good to answer a number of questions: In what sense is this text really a unit or unified? Does it have a specific or clear theme? The preacher must guard against arbitrarily selecting a text that leads to improper study. Particular sermons or series can impact the length of the text selected. That is understood. But the preacher needs to be fair in handling the text. The sermon may, in fact, focus on a section within the literary unit, or it may combine several units, sections, or divisions within the biblical book. Awareness of these facts will help the preacher prepare his message.

Let's look at an example. Take a text like the first chapter of 2 Peter. An overview of this chapter could be presented; two sermons could be preached, dividing the chapter into verses 1–11 and 12–21; two sermons could be preached dividing the text into verses 1–15 and 16–21; or an entire message could easily be devoted to each of the following: 1–4, 5–7, 8–11, 12–15, 16–21. In text selection, one needs to consider the literary genre and the "doctrinal density" of the text. This chapter, although only twenty-one verses in length, lends itself to a number of messages. The author actually lists seven "things" that need to be added diligently to the believer's faith. Running through such a list is a possibility, but each word in such a context merits careful attention.[10] Growth in Christian character and conduct is the outgrowth of verses 1–4, the results of such growth are given in verses 8–11; the importance of "these things" is stated in verses 12–15, which leads into the apologetic given in verses 16–21. It is plain to see that the text itself encourages you to slow down due to genre and doctrinal content.

A contrasting text would be the account of King Asa found in 2 Chronicles 14:1–16:14. The preacher needs to consider the concerns of the chronicler in presenting the various kings and events throughout this portion of Scripture. Certainly one could preach a number of messages on the account of this king of Judah. But two periods of his life are presented: the period when he sought the Lord and encouraged Judah to do so (14:1–15:19) and the period when he did not seek the Lord (16:1–14). A contrast is clear as you read the prophetic challenge of the seer Hanani and Asa's response (16:7–10). Given the genre of Chronicles and the overall message and impact, the nature of the text lends itself to one or two messages even though the narrative is made up of numerous paragraphs. Certainly more messages could be preached from the three chapters; but the flow of the text, the important contrast within the text, and the doctrinal focus of the text make one or two messages adequate in our opinion. We recommend that the preacher consider the literary genre and the "doctrinal density" of the text as he considers the textual dimensions of the message.

We recommend that the preacher consider the value of a *primary text for focus*. Other texts need to be studied and used appropriately throughout a message, but a primary text helps to provide a textual focus for study rather than just a thematic focus. A message can be developed on the basis of more than one text. Sometimes two contrasting texts or complementary texts may form the basic textual dimensions of a message. In such a case, the preacher actually prepares two "textual expositions" within one message and theme. The same could be argued for more texts. The problem comes when one seeks to explain carefully the text in context, because one's time is limited.

The text for study is the beginning place for specific sermon preparation. After study has commenced, other decisions will be made, including what amount of text will be read, when it will be read, and by whom. Sermon preparation can proceed when the "working" text has been chosen.

Conclusion

We started our discussion of text selection by presenting the example of the apostle Paul as recorded in Acts 20:17–38. He had fulfilled his responsibility before God so that he could say that he was "innocent of the blood of all men" (v. 26). Other examples could be given to show the need for accountability in preaching as well as sensitivity. God has set the agenda, and God can be relied upon to direct in the carrying out and proclaiming of His agenda. It is our fundamental conviction that the Word of God and the Spirit of God never stand in opposition to each other. The preacher has the revelation of God to open up and proclaim. That "Word" also is the objective standard by which and before which a preaching ministry must be viewed. If a preacher contradicts the Word of God consciously or continuously, he does not have to ask if God's Spirit is pleased—He isn't!

At the same time, there must be submission and dependence upon God's Spirit in every aspect of preaching. This includes being sensitive to His leading and working in the study, as well as in the pulpit. Planning and preparation are recommended, but they must be submitted to God and entrusted to Him for His sovereign guidance, working, and overruling if He should so choose. Our concern, our passion needs to be God's approval and His blessing upon what we offer and do. We are accountable to God in the light of His eternal truth and our assigned task. We, therefore, need to be faithful to Him as we seek to proclaim that Word and fulfill that responsibility. This sense of accountability should impact each opportunity to preach the Word, as well as the character of a whole ministry.

CHAPTER EIGHT

THE PREACHER AND PREPARATION: INVESTIGATION

Open my eyes, that I may see
Wondrous things from Your law.
—Psalm 119:18

After the preacher knows the text for the message, the next step and obligation is to make sure that the truth of God revealed in the text is in fact the *basis for* and *master of* the sermon that is to be preached. At the heart of expository preaching is a commitment to expose and proclaim the truth that is *there*

101

in the text of God's Word. A primary and fundamental concern in sermon preparation is to discern accurately the truth that is really in the text.

There are many styles of preaching and styles of preparation. We need to define and explain the particular style of preaching that is being presented here, and the particular process of preparation that relates to it.

"Textual-thematic exposition" is the type of preaching we are presenting and promoting in this book. The term "textual-thematic" is borrowed from Sidney Greidanus. Professor Greidanus explains: "By the term *textual-thematic preaching* I mean preaching in which the theme of the sermon is rooted in the text."[1]

The preaching we are presenting is *textual*. The issue for preaching is not the length of the text, but an attempt to be faithful to the meaning and teaching of the text in context. The preacher is required to be a voice for the dominant truth and truths of that selected text. Preaching styles and lengths of sermons can lend themselves to certain amounts of text. But cautions need to be heeded. If the text is less than a paragraph or literary unit, the preacher must be aware of the immediate context, and the primary truths within the context must be viewed in relation to the sermon text. The danger of single sentence or verse preaching is the possibility of missing the contextual significance of the text and moving to a broad biblical significance that may miss entirely distinctive emphases intended in the text. On the other hand, the danger of "overview" preaching is that the preacher often generalizes or systematizes a large text without careful attention to the real details and flow of the text. Whether the preacher leans towards the micro- or macro-approach, the real issue is faithfulness to the text in context.

The preaching we are presenting is also *thematic*. Greidanus defines the theme as "a summary statement of the unifying thought of the text."[2] The selected text is to be studied, but what is to be proclaimed? What is the message? Is it a series of observations or miscellaneous applications? We encourage preachers to focus the sermon on the theme, the dominating teaching of the text. There are many angles one can take, depending on our study, theological framework, and the specifics of the message and occasion. But, what is the primary truth of the text? This primary truth, teaching, or theme within the text is to be the objective guide for proclamation.

We will say more about finding, clarifying, and articulating themes later. Here we are explaining our approach to preparation and preaching. So, as we study the text, the goal is to discern the intended truth or truth(s) expressed in the text. This will form the basis for the theme, the essential message that is to be communicated.

Exposition with the term "textual-thematic" in front of it speaks of that preaching which proclaims the theme of a given text (or texts) on the basis of textual authority and explanation. To declare a theme without textual authority or explanation is simply to give a testimony or an opinion. We need the word of testimony in the body of Christ, but this shouldn't be confused with expository preaching. To declare a theme or message on the basis of a quoted textual authority is to give a biblical exhortation. A statement of truth is given and biblical authority claimed; but then the communication could move in many directions. It could be a "prophetic" denouncement, a word of encouragement, a personal testimonial to biblical truth, etc.

The purpose of textual-thematic exposition is to communicate the essential truth (or truths) of a text (or texts) of Scripture on the basis of the authority and explanation of the Scripture. The Scripture itself is not only stated to be the authority for the truth, it is *shown*, or exposed, as the authority for the truth. The truth of God is proclaimed and explained on the basis of textual explanation. The preacher is concerned that the message accurately corresponds with what God has said in His Word. He then seeks to declare and explain this truth in a way that can be shown from the text and understood by the hearers. This should be done in such a way that people can respond to the God who speaks in and through His Word and by the Holy Spirit. The preacher calls for the appropriate application and response to what the truth demands.

Why do we emphasize and value this approach to preaching? First of all, this approach to preaching makes *textual authority* a priority. Secondly, *thematic clarity* is a priority as well. The preacher says "something," something specific, that in fact corresponds with the primary truth(s) of the text. A third value of this approach relates directly to preparation: the text and theme provide *a helpful framework and an appropriate master for the preparation process.* How does a message develop? How should it develop? There is a sense in which no two messages are the same, or should be. What to include and exclude from any given message is a practical and ongoing concern. The text, in a sense, gives the initial parameters for study while the theme gives the focus for study. How this works in practice will be seen as we move into the details of the preparation process.

THE PRINCIPLES OF INVESTIGATION

The text before the preacher needs to be studied with dependence upon the aid and anointing of the Holy Spirit.[3] In addition the text needs to be studied in the light of how God chose to reveal Himself. God has set the agenda for preaching, and He has also set the agenda for study. The nature of the Scriptures themselves guides the preacher into the process and procedure of preparation. What do we mean by "the nature of the Scriptures themselves"? What do we see when we view a particular text of Scripture? We see words—specific words, written by specific people, given by inspiration of God. We see words joined together in definable ways syntactically, within syntactical frameworks that have a literary context and historical setting. These words within such frameworks, contexts, and settings have theological meaning and significance because they are God-breathed. Therefore, when such technical terms as *linguistic-syntactical-literary-historical-theological* study are mentioned, they are a response to the way in which divine revelation has been given to us.

We see then that the particular text selected needs to be studied spiritually and practically as a specific part of God's revelation in the Scriptures. Therefore, study or investigation should take into account: (1) the historical and literary settings of the text; (2) the syntactical and verbal specifics of the text; and (3) the doctrinal and theological significance of the text.

God has spoken! God speaks to us through His Word! It is hearing God speak through what He has spoken that is the goal of investigation. The assumption here is that it is important to understand what God has said in order to hear and authenticate what He is saying. God's critical and irreplaceable revelation for us is the Scriptures, and this is what should be communicated through the preaching ministry.

Let us remember that the risen Lord Jesus used the Scriptures to explain Himself. He was in the very presence of His disciples. He spoke as the Living Word. Yet, on the road to Emmaus

(Luke 24:13–43) and at a later gathering, He specifically used the Scriptures to explain Himself (Luke 24:44–49). What does that imply in terms of the self-revelation of the Son of God? It affirms that the Scriptures are not replaced or ignored in the context of direct communication by the risen Lord. The apostle Paul, and indeed the rest of the New Testament, also bears witness to the abiding significance and the unique authoritative character of the written Word of God (for example, see 2 Tim. 3:16–17). It is not our purpose to discuss, probe, or question the ways God chooses to speak, move, and work today. Still, we must answer a potential question: Why should the preacher study at all? Why not chair committee meetings, visit people, oversee ministry projects, counsel, and then show up in the pulpit? The answer is simple: God has set the agenda for study by choosing to reveal Himself in and through the Scriptures. Not only is this revelation authoritative and binding, it is irreplaceable and profitable. Therefore, let's begin the task of investigating.

PRACTICAL AND PRELIMINARY CONCERNS

The preacher must do those things that enable him to listen to the text and discern the truth of God. All study methods, habits, practices, procedures, etc., should assist the preacher to hear what God is saying in His Word. Once that goal is established, then the determination of the preacher will need to match his awareness of how he best listens, understands, records, and retains. No two people are the same. The preacher must determine how to maximize his time and utilize tools in order to listen intently, understand accurately, and record purposefully so he can retain meaningfully.

Time

Although there is a real sense in which sermon preparation is a twenty-four-hour-a-day process and program, the preacher needs to think about specific preparation time. We are not talking about general reading time, planning time, or even personal prayer time as such. *Time* must be set aside for the preparation of specific messages.

Quality time must be *guarded* for sermon preparation. Although many would encourage the morning hours for such study, the critical issue is making time a priority in the schedule and seeking to use those hours when you are at your best. You may be able to accomplish twice as much on certain days or during certain hours. Life and lifestyles have patterns and rhythms, and the preacher needs to assess time for preparation within the variables of life. A preacher who works a night shift at a factory may find the morning hours a hard time to concentrate. A few hours a day in the early afternoon may be guarded before the children come home from school. Both the *quality* of the time as well as the *maximum time* possible need to be considered.

How much time is enough? You'll hear many examples and suggestions. If a preacher regularly preaches four or five times a week, the study time needed will be different from his colleague who has one or two preaching commitments a week. John Stott suggests as "a useful rule of thumb" the need for one hour of study for every five minutes of preaching.[4] This sounds conservative, at first, and certainly cannot be a guide for everyone. Nonetheless, if a preacher preaches two hours a week, Dr. Stott's suggestion works out to twenty-four hours needed for preparation! The key is to "block out" quality time to be able to pray, listen, think, record, etc.

Haddon Robinson shares a pattern for preparation that he has found helpful.[5] The pattern begins ten days before the sermon is to be preached. So, if the commitment is on a Sunday, the Thursday ten days before is the day for initial exegetical study. Then on the Tuesday, five days before the Sunday, the exegetical work is finished and the sermon is organized. The Friday before the Sunday, the message is finalized. Establishing a pattern for study, to maximize time and to give focus for study, is extremely important. We recommend beginning specific preparation as far ahead as possible. Messages mature over time. The preacher is helped greatly if he can dwell on a text, a theme, and the specific message. Relevant thoughts and insights can come to mind while driving the car, waiting in a line, or even in the middle of an important conversation. Stretching out the preparation time also allows the preacher to *live with* and begin to *live out* the message. Some of the practical issues related to the truth will be seen and experienced in the preacher's own response to the truth. This personal involvement with the message enriches the message and is part of the "incarnational" process that makes ideas, truths, and thoughts become part of the preacher. Time *with* a message is as important as time *for* a message. So, think about using time, ahead of time, to prepare.

Establish a pattern and plan for study time. Then, try to use it and maintain it.

If the preacher is responsible for a number of messages each week, then the study time must be divided and allocated accordingly. Some may find working on two or three sermons within the same day to be refreshing and helpful. Others will find it confusing and will prefer to finish one message's primary preparation time before starting another. Each preacher must make decisions for himself and then act accordingly. Time must be allocated carefully so that each message receives adequate attention.

Location

In real estate matters location is important. It is also very important for sermon preparation. The preacher must find the best place to listen, study, write, etc. It may be the church building, possibly in his own office or study. For some, an available room or corner at home will provide the best place. For others, an alternative may be necessary, a local library, some quiet "somewhere." We know a pastor who ended up doing a lot of study at a restaurant near the church. (Because the restaurant was east of the church, he referred to it as his "east office.") A quiet table, no telephone, and a different atmosphere, in contrast to the "availability" of being on location at the office, helped this pastor. Sometimes we need to be creative; but more importantly, we need to be determined to find the right place for the type of preparation we must do.

Procedures and Tools

There is a uniqueness to every message, and one certainly does not want to become mechanical and machinelike in preparation. At the same time, having a regular procedure that enables the preacher to eliminate waste and fog is something to consider. "How do I waste time?" is an important question to ask and answer. Eliminating time-wasters is what procedures and tools are all about. The biggest time-waster may be interruptions—the telephone or knocks on the door. These can be dealt with pretty ruthlessly by first choosing the best times for study, then disconnecting the phone if necessary and being as "unavailable" as possible. Sometimes unrelated thinking or worry can be a problem. The preacher may need to pray purposefully and fervently to make a transition into study time, and then read, think, and even pray with a pencil in hand. The pencil or pen will help to keep the mind focused.

Getting started can be the toughest thing. Knowing what you are preaching on is a real help in this regard. Also, knowing what you are trying to accomplish in the allotted time is important. What must be completed at the end of this period of time? Ask that question and then do what is required to accomplish it. (We will look at this matter further as we present a pattern for study.)

Tools simply help you get a job done better and faster. Original-language texts help you save time so that you are not trying to read the ancient manuscripts themselves! Interlinear Bibles, providing original language and English translations, can be very useful. English translations help to provide quality translation work without starting from scratch. Concordances, lexicons, word-study books, Bible dictionaries and encyclopedias are reference tools that strengthen the preacher's grasp of biblical words and details, while saving time. Then, of course, there are specific commentaries[6] and many other helps available in print and electronic media. But time can be wasted if you want a tool and it is not available when you need it. Therefore the preacher must surround himself with the tools he finds helpful, keeping files and resources nearby. The young preacher can learn much from those who have heavy preaching responsibilities, yet maintain a high quality of solid, accurate, and authoritative biblical preaching. We need to learn from others, discerning always where we must adjust, adapt, or do things differently.

THE PROCEDURES FOR INVESTIGATION

Now that a sufficient amount of quality study time has been set aside and the preacher has surrounded himself with the necessary tools he may need, it is time to begin the investigation of the text.

The Reading(s) of the Text

A good place to begin study is to read the text! We need to come to the text prayerfully, openly, and alertly. We must depend upon the Spirit of God to aid our understanding and our response. Initially our immediate need is to see, to hear, and to sense what the text says, means, does, and in fact *is*. We must be open to the Word and the Spirit, rather than assume we already have a complete handle on the text.

Such an openness to the Word and the Spirit calls for an honest assessment of the "self" we are bringing to the text and vice versa. There are potential barriers to our openness and understanding of the text and the truth. At the surface level, linguistic, literary, historical, cultural, and even geographical distance must be acknowledged. To be open to and to understand deeply the words in the text, they must be heard and read as they were intended to be heard and read. Often in regular daily conversations we have to *work* at clearly understanding what is being said. When engaged in cross-cultural communication, the potential barriers to understanding are even greater, requiring us to acknowledge the differences in language, thinking, customs, etc., that exist. Acknowledging these differences does not hinder communication or understanding; rather, it is part of seeking to really understand another person. The same acknowledgments are necessary when reading cross-cultural texts. Since biblical literature is foreign to us and distant to us in this basic sense, the essential distance from the text needs to be accepted. We need not be pessimistic or defeatist about moving towards understanding, because the Scriptures are God-breathed and ordained to be profitable. An understanding and a joyful acceptance of the realities of the text are simply a part of the openness needed.

The potential for *personal* and *spiritual* barriers to understanding must be admitted as well. We must be willing to lay aside and continue to watch out for personal bias or spiritual blocks to "hearing" the text. So, how is this done? Be open, and read the text with dependence on the Holy Spirit. Personal spiritual issues, also, must be dealt with in this regard. In fact, certain issues in the preacher's life should be dealt with as a part of sermon preparation. If not, the spiritual blocks can remain, denying the preacher the liberty to hear, see, respond to, and rejoice in the truth personally.

Reading in the original language of the text is a wonderful practice and privilege, although many may not be able to do this. Writing out a personal translation is a good way to force oneself to read carefully. At the same time, textual issues must be dealt with. The preacher has to be satisfied in his own mind that he is reading the text in its best form. There is much debate about textual criticism, manuscript traditions, versions, and translations. If this were a book on Old Testament Introduction or New Testament Introduction, we would need to address these matters thoroughly. All we can say here is that the preacher needs to be as informed as possible and be satisfied with the textual decisions that relate to the text being studied.

The preacher who has had little or no knowledge of the ancient languages need not despair. We believe in a sovereign God who has given gifts of scholarship and translation to men, including Christian tradition, to enhance understanding. Most preachers, even with a few years of language study, will not come close to the language knowledge of those scholars who eat, sleep, and work at the original texts constantly. We sometimes sense an inward check when we hear a preacher questioning the translation being used, preferring a meaning offered through his own personal study. No translation is above criticism, but careful study went into producing legitimate translations.

Be aware of the specifics of the translation you are using: the date, those responsible for the translation, the methods used, the type of translation it is. The preacher must be certain of the reliability of the translation, particularly in its efforts to conserve the original meaning and distinctives of the text. The primary original manuscripts or textual tradition followed by the translation is also important to know.

Our discussion thus far has focused on the initial reading of the text. We recommended that you give this as much time as you can. It may be helpful to read the text in different versions to gain a sense of common ground as well as variations that may be noted. Read and reread the text! After you have gained a basic sense of the "flow" of the text, it may be helpful to read the text aloud, with careful expression and enunciation. This practice may help you to focus on textual details.

For the busy preacher, the most important thing will be to pause from other activities, quiet the mind, and prayerfully read the text with a sense of peace. If the mind is cluttered with "stuff," a careful reading and listening to God's Word and message is almost impossible. We are sure you have been in conversations with people, speaking face to face, when you *knew* that they were not listening to you! We can equally be distracted in our study, just going through the motions of reading and preparing. We must make sure that we are really listening to the text and concentrating on the task at hand.

The Investigation of the Setting(s) of the Text

After the initial reading of the text, the preacher should have a sense of the theme and flow of the text. Significant thoughts and facets of the text may stand out or draw special attention.

Certainly one could jump right into a time of careful study devoted to the specifics of the text. Yet we recommend a prior step in the investigation process. Before getting to the heavy and detailed study of specific elements of the text, it is helpful to step back from the text and ask some contextual questions.

We begin serious study by seeking to describe the setting of the text.[7] Our purpose is to gain a sense of the relationship of the text to its literary context, and to place the text in its historical realm. Doing this helps the preacher avoid moving too quickly to apparent meanings, themes, emphases, and even applications that are not in keeping with the nature and purpose of the text in context. Questions concerning the setting of the text enable the preacher to describe both the nature and purpose of the text.[8]

The Literary Setting. The nature of the literature and the literary genre will impact the way you view your text. Different literary genre have their own distinctive features. The preacher is aided greatly by an understanding of these basic features and characteristics. Also, he should be aware of how the text fits within the broader biblical context. So, how many concentric circles of context does one need to be aware of? The following are helpful: the immediate context of the text, the section or division of the biblical book in which it is found, the book itself, the section of the Testament in which it is found, and its canonical "role."

Working from circumference to center, let us make some suggestions. At this point the preacher begins by acknowledging the canonical setting of the text and the section of the Old or New Testament in which it is found. Then genre recognition helps the preacher be sensitive to how the literature works and what to look for in the more detailed aspects of study. If the preacher's text is a psalm, familiarity with psalms and Hebrew poetry is very helpful. Correct interpretation of a proverb may be facilitated greatly by understanding proverbial literature in general. The same can be said for Old Testament narrative texts, prophetic texts, gospel pericopes, and texts in other forms of biblical literature.[9]

Next, having a sense of the biblical book and its major divisions calls for some attention. The preacher is helped by having a basic understanding of the whole. For example, the Book of Esther is a fascinating account of the preservation of the Jewish people from an evil plot, with the human instrumentality of Queen Esther and Uncle Mordecai. The book really stands as a witness to the hidden hand of a sovereign God preserving His people. Such a perspective helps to guide one through the book, and helps the preacher avoid going down serious tangents and side streets. Other biblical books can be summarized in a similar fashion and that summary description can serve as a framework for viewing the divisions within the book and each section. The preacher has many resources for assisting him in viewing divisions and sections of books: study Bibles, articles in Bible dictionaries/encyclopedias, and commentaries of all types. Nonetheless, it is certainly a worthwhile activity to present your own outline for the book you are studying.

The basic themes, unifying features, patterns or movements within the book, key words, emphases, and "hinges" within the book are all important. An awareness of the genealogies in the Book of Genesis, for example, helps one to get a sense of the purpose and structure of that book.[10] The cycles and key phrases in Judges certainly help provide the preacher with a framework for tackling the texts within.[11]

An awareness of primary features and dominant themes helps to give *perspective* for the textual study to follow. Such perspective is critical because it helps the preacher to have an appropriate framework for viewing the text.

Having a sense of the whole book, its divisions, and then the immediate context helps the preacher to get at the *purpose* of the text in context. The preacher should ask: What role does this text play within the flow of the book? Why is this text there?

The Historical Setting. Closely connected to literary concerns are the historical concerns and questions. Who is writing? To whom? About what? When? Where? Why? How? Broad introductory questions of authorship, date, location, purpose, structure, themes, as well as textual and canonical issues obviously overlap with literary concerns. Since we are talking about sermon preparation and not doctoral research, our goal here is to have a sense of the historical realities both *around* and *within* the text. We believe that the historical realities within the words of Scripture themselves should be our focus in sermon preparation. Our focus needs to be on (1) what is explicitly given to us in the text, and (2) what is within the various concentric circles of context. The preacher can get preoccupied with external matters, often opinion and speculation.

These historical frameworks can actually impose on the text a way of viewing the text that is secondary to what is actually emphasized in the text itself. In other words, be careful. We recognize that there is a hermeneutical interplay between internal and external textual realities, but we can miss what is there in the text all too often. So look for historical indicators in the text itself. Use the Scriptures to support and supplement the text being studied in this regard. As necessary, use generally accepted introductory positions on biblical books that are in keeping with a high view of Scripture as well as sound scholarship. Then, make sure that you can place the text chronologically, geographically, situationally, and generally within the historical realities surrounding it. Such questions as these should be answered: How does the "occasion" of the biblical book as a whole impact the text to be studied? What historical factors, within the biblical book or external to it, are relevant to the understanding of the text to be studied? What is the real life-situation, as best as can be determined, that surrounds the text?

Now, why do all this? Because such study responds to the literary and historical realities of the way God chose to speak and reveal Himself. If the preacher leaves this part of the preparation process with a sense of the *nature* of his text in context, a sense of *perspective* on the text, and some insight into the *purpose* of the text, then the time was worthwhile indeed. Because the text has already been read carefully, this type of contextual study is not done in a vacuum. The prior reading of the text may even point to some issues and questions that context can answer immediately. Our text is not forgotten; we are simply making sure that we understand what it is, where it is, why it is, etc.

Many examples of historical context could be given. Consider 1 Kings 11:1–13, which describes King Solomon's disloyalty to God and His covenant, expressed in initial and continuous disobedience. This narrative passage clearly presents the turning of King Solomon's heart after other gods. You see the initial causes (vv. 1–4), the developing condition (vv. 5–8), and the devastating consequences of King Solomon's "heart problem," a heart problem that is contrasted with his father David's faithfulness (vv. 9–13). Now, we've already moved into homiletical expression, but that's just to summarize the text. What we seek to illustrate here is the importance of the setting or context. This passage occurs at a significant point in 1 and 2 Kings. Chapters 1–10 of 1 Kings describes a king that is glorious, wise, wealthy, and powerful. This is a man who has experienced abundant privileges and blessings, even having "the LORD God of Israel" appear to him twice (v. 9). The temple has been built and dedicated. The kingdom is strong and expanding. After this text, things start to fall apart. God raises adversaries against Solomon (11:14, 23).

Jeroboam is introduced, and the rebellion of Israel takes place. When one views a summary statement such as 2 Kings 17:5–23 (21–23), one can see that the movement towards tragedy began in the wake of Solomon's sins and God's response. Jeroboam is attributed with driving Israel "from following the LORD" (2 Kings 17:21), and his rise was part of the consequences of Solomon's sin. So the context reveals the seriousness of Solomon's sin, both in the light of the glorious period of time in chapters 1–10, and the development from 11:14 to the end of 2 Kings.

First and 2 Kings is concerned with kings, chronology, and covenant. The literary positioning of this text, and the historical realities reveal the significance of the text directly. This 1 Kings 11:1–13 text is a "hinge" text in the flow of the literary content of 1 and 2 Kings. Keeping in mind that the ordering and selecting of material is a key literary feature, one can sense the strategic role of this text. Historically, the text stands at the dividing line between the glory days of the nation of Israel and the divided kingdom. The text tells what happened at this critical point in the nation's history, written in the light of the downfall to follow. Such observations help to move the preacher towards a basic perspective on the text, and towards a sense of the text's purpose.

Now, how does one do all this within the pattern and procedures of sermon preparation? First of all, the preacher must rely on previous study and his broader knowledge of the Scriptures. Certainly some type of ongoing macrostudy of the Word of God is recommended. Consistent reading of the Scriptures with a sensitivity to "big picture" issues is important. The preacher cannot expect to spend lots of time doing what we have outlined above. Past study, insights, notes, and the use of basic reference helps can give the type of information that one looks for generally.

We recommend that the preacher briefly but carefully consider contextual issues specifically when doing sermon preparation on a given text. Being realistic, we suggest using one tenth of the total preparation time for doing what we've outlined above. The preacher will need to be a good observer and a fast worker. It may be helpful to have a sheet of paper and write the word *setting* or *context* on the top. Then, make as many observations about both literary and historical contextual issues as possible. At this point in preparation, the need is not to draw final conclusions concerning perspective and purpose. There will be time for that later. Here the concern is for observations that have a bearing on how to view the text you will be preaching.

The Investigation of the Specifics of the Text

This is where the heavy "detail" work is done. Approximately 30 percent of one's preparation time may need to be used here. Attention to detail is now the priority. God chose to use specific words to communicate His truth; therefore, we need to study those words. It is possible, and even easy, to miss details. Just as details of a conversation can be missed, so the student of the text can miss what is there. The concern of the preacher in this part of the preparation process is to see, view, and seek to understand what is written, in *detail*.

The preacher seeks to understand the original intended meaning of the text in context. *What* is actually said in the text? What is the text about? *How* does the text say what is says? *Why* does the text say what it says? What does the text *do* as an active form of communication? Such questions and many more are to be raised and answered at this time. We are working towards a description of the main theme or themes of the text, the thoughts or movements that make up the theme(s), and the thrust or impact of the text. These will be homiletical categories later, but here we must first seek a basic understanding of the text. That understanding is based initially upon the original meaning of the text as intended by the human author under the inspiration of the Holy Spirit.

To "get at" the meaning expressed in and through the details of the text, we must consider the text syntactically and verbally. In other words, we must view the text as a *meaningful combination of words* as well as *individual words that have meaning*. Syntax has to do with "the way in which words are put together to form phrases, clauses, or sentences."[12] We must read the text as it was intended to be read, recognizing the flow of words and their interrelationship. Within that flow, individual words make their specific contributions to the meaning of the text. For the preacher to understand the text as a whole, the parts of the text must be viewed along with the words within the parts. Details within details within details! These are the basic data for the investigation.

Syntactical Specifics. The preacher needs to study the sequence, the flow, and the interrelations evident in the text between words, phrases, clauses, sentences, paragraphs, etc. This leads to discovering the overall themes or theme, the thoughts that express or convey that theme, and the purposeful challenge or thrust explicit or implicit within the text.

The preacher is encouraged to do whatever helps to give attention to syntactical details in this regard. Certainly time constraints are a reality. The time available, the type of text, the length of text, and the kind of message to be preached may impact the procedures that need to be followed. Our focus is on basic syntactical analysis and word studies. This study needs to be done with a sensitivity to broader contextual concerns, including the type of literature being studied. Broad macrostructures within the literature, as well as the basic sentence and paragraph syntax, need to be recognized. Different types of texts will call for special treatment in keeping with the distinctives of the genre represented.

Simply *reading and rereading* the text in the original language, interlinears, and/or different translations will often get the preacher a long way down the discovery road. It may be helpful to summarize the essential thoughts within each paragraph, if not each sentence. The biblical text can be written or typed with wide margins so that the preacher can make comments and summary statements for easy reading and reference. "Visualizing" the text with its sections and relationships can be very helpful. Besides summarizing main thoughts, it will be helpful to identify movements between paragraphs and even sentences. Try to get a feel for the text. Read it out loud to listen to the flow of words and structure. Such reading will force you to "hear" the text and make choices concerning how the text needs to be read in general, as well as how it should be read in the pulpit. Issues for further study will arise.

Ask structural questions that force you to assess the relationships between paragraph and paragraph, sentence and sentence, and even words within sentences. Identify key connecting words. Clarify the main thoughts that are being connected together. Then, if practical and helpful to you, label as many words, phrases, and clauses as possible. You may even want to label grammatically so that you recognize the role that certain words, phrases, or clauses serve. Such labeling or other practical activities help the preacher attend to what is written without assuming anything. The aim here is to think in terms of what the specific details of the text contribute to the meaning of the text as a whole.

Making a simple indented *outline* or a diagram of the text can help display the basic roles and relationships evident in the words of the text. Seeking to present the text in this fashion is just another way to make sure we are thinking at all, and thinking specifically about the specifics of the text. There are numerous ways this

Romans 12:1–2

I beseech you therefore, brethren

      by the mercies of God,

    that you present your bodies a   sacrifice,

            living

            holy,

            acceptable to God,

      which is your reasonable service.

And do not be conformed

       to this world,

but be transformed

       by the renewing of your mind,

     that you may prove what is that   will of God.

             good

             and acceptable

             and perfect

can be done, but we offer here a simple indented outline of Romans 12:1–2.

We have placed the main clause, "I beseech you . . . ," furthest to the left. This indicates that it is the primary clause. These two verses are a direct personal exhortation on the part of the apostle. This text is, in fact, a direct exhortation in the light of what has been said already (Rom. 1–11). The next line of indentation indicates the main aspects of the exhortation expressed in the main actions/verbs that are called for (that you *present, do not be conformed, be transformed*). The next movement in the indentation indicates key descriptive phrases that relate significantly to the action called for (v. 1, "which is your reasonable service"), (v. 2, "that you may prove . . ."). The other distinctive elements in the outline show modifying phrases or words. Such an outline helps you *isolate* and *relate* words in the text.

Any sort of rewriting of the text, outlining, or diagramming will help the preacher to look again at the text, which in and of itself is helpful. "Major," "minor," and "modifying" categories can be applied, recognizing that nothing is unimportant or arbitrary in the text. Key sentences will stand out more, as will key clauses or phrases. Certain words will be displayed as especially crucial to an understanding of the whole. And just as important, the roles and relationships within the text will be viewed in the process. If the preacher can basically accomplish this by a careful reading and rereading of the text, that's great. But we mention this practice or procedure as a tool (or an option) to view the details carefully.

More sophisticated diagramming can help the preacher isolate and relate with more technical precision.[13] The key element to diagramming is to diagram in a way that helps you "see" the text and define the details. The elements of the text that are hardest to define and relate are obviously the ones that you struggle with. Such diagramming and labeling will test your knowledge of grammar as well as the flow of words in the text.[14]

A careful assessment of the details of the text within its syntactical shape helps the preacher understand the text on and in its own terms. You are not imposing meaning, structure, and theology; rather, you are discovering meaning and structure along the route towards the theology or doctrine to be preached. At the same time, the preacher wants to avoid a "bits and pieces" sermon, a sermon that uses some textual specifics but misses the point of the text and the flow of thought. All sermons have to be

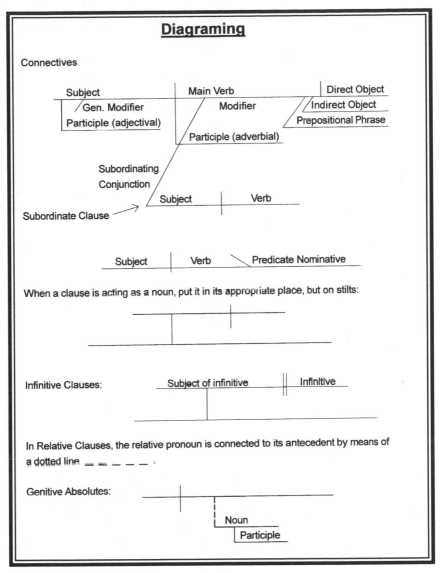

Diagraming

Connectives

Subject | Gen. Modifier | Participle (adjectival)

Main Verb | Modifier | Participle (adverbial)

Direct Object | Indirect Object | Prepositional Phrase

Subordinating Conjunction

Subordinate Clause

Subject | Verb

Subject | Verb | Predicate Nominative

When a clause is acting as a noun, put it in its appropriate place, but on stilts:

Infinitive Clauses:

Subject of infinitive | Infinitive

In Relative Clauses, the relative pronoun is connected to its antecedent by means of a dotted line _ _ _ _ _ .

Genitive Absolutes:

Noun | Participle

selective in the presentation of textual specifics, but the selection process should be appropriate to the text. What dominates the text should come through loud and clear in the message, whereas subordinate and supportive phrases, clauses, and thoughts should be viewed accordingly. The preacher will gain much by viewing the text as "a whole with significant parts." Such a perspective aids in the recognition of the primary or dominant theme(s) in the text and how they are expressed. Discerning the major "what" of the text and the related "hows" will help in the assessment of the "why" of the text as well. We recognize, though, that meaning is expressed in specific words. Therefore we now turn our attention to the study of specific words.

Verbal Specifics. As one is involved in the study of the text, certain words will call for special attention. Obviously, if one had many hours and/or a very short text, a high percentage of the words in the text could receive thorough investigation. But, generally, a selection process will be needed to identify words that merit special attention. What words ought to be studied in more detail, and what are you looking for?

Study Unknown Words. If a word is unknown, either in original language study or in English Bible study, an effort should be made to understand its basic meaning. In all word studies, you are seeking to discover/discern the meaning of the word in its particular context. What does the word mean right where it is in the text? At the same time, the preacher needs to be aware of the general or usual options of meaning, the semantic range of the word. Two tools help a great deal in this type of study: the dictionary/lexicon and the concordance. The dictionary/lexicon gives definitions of words based on different usages, sometimes giving examples. It focuses in on usual meanings. The concordance gives you uses of a particular word in different contexts. Large concordances give all the uses of a particular word in the original language text or in the particular translation on which it is based. Such study helps you gain a sense of the different uses of the word and its range of meaning. So, look up your unknown words and get a sense of "dictionary meanings," and find in the concordance a good sample of uses elsewhere to consider.

Because the goal of such study is to understand a word in the specific text you are studying, we recommend a pattern for word studies. In a sense, this is a pattern for "weighing" the evidence. There are ever widening circles of evidence and we start at the center. First you need to view the word within the syntactical shape of the text itself. Then consider other uses of the word within the immediate context. There may be a particular emphasis within the context that helps in the assessment of the meaning of the word. A nuance or shade of meaning may be evident as you study the flow of the text in its immediate context.

It is evident that biblical authors maintain their own characteristic styles and word uses in the writing of "God-breathed" Scripture. Therefore, the next two circles of evidence are (1) the whole book that the text is in, and (2) other books by the same author. From there you move to other biblical examples of the

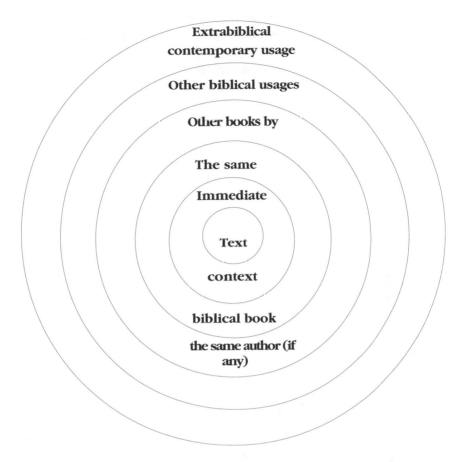

word, and, finally, to contemporary extrabiblical usage.

The history of a word (its etymology) can be of interest, and its diverse forms (morphological analysis) can provide helpful insights. All of this study aids in assessing a word's most probable meaning in the text. Word study, along with syntactical analysis, has guidelines, but it is not a mechanical science. The preacher needs great sensitivity to the text in order to discern the best reading. Although we have drawn concentric circles, that does not mean that an outer circle cannot be very significant. Generally speaking, though, you want to make sure that within the biblical book and the immediate context, the meaning of the word makes good sense—indeed, best sense.

Study Significant Words in the Text. Here the concern is with words that occur within the primary and dominant elements of the text. Subjects of sentences and main verbs are a good place to start. Connecting or disconnecting words are worthy of careful study, and they stand out as you study the flow of the text. The text itself will, as it were, point to certain words, saying, "This is important."

Study Key Words in Context. If a word is used significantly throughout the context of the text being studied, this should draw attention. Key words and phrases are a critical means of communicating the primary thoughts of the author. Such consistent, significant usage of the same word or words should draw us like a magnet to give attention.

Study Other Words That May Be of Special Significance. Repeated words in a given text need to be viewed. Repetition is an important tool in both written and oral communication. A word or phrase that occurs many times or a few significant times within the text is worth special attention. Contrasting words are another means of emphasizing meaning. When explicit contrasts are evident in the text, we need to understand the meaning of these contrasting words and the point or nature of the contrast. The contrast—whether emphasized in the text or just present—should be noted. "Similar but different" words can be an interesting focus for study, as well as speculation. It may be that the writer wanted to stress a slightly different meaning. On the other hand, the writer may have viewed the words as being synonymous, with overlapping semantic ranges. The change could have been stylistic, or very purposeful. Therefore the investigator needs to be cautious. Unusual words need attention because we may not be as certain about their normal usage. They are also a potential camping ground for speculation, but having given that warning, clearly such words need attention and explanation. The writer may have wanted to convey a specific meaning that was only captured in that unusual word. Also, an unusual word could indicate a "borrowed" word or phrase from another author or text that was not part of the author's usual vocabulary.

Study Difficult Words. Difficult words merit attention, even if your conclusion is that "this is a difficult word to translate and understand." It could be a word that has received a diversity of interpretations over time or little interpretation at all. If exposition involves explaining what is in the text, then certainly the expositor needs to attempt to tackle the difficult words in the text. Very often words are difficult because they come in a phrase, clause, or sentence that is difficult. Nonetheless, the commitment to proclaim the truth accurately encourages the preacher to read and reread these difficult words; analyze them syntactically and contextually, etc.;   and consult reliable helps and sources for various possible interpretations. Second Peter 3:16 makes clear that "some things" that Paul had written were "hard to understand." Indeed, "untaught and unstable" people twisted Paul's teachings. Peter does not deny that there are some difficulties in Paul's epistles and that such texts may have been a campground for false teaching. This is both an encouragement and a warning to us today, so don't lose heart!

Humility and determination need to go hand in hand as we wrestle with difficult words, tough truths, and syntactical tangles. The warning comes to us as we recognize the potential for erroneous interpretation and false teaching. It is better to admit the difficulty and focus on the clear teaching within a text than to give dogmatic opinions on textual difficulties. Share what you believe is the best understanding of the difficult word, phrase, etc.; acknowledge that there are orthodox alternatives (if there are); and view that part of the text in the context of the whole. One need not get preoccupied with difficult words or phrases when the teaching and flow of thought in the text is clear, regardless of the final assessment of the textual difficulty. If the difficult word or phrase is at the center of the text's meaning, teaching, import, etc., then you have two options: do the best you can, relying on the Word of God, the Holy Spirit, and solid Christian witness; or preach on another text.

Study Names, Places, Dates, Numbers, and Historical Data. No biblical word should be treated lightly; therefore, special attention should be given to people named or described, places named or described, dates or time frames mentioned, numbers specified, and other historical data written. Such information is not wasted in Scripture. It is provided purposefully. Significant facts need to be understood clearly, and the significance of names, designations, or of descriptive details need to be viewed in the light of the purposes and patterns of the author. Of special importance, of course, are the names, characterizations, and modifiers associated with God Himself. This is true from Genesis to Revelation and regardless of literary genre.

Thinking practically, the preacher may only have an hour or two for special studies if ten hours for preparation are available.[15] One thorough word study could take all of this time if numerous texts are studied and various meanings are assessed. Previous familiarity with the words of the text will obviously help in the use of time. Using available resources such as concordances, lexicons, word study books, and commentaries can give quality information within a brief period of time. Still, study will probably have to be selective. Here is where judgment calls are needed to discern the priority ideas and issues in the text. Sometimes a particular word or phrase may "strike" you in study and call for extra attention. Make sure, however, that you do not go off on a tangent by making that word the whole focus of your study. If it is vital to the text, then obviously investigate and reap the benefits of the new insights and deeper understanding.

Note our indented outline of Romans 12:1–2. All the words in this apostolic exhortation need attention, but time constraints may necessitate focusing on certain words, leaving less time for the rest of the words. Past study and basic familiarity may have to suffice for "the rest of the words."

Key nouns, verbs, and connectives are circled. Other key phrases, contrasting words, and modifiers have been circled for special study. For example, the modifiers of *sacrifice* are *living, holy, acceptable to God. Holy* and *acceptable to God* are very important, but would be anticipated when speaking of a sacrifice. *Living* is unusual usage, and a key word in Romans. So, *living* could merit attention.

The goal in this part of preparation is to have a good understanding of the essential *details* of the text. The preacher must take advantage of this time to dig as deeply and think as sensitively as possible. Our dependence on the Holy Spirit and our need to search the Scriptures are essential as we wrestle with the issues of word meanings and structural relationships. We do all this as we endeavor to arrive at an accurate understanding of what the text says and means. With our findings, we can describe the overall theme within the text because that description is based accurately on the details of the text. We understand the text's content in the light of its own terms. An overall theme, subject, or emphasis should emerge as well as the sense of the impact or force of the text. *The uniqueness of the text will likewise translate into the uniqueness of the preached message.*

At this point in the process, you still are not putting the sermon together—even though you may actually see a subject and a structure emerging! There's nothing wrong with putting that subject and structure down on paper and saving it. Take advantage of insights as they come. It's so easy to forget valuable thoughts. It is best to write down and save your syntactical analysis and word studies; it is good stewardship of valuable time. You have completed research that you will want to use again and again.

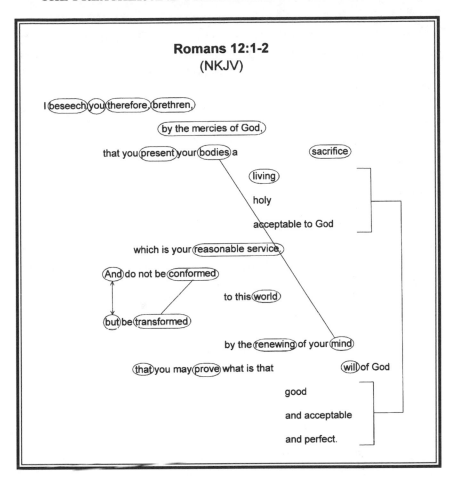

Romans 12:1-2
(NKJV)

I beseech you therefore brethren,

by the mercies of God,

that you present your bodies a   sacrifice

living

holy

acceptable to God

which is your reasonable service.

And do not be conformed

to this world

but be transformed

by the renewing of your mind

that you may prove what is that   will of God

good

and acceptable

and perfect.

At this point in your preparation you must turn to what all the specifics really mean collectively. The specifics, the details, now need to formulate doctrine and theology. What in fact does this text, in terms of its specifics, teach? What truths are taught in and through this text?

The Investigation of the Significance of the Text

The preacher's careful investigation of the specifics of the text helps to lead to an accurate assessment of the doctrinal and theological significance of the text. He is not interested in simple moralizing, psychologizing, or politicizing of the textual facts. Rather, the preacher is concerned with the intended truth (doctrine) in the text and that truth viewed (theologically) as part of

God's purposeful revelation. Our goal is to discern the truth claims of the text. The preacher must now take time to summarize, synthesize, and, ultimately, state clearly what, in fact, the text reveals or teaches. The preacher asks: what is God saying in and through this text?

Hermeneutical Principles and Procedures. Hermeneutics is a vast discipline, and our comments only scratch the surface of the hermeneutical landscape.[16] What is presented here is not so much a specific set of steps, but rather a "helps menu" or checklist to guide the preacher as he tackles the awesome responsibility of discerning truth. Such a responsibility should cause us to seek the Lord's enabling through His Holy Spirit for spiritual discernment. This is the time for reflection, assessment, and waiting on the text and the Lord. The preacher must "think through," to a point of conviction, the essential meaning of the divine doctrine purposefully exposed in the text. Texts will by nature have theological foundations or underpinnings, and it is helpful for these to be discerned. Walter Kaiser emphasizes the need to discover the "antecedent theology" upon which the textual teaching is based.[17] The text will express specific truth, but that truth is not in a theological vacuum. God has revealed Himself, His truth, and His Word previously, and this theological seed blooms in such soil. Depending on the text, God may say much more diachronically and christologically speaking. There is a *before* and *after* to most texts that the preacher needs to be aware of. The preacher seeks the essential teaching of the text and then views that teaching theologically, biblically, and christologically.

At the risk of being simplistic, the preacher *will* inevitably view the text from a particular perspective impacted by every factor that influences his thinking. Discerning between what is spiritual reflection and what is merely personal reaction is not always as easy as it sounds. An immediate off-the-cuff response to a text may not be a "genuine response" to the text. Hermeneutical principles and procedures should help the preacher be "in step" with the text. That's their function and purpose. At the same time, we need to depend on the Holy Spirit Himself to aid in our thinking as we encounter and reflect upon the text.

Describe the Original Intended Meaning of the Text in Context. The study of the specifics of the text should have brought the preacher to this point in the preparation process. The preacher does not now *ignore* all of this study and move to some higher, deeper, wider, greater truth. There is a real significance to the "facticity" of the text. God chose to speak specifically, and we lose something important if we act as if the text never happened or never meant anything. Now, in the preparation process, we must describe as clearly as possible what the text meant as written.

Practically speaking, it may help the preacher to write an outline or series of sentences to describe the original meaning of the words of the text. This presentation of the original meaning of the text could take a shape similar to our homiletical structures discussed in the next chapter.

Original dominating theme of the text: _____

_____

Supporting/integrating thoughts within the text: _____

_____

_____

_____

_____

_____

Original purposeful challenge or thrust intended for original readers that is expressed or implied in the text: _____

_____

_____

_____

The result would be an outline or synopsis of the text, depending on the length of the text. The main themes, actions, and/or statements in the text need to be represented. Significant thoughts, words, structures, and movements ought to be reflected in such a restatement. Distinctive emphases should be evident. This is done with a sensitivity to the text as a purpos   eful, written communication that is revelatory by design.

Seek to Recognize the Essential Truths of the Text (View It Theologically). On the basis of a clear understanding of the original meaning of the text, the preacher can assess the essential truths within the text. One's theology will impact what is viewed as essential, significant, purposeful, intentional, and meaningful within the text. We grant that. And yet, the careful exegetical-theological preacher will seek for *real indicators within the text* that express priority truths and emphases. These textual emphases need to be viewed in order to express the doctrine and theology of the text, rather than simply imposing a theological framework on the text. The goal is exposition of the truth(s) that is intrinsic to and intentionally expressed by the text. In a sense, you view the text as proclamation. What is being proclaimed in and through the text? What is being proclaimed about God and man's relationship to Him? There may be foundational truths that are assumed by the text, expressed in the text, but not emphasized. These are important and may be foundational to other truths that are clearly presented, emphasized, and proclaimed by the text.

Both the implicit and explicit truths of the text are important, but the preacher wants to identify the clearly expressed truths of the text. Often this will not be a struggle at all; the truths will be clear and already explicit in the description of the basic original meaning of the text. Be encouraged at such times, and move on. Other times, particularly with literary genre more difficult to mentally "propositionalize," the thoughts and truths of the text need to be extracted without destroying the uniqueness and dynamic of the text. A narrative may show a truth. It may be part of a larger historical account revealing the nature of God's active relationship with His people and their response and the subsequent consequences, etc. The "showing" of a narrative, although "scenic, subtle and succinct" is not a playground for the potential truths of your choice.[18] The text is intentional and such truths can be discerned and stated for further sermon preparation. Other genre have their distinctive qualities, and the preacher will need to be sensitive to these distinctives when interpreting a proverb, psalm, prophetic oracle, gospel message, apostolic exhortation, apocalyptic symbol, etc. What essential truths are evident in and through the text and its distinctives? What is taught and proclaimed dynamically within and through the language of the text? You may have identified the central or dominant truth or theme of the text, plus multiple other truths expressed in the text in step one above. It may help to write them down separately, expressing each one as clearly as possible in meaningful sentences or phrases. You are focusing now on what this text proclaims and teaches doctrinally and theologically. A warning sign should appear if your sentence or phrases make no reference to God Himself or fundamental truths that are part of God's special revelation to man. It may be helpful to take your description of the original intended meaning of the text and see if it needs new expression doctrinally/theologically.[19]

Use the Clear/Major/Numerous to Give Insight into the Less Clear/Minor/Few. Although we are dealing with major truths and themes at this point, the preacher will at times face difficulties in the text or with aspects of the truth. Sometimes prayer, time, study, and struggle must take place to work through to a satisfactory understanding of the truth(s) in the text. In general, though, the preacher can gain perspective on those textual and theological difficulties by focusing on what is clear, dominant, and repeated within the text, the biblical book, and, in fact, within the canon of Scripture itself. The clear gives perspective for the study of the less clear. Dominant truths give perspective to the supportive or subordinate. The numerous references, restatements or repetitions of truth, particularly within a given text or biblical book, are certainly helpful in arriving at essential doctrine that we must proclaim. This is not to say that all due diligence shouldn't be given to unwrap the tightly packaged difficult phrase, clause, text, truth, etc., but we want to be very practical at this point. There are tough texts and tremendous truths that could take months, years, and almost a lifetime of study. As we have already noted, Peter refers to "some things" in Paul's writings that are "hard to understand" (2 Pet. 3:14–16). The preacher needs to study with diligence and humility. This humility not only leads the preacher to admit that he doesn't understand all texts and truths completely, it also allows him to be honest before God and his people. The preacher can faithfully and fervently preach the truth that is clearly evident in the text, even though he knows that he doesn't understand all that it means or could mean. This is not an excuse for laziness; nor is it a cop-out for not proclaiming the whole counsel of God. What we are speaking of here are those potential preoccupations in study that should not dominate the preacher's time and efforts. The preacher can always say, "Some other time I would like to return to this text for further study, because there are depths and dimensions of truth that I don't believe I fully understand. But today I am proclaiming to you the clear dominant truth of this text, which will certainly and adequately demand our focus and response." There is always room for more study.

Use Scripture to Interpret Scripture (View It Biblically). To understand more fully what we have stated above, it is important to view the truth(s) of the text in the light of the broader teaching of the Scriptures. Certainly studying the same truth, within the *same biblical book* is critical. Such a study will give depth and breadth of understanding as well as a more complete picture of how the truth being proclaimed relates to other truths and themes in that biblical book. How that truth is presented by the *same biblical author(s)* is significant. God used the writers in such a way that they expressed their own vocabularies and theological emphases. Therefore, it is important to see the truth(s) of your text within the mind-set of the author's purposes and themes.

Antecedent theology is certainly important. One can be helped by finding the first biblical reference to the same words, concepts, or truth. A tracing of the same truth or theme historically would be ideal, if time allows.

Seeing further developments of the truth can also be important. If you are dealing with a text from the Law of Moses, there is much to examine in subsequent Scripture historically and canonically. The Bible is a unity within diversity and progression. Having a sense of biblical perspective (historically) is both strengthening and corrective to wrong theological conclusions.

Other possible studies abound. There may be a *key biblical text,* what we call a "full-mention text," that needs to be consulted. That text treats the same basic truth found in your sermon text in its fullest form in the Scriptures. The purpose is not to read into your text what is not there, but to be able to view your text with an informed biblical perspective.

Other types of texts may prove especially significant in seeking a broad biblical perspective. *Contrasting texts* may help to balance the truth. This is especially important if the biblical book itself states or suggests a contrasting truth to add clarity or emphasis. *Parallel texts* that add supportive insights to the truth are worthy of study. *Illustrative texts,* particularly narrative texts, that actually *show* truth(s) can be extremely helpful.

Scripture helps to interpret Scripture. Be aware of the contextual aspects of each text being used in such a study so that the texts are understood as accurately as possible.

This type of study needs to be saved on paper or in some retrievable form for future use. Supportive biblical material will not only inform the preacher as he seeks to arrive at the teaching of the text, but such material can be drawn on when developing the actual content of the sermon. Explanation, illustration, application, argumentation, amplification, etc., can all be benefitted by having supportive biblical material at hand.

Have a New Testament Perspective (View It Christologically). "But now," Paul says (Rom. 3:21). Although there is an essential and glorious continuity within the Scriptures, there is a "but now" evidenced and proclaimed in the New Testament.

In a very real sense the New Testament is fulfillment. This does not simply make the Old Testament a book of promises or predictions, but it does make the preacher look at how an Old Testament truth is to be viewed in the light of the New Testament and Christ Himself. The word spoken "by the Lord" and confirmed "by those who heard Him" stands in a primary position within God's special revelation (Heb. 2:1–4; 1:1–4).

The New Testament's use of the Old Testament is a fascinating study and certainly merits attention. Hermeneutical systems differ as to how to put God's purposes, dispensations, and covenants together. Our concern here, though, is to make sure that the preacher always remembers that he is *a minister of Christ Jesus* (Rom. 15:16). The centrality and preeminence of Christ must be appreciated. We preach *in light of the gospel*, even if we are not technically preaching a "gospel message"! "The Lord Jesus Christ," "gospel," "now," and "new" all go together to express a glorious explosion of divine activity and proclamation that separates "these last days" from all previous days. And we can reduce our "message" ultimately to one word—"Him" (Christ)—as Paul did (Col. 1:28).

So what does the preacher do with the fact that a majority of our "Bible" is found in the Old Testament? First of all, God's revelation now referred to as the "Old Testament" was the authoritative revelation to which Jesus and the apostles turned. The foundation of New Testament truth and theology is the Old Testament. "This is that" declares Peter on the day of Pentecost (Acts 2:16, KJV). But there is more than a relationship of promise and fulfillment between the Old and New Testaments. The Old Testament maintains, as inspired Scripture, its profitable status to communicate and challenge God's people in Christ (2 Tim. 3:16–17).

When preaching on Old Testament texts, we should use the hermeneutical "helps" already mentioned. As a final aspect of using Scripture to interpret Scripture, the preacher needs to consider: (1) any New Testament use of the text, (2) any New Testament fulfillment of the text, (3) any New Testament parallel or contrast to the text, (4) any New Testament development on or perspective for the text.

When preaching on an Old Testament text, a direct New Testament quotation or clear allusion to the Old Testament text is significant. The preacher might find that the New Testament writer uses the text in an apparently "distant way" to the context of the Old Testament text. The preacher in such instances needs to work carefully with the New Testament text and avoid casual or careless interpretation, while still appreciating the original meaning of the Old Testament text. The various ways in which the New Testament uses the Old Testament causes the interpreter to be slow to jump to conclusions.

More generally, the preacher needs to consider how an Old Testament text and truth needs to be viewed in the light of the New Testament and Christ Himself. There may not be explicit quotation of an Old Testament text within the New Testament, but there may be a clear New Testament perspective within which to view this Old Testament text. This type of study is done to gain perspective on the Old Testament text, not to rob it of its intrinsic or essential truths.

There is sometimes clear continuity and sometimes definite discontinuity between aspects of the Old Testament text and New Testament teaching and truth. Such a recognition is critical, especially as you move towards application and the challenge of a message. New Testament continuity with Old Testament truths will often involve intensified development in the light of the revelation in Christ Himself. Look for this! The interpreter needs to be especially observant when there is apparent discontinuity between the Old Testament text and the New Testament "situation" in Christ.[20] Don't be quick to discount the value of the original meaning of the text. The same God who spoke those Old Testament words sent His Son and spoke through Him. There can be clear theological and practical "truth links," although specific details of the Old Testament text may be fulfilled or need to be viewed specifically in the light of the coming of Christ. The original meaning of a given Old Testament text does not change, but its significance within the canon and specifically in the light of the New Testament should be assessed.

What do you do with an Old Testament text that evidences some discontinuity with New Testament truth? Can we preach on a text like Deuteronomy 32, especially verses 44–47? Do these challenging verses have something to say through the Christian preacher to a local congregation, for instance?

Yes, they do! This text had an original audience and context that must be recognized. A direct connection is declared between allegiance and obedience to "all the words of this law" (32:46), and life and prolongation of days in the land (32:47) for "all Israel" (32:45). This is a literal command/promise. A responsibility was given to Israel on that occasion, and a result was declared, promised. What an awesome text capturing vital words at a critical point in Israel's history!

The New Testament Christian preacher needs to recognize the original meaning of this text and consider the essential truths, the abiding biblical-theological truths that can be preached as a part of a "Christian" message. This text in Deuteronomy 32 teaches the vital importance of the "Word of God" (speaking theologically and biblically), and allegiance and obedience to that Word. The preacher must ask how that Old Testament truth, with its specific promise, is to be viewed in the light of the New Testament and as a part of New Testament preaching. Reference to the literal truth of God's promise to Israel to bless them in the land according to their obedience to the law should be made. But, what abiding truth for the church today that can be preached?

The continuing importance of God's Word in His dealings with His people. The truths of (1) the importance of God's Word, and (2) God's blessing in relation to obedience to the Word (James 1:25) can be declared as aspects of Christian truth and life in Christ. God's Word is still vital. Personal allegiance and perpetual obedience are still critical to fulfilling God's purpose as His children. These truths can point further to the vital importance ultimately of the saving Word (Rom. 10:17). Yet, even if we don't move to this specific gospel implication, the abiding general truths concerning the role of the Word of God and the need for obedience stand as preachable truths, applicable in any setting. Implications and applications on the basis of these basic truths must be evaluated individually and carefully.[21]

It is possible to view the Old Testament itself as less than it was and is. One should not view Deuteronomy 32:44–47 as a command/consequence text in a vacuum. It is a command and consequence based on God's elective-redemptive-protective-purposeful dealings with His people to date. The context of God's salvation, purpose, and promise is there, even in the Old Testament text. The Old Testament is filled with God's mercy, grace, saving words, promises, and fulfillments, as well as His discipline, judgments, and punishments. These are points of continuity between the Old Testament and the New Testaments. God is God. There is a "but now" and there is the "new" that came with Christ, and in Christ; but God is consistently God, revealed in all His wondrous characteristics and activities. Look for these truths both in the Old Testament and the New Testament.

Bryan Chapell has expressed serious concern about preaching a "sub-Christian" message, even in expository form.[22] He identifies types of messages that can easily fit in this category.[23] His comments do not only refer to messages on Old Testament texts, but also to any biblical text. It is possible to preach commitment, responsibility, lifestyle, or challenge without any significant reference to Christ Himself, His redemptive activity, and the resources available in Him. To put it another way, just as you can miss the glorious foundational truths of God's mercy, grace, and promise in the exposition of an Old Testament text, the same can be true in one's approach to the New Testament. We are not so concerned about one such message to committed Christians who understand God's mercy, grace, and promise in Christ; but, to consistently preach "Be," "Do," "Change" messages without the essential truths that make such directives *meaningful* and obedience *possible* is to miss the forest for the trees.[24] We are not talking about imposition, we are talking about appropriate interpretation. It is appropriate for the preacher to discern the theologically and christologically explicit truths in the text, plus those that *undergird* the primary truths of the text. This is where viewing the Scriptures as a whole, Old Testament and New Testament, becomes practical. Once you determine the original meaning of the text, focus in on the essential truths within the text; look at the Scriptures to sharpen, broaden, and gain perspective; and determine what to preach.

Chapell writes: "In recognizing that all Scripture predicts, prepares for, reflects or results from the ministry of Christ preachers unfold the road map that keeps them traveling to the heart of the Bible no matter where they journey in its pages."[25] We have sought above to show that *the journey is not always the shortest distance between two points*. To view a text christologically is not a license to preach the gospel by misinterpretating the text! We must be faithful to the text, but view it legitimately as a part of God's whole counsel that is centered in our preeminent Lord Jesus Christ.

It is possible, for example, to take a text like 2 Corinthians 8–9 and establish new "laws" for Christian stewardship without an appreciation for the theological truths, principles, and perspectives within the text. If one wants to be narrowly legalistic with the text, then he had better send the next offering to the poor among the saints in Jerusalem—because that was Paul's *literal* concern. No, the particular historical occasion of the text is limited to a specific church and a specific collection project. Yet Paul, in this circumstantially motivated set of directives, uses numerous examples, principles, incentives, etc., to call the Corinthians to accountability in this stewardship matter. Within the specifics of the text are clear foundational principles. The *sincerity* of the

Corinthians is a concern (2 Cor. 8:8). To show that he is not going overboard, Paul makes clear that *equality* (8:14) is a principle in God's economy. *Integrity* is shown to be critical in the way this gift is to be handled (8:21), and this impacts the practical administration of the project. Also in the text is a call for *generosity* (9:5–7), and further truths concerning *divine accountability* (9:6), *sufficiency* (9:8–11), and *productivity* (9:12–15) in relation to this matter of love and obedience. Furthermore, we need to note that this passage begins with the "grace of God" (8:1), significantly presents the grace of our Lord Jesus Christ (8:9), gives challenges for Christian grace and love (8:8, 24, 9:13), and ends with an amazing exclamation, "Thanks be to God for His indescribable gift!" (9:15). There is an interweaving of theology, principle, attitude, practice, particulars, and the very "incarnational" model of the grace of our Lord.

One could bluntly say that the bottom-line issue here is for the Corinthians to "get moving" and follow through on their promise to give to the collection project and avoid any embarrassment and any sign of lack of love. The preacher needs to appreciate this original, practical motivation. In addition, the essential truths that move beyond this one historical situation need to be gleaned. These truths can be viewed helpfully in the light of the rest of Scripture and, specifically, God's grace in Christ. This text glows with basic Christian truths and graces, with direct references to the grace of God and of our Lord Jesus Christ. For people to give "convictionally" they need to appreciate the essential truths, the theology, the christological insights that such a text proclaims.[26]

If the preacher believes he is moving beyond Paul's explicit original intention, he needs to make such a notation. That does not mean that such broader New Testament truths or christological insights cannot be preached. But a helpful distinction should be made between Paul's explicit teachings and the broader implications supported by the rest of the New Testament. This is recommended in the handling of all texts within a preaching context. The preacher cannot always take his audience through the hermeneutical process. Still, the preacher should make plain before his people when he is, as it were, seeking to express the explicit theological truth of the text, and when he has moved to broader theological considerations and implications.

Practically Speaking. Now for the shocker! Probably about 10 to 15 percent of your preparation time can be given to this critical point of sermon development. We referred to the various comments above as hermeneutical helps or a checklist. The use of such helps or checks will take more or less time depending on the type of the text, past study, and any specific issues that are unique to the text. Sometimes there will be an immediate or smooth transition the from original intended meaning to essential truths—to a New Testament Christ-centered perspective. Other times the movement will be slower.

The preacher may move through this process almost instinctively. If it helps to write out the process, it could be done in the following fashion.

Summarize the thoughts of the text under the heading "Original Intended Textual Meaning." Then on a separate sheet and/or under a separate heading write down "Essential Theological Truths in the Text." The next heading and/or page would have something like "General Biblical Perspectives on the Essential Truths," and the last heading or page would be "Specific New Testament Perspectives on the Essential Truths."

The more clearly and succinctly these doctrinal truths and principles can be expressed the better. The results of careful investigation are at the heart of the sermon preparation process. The preacher must discover textual truth to proclaim before he can focus on how to preach the truth!

CONCLUSION: THE SIGNIFICANCE OF THE TEXT AND HOMILETICAL PRINCIPLIZATION

Walter Kaiser uses the term *principlize,* by which he means "to state the author's propositions, arguments, narrations and illustrations in timeless abiding truths with special focus on the application of those truths to the current needs of the church."[27] Dr. Kaiser moves through a series of *steps* that take the preacher from the subject and emphasis of the text to the main points and subpoints of the message. In the process, the preacher should determine what is "the permanent, abiding and doctrinal part of the passage."[28] Dr. Kaiser is very concerned that one should not import other or later doctrine or theology into the text. He values what he terms "emerging theology"[29] in the text, rather than systematic expression of theology that robs the text of its place in biblical theology. He goes on to say, "Systematic statements are

Text:	Original Intended Textual Meaning	Essential Truths in the Text	General Biblical Perspectives on the Essential Truths	Specific New Testament Perspectives on the Essential Truths
Dominating Theme ↑ Supportive/Integrating Thoughts ↑ Purposeful Motivating Thrust ↑				

useful only when we have completed exegesis of a passage. Then in our summaries of each main point, in the sermon outline, or in the whole passage, we may jump over the centuries and bring to bear all that God subsequently revealed on the theological issue being examined. In no case should later doctrine be used as an exegetical tool to unlock an earlier passage."[30] The principlizing that Dr. Kaiser recommends is very sensitive to the specifics of the text, including its historical realities which give it a specific setting in biblical theology.[31]

We want to relate this process of principalizing to the methodology we have presented. By the end of the study of the specifics of the text (above) one should be "getting at" the original meaning that is there in the text. Then, that original meaning is clarified in our study of the doctrinal and theological significance of the text and "principlized" as the preacher gets at the essential truths in the text based on the original meaning of the text. We emphasized the need for the broader biblical and christological perspective, which the preacher can, and should, eventually have. But this does not mean that the insights of such broader study are read into the text in such a way that the text loses its meaning, theology, and dynamic. Seek that fair understanding of the theology and principles of the text, and then consider the broader biblical and christological perspective.

At the end of the investigation process, the preacher ought to be able to express the abiding truths, the principlized truths that arise from the original meaning of the text. These essential principles or truths, expressing the doctrine and theology of the text, are given perspective by viewing them biblically/canonically and specifically christologically. They may be shaped by expressing the dominating theme (truth), the various supportive/integrating thoughts (truths/principles), and the purposeful thrust essential to the text in its contextual and canonical contexts.

Essentially our concern is to discern the truth of God in the text. We want to hear His "voice," and understand the truth and its implications. "What God is saying through what He has said" is our concern and goal. The procedures outlined above are shared to help us have "listening ears" to hear. At the same time our hearts must be ready and right to truly receive and understand that truth.

CHAPTER NINE

THE PREACHER AND PREPARATION: ORGANIZATION

Be diligent to present yourself approved to God, a worker who does not need to be ashamed, rightly dividing the word of truth.

—*2 Timothy 2:15*

"Must I not take heed to speak what the Lord has put in my mouth?"

—*Numbers 23:12*

S o far, our primary concern has been to listen to the text, to listen to God's voice in and through the text. To do this we have sought to interpret the text as a specific part of God's revelation, seeking to discern God's proclamation in and through the textual specifics in context. The meaning of the text is sought and the essential truths within the text have been viewed theologically, biblically, and christologically. During this process, the preacher has been aware of the fact that a message needs to be preached (at some point), but the main responsibility has been to "get the truth." Preaching should be message-driven. The message should dominate the preacher, calling for expression. Before a message can be shaped for communication, the preacher needs to "get the message." This should have taken place by this time (even though learning never ends).

Now there is a change of priority in the preparation process. We move from what the text says (what God has said through what He has said) to what *the preacher must say* in the light of what God is saying. We move from the process of learning and understanding to the process of presentation and communication about what we understand of God's truth. The hermeneutical hat is replaced by the homiletical hat, and the preacher now thinks about what needs to be preached.

If one has sought to study along the lines outlined above, much information has been gathered along with the truths of the text. The preacher must be selective in preaching; everything cannot be said about everything, even when preparing a sermon on a short text. Selection and limitation are realities. Alongside these practical realities is the spiritual reality of the Holy Spirit's leading and directing in the study and when preaching. The humble preacher seeks to preach what God would have him preach—what should be preached to the particular people on the specific occasion. Therefore, faithfulness to the Word of God and sensitivity to the Spirit of God are called for both in the study and while preaching.

Principles of Organization			
Truth	Unity	Theme	Subject
Clarity	Movement	Thoughts	Structure
Passion	Purpose	Thrust	Significance

For now we are still in the study. We need to take what we have learned, and prayerfully and carefully seek to *organize* and *finalize* what needs to be said. Some may argue that such further preparation is not needed, that the preacher should just let the message happen under the leading of the Holy Spirit. Well, there may be times when such lack of full preparation is necessary. Nonetheless, we strongly recommend the final stages of preparation that we are presenting. Not only will such preparation, Lord willing, be a blessing to the listeners, it will be a blessing to the preacher. With that in mind, take the information you've accumulated through the study of the text, put on the homiletical hat, and consider the best way, under God, to say what must be said.

PRINCIPLES OF ORGANIZATION

The theme, thoughts, and thrust of an expository message should be governed by the text(s) as studied. The preacher is to become a proclaimer of the text's "message." He is to proclaim what the text proclaims. The sacred text, given by inspiration of God, becomes the *master of the message.* A good place to start the formulation and presentation of a message is to structure or organize the truths of the text that need to be proclaimed. (As we present our recommendations, we must express our indebtedness to W. Graham Scroggie. The wording of this material may be different, but the inspiration and ideas were his.[1]) Ask the following questions of the text:

1. What is the dominating theme?
2. What are the integrating thoughts?
3. What is the motivating thrust?

The Dominating Theme

The dominating theme is the truth that the text proclaims. It is the central idea of the text.[2] It is the "big idea,"[3] and it is the unifying element of the sermon. Here we want to show the importance of a clear, precise, accurate dominating theme to the message. A message is enhanced by *unity* and unity is aided greatly if the main idea (also called the subject, the proposition, the sermon in a sentence, the central idea, or the dominating theme) is stated clearly. It becomes the primary "sound" that is heard. We believe that the best unifying factor in the message is the *truth* of the text. G. Campbell Morgan expressed the need for "truth, clarity, and passion" in preaching, with truth preeminent.[4] Truth ought to master the message. A practical way to make sure this happens is to allow that dominating theme, the primary truth proclaimed in and through the text, to guide in the rest of the preparation process. As we have stated, we are promoting textual—thematic—exposition. The text has been studied and the truth has been recognized, even if it is not yet been stated clearly by the preacher. Now is the time to write down that dominating theme in as accurate a form as possible. The dominating theme should come right out of the text, right off the pages of the work already completed on the significance of the text.

The Integrating Thoughts

The integrating thoughts should likewise come right out of the text, expressing what the text says about the dominating theme. A list of such thoughts, as we will see, helps to provide structure, movement, and interrelatedness to the message. A message must move; you can't say everything at the same time! There has to be sequence, and the guiding principle for the sequence and movement of a message should be the truth-movement of the text. G. Campbell Morgan cites the need for clarity in preaching. A clear identifiable sense of movement can aid greatly in providing clarity. The more complex the message, generally speaking, the greater the need for clear movements to guide the listener through the expository sermon. The integrating thoughts are to be exactly that—*integrated* and *thoughts*. They are integrated in the sense of relating to the theme clearly and to each other sensibly, while accurately reflecting the thoughts of the text. They are to be thoughts, not just words or changes of pace. These stated points express the "thinking" of the text.

The Motivating Thrust

The motivating thrust has to do with the challenge, the call, the appeal, the appropriate cumulative application of the text. G. Campbell Morgan refers to the need for passion in preaching. The two words *motivating* and *thrust* are passionate words. They are also purposeful words. The motivating thrust or the "call" of the text, guides the preacher in clarifying the *purpose* of the message. What is this message *to do*? It is good to clarify this motivating thrust, to indicate where the message is going from first to last. This indicates the purpose and the passion of the message, and hopefully of the preacher as well.

So, in organizing the message, we seek to recognize "obligations," as Dr. Chapell has put it, that guide the preacher.[5] Truth must dominate and permeate the message. There must be an unfolding, an explanation of the truth in some form of sequence. We believe that clarity is a goal in this regard, a clear presentation of integrated thoughts. The motivating thrust, although possibly emphasized in the conclusion, should impact the purpose and passion of the message.

PROCEDURES FOR ORGANIZATION

Determine the Dominating Theme

The first assignment is to determine what really is the theme, the dominating theme of the text. Work at clarifying this dominating theme. You may need to reword, rephrase, or restate the theme later as the sermon develops, but seek to express the dominating theme as clearly as possible for communication. Can the dominating theme be captured in a word? Can it be adequately expressed in a phrase? Should it be stated in the form of a sentence with a subject and predicate? All of the above are helpful, but the preacher may need to start at different points with different texts. Answer the question, What is the text about?

Donald McDougall has pointed out that the "central idea of a passage" may be discovered in a "simple statement" in the text. That statement stands out and the text, as it were, presents that statement as its key thought or idea.[6] For example, take a text like Matthew 8:5–13. This Gospel pericope is a fascinating text (especially in the light of the different details and emphases in Luke's account). This miracle account, in a series of miracle accounts in Matthew's Gospel, stands out because of Jesus' statements. Jesus' response to the centurion's display of humble faith is to marvel and say, "Assuredly, I say to you, I have not found such great faith, not even in Israel" (8:10). This statement seems to point to the theme or distinctive point of this account. The pericope is about "such great faith." The centurion's faith is demonstrated, Jesus marvels at it, and then we see the significance or results of such great faith in both Jesus' words and in the miracle to follow. Such great faith leads to the healing of the centurion's servant, but it also has a kingdom significance. Although one could focus on the *authority* of Jesus, the *healing* itself, or some other aspect of the text, the fact that Jesus makes such an amazing statement causes us to look very closely at the words *such great faith.* In this case, *such great faith* is a subject, and the predicate is supplied by the flow of the text. The theme can be expressed as a subject only or expanded to form a complete sentence.

Another indicator of the dominating theme, or central idea, in a passage is a recurring theme, phrase, idea, etc.[7] Repetition in the text needs to be viewed carefully. When God gives an exhortation *three times* (with only slight variations) to Joshua (1:1–9), one senses the challenge God presents to His servant: "Be strong and of good courage" (1:6); "only be strong and very courageous" (1:7); "be strong and of good courage" (1:9). In fact, this is reinforced by the people in 1:18. The need for such strength and courage is certainly made clear in the text, as are the resources upon which Joshua could depend. The challenge is clear and is in keeping with the major themes of the book as a whole.

Sometimes the theme or central idea does not "stand up to be counted"; rather the preacher must gain a sense of the theme from the context. The larger context may be the indicator of the theme, especially if numerous themes and ideas seem to intermingle in the text.[8] Other times the preacher needs to look at the text in terms of its different thoughts or parts and ask, "What are the sum of the parts? What do the parts add up to say? What is the cumulative message of the text in context?" Two familiar texts come to mind in this regard. Matthew 28:16–20 presents Jesus' final resurrection appearance and statements in Matthew's Gospel. At the center of Jesus' words is His command to "make disciples" (v. 19). But one certainly does not want to minimize the declaration concerning Jesus' authority that sounds forth at the beginning of Jesus' words. Nor does one want to minimize the promise of His presence, or the different directives that are expressed grammatically in participial form. We would not quibble with someone for focusing in on "discipleship" as the core challenge of this text. At the same time, this text has a number of points and moves from our Lord's authority to His specific directives and promise. If you add these parts together, you end up with a descriptive statement concerning the text, such as "Jesus' Final Words," "The Great Commission of our Lord," or "Jesus' Final Charge to His Disciples." All are attempts at stating what the text is, viewing it as a sum of its clear parts. From this descriptive summary of the text it is then easier to move to a more refined thematic statement.

The second text that illustrates the cumulative message of a passage is Romans 12:1–2. It is clearly an apostolic exhortation based upon Paul's gospel presentation in chapters 1–11, and it leads into his practical community instructions in 12:3–15:13. The words of the text are rich with significance and give every evidence of being carefully selected. Sacrificial bodily presentation is called for (12:1) and then purposeful mental transformation is exhorted (12:2). The exhortation clearly functions as a whole, being set apart by the "therefore" in 12:1, and Paul's use of *"lego gar . . ."* in 12:3. So, what is this text about? What does the text add up to say? Is it not about the life response, the commitment, the appropriate response that the "mercies of God" call from the "brethren." Is it not the apostolic exhortation to total commitment in the light of the mercies of God? This can be worded, stated, propositionalized in a number of ways, but the sum of the parts in context gives you the starting place.

So again, write down the dominating theme. The more precise and specific the theme is, the better. Practically speaking, you may need to start with the apparent theme, worded as simply as possible, and move on. You have a lot more to do, and what follows could impact the way you express your theme in the end.

Outline the Integrating Thoughts

The next aspect of organization is to isolate and outline the integrating thoughts. What integrating thoughts relate to that dominating theme expressed in the text? The integrating thoughts may move according to narrative sequence, or flow of argumentation in an epistle. There may be key words, grammatical indicators, or other textual specifics that help the preacher see movement or sequence actually supporting textual evidence for the dominating theme. Write these thoughts, points, or movements in a sequence. You may need a worksheet to develop this list of thoughts into an outline that expresses the truths of the text in relation to the theme.

The Outline of Integrating Thoughts Should Be Biblical. The outline should be faithful to the text. The integrating thoughts should come out of the text. They should not be imposed on the text. Thus, a good outline should reflect the primary integrating thoughts of the text. The minor modifying phrases, or subordinate movements or thoughts, should be reflected in subpoints or in the flow of the message, but not in the main points. It may help the preacher to put the paragraph, verse, sentences, phrase, or word—the specific *textual basis* for the point—right beside the point as you write it down. Such an outline can be checked against an exegetical outline; indeed, this homiletical outline should flow out of the results of your textual investigation. It does not matter how beautiful or logical an outline is if it does not express the textual thoughts. The preacher has to be selective, and he has to seek for clarity, especially in the presentation of the truth of the text. But the need for clarity and selectivity is not a license to ignore or miss the primary emphasis of a text. Therefore, be biblical *and* textual.

The Outline of Integrating Thoughts Should Be Logical. We are not speaking of a sophisticated or philosophical logic. Rather, the outline of integrating thoughts should be understandable and a good representation of the flow of thought or movements in the text. The "logic" of the text should be captured in the outline, and there should be clarity of thought and movement in the outline itself. How do you develop such an outline? First of all, keep each point distinct and mutually exclusive.[9] Make sure that each point is indeed capturing a specific distinct emphasis, thought, or move-ment in the text. As we move towards the sermon itself, we are trying to develop *homiletical distinctiveness.* We want to be able to clearly and definitely proclaim this thought or point. It is best to write down each point clearly before being concerned about form or style. Muddled thinking about the main thoughts of a message can easily result in a muddled message or a message that takes on its own priorities and agenda.

To express textual-thematic "logic," the outline should also be connected to the theme. This aids in developing what we call *har-monious relatedness.* The thoughts of the message are all related to the theme and, therefore, can help to present that theme logi-cally. For example, let's say that the preacher is developing an outline on Matthew 28:16–20 and has chosen the theme "Our Lord's Great Commission," or "Our Lord's Great Commission is given to His disciples." An outline could be developed that pre-sents miscellaneous thoughts or points:

1. Eleven disciples
2. The appointed mountain
3. Are you worshiping or doubting today?
4. Jesus has all authority
5. We should make disciples Jesus' way
6. Jesus is always with us
7. Be a discipler
8. To be a discipler you need to be a disciple

This outline certainly could be used in preaching without promoting error, but it lacks *harmonious relatedness* because the points lack "relatedness," both to the dominating theme and between themselves. The points are a combination of: textual specifics (1, 2), a question (3), a principlized statement (4), applications (5, 6), a direct exhortation-command (7), and a concluding observation-application implied by the text (8). Many or all of these words could be used in a sermon, but as an outline it lacks logical flow. Remember, we are trying to develop an outline that maintains our focus on the dominating theme and moves us through the primary integrating thoughts in the text. This outline is not an exegetical outline, nor is it a list of "prompting" words to keep us preaching. It is an attempt to *organize* the primary thoughts of the text (initially), especially as they relate to the theme of the text.

Consider the outlines of integrating thoughts below:
1. Our Lord's Authority for the Great Commission (28:18)
2. Our Lord's Strategy for the Great Commission (28:19–20a)
3. Our Lord's Availability for the Great Commission (28:20b)

•••

1. The Power of the Lord for His Great Commission (28:18)
2. The Program of the Lord for His Great Commission (28:19–20a)
3. The Presence of the Lord for His Great Commission (28:20b)

Some details of the text (28:16–17) not reflected in the outline may need to be covered in the introduction or at an appropriate point in the movement of the message. But these two outlines help to display the *primary thoughts* of the commission and they keep our focus on the commission.

To "tighten up" a sermon and keep it moving with a logical flow, there are two simple tests to apply to your outline. First is the "key word" test.[10] This word, generally a plural noun, can be identified to tie your points together. Let's look at a sample statement: "As we consider 'Our Lord's Great Commission,' the text presents three motivational *truths* that we need to understand and respond to today." The key word is *truths*. This plural noun identifies each point as a truth, and each truth relates to the theme. In other statements the plural nouns could be *lessons, facets, reasons, dimensions, directives, pictures,* etc., whatever the text gives you. Our aim is to order the thoughts and organize them so that they move logically and clearly.

Another test for the clear "thinking" of an outline is to put each point in a sentence relating the point to the theme. Consider this example: "As we consider these dynamic closing words to Matthew's Gospel this morning, we will see that

1. Our Lord declares His authority/power for the Great Commission
2. Our Lord presents His strategy/program for the Great Commission
3. Our Lord assures His availability/presence for the Great Commission"

These sentences could, in fact, be the full expression of the integrating thoughts in outline form. The sentence form may be helpful throughout the actual sermon, or an abbreviated form may be preferred for simplicity and clarity. But certainly, putting integrating thoughts into sentence form helps to clarify the full thought being expressed.

The Outline of Integrating Thoughts Should Be Applicable. Preaching involves the "contemporization" of the textual message.[11] We encourage preachers to formulate outlines that allow for a simple movement towards application on the part of the preacher. You might adapt the simple outlines above in the following fashion:

1. We must respond to Our Lord's Great Commission *in the Light of His Authority*
2. We must respond to Our Lord's Great Commission *in the Light of His Strategy*
3. We must respond to Our Lord's Great Commission *in the Light of His Availability*

This outline is a series of exhortations and applications of the text, but it maintains contact with both the theme and thoughts of the text. One can present an applicable outline without actually making the points applications. How is that done? Make sure that the points are principles or statements put in the *present tense*.[12] Avoid past tense, past proper names, or past details. You are stating your point in such a way that it is true and applicable for the contemporary listener, even as was for the *original* listener. To facilitate easy movement from then to now, text to sermon, Bible to life, we should also avoid technical terms and complicated wording that call for a lot of unpackaging or explanation.

When you present an outline on Joshua 1:1–9, it does not detail what God said to Joshua only, it expresses the truths that are true and applicable for both Joshua and for us today. Romans 12:1–2 can be outlined in such a way that the commitment called for is not unique to the believers in Rome in the A.D. 50s; it is applicable to us today.[13]

An Authentic Call for Total Commitment
1. There is an Authentic Call we must Heed
    1) Backed by gospel ministry (12:1a)
    2) Based upon divine mercy (12:1a)
    3) Basic to Christian community; "brethren" (12:3ff)
2.There is a Total Commitment we must Make
    1) The Sacrificial Dedication of our Bodies (12:1)
        (1) the contents of the sacrificial dedication (12:1b)
        (2) the requirements of the sacrificial dedication (12:1b)
        (3) the significance of the sacrificial dedication (12:1c)
    2) The Radical Transformation of Our Minds (12:2)
        (1) the principles of radical transformation (Rom. 12:2a)
        (2) the process of radical transformation (Rom. 12:2b)
        (3) the purpose of radical transformation (Rom. 12:2c)

The outline above could be simplified, but it illustrates an attempt to maintain textual distinctives behind the truths while stating them in an applicable way. It would be much simpler to describe the commitment in this way: Be Devoted (12:1); Be Different (12:2), both in the light of Romans 1–11 and the mercies of God. The theme could be "Responding to the Mercy of God." The preacher will have to decide how far he moves from textual expression depending on the type of message and the audience. It can be said, though, that the earlier you are in the process of organization, the closer the outline probably needs to be to the textual wording and expressions.

The Outline of Integrating Thoughts Should Be Memorable. By memorable we mean both "worth remembering"[14] and also that it can be remembered, it is memorizable. This helps both the preacher and the listener. If something is worth remembering, we should try to express it in such a way that it can be remembered. We are not delving into memory theory or what it means to remember. We are just making practical suggestions from observation and experience that may be helpful. Also, at this point in our preparation our focus is still on the *outline* we are formulating, not the sermon itself.

First of all, strive for simplicity. We don't want to sacrifice truth, but we do want to simplify truth. You can simplify by avoiding detailed complex sentences or thought structures. Simplicity in word choice when possible is encouraged. We have found that complicated expression is often a reflection of lack of understanding. The better we understand a truth or thought, the clearer and simpler the expression and/or explanation. Generally speaking, select the most understandable words of the options you have and limit the length and complexity of your outline points.

Then, as much as is possible, limit the number of primary points and levels of structure. Common sense, and possibly experience too, will tell you that a sermon with seventeen main points and three substructures for each point will present a problem. Not only will the points be hard to remember, but the sermon will be a skeleton with little else to help it live. The text needs to dictate the type of outline that comes forth, but the preacher may need to look for ways to combine, summarize, and simplify legitimately to make sure that the primary truths are declared and understood. Sometimes it will become apparent that more than one sermon will be needed to proclaim the theme and related truths clearly and simply. Often, it's just hard work under the anointing of the Spirit that is needed to extract accurately from the text what should be said. Charles Koller suggested limiting the number of main points to five.[15] Although Dr. Koller was promoting preaching without notes, such a limitation is certainly a help for the preacher as well as the listener. Yet, having said this, certainly no number can be given as an absolute cutoff point; the preacher just needs to avoid needlessly piling points on top of each other.

Thirdly, help the people to "hear" the outline. This takes place during the delivery of the message as well as in the study. Presenting your points in similar form helps people to hear and recognize the fact that each point is in a sequence or series. Simple practices such as using the same number of words in each point, repetition of key words or phrases in each point, symmetrical constructions, rhyme, alliteration, etc., all can be used to help people "hear" the outline. Certainly the preacher can ask the congregation to repeat the point after he has already repeated it, but right now we are talking about word choice and outline construction itself. Beginning each point with the same words or phrases or the same first letter in words, etc., draws "audio" attention to a pattern, a sequence. You are drawing attention to parallel thoughts by placing them in parallel form with distinctive characteristics. There is nothing wrong with creativity to enhance clarity. A little work to shape an outline in this regard may be very helpful for the communication of the message.

John Phillips has used the image of a bridge to explain useful and appropriate alliteration. The bridge is the alliteration, but what's important is that you use the same entrance or exit when using the bridge. There must be grammatical consistency (as well as textual integrity). If you have an entrance and exit, they both need to be parallel.

1. There is the Lord's Power for the Great Commission
2. There is the Lord's Program for the Great Commission
3. There is the Lord's Presence for the Great Commission

The words *power, program,* and *presence* are all nouns and are grammatically parallel in these phrases or sentences. There is the same entrance ("There is the Lord's . . .") and the same exit (". . . for the Great Commission") in these three statements.

With all the possible distractions, as well as the regular details of a good message, drawing attention to the primary truths of a message is needed. The outline can sound forth with more clarity and distinctiveness if attention is given to the way the points sound. Parallelisms, repetitions, alliterations, use of rhyming words, and other means to show sequence and similarity are just creative ways of saying 1, 2, 3 or a, b, c. Few would question the value of numbering your points, indicating sequence and similarity. Helping people hear your outline is all we are encouraging you to do.

Lastly, help people when possible to see the outline. I'm not primarily talking about the use of an overhead projector, video projection, computer generated outlines and images, or handing out outlines, synopses, or manuscripts. All of these may be useful, as well as having someone stand up with your points written on sheets of cardboard at appropriate times in front of the congregation! The setting, the type of service, the size of the audience, available technology, and finance determine the various helps that can be used. The preacher needs to keep in mind, though, that these "helps" can also be distractions. They should be used meaningfully and carefully within appropriate settings.

The primary point here, though, is that the preacher needs to word and emphasize the outline in such a way that people are able to see it. In the study, this means attention to word choice and especially word choice that, in a sense, captures the truths of the text and shows them. Consider the following four points of a message on "The Call to Action": *wake up, get up, dress up, line up.* The text is Romans 13:11–14. The text essentially is a call for response, a call for immediate attention to matters of obedience. It is a revival/renewal text. Verse 13:11 basically tells us to *wake up.* What that means and why are revealed in the verse. In verse 13:12a we are told to "cast off the works of darkness" because "the day is at hand." The point *get up* captures the idea of the day being at hand and the need to throw off the nightclothes (as it were). Although the wording is somewhat "distant" from the original wording of the text, it captures the exhortation given. *Dress up* captures "let us put on the armor of light" (13:12c), and "put on the Lord Jesus Christ" (13:14a). *Line up* expresses the thoughts of 13:13, the exhortations to proper behavior in contrast to behavior dominated by the flesh. This outline is biblical, logical, applicable and memorable. It captures the basic truths of the text, and communicates the exhortatory role and purpose of the text. Furthermore, it captures and uses the images and pictures explicit and implicit in the text.

Warren Wiersbe, who has contributed much to the field of preaching and homiletics, has written specifically and thoroughly on the matter of finding, understanding, and using biblical images and pictures in preaching.[16] He sounds an appropriate warning against dry skeletal outline sermons that do nothing but list thoughts devoid of meaningful explanation and illustration. Dr. Wiersbe's study will be referred to again later, but here it is mentioned in relation to the point at hand. If the preacher is going to use an outline, and indeed preach an outline in the midst of the sermon, how helpful it is when the outline can reflect the pictures and purpose of the text. If picture language explicit or implicit in the text can be drawn on, that will help to make the outline *see-able*. Outlining need not hinder the appreciation of the life and creativity of the text; it can build on it and express it, albeit in outline form.

Our main point here is to help people "see" the outline. Avoiding technical or philosophical language is important, but just as important is the use of language that captures and pictures the truths in the text. Look for such picture language as an option for developing the outline.

Preaching itself is a visual as well as a vocal presentation. The preacher is part of the message. When preaching, attention can be drawn to the outline through gestures, body language, pause, repetition, intonation, facial expressions, etc. Then, of course, all of the other possible visual aids may be used to reinforce the basic vocal and visual message. In the study, though, the preacher needs to formulate the outline to express the primary thoughts of the message, and to act as a guide for the sermon finalization to come.

Express the Motivating Thrust

The third part of the organization process is to focus in on *the thrust*-the challenge, the issue, the purposeful function of the text. Going back to the late W. Graham Scroggie's trilogy, we encourage the preacher to ask the question, What is the motivating thrust? The dominating theme has been determined and displayed. The integrating thoughts provide "sequence" for the sermon. Now, we focus on what the text, and indeed the Lord of the text, would have us do with the truth proclaimed. From the exegesis stage of preparation we are aware that the text is intentional and that the purpose of the text needs to be viewed. But here we are thinking homiletically, and we are thinking about what the sermon needs to call forth in response to the truth today. What does the truth demand and deserve in response? What is the appropriate response that is either clearly expressed, implicit within the text, or intrinsic to the text due to its genre, context, subject matter, overall themes, etc.? This sense of call, purpose, and thrust should permeate the message and it will usually be the focus of the conclusion of the message. We will discuss the different aspects of the conclusion later, when we are finalizing the message. Here, the need is to clarify what that truth-thrust is, and how it can best be expressed in this sermon.

The dominating theme and the motivating thrust may be similar in the texts that are basically exhortatory. A text like Romans 12:1–2 is an exhortation. In the case of this pivotal text in the epistle to Rome the theme and the thrust could be very similar in wording. One would be descriptive or indicative (the theme) and the other would be prescriptive or imperative (the thrust). The theme could be stated as "An Authentic Call to Total Commitment." The thrust could be "Hear the Authentic Call and Make the Total Commitment." The theme summarizes the substance of the text; the thrust expresses the "call" of the text in response terms.

Consider a text like 1 Kings 11:1–13. There is no direct exhortation presented. The narrative flow and God's Words to Solomon due to his disobedience are clear in the text. The theme is disobedience, but more specifically, the turning of the heart from the Lord God.

One could title such a message in a lot of interesting ways, but at the heart of the text is the seriousness of disobedience leading to the turning away of the heart from God. Indeed, the theme of this text is the seriousness of spiritual heart trouble. The thoughts of the text flow as follows: (1) the facts or the causes that lead to the turning of the heart, (2) the detailing of the evidence and extent of the disobedient acts that were part of the condition of Solomon's heart, and (3) the response of God to Solomon. These could be reworded in the following matter:

1. The Causes of Spiritual Heart Trouble
2. The Condition of Spiritual Heart Trouble
3. The Consequences of Spiritual Heart Trouble

But what would be the thrust? This is the type of text that would seem to have an obvious thrust, but it needs to be viewed in context. The themes of 1 and 2 Kings will help in this regard. Certainly the preacher must issue a warning against disobedience that leads to such duplicity and half-heartedness in our lives. So, there is a *warning* thrust, and this is certainly in keeping with the intention of Kings as a whole. The book ends with Israel in exile and Judah following them into captivity. The commentary in 2 Kings 17:7–41 is clear. The warning thrust of the sermon then would call for obedience rather than disobedience, covenant allegiance rather than a divided heart, and a recognition of the real consequences of sin. But is that all there is? We think such a thrust would be appropriate, but there is something implicit in the text that could also be significant as a balancing truth. Twice in the first part of the text Solomon is contrasted with David (vv. 4, 6). Twice in God's words to Solomon, He refers to an adjustment in punishment "for the sake of" David (vv. 12, 13). Such references in the text are not incidental and express an obvious contrast. Despite King David's serious sins, his heart was loyal to the Lord God. King David fully followed the Lord; Solomon didn't. Besides the warning of the text, which is in keeping with the whole message of Kings, the exhortation to wholehearted devotion and obedience would seem to be an appropriate thrust implicit in the text. Certainly these are the "calls," the "challenges" of the text: a warning against disloyalty and disobedience and an exhortation to be loyal and obedient.

This warning and exhortation can be presented within the context of God's promises and blessings towards Solomon, which chapters 1–10 of 1 Kings make clear. Even God's "adjustment" of punishment for the sake of David indicates divine mercy and covenant faithfulness alongside of God's necessary judgment. We are not exploring the biblical and christological perspectives in depth, but these contextual and textual indicators clearly point us to the framework of the grace, blessing, and faithfulness of God, and the seriousness and sadness of faithlessness in response. The Book of Hebrews would indeed offer many parallel truths within a New Testament context.

There are many ways of presenting the substance or essence of a message. In short, though, you need to start somewhere, move, and end somewhere. The dominating theme, integrating thoughts, and motivating thrust help to move you from beginning to end. If a person wants the sermon in a sentence, the theme, thoughts, and thrust can be condensed to do that. In the Romans 12:1–2 text, we hear an authentic apostolic call backed by gospel ministry, based on divine mercy, and basic to Christian community; a call to total commitment consisting of a sacrificial dedication of our bodies and a radical transformation of our minds; and a commitment resulting in authentic worship and discernment of the will of God, which we need to hear and respond to in total commitment. Omit the integrating thoughts and you have in Romans 12:1–2 an authentic call to total commitment, which we must hear and to which we must respond. In 1 Kings 11:1–13 the seriousness of spiritual heart trouble is portrayed in terms of its causes, its condition, and its consequences warning us against disloyalty and disobedience (and exhorting us to faithfulness and obedience). Matthew 28:16–20 could be presented as follows: the risen Jesus presents His Great Commission to His disciples in which He declares His authority, strategy, and availability for fulfilling the Commission, a commission we must respond to as disciples committed to making disciples.

The above formulations of theme, thoughts, and thrust should be abbreviated and sharpened for homiletical purposes. The preacher may want to use a worksheet to put the theme, thoughts, and thrust on paper initially and then fine-tune them to make sure of their textual, logical, applicable, and memorable qualities.

Such a process of initial formulation, transition, and sermon organization will probably need to be done within one tenth of the preparation time that the preacher has. *The turning or hinge point in the whole preparation process is the move from the truths of the text to the theme, thoughts, and thrust of the text expressed homiletically.* You are making a transition from revealed truth to what needs to be said to proclaim and explain that truth. You are making a transition from the exegetical-theological process to the homiletical process. The preacher is thinking of communication now. How can the theme, thoughts, and thrust of the text be expressed, not only biblically and indeed textually, but logically, applicably, and memorably. With this attention to expression, the theme, thoughts, and thrust of the text become the theme, thoughts, and thrust of the anticipated sermon. The sermon itself is now organized at a basic level and can be developed further. The text must still remain the master of the sermon, even though the emphasis now is on the communication of that sermon.

CHAPTER TEN

THE PREACHER AND PREPARATION: FINALIZATION

Give attention to reading, to exhortation, to doc-
trine. Do not neglect the gift that is in you, ...
Meditate on these things, give yourself entirely to
them, that your progress may be evident to all.
Take heed to yourself and to the doctrine.
Continue in them for in doing this you will save
both yourself and those who hear you.
—1 Timothy 4:13-16

The essential truths of the message have been translated into the dominating theme, the integrating thoughts, and the motivating thrust. These organizing elements provide the framework for thinking through the specific form and words of the message. We recommend that the preacher give as much time, thought, and prayer as possible to the next aspect of preparation: message finalization. This time can be aided greatly by the writing of a manuscript.

PRINCIPLES OF FINALIZATION

The *process* of writing a manuscript is as important as producing the manuscript. Writing a manuscript helps the preacher think through the message and capture it in specific words. The manuscript can then become a tool for reviewing, relating, and rehearsing the message. It can be filed or kept in some form for future reference as well. But before you preach, it is critical that you have a *vital biblical message*, not just a written manuscript to present. We will present a process or discipline designed to help you proclaim an "incarnate" message, whether you use a manuscript, notes, or no notes at all in the pulpit or on the street corner.

Certainly there are times when the writing of a full manuscript is difficult or even impossible. We understand that. But we recommend this as a discipline and practice for the preparation of new messages especially. The actual manuscript may never appear in public; it may simply be a means of preparation for and preservation of the message, which in itself is a valid stewardship of time and thought. This discipline forces the preacher to think through the message and to give attention to the actual communication of the message. Every word presents a choice and a commitment on the part of the preacher. He, therefore, has to select and record the details of the message. Such a process will not only make sure that the preacher has thought through the details of the message, it will aid in the preacher's ability to choose the best ways to "word" the message.

The preacher is not preaching to demonstrate rhetorical ability or to impress people with a vast vocabulary. On the other hand, the preacher is seeking to choose the best way to word and communicate the truth for which and to which he is responsible. Words are tools. The discipline of wording a manuscript can strengthen the preacher's vocabulary and the ability to choose the most appropriate ways to explain, apply, and illustrate the message.

PROCEDURES FOR FINALIZATION

Prayerfully Write the Sermon

Pray, think, write! You have the theme, thoughts, and thrust as your guide. A message can develop and be formed in many ways, but the priority is to proclaim the truth of the text(s) on the basis of textual authority. For the purposes of our discussion, and as a simple pattern to consider, we will divide the content of the message into the introduction, exposition, and conclusion (peroration). Depending on the type of message, and the preacher's preference and need, he may decide to start his writing at either one of these three break points in the flow of the message. If the preacher gets "stuck" as he struggles with introductory matters, it may be wise to move to the first main point in the message, which is already known from the previous aspect of preparation. If one has a tendency to rush the writing of the conclusion and not to think it through, then starting with the conclusion is something to consider. Our presentation below moves from the introduction through the exposition, to the conclusion.

The Introduction. The introduction is more than just the first words or sentences of a sermon. It is the wording that presents the message and the messenger to the particular audience being addressed. The introduction serves, also, as a verbal transition from whatever has taken place in the experience of the listeners to the event of preaching. So, besides introducing the dominating theme of the message appropriately, the introduction actually begins a new activity to which people will and must respond. Because of the unique nature of every preaching occasion, the introduction to the same basic message may differ substantially on different occasions. And indeed, a planned introduction may differ greatly from the actual introduction presented. Nevertheless, it is helpful to think through the introduction of the message carefully to make sure that essential elements are included.

Generally speaking, the introduction should introduce the subject (the dominating theme) and the object (the burden, the purpose, the motivating thrust) of the message to the listeners. What are you preaching about, and why are you preaching? The preacher is not, as it were, giving "all the answers" in the first few sentences in the message, but he is saying that he has "an answer" on the basis of the Word of God. A clear, honest, and bold proclamation of what is to be expounded and what is the goal of the message is needed.

Depending on the occasion and the audience, there may need to be an introduction of the messenger and the activity of preaching as well. There are a number of accepted givens on the part of informed members of a congregation at a regular church service or function. When a preacher walks up to a pulpit at a specific time during a worship service, opens a Bible, and begins to speak as indicated in a written "order of worship," expectations are already established. For many, basic questions concerning the role of the preacher and the nature of preaching are answered, and many know at least in part what is taking place. But in unique situations, and even in regular church services, the preacher may need to explain what he is doing as a preacher and why he is doing it. The message and the messenger cannot be separated, and when the messenger is not known or his role is not understood, there could be the need for a careful and brief explanation.

The focus of the introduction is the presentation of the dominating theme of the message. This theme is the truth of the text now worded for the sermon and the preaching event. The theme should be distinguished from a title, which may only introduce people to the real theme. There is nothing wrong with stating, "The theme of this message is . . ." "The subject of the sermon today is . . . " "The wonderful truth we are proclaiming today is that . . . " "I want us today to hear and respond to the text of God's Word as we consider the dynamic truth . . ." Sure, there is room for creativity and the need for care as one begins the message. We recommend, though, that there be clarity from the beginning. The theme of the message, which is based upon a dominating theme in the text, is presented as the subject matter of the sermon.

Alongside the clear stating of the theme are two other ingredients we recommend in the introduction: the background of the text, and the burden of the message. The background information concerning the text introduces the listeners to the textual source of and authority for the truth being declared. The amount of background information will differ depending on the type of text, message, occasion, and audience. Some background can be shared before the text is read, or it can be presented later. Certainly what is desired in all situations is a creative presentation of contextual and historical matters in order to help the listeners understand both the text and the truth of the text. The same potential barriers that the preacher faces in the study are faced by the people when they hear the sermon. A commitment to biblical inerrancy and relevancy does not mean that such an explanation of the background of the text is not necessary. On the contrary, the preacher is revealing the very nature of the Scriptures as given by God. A historical/contextual setting is explained in such a way as to enable the people to understand the text more fully, while helping them to appreciate the abiding and indeed critically relevant truth that is being declared. As we have indicated in our discussion of text investigation, often the original purpose of the text can lead directly into the purpose of the preacher's message. This connection is a good focus point for the presentation of background information. The "what" and "why" of the original text can be introduced against a creative description of the text.

A Bible study context may call for detailed background information in keeping with the purpose of the occasion and the length of time available. On the other hand, a street corner evangelistic message may call primarily for the simple declaration of the fact that the words, which the preacher is about to quote, are authoritative words from the Word of God on a particular subject. In either case a textual-thematic exposition will seek to draw attention to the text of the Word of God as the authority for what is being proclaimed. The preacher is presenting the text as a "living" text that is relevant to the listeners. Allowing the common denominators between the historical/contextual framework of the text and that of the listeners will help to point to the abiding significance of the text to the contemporary audience. The text is authoritative and relevant because it is part of the Word of God— period. That authority and relevancy are affirmed and illustrated as the connection between the realities of the text and the realities of the audience is shown. This connection is not ultimately based on existential similarities, but on the foundations of the changeless nature of God, the "constants" in the nature of man, and the abiding truth of the Word of God.

We recently heard a message based on the first few verses of Hebrews. One could spend time discussing various issues concerning the dating and authorship of this wonderful epistle. Many of the challenging features of the epistle could be referred to, but for what purpose? The goal is to affirm the authoritative nature of the text and to make the text understandable to the listeners. The preacher in this instance, creatively and with simplicity explained when and for whom the epistle was written. The possible date for the epistle was presented simply, without academic discussion. A vivid personal experience was shared illustrating the real issues facing Jews exposed to Christianity or converted to Christianity. The theme of the epistle, captured in the word *better*, was explained succinctly. The introduction helped us to see the text within its original context.

Expository preaching need not present background information in an academic way. The preacher should not take the listeners back into the study. That is the lazy way to present such information. No, the preacher must present the fruits of his investigation in such a way that the text is seen for what it really is, the living and abiding Word of God. Generally speaking, the preacher should avoid purposeless presentations of background trivia and tedious listings of options and possibilities that could give the wrong impression. A specific Bible study setting or classroom situation may call for more thorough presentations, as we have noted, but the congregational setting does not demand this. Another possible exception could be if the preacher is beginning an expository series through a biblical book and he wants to devote a significant amount of time in one message to the background and the "big picture" of the book. Even so, care should be taken to present this material purposefully and practically.

The introduction should include, also, the burden of the message. In other words, the preacher should communicate why the message is being preached. Every message of the preacher should be critical, and a sense of the critical nature of the message should be expressed. If the preacher is preaching incarnationally, this critical and vital aspect of the message will be sensed personally and passionately by the preacher. It is of utmost importance to the preacher that the message be declared, and that the message be embraced. The latter concern is not driven by a concern for popularity or success, but rather because the preacher longs that the truth be received and responded to with appropriate obedience. The preacher knows that the truth is worthy of obedience, and he knows that obedience to the truth will have a significant impact upon the lives of the listeners. The Christian preacher is not a detached voice, sounding a message with neutrality. He knows the value of the truth he declares, first of all because it is God's truth, but also because of the benefits of that truth in the lives of those who respond as God requires.

The burden of the message can be communicated in various ways. The preacher's personal concern can be expressed, an illustration of the need for the truth can be told, biblical material can be drawn on, etc. The preacher needs to let the audience know that this message is, in fact, for them, and it will make a difference in their lives. The listeners should sense that the preacher views the preaching of this specific message as a purposeful activity. It is vital that the preacher's audience hear this message and respond. Indeed, the purpose of the message can be communicated clearly and directly—and this need not be saved for the conclusion. "My purpose this morning, on the basis of the truth of God's Word, is to call all who hear me to . . . ," "My burden in this message is to help each of us avoid the serious consequences of . . . ," "All of us today have to make a decision concerning the truth I am declaring. I am calling for obedience today . . ." In the last chapter we discussed the motivating thrust of the message. This is the call, the challenge, the demand, the necessary response appropriate to the truth of the text. The burden of the message and the preacher will lead to the motivating thrust of the message. The preacher may not express fully or stress heavily the motivating thrust as he introduces the message, but the basic or simple burden of the message is important.

It may be that the preacher will express the full theme, thoughts, and thrust of a message in the introduction. An abbreviated sermon overview would include a clear presentation of the dominating theme and the motivating thrust. Placing these two within a sentence or two would put together the subject and the object of the message. Certainly the preacher should have a good understanding of these organizing elements, even if they are not all stated clearly at the beginning of the message.

Great emphasis could be placed on the introduction from the standpoint of communication, since it is the first critical contact with the audience. Care must be taken not to waste these precious moments. (We will touch on this again in a coming chapter.) Here, though, we want to emphasize what needs to be written in the manuscript. The introduction need not be elaborate. Indeed, a common problem with introductions is that they are too long. This tendency can be curbed by placing some of the material from a long introduction within the body of the exposition, or eliminating it altogether. Suggested time limits could be given for introductions, but obviously the lengths will vary from message to message. The key is to say what needs to be said and then move into the body of the message. There should be a sense of movement, and significance must be given to the actual explanation of the text itself. Focus in on the communicating of the dominating theme, the background of the text, and the burden of the message.

If the Scripture has not been read already, the reading of the text will need to precede or be a part of the introduction. This needs to be thought through carefully, with great importance placed upon the actual reading of the text. Time must be allocated adequately for a meaningful reading without any sense of rush. The preacher will need to know when the Scripture is to be read as he puts his introduction together. Prayer is another important consideration. We recommend offering a specific prayer in relation to the preaching of the message. Certainly this takes place separately before the preaching event, but acknowledging the Lord and the preacher's dependence upon Him is appropriate in any preaching context. Study the apostle Paul's thanksgivings and prayers in his epistles and note how they relate to the content surrounding them or to follow. It is appropriate for the theme and burden of a message to be lifted to the Lord in prayer with a sense of complete dependence upon Him.

The preacher may develop a preference in the way he proceeds at the start of the message. He may read the Scriptures (with or without background or explanatory comments), then pray, and begin the actual introduction of the message. Another pattern may be preferred. What is important, though, is that each one of these significant activities is given careful attention. The preacher should plan to proceed in a particular way, even if the plan is changed when standing before the people. These matters should be thought through, and a good time to do this is when you are writing the introduction.

The Exposition. The exposition itself seeks to proclaim the truth of the text on the basis of textual authority and explanation. The outline that has been formed serves as a guide as the preacher now seeks to write out the substance of the sermon. The preacher needs to go back to the outline and view it in relation to the introduction. A transitional statement or series of statements may be needed to move from the introduction into the first major movement of the exposition. The expectations that the preacher has raised through the introduction need to be met through the content of the exposition itself. If the preacher is struggling for the right transitional sentences, a good way to proceed is to tell the people how you are going to address the theme in the body of the sermon. The "what" of the sermon has been presented, and the "why" of the sermon, at least in part, has been presented. Now you are telling them "how" the message is going to proceed, how the truth is going to be proclaimed and explained, how you are moving from this point forward.

Expositions can take many shapes. Haddon W. Robinson presents a number of these shapes helpfully.[1] He discusses "An Idea to Be Explained," "A Proposition to Be Proved," "A Principle to Be Applied," "A Subject to Be Completed," "A Story to Be Told," and other forms. The very diversity of the Scriptures themselves, of truths that need to be declared, and of audiences and circumstances causes the preacher to consider carefully how the exposition should unfold. The outline already developed will represent the main movements of the message, and will point to a particular shape for the exposition. This outline has come out of direct textual study and should represent the flow and pattern of the text as it reveals, declares, explains, demonstrates, etc., the truth of the text. If at this point in preparation the preacher thinks he ought to adopt another sermonic shape, he can adjust the outline accordingly. Sensitivity to the truth and the text are called for, and the preacher should seek to form the message in a way that preserves the truth and the purpose of the text. There is room for much creativity, especially that creativity that seeks to take its lead from the text itself.

Once the dominating theme, the integrating thoughts, and the motivating thrust of the message are in final workable form, they will be the basic affirmations of the message as well as the practical guides as you write out the body of the exposition. The dominating theme (DT) should always be in the preacher's mind while the sermon is being written. This is the unifying element to the proclamation and the content. When the preacher is tempted to go off on a tangent, he needs to ask, "Am I still proclaiming my theme? Am I still presenting the message?" The integrating thoughts (IT) make sure that the preacher is moving in the exposition, affirming aspects of the truth to be declared. If the IT are carefully related to the DT, then the movement will be unified. The IT will lead meaningfully and purposefully towards the final expression of the motivation thrust (MT). Awareness of the MT will help the preacher to stay purposeful throughout the exposition, especially as he moves to the conclusion.

The body of the exposition moves with the help of the IT. Review the flow of the IT previously formulated. Do they need any adjustment as you now seek to write out the flow of the message? The writing of the introduction may have brought certain new insights to mind. You may now think that the message will take a slightly different shape, and the outline is adjusted without sacrificing truth. Once you are clear concerning the flow of the IT, then you make the transition into the first point, state the first point (the first IT), and write out the development of that point, principle, truth, which is your first main movement in the body of the exposition.

Each point or movement in the exposition will generally represent an integrating thought with textual support. The truth masters the sermon and the text masters the truth. But the preacher has many ways to express the truth on the basis of textual support. To simplify the presentation of all the possible options that the preacher could use to word the message, we will deal with four categories of material: explanation, application, illustration, and transition.

Explanation. The point in the outline will represent the essence of the textual truth that is being declared and explained at this time in the sermon. The preacher will be limiting himself at this point to that section, verse, sentence, clause, phrase, or word that supports, expresses, demonstrates, represents, declares, indeed authorizes the truth or point being made. The preacher will focus in on that part of the text and expose it to the people. Rereading the text may be called for. Helpful rephrasing of difficult words or sentences may be useful. The preacher wants the people to grasp the flow of thought within this specific section of the text. Helpful expository insights that clarify and picture the meaning of significant words can be offered. The goal is to explain the text, and explain it in a way that will open it up to the hearers, depending always on the Holy Spirit to do the work only He can do.

The preacher needs to pay attention to the type of text he is dealing with. A narrative text may call for a retelling of the account to give the listeners a sense of the whole. The main characters may need explanation in terms of their roles within the narrative. Significant actions, speeches, names, or places may need special explanation, since the role of these details may not be obvious at an initial reading. The preacher must always remember that although he has been working with this text in preparation for this message, the audience may only have thought about the text for the last few seconds! To explain a prophetic statement, the preacher may need to present creatively the historical setting and ethos within which these words have their original meaning and impact. Gospel pericopes may need to be retold with an eye to detail that the audience would not see on an initial reading. Epistolary material may need to be unpacked with a careful attempt to express the main concepts and directives and to argue or defend the truth as the apostle did.

Accurate, creative, and dynamic explanation is what we are striving for. Words will need to be defined accurately, simply, and vividly. Difficult phrases, clauses, sentences, or even paragraphs need helpful discussion. How the text expresses the truth you are declaring needs to become evident as you proceed. Ideally, the listener should be able to go back to the text and recognize the meaningful connections that you are making. Ask the question, How can I best explain this section of the text? Avoid unhelpful exegetical comments or details that are not critical to the truths being exposed and proclaimed. The preacher will inevitably need to be selective; he cannot say everything about everything in the text. That is why time was spent to develop an organizing outline. That outline focuses on the primary concerns of the text as they relate to the primary truth within the text.

Developing your skills of explanation is a worthy pursuit. Note how the biblical material explains truth itself. Learn from great preachers and teachers by examining how they actually explain the truths, concepts, and points they are making. Consider the value of explaining the point in a number of ways to reinforce the meaning. You may seek to retell, rephrase, and provide exegetical insights that you yourself have gleaned. Parallel or contrasting biblical wording may be used to support and further explain the textual specifics. The selection of a helpful quotation may shed light. Providing a question/answer framework for the explanation may keep the listeners on track. You are seeking to help the people think about the truth in focus, and to help them think through the text as well. Obviously, the level of exegetical exploration and discussion will depend on the text, audience, and situation. But the preacher should enable his listeners to understand the essential elements of the text as they relate to the truth being declared. In one way or another the preacher is going to isolate these elements to draw attention to them and then show how they relate to the flow of the text.

Illustration. Closely connected to explanation is illustration. Under the category of illustration we will discuss various means to shed light on the truth, the text, and even the application. The preacher needs to determine when further explanation is needed by means of a vivid illustration, example, or picture. Certainly the preacher ought to consider whether or not an illustration is needed in relation to major truths being expounded. Illustrations are particularly helpful when the exposition calls for careful explanation and detail. Theological concepts, direct commands and exhortations, and heavier didactic material often require illustrative expression. On the other hand, I have heard messages on Old Testament narratives and from the Gospels that needed very little additional illustrative material. The very expounding of the text paints the picture. Ask the question as you prepare, Do I need to help them further to see the truth? Make sure the illustration does in fact illustrate clearly the point you are seeking to illustrate! Generally speaking, illustrations should be communicated as simply and clearly as possible so that the point will be obvious. That is the purpose of an illustration. If the point of the illustration is not obvious, then the illustration has obviously not make obvious what should be obvious!

Sources for illustrative material are numerous: personal experience, common community experience, current events, historical accounts, literature, hymns and poetry, parables, and material created for the occasion. Other preachers often are a good source or at least good catalysts for thinking through possible illustrations. Resource books and computer programs are all available to help the searching preacher. If the illustration is found, make sure it is credible. Be accurate in the retelling of an illustration, give credit succinctly as appropriate in the context of the message, and make sure that the point is clear. If you have to illustrate your illustration, then you may have the wrong one!

It is hard to generalize when dealing with the matter of illustrations. The preacher needs to know his message, his audience, and his own preaching strengths and weaknesses. An illustration that really impacted you as the preacher needs to be considered. At the same time, a good variety of illustrations is helpful. Once an illustration has taken a significant place within a sermon, leave it there. It is best not to constantly use the same stories from sermon to sermon. Look for new illustrations. Generally speaking, the illustration should be told as simply, vividly, and carefully as possible. Some of the best illustrations we have heard have been simple retellings of everyday experiences in a way that vividly portrays the point. The preacher should be sensitive to the lessons of everyday living. Meaningful personal experiences that are not self-promoting or needlessly self-deprecating can be of great help.

They illustrate the truth, but also remind the people of the fact that the preacher is a real person, not just a talking head. The audience has the right to ask the question, How has the truth you are declaring made a difference, impacted, or been processed in your experience? How does the experience of the preacher relate to the truth being preached?

A special word is needed about the use of the Bible for the purpose of illustrating truths in the primary text. The Bible itself is a wonderful source for illustrative material. By using biblical material you expose or remind people of other biblical texts and help them see how Scripture can interpret Scripture. In the process of using biblical illustrations, great care should be taken to make sure that the text is being explained appropriately. Also, the authority of the Word should be maintained. While the Bible is a sourcebook for helpful stories, it is still the authoritative Word of God. Numerous narrative texts are available to give a picture of a truth, a wrong or right behavior, and most of all, the dealings of God with His people. God is always the hero in biblical narrative. All human examples break down; so, beware! Ultimately the main concern in using biblical illustrations is that the text is treated fairly and accurately. But to ignore the vast amount of truthful, accurate, vivid, dynamic, and indeed God-breathed illustrations within the Word, in our estimation, would be a shame.[2] Narrative texts are certainly not the only type of texts that are appropriate for illustrations. Sometimes a pithy proverb, a passionate declaration from the Psalms, or some other quotation from the Scriptures can capture, in a different word-picture, what you are trying to illustrate.

Avoid preaching a separate mini-sermon based on the illustration! Also, try not to deaden an illustration with qualifications, disclaimers, etc. For example: "I heard about a terrible event that happened the other day, or week, maybe it was three weeks, I can't remember, but it was a terrible event that was told to me, actually it wasn't told to me directly, I overheard it while getting a haircut at Smith's Barber Shop. Two men were talking and I thought I heard one of them state that a terrible thing had happened the day before according to a recent report from a teacher at a local school. I don't want to name the teacher or the school, and in any case it doesn't make any difference to the report . . ." Such an illustration amounts to the terrible event itself!

Let the illustration do its work and move back to the flow of the message. A pause may be needed or some type of transitional statement may be needed to move on in the exposition. It is better to present carefully a limited number of point-making, vivid illustrations than to pile up story upon story without real value to the truth of the message. Instead of piling up illustrations, the preacher can work towards improving his choice of words in an attempt to simplify and make truth more "see-able." Selecting words that "picture" the truth can be just as helpful to the listeners.[3]

Application. Also included within the content of the exposition should be application. We have devoted a whole chapter to the subject of application in the next section. Here we want to point out the need to write down this aspect of the exposition as well. Preaching should be application oriented throughout, but there also needs to be specific applications. Application relates the truth of the text to the life of the listener. What may have seemed general, or biblical, now becomes personal. Questions often help to make a transition to direct application. For example: "What relevance does this truth have to you this morning?" "How does God want you to respond to His will as revealed in this portion of the text?" "What difference will your obedience to this truth make in your life today?" "We've viewed what the apostle was saying to his beloved Timothy, but what would he say to you, and in fact what is God really saying to us today through His Word?" If such questions are asked, it is critical that they be answered carefully and be made relevant to the lives of the hearers. Not only is it helpful to put the biblical truth, directive, promise, etc. in accessible personal terms, it may be appropriate to give response steps as well.

We definitely encourage applying the message throughout the exposition. The personal relevance of the truth should be sensed as the message proceeds. It may be helpful to think through how the truth you are declaring relates to the lives of different groups within the church or audience. Be careful not to stereotype individuals in some unfair or naive way. At the same time, often the Christian and the non-Christian are at different points in terms of the response that the truth demands. Also, the application may need to be pictured slightly differently for singles, married couples, parents, children, young, middle-aged, and older adults, etc. If application is not the strength of the preacher, then writing out the applications is even more important. This will help the preacher to think through this aspect of the exposition carefully.

Of utmost importance is making sure that the application is, in fact, based on the text, and is appropriately applied to your hearers.

Bryan Chapell states, "Preachers who cannot differentiate between a scriptural mandate and a good suggestion drain biblical power from their ministries. You must make sure the Scriptures—not you—demand what your application requires."[4] It is important also to tell people not only how they should respond to the truth, but how they are *able* to respond to the truth. To place a demand on the hearer, even if true to the Word, without giving guidance and the resources available in Christ, can lead to frustration and defeat. So, the providing of application is a challenging aspect of sermon development. Examples, pictures, and illustrations for your applications can help to clarify what adjusting one's life to the truth looks like. Even sharing how the preacher has sought to respond to the truth can be very instructive to the audience. People need to know that the preacher is under the Word he is declaring and that he is motivated to respond to the truth in his daily life.

The careful and creative connecting of explanation-illustration-application is a challenging dimension of textual-thematic exposition. We recommend that this be done for each major thought, truth, movement in the message. There should be a sense of completeness to each point. When you move on to the next facet of the exposition, you really do move on! There is a sense of movement, and also a sense of the importance of each section of the message. Although you will tie the message together in the conclusion, people will miss something if they do not follow you all the way through the message. Each IT is critical, calling for textual explanation, illustration when necessary, and application. Nothing is extraneous or insignificant. If in the writing of the message you sense that something is unnecessary for the proclamation of the truth in this particular message, then you should delete it. You want to cover the text fairly, but you also want to maintain thematic clarity throughout the exposition.

Transition.—Unity and clarity are served well by transitions between the major movements in a message. These transitions are particularly helpful in oral communication. Transitions within an exposition give opportunity to clarify for the audience how the message is moving. It may be helpful to restate the DT and the IT to this point in the message, and then clearly state the next movement in the exposition. The very progression of the message should encourage the listeners to continue following the preacher as he seeks to move to this next critical section of the exposition. The more detailed the exposition and the more supportive thoughts that compromise the DT, the more the transition points need to clarify what has been said and what is about to be said. Repetition is a critical tool in oral communication, and these transition points in the message are strengthened by the repetition of the DT and the relevant IT. We don't realize how helpful clear transitions are until they are absent. Each IT provides an opportunity to tie the message together in a meaningful way.

Explanation, illustration, application, transition—these are the basic ingredients that need to be blended together within the body of the exposition. This type of presentation, as guided by the organizing elements of the sermon, will help the preacher maintain thematic clarity while attempting to expound the text. We certainly want to see the text fairly and carefully expounded, but we also want a message to come through that leads to an appropriate conclusion. It may take the preacher a number of hours to write out all of the above. Careful attention should be given to word choice, clear sermonic development, and a sense of unity throughout the message.

The Conclusion. When the last integrating thought has been presented with expository support, the movements in the message have been completed. The DT has been proclaimed, and the IT has served to aid in the proclamation while providing a framework for the exposition of the text. The conclusion is not tacked on to add material to the message. The conclusion clarifies, exhorts, and invites response appropriate to the truth that has been declared. The motivating thrust (MT), which has already been identified, becomes the focus of the conclusion. Although applications have been made along the way, now the preacher is seeking to call for the basic response to the total message. The MT really represents the issue, the challenge, the call of the theme and text to the listeners. The purpose of the exposition is to proclaim the truth and to call for the response that the truth deserves and demands.

When writing a conclusion, three separate movements are worth considering. This is especially true for those who find it difficult to conclude a message. The first movement is *clarification.* Here the preacher brings the whole message together and relates it to the MT. A summary statement concerning the message may be formulated. This statement or series of statements may include the DT, each integrating thought, and the MT. In any case, this is a good time to review the theme and main points of the message with a view to showing the appropriate response that the biblical text calls for. Options remain to the preacher to reinforce what the challenge really is. He may go back and reread the text, asking questions that relate the text directly to the listeners. A key thought or phrase within the text may be used as a focus point to drive home the heart of the matter. Another text can be used if it has the exact wording that the preacher is wanting to use to summarize the response, but the preacher needs to be careful that he does not start to preach another sermon. In general, this is not the time to bring in significant new biblical material that could deflect from the focus of the message. An illustration, quotation, or some other significant wording can be drawn on to express the essence of the message in such a way that it leads to or reveals the MT. Questions can be used to help the listeners face the challenge of the message, such as "Will you commit yourself today to . . . ," "How will you respond today to the truth of God's Word? Will you . . . or will you . . . ?" Questions help to clarify what the issues are, and they encourage the people to think about their response. The purpose of this aspect of the conclusion is to erase any doubts as to what the message is really about and what the hearers need to do in response. Indeed, a valid purpose of this part of the conclusion is to make sure that people realize that a response is needed, appropriate, and required.

Clarification leads to *exhortation*. The apostle Paul exhorts his readers in Romans 12:1 as follows: "I beseech you therefore, brethren, by the mercies of God, that you present." On the basis of the "mercies of God," which really summarizes or clarifies the nature of God's dealings with man in chapters 1–11, the direct exhortation is given. It is interesting that the apostle uses the word *b r e t h r e n* as he appeals for specific and total response to the presentation in the epistle. The preacher is not neutral about the DT or the MT of the message. The preacher should exhort the type of response that is appropriate, that which is desired by God. It should be apparent to the audience that the preacher stands under the Word himself and that he has to respond to the message. But, this should not get in the way of direct exhortation needed. The preacher may refer to his own response or let the audience know that he has had to face the challenge of the message during the preparation of the sermon. The focus now, though, is on the congregation or the audience: "On the basis of the truth of God's Word, I exhort you to . . ."

The preacher may need to explain the "you" in his exhortation so as to make sure *everyone* recognizes that they come under the sentence of the Word. In fact, the exhortation may need to be addressed to various subgroups within the audience, as was the case when applying the message. The two primary groups are those who are "in Christ" and those who are not! At the same time, if the message has been addressed primarily to the people of God, they should be exhorted to respond, even if there is a special word for those who need "repentance toward God and faith toward our Lord Jesus Christ" (Acts 20:21). What is of utmost importance is that the exhortation is in keeping with the biblical truth that has been declared. People should only be exhorted to respond to what has been proclaimed clearly.

There are many words that can be used to encourage response. The *ethos* of the challenge of the message should be in character with the *ethos* of the message. The preacher is not, as it were, switching hats at this point in the sermon. He is following through with his responsibility and fulfilling the purpose that he had when he started to speak. It may be helpful for the preacher to think in terms of Whom he represents, rather than a specific message only. In other words, the preacher is calling the audience to respond to the truth and to the God of the truth. People are not just to adopt a new set of principles or behavior patterns. They are to respond to God in the way He directs through the truth that has been declared. The response should be God-directed and God-centered; indeed Christ-directed and Christ-centered.

Exhortation leads to *invitation*. In the exhortation a call for response is issued; in the invitation that response is encouraged and a means of response is provided. The challenge of the message is personalized in the exhortation; it can be actualized in the invitation. In using the word *invitation,* we are not focusing in on methodology. We are speaking more fundamentally about allowing people the opportunity to respond in a meaningful way to what has been declared. A chapter on the invitation appears later in our study, so we do not need to labor our discussion here. There are a few observations, though, that may be helpful to consider as we prepare the message and finish the manuscript. The preacher needs to know how he intends to actually conclude the message. This is a holy and significant event. Sensitivity to the Holy Spirit is needed both in the study and when preaching to invite people to respond. Life transformation is the practical purpose of the message. It is awesome to realize that the Holy Spirit can take the preached word and use it to accomplish saving and sanctifying activities.

After a clear call or exhortation has been presented, the preacher should then instruct, guide, and invite the response. A good question to ask in the study is this: If someone desires to respond to this message as the Holy Spirit works in their lives, what should they do immediately at the end of the message? If anyone is asking privately or publicly, "Men and brethren, what shall we do?" (Acts 2:37), you need to have an answer. People should have an answer to that question. Make the answer personal so that any individual will know what to do. You may want to picture yourself sitting next to that individual. They have just said, "I heard the message. I need to respond. What does God want me to do?" The invitation time provides an opportunity for people to make a definite decision, to settle a spiritual battle, to make a first step in faith and obedience, to focus specifically on their relationship with God, and depending on the methodology, to confess in one way or another that they have responded or desire to do so.

There are limitless ways to conclude a message and invite response. The preacher needs to think and pray through what God desires and deserves in relation to the specific message being prepared. We recommend that the preacher clarify the appropriate response to the message and lead in prayer before other aspects of an "invitation time." Even the singing of a hymn, although a wonderful way for the congregation to respond corporately, can cause a shift in focus from one's own personal response to the Lord. The practicalities of finding hymnals, finding the hymn, standing, looking around, etc., can disturb these moments. Therefore, before there is a transition to other activities, give individuals the opportunity to present themselves before the Lord, especially in relation to the truth that has just been declared.

An appropriate way to proceed is to give specific steps of response and then to lead in prayer. Avoid using religious jargon that may or may not be understood. If you are exhorting and inviting true repentance, explain what that means. If the emphasis is on faith, indicate how faith can be actively directed towards the Lord. If obedience is the thrust, then give a first step within the context of the enabling grace of God. If people are to flee the wrath of God, tell them how and invite them to look with faith and deepest gratitude to the one who took the wrath of judgment upon Himself.

Write down the concluding words of the sermon. Although there are basic aspects of responding to God, try to make the invitation appropriate to the specific exposition you have delivered. Then, lead in a prayer of response. Here's an example:

> I want to give an opportunity right now for response to this message on . . . We are going to go before the Lord in prayer. I encourage

you to pray honestly and personally. Don't ignore the truth of God's Word that has come to you today or the work of His Holy Spirit. I will lead in prayer, but you direct your mind, heart, and will towards the Lord in these precious moments. You may need to make a definite decision this morning. You may need to settle matters between you and God. Don't wait. Let's go to the Lord meaningfully, prayerfully right now.

These moments should not be rushed. This is a sacred encounter. If people reject the message or do not use this time to respond in some way to the Lord, they have at least had the opportunity. For those who respond, it may be a saving moment(!), or another step in their walk with the Lord (a growing moment!).

God is sovereign. His Word will do its work. The preacher is not to manipulate response in any way. (We speak about that more in the chapter on the invitation.) At the same time, there is an urgency intrinsic to preaching. Now is the appropriate time to respond to the truth. Certainly there will be some who cannot honestly respond or arrogantly will not respond at the time of preaching. But at least they know how to respond, and their time of response may be later, Lord willing.

What happens after the prayer time we have recommended is very significant, but the preaching situation will impact greatly the specific activities to follow. The preacher may call for some form of an open confession of response. This may take place while a hymn of response is sung. Whatever takes place should be done as meaningfully as possible with careful explanation. People should not make a public confession of something that they are not sure of. The open invitation could include those who are still uncertain of their faith or obedience, but want to make that step. But still the preacher has clarified exactly why the open confession is taking place and what each individual is saying if he/she stands, comes forward, stays after the service, receives follow-up counsel, or all of the above.

The preacher need not write down all these details. The manuscript can contain some of these matters, but in essence, the message itself is completed as you enter into prayer or with the prayer itself. The preacher who is involved in regular pulpit or itinerant ministry must think through the end of the preaching event carefully and with conviction. Although you have reached the end of the sermon, the response to the sermon is just beginning. If people respond and there is open confession, what happens next? This may be one of the most significant moments in a person's own experience. What guidance, counsel, and support will they receive? Our chapter on "Conservation" will address these matters.

Prayerfully Review the Exposition

The final stages of preparation are to review, relate, and rehearse the sermon. These activities may overlap in practice, but there are three different goals that are being pursued. We will address each one of these separately as we complete our discussion of message finalization.

The manuscript becomes a great tool for reviewing the content of the message. The preacher can familiarize himself with the flow and wording of the message, making deletions, additions, and other adjustments as necessary. The real goal here is editing. You want to strengthen the message as much as possible in the time available. Each part of the sermon can be reviewed. The major issues of unity, movement, and purpose; truth, clarity, and passion can be assessed. Is the truth coming through the whole message? Do I go off on unnecessary tangents? Is the DT expressed in the best possible way, and is it sensed throughout the message? Is the treatment of the text fair and sufficient? Is the message accurate and truthful in every sense? These are major issues. Then, are the IT distinct and carefully related to the DT? Is there clarity and a sense of movement throughout the body of the exposition? Do I get bogged down in some matters of explanation that will not really add to the message? Is there the right combination of explanation, illustration, and application under each integrating thought? Do the introduction, exposition, and conclusion accomplish what they should? Does the burden of the message come through in the introduction? Is the message characterized by purpose and passion leading to the MT?

Along the way, the preacher has the opportunity to check specific wording and phrasing. It may be that a better way to express a thought or sentence comes to mind as you review the content, and you can adjust the manuscript accordingly. Jay Adams encourages preachers to "put to better use the vocabulary [they] already possess."[5] This will call for hard work on the part of the preacher to "search for the best" words to use, rather than to settle for old and overused words and clichés. Dr. Adams exhorts the preacher to "be concrete." Avoid abstract and general words; rather, use concrete, specific words, expressions, and details that paint pictures for the people. Then "be precise." Precise words add clarity and accuracy to expression and tend to be easier to see. Dr. Adams calls the preacher to "be ruthless." This ruthlessness involves the cutting out of all "trite expressions, clichés, vague terms, meaningless repetitions, long, complex sentences, abstractions, and jargon." The preacher must be critical of his own word choices and strive for the best.

Lastly, Dr. Adams exhorts, "Be persistent."[6] In short, this means practice, consistent practice. Such advise is needed because words are the tools of communication. And while we often are concerned to improve other dimensions of sermon preparation, word choice may be taken for granted. If time allows, you may want to read the manuscript out loud to check the sense of oral flow and sound. Sometimes words look good on paper, but they don't "sound" right or as good as they look. Reviewing the manuscript prayerfully allows the preacher to check his work. The preacher wants to be accurate to the Word of God and sensitive to the Spirit of God. The preacher wants to say what he says in the best possible way for the audience and the occasion. This type of reflective editing can improve the manuscript greatly and, in so doing, can impact the message.

Prayerfully Relate the Exposition

The preacher should respond to the truth as he prepares the sermon. In a sense the preacher is being preached to as he prepares, and he needs sensitivity of spirit to commit and conform to the Word of God as the message develops. We recommend that the preacher in viewing the message as a whole should hear it, respond to it, and then own it as a message to the preacher and then through the preacher. This process or act is vital if the manuscript is really going to become a message in and through the life of the preacher. Here the goal is not editing the manuscript, but editing the preacher! The preacher must be submissive to the Lord and ready to respond to the message himself. In a future chapter we deal directly with the "incarnation of truth." Right now we are just touching on a practical discipline that can assist in this incarnational process.

The manuscript must become a message in and through the life of the preacher. Dr. Chapell speaks of "Word and Witness" as he develops the very definition and concept of Christ-centered expository preaching.[7] The preacher is not just passing on a message, he is bearing witness to the message. It is intrinsic to true Christian preaching that the preacher is a witness to the truth he declares. This does not mean that the preacher has the ultimate level of spiritual experience in relation to everything he preaches. It does mean that the preacher is committed to the truth he is declaring and that he is personally bearing witness to truth that has touched his life and to which he has submitted. Think for a moment of the alternatives! Parroting words that are doubted and/or are in no real way a part of the life of the speaker is not Christian preaching. Another alternative is a kind of lifeless detached presentation of truths without real personal commitment or knowledge. We encourage prayerful relating of the message to the life of the preacher. It is marvelous to come out of the experience of submitting to the truth and stand before others to call them to do the same. We cannot be hypocrites in the pulpit! We need to be proclaimers of the truth out of our own experience of submission and obedience aided by the Holy Spirit. These are precious moments with the Lord. We submit ourselves afresh to Him, particularly in regards to the message that is to be preached. We ask that the Holy Spirit make this message a part of us, so that we can be incarnational preachers, rather than getting in the way of the very message we are to preach.

This activity of relating the message to the life of the preacher is especially significant if the preacher is preaching a lot of material he has gleaned from others. There is nothing wrong with learning from others. The Holy Spirit speaks and works through others besides yourself! A sermon idea, exegetical helps, a sermon outline, and even the basic content of a sermon may have had significant impact upon the preacher in his preparation. Obviously, we encourage preachers to do their own preparation, but it is unrealistic and in fact *wrong* to deny the value of others' work and insights. Of course appropriate credit for other material needs to be recorded and shared when necessary, but there is a bigger issue. The bigger issue is that the "borrowed" material needs to become a message that can be preached authentically through the preacher. Here is where the relating of the message becomes particularly significant. It is more important to submit personally to the message and ask the Lord to burn it into your heart than to try to rewrite material that you think is tremendous. You can use it, giving due credit; but make sure you have "heard" it and responded to it, that the message is yours by virtue of personal submission and commitment.

Relating the message is a critical, vital, and indeed, practical way to be fresh in the pulpit. The message comes out of your own relationship to God, and you bear witness to that truth. Should you preach the same message more than once? Well, it depends what you mean. There is nothing wrong with preaching the same truth, the same text, the same basic thoughts, and the same thrust of a message. As has been said often at our center, if a message is worth preaching once, it's worth preaching again. But there is a sense in which you won't preach the same message again if you seek to constantly relate the message to your own life, asking the Holy Spirit to burn it afresh into your being. You may preach the same basic message, but it is as fresh as the Spirit's work in your life and your fresh commitment to the truth you are declaring. Preaching is an event! Every preaching occasion is unique. Our prayer needs to be that God will speak through His Word on any given occasion. God may use the same basic message on different occasions to do completely different things in the lives of individuals or a congregation. We need to be incarnational preachers who are sensitive to each occasion and to what God is seeking to say at this time in this place.

Prayerfully relating the message could take hours, and it may need to on certain occasions. The preacher should, though, be preparing with an attitude of prayer, desirous of relating truth to his life even as he studies the text, formulates the message, and writes the manuscript. Although a life of prayer is more important than just praying over a specific message, we do recommend, as part of preparation, praying specifically to make sure that the *manuscript has become a message*. The length of time is not as critical as the reality of the experience. The preacher must be in harmony with the truth he is declaring. The truth needs to come through a submitted servant who seeks to be true to the truth he declares. Therefore, pray about your own response to the message. Pray that the message will be burned into your life by the Word and the Spirit. Pray that you can preach "incarnationally," bearing witness to the truth in the power of the Holy Spirit. Pray that God will make the preaching of this sermon a redemptive event, as that same Holy Spirit takes the Word and uses it in saving and sanctifying ways in the lives of those who hear.

Prayerfully Rehearse the Exposition

There are a number of benefits to actually rehearsing the message, either out loud or mentally. The concern here is to go through the message as a whole without continuous stops or editing. You want to think through or speak through the message from beginning to end. This serves as another opportunity to review and relate the message. If the preacher is pressed for time, he may need to prayerfully review and rehearse at the same time. But, ideally, the preacher is now rehearsing the message, not anticipating major changes or editing. He may visualize the audience, or he may, as it were, present it to God alone. The goal is a sense of "approval" concerning the message that is to be preached. The preacher ultimately has to please One only, and that is the God of the message he is declaring.

There are a number of practical benefits to rehearsing the message. The preacher will become more familiar with the essence and the specific expression of the message. If the preacher rehearses out loud, he can hear the message. Words, phrases, sentences, and whole sections that seemed great on paper may need to be changed or eliminated. Not only can the preacher hear the message, he can time it. This is especially helpful if this is a new message, or if time limits are very exact on a given occasion. Although the preacher is not thinking specifically at this time of strengthening his oral skills, this type of rehearsing will also do that.

What is important in the three movements we have discussed is that the preacher improves the message as written, and submits himself to the message obediently and dependently. Only God can take the words of man as based upon His inerrant Word and use them powerfully to effect saving and sanctifying change. The preacher must be a willing and obedient servant, longing that God will do His mighty work for His glory through the preaching of the Word. With integrity, honesty, and dependency the preacher should make sure that he is a ready vessel for the Lord's use, and that the message can come through accurately, clearly, and passionately, indeed incarnationally and redemptively, because the manuscript has become a message.

The preacher must depend upon the aid and the anointing of the Holy Spirit as he preaches the Word.[8] Such prayer and dependence is not an excuse for sloppy preparation. Indeed, the preacher should have been dependent on the Holy Spirit in the study as well. Such prayer, both in the study and as the preacher preaches, should come out of one's concern for accuracy, clarity, and passion in seeking to faithfully proclaim the truth of God. Praying for the aid and the anointing of the Holy Spirit goes hand-in-hand with conscientious preparation. Text selection, text investigation, message organization, and message finalization should not have been a mechanical process devoid of spiritual sensitivity and activity. Rather, the spiritual activity in the study should lead to the spiritual activity in the pulpit or on the street corner.[8]

A final consideration in this chapter is whether or not the preacher should take the manuscript into the pulpit or the preaching situation. As is so often the case, there is not any easy answer to that question for every preacher and every preaching situation. Let us say, first of all, that the preacher will need to depend on the Holy Spirit whether or not he has any type of manuscript in the preaching situation. Also, the preacher can always depart from the manuscript if he senses that is what the Lord would have him do. Examples can be given of great sermons with a manuscript and great sermons without a manuscript. So where do we go from here? This is a matter that the preacher himself must decide in the light of his gifting, his training and tradition, and the different preaching situations he faces.

Let us make some suggestions that are based on our approach to delivery. Truth, clarity, and passion are desired in the delivery of the message. One has to assess how the use of a manuscript impacts each one of these three important aspects of the delivery of a specific message. For example, if a preacher feels that he is freer in delivery without any notes, but he loses some clarity in the exposition, this needs to be viewed very carefully. Let us share some options.

Option #1: Enhance the written manuscript. Use underlining, color coded main points, or some means of making the main movements stand out in the text. It would be helpful for the preacher to develop or use an outlining system that can be included within the written or typed manuscript. This way the preacher does not need to prepare any additional notes; he can use the manuscript as an outline most of the time and refer to it carefully for tighter points of exegesis, for quotations or statistics, or when he wants to make sure of some specific wording. In this case, the preacher would take the manuscript into the preaching situation, but it is a manuscript prepared for the preaching situation. There is no need for the production of other preaching notes.

Option #2: Develop simpler preaching notes or preach from an outline. There is no possibility of being tied to a manuscript in this case. The preacher eliminates that option, but keeps the DT, the IT, and the MT in front of him to help him focus on the unifying truth, the movements of the message, and the motivating thrust while preaching. The preacher can add to the bare outline some additional wording where he may think he needs it, such as key words in the introduction, some exegetical details, leads into key illustrations, and/or the careful wording of the final exhortation and invitation. This will call for additional work on the part of the preacher if he is already producing a manuscript in complete or near complete form. However, the benefits to certain preachers may be worth the extra effort.

Option #3: Work at preaching basically without notes. More time may be needed to review, relate, and rehearse the message. The more the preacher can think through, listen to, and speak out the message, the better. A simple help that the preacher may consider is to write a few abbreviated notes beside the text in the margin of his Bible. Another possible help would be to put on a small card or a small sheet of paper a few items that the preacher may not be able to recall in the flow of the message: a key quotation, a specific exegetical insight, a detailed illustration. In this case, the preacher is not following an outline as such, he is just using a written source for a few moments in the message.

These options and others are available to the preacher. As technology advances other visual helps for the preacher and the audience will increase. The overhead, video-projection, computer-generated images, outlines, and graphics, etc., are certainly there for the using in many situations. But let's consider some other basic factors. Generally speaking, the more intimate, informal, or circumstantial a preaching situation, the less the preacher should be tied to notes. The more structured and didactic the situation, the more notes or a full manuscript will be appropriate. Simpler or well-known messages will not demand the same use of a manuscript or notes as will heavier or new messages. There will be some situations that will make the use of notes almost impossible, so the preacher should be able to adapt when necessary. At the same time, the preacher should establish a pattern for his regular preaching ministry. This is a personal matter before the Lord, and the preacher should be convinced that what he is doing is the best way for him to preach.

Lastly, the preacher needs to be RFA—ready for anything! The "anythings" in life and ministry call for personal adaptability and adjustment. The preacher may go through all the steps we have shared, be ready (generally speaking) to preach, but know as he enters the preaching situation that another message is needed. Sometimes a crisis calls for a change of message. Sometimes an urgent invitation to preach allows no time for a new message and you don't have any notes with you. Sometimes an unexpected meeting is added to your preaching program on a trip, and there is no time for further preparation. You may even find yourself in the rare situation of having to borrow a Bible! It is wonderful to know that God is sovereign, His Word is powerful and sufficient, and that the Holy Spirit is still working.

CHAPTER ELEVEN

THE PREACHER AND COMMUNICATION

*Praying also for us, that God would open to us a
door for the word, to speak the mystery of
Christ, for which I am also in chains, that I may
make it manifest, as I ought to speak.*
                                    —Colossians 4:3–4

*And for me, that utterance may be given to me,
that I may open my mouth boldly to make known
the mystery of the gospel, for which I am an
ambassador in chains; that in it I may speak
boldly, as I ought to speak.*
                                    —Ephesians 6:19–20

How ought we to speak? What are our priorities to be when
we deliver a message to any particular audience? Are we to
seek to be "good communicators," and in what sense? Paul's
exhortations to Timothy concerning his ministerial responsibilities
and practices include a call for growth and progress "evident to
all" (1 Tim. 4:15). In the various aspects of our Christian lives and

ministries, there should be improvement in the deepest sense of that word. In this regard, the preacher should be giving attention to and seeking to improve every aspect of ministry before the Lord and before His people. However, the motive and means of improvement need to be checked carefully, particularly in the area of communication. There is plenty of communication theory around, and certain results are more predictable if certain methods and means are adopted. The Christian preacher must be careful to examine his preaching in the light of the priorities and practices evident in the Word of God.

Against the background of a detailed study of Greco-Roman rhetoric, Duane Litfin presents Paul's perspective and theology of preaching, especially as presented in 1 Corinthians 1–4.[1] The thrust of Dr. Litfin's careful study is that Paul's "view of the role of a preacher contrasted sharply with that of the Greco-Roman orator."[2] Paul did not view himself as being a persuader in the tradition of the rhetoric of his day. "It was not the herald's task to persuade, but to announce."[3] "It was the proclaimer's function to be sure that all heard and understood, but it was not the proclaimer's role, as it certainly was the orator's, to engage his rhetorical skills in order to induce his listeners to yield to the message, however much he might desire them to do so."[4] Paul was concerned that he not rob the message of the cross of its power, that he leave to the Holy Spirit what only He should and could do. Paul believed that adopting the rhetorical practices of his day would impact negatively, even negate, both the message of the cross and the dynamic of the Holy Spirit. We cannot do justice to Dr. Litfin's thorough presentation here. We draw it to the reader's attention for their own study, but also to give caution concerning the means and methods we adopt as preachers.

So, in what sense should we try to strengthen or improve our preaching? What should be the priority concerns of the preacher in this regard, and what are the practical implications? Can we determine basic principles that relate to the actual delivery of the message?

The apostle Paul requested prayer at the end of both the Colossian and the Ephesian epistles. In both letters Paul reveals a deep concern for his speaking, implicitly his preaching. In and of itself, this is instructive to us; it should challenge us to pray about our preaching and to ask others to do the same. As we view Paul's requests, there is an "oughtness," a sense of necessity, in both of these requests. Paul is not dealing with trivial or optional aspects of his speaking; he is concerned with the basics, and he presents these basics before others to support him and his ministry in prayer. *Whatever other means we use for strengthening or improving our preaching, prayer is fundamental.* We should pray and invite the prayer of others. Let us now consider the foci of Paul's prayers as related to his preaching.

In the Colossian text we see Paul's request and dependence upon God for even the opportunity to speak. His concern in relation to the actual speaking is that he would make "manifest" the mystery of Christ (Col. 4:3–4). The verb *phanaroo* means to "reveal, make known, show."[5] Paul saw himself as an apocalyptic preacher, making known the mystery of Christ, the mystery of the gospel (Eph. 6:19–20). At the heart of Christian proclamation is the purpose of making known what otherwise would be veiled, revealing what God has revealed, showing or making clear what is in fact the truth of God. For this to be done the Holy Spirit must work, but here Paul is speaking of his own responsibility. We have not exhausted the significance of this request, but we need to move to some implications for the preacher. The preacher is concerned to communicate in the sense of making something known. In that sense making clear or clearly presenting the truth is a priority concern of the proclaimer. It is awesome to think that the preacher is actually opening up and making known truth as the Holy Spirit works. Preaching is apocalyptic! In fact, that apocalyptic nature of preaching is at its heart, the very purpose of preaching is to reveal a mystery, to make known Christ and the gospel. Paul sensed the necessity of doing just that. We can pray similarly, request that others pray for us, and then seek to proclaim the revelation of God in His Word clearly in each given context, in such a way as to make it manifest.

Paul's request for prayer in the Ephesian text has a number of similarities to his request in the Colossian epistle. What we want to draw your attention to, though, is a different feature, although it may be implicit in the Colossian epistle as well. Paul reveals his concern here for "outspokenness, frankness, plainness, courage, confidence, boldness, fearlessness" as he speaks.[6] The NKJV uses the word *boldly;* the NIV, *fearlessly* both in relation to the descriptive phrase *en parresia* and the verb *parresiasomai*. It is interesting and not incidental that Paul has been presenting in full the need for divine power and protection in the face of spiritual conflict.[7] He moves into his personal request for prayer, having called for prayer in general in Ephesians 6:18. In his personal request, he expresses his concern that *logos* be given to him. He wanted his words to be God's words when he opened his mouth. Alongside of this was his concern for making "known the mystery of the gospel," a similar concern to that expressed in the Colossian epistle. Then the request is repeated for "boldness" or "fearlessness" in speaking. The apostle prayed to be bold in his speaking! In fact, he asked others to pray that he would be bold in his communication of the gospel. This should be an encouragement to any preacher, and it should remind us from whence our sufficiency comes. Paul did not seem to take much comfort or find boldness in his own ability or position. He thrust himself upon the Lord for the kind of proclamation that would make clear the mystery of the gospel with boldness and courage. The implication we draw from this text is that such boldness seemed to have been a priority concern of the apostle as he concluded this majestic epistle. It is a legitimate application, we believe, to say that such boldness should be a concern and characteristic of Christian preaching in the face of opposition and personal weakness.

If we put the prayer requests in the two epistles together, we see a concern for making known a mystery and a concern for boldness in speech.[8] These two facets of delivery are in keeping with Paul's basic perspective on his own preaching ministry as set forth especially in 1 Corinthians.[9] The herald's fundamental responsibility is to announce the truth clearly, with directness and boldness.

PRIORITY CONCERNS FOR THE COMMUNICATION OF THE MESSAGE

The preacher (proclaimer) is a messenger/herald (2 Tim. 4:2; 1 Tim. 2:7). Therefore, the preacher is to become a "mouthpiece" for the message God has given. In textual-thematic preaching that means that the text and theme (truth) are to be "heralded" to the specific audience addressed. The manner of preaching should assist in the proclamation of the message clearly and passionately (boldly). Whatever helps to communicate the truth of the text clearly and passionately is encouraged. What distracts from the meaning of the text or hinders a clear and passionate communication of the theme (truth) of the text is discouraged. We seek a clear and passionate proclamation of the truth with dependence upon the Holy Spirit.

The paragraph above seeks to combine the applications from the two Pauline texts with the language of G. Campbell Morgan.[10] The priority concern is that the biblical and indeed textual truth be communicated. The preacher in full dependence upon the Holy Spirit seeks to preach clearly to make the truth understandable. Also, the preacher ought to preach with a personal passion, a boldness within the context of preaching. We are not speaking simply of emotion or a particular style of preaching. We are talking about that convictional passion based upon the preacher's commitment to the Lord, the truth, and the task of declaring the truth as it ought to be declared. A convictional passion translates into a boldness and authority as one preaches, especially in the face of opposition or hardship. There are other aspects of Christian commitment and character that ought to impact one's preaching, but we focus on these as a starting place for discussing basic concerns in the delivery of a message.

The practical aspects of delivery ought to be viewed in relation to these fundamental aspects of the herald's proclamation. The truth needs to be declared clearly and passionately. The message needs to be accurate and understandable, and it needs to be proclaimed with authority, boldness, and passion as the herald speaks on behalf of his Lord. The preacher may preach in weakness, but passion and God-given authority are deeper and beyond personal weakness. In fact, such weakness is the resting place of true passion and authority in preaching because of the work of the Holy Spirit. The passion we are speaking of is directly related to the preacher's commitment to the truth and the work of the Holy Spirit. Prayerfully reviewing, relating, and rehearsing the message helps to plant the message (the truth) deep within the heart of the preacher so that he can preach incarnationally and convictionally. The truth is "real" to the preacher. By prayerfully seeking the aid and the anointing of the Holy Spirit, the preacher places his dependence and confidence in God rather than in his own ability to preach. Then the preacher's boldness and passion are based upon the Word of God and the work of God, the truth and the Spirit. Prayer and dependence should be expressed as one prepares to preach, and the attitude of prayerful dependence should accompany the preacher throughout the preaching event. This prayerful dependence is a priority matter for the preacher, regardless of the other dimensions of sermon delivery. The apostle Paul indicates prayerful dependence on the Lord even as he anticipates potential ministry in the future.

PARTICULAR MOVEMENTS IN THE COMMUNICATION OF THE MESSAGE

We now consider the various parts of a given message. It is important to remember the uniqueness of each and every preaching event. A message is to be preached for a particular people at a particular time. The occasion will never be repeated. The audience and the dynamics of that particular occasion will never be the same. The preacher needs to be sensitive to the uniqueness of each opportunity and then preach with an appropriate urgency since the time is "now" for the truth being declared. The preacher should not allow the routines and patterns of ministry to rob this sense of the uniqueness and urgency of the moment. He needs to be aware of the specific audience that is being addressed. Who are they? Why are they present? What dominant concerns do they have at this time? What potential barriers are there to understanding and responding to the message? These questions should be asked and answered on the deep and theological level as well as on the personal and practical level. The preacher asks these questions, not in order to compromise the message, but rather to make sure that the truth is presented as clearly and as passionately as possible to these people on this occasion. One only has to read the messages recorded in the Acts of the Apostles or to reflect on the nature of many of the New Testament letters to recognize the importance of addressing the message specifically to the audience that is hearing or reading the message. On the theological and practical level, the audience needs to know that this message is specifically for them. This preached truth is being heralded at this time so that these particular people can hear and respond to the truth.

Initial Comments

Now let's consider some of the usual parts or facets of a preaching event. The preacher's initial comments or "bridging" are of utmost importance in preaching. These are the very first words that are spoken, and they can impact the message and the audience greatly. The context will clearly affect what needs to be said to transition into a preached message from whatever has happened before. Sometimes a response is needed to words of introduction. Sometimes it may be appropriate and even necessary to reflect on and respond to what has just happened before you started speaking: a testimony, a hymn, music ministry, or some other planned or unplanned activity. The preacher should seek that spiritual sensitivity to discern what God is saying and doing on the specific occasion, outside of the message prepared. At the same time, the preacher needs to be aware of those relational and practical matters that may need mentioning as one begins to speak: a thank you, a word of greeting, an expression of praise, or some comments appropriate to a special occasion. Such words respond to the evident working of God in the context of preaching, and they are appropriate to the "occasional" nature of preaching. These initial comments are particularly important if the preacher is unknown or hardly known to the audience. They are important also if the preacher has not said anything to that particular audience before he gets up to preach.

In general, the preacher must seek to be sensitive, appropriate, and as brief as possible when involved in bridging or making initial comments. Sensitivity is needed in relation to the spiritual and personal dynamics of the audience. Whatever is said should be appropriate and necessary to the occasion, not flippant or just a filler. Whatever is said should be in good taste for a servant of the Lord right in the context of preaching the Word. Nothing should be said that would be or appear to be inconsistent with the preacher's role or message. There is nothing wrong with being personal, but make sure that the personal remarks are significant to the audience as a whole and that they do not betray any confidences or take advantage of any relationship. There should not be anything offensive in such comments or remarks. This would be a distraction from the message itself. Also, the preacher does not want to be abrupt or rude in any way. This can be communicated through what is said and what is not said. If a personal response is needed to some kindness towards or comments about the preacher, the preacher must seek to be kind in return and to express the love of Christ sincerely and sensitively. The same is true if some response is needed to what has taken place already in a worship service or in a special event where ministry has preceded the preacher. The wrong words can hurt, hinder further communication, and turn off the ears of some people before you even start the message.

Another caution about initial comments and bridging is to make sure that whatever is said *does not take away from the time needed for the faithful proclamation of the message.* In general, you want to be as brief as possible in introductory remarks. People need to know that the preacher has a priority, and that is to deliver the message. Without being abrupt, the preacher should seek to get to the message itself as soon as is appropriate and possible. Recently we heard a testimony that touches on this issue. The testimony had to do with the impact of a particular preacher and sermon on one occasion many years in the past. What struck the individual who was sharing the testimony was the eagerness of the preacher to preach the message on that occasion. The preacher seemed almost to run to the pulpit to preach! That initial impression of the preacher was a lasting one, and although testimony was shared about the message itself, that initial movement to the pulpit is what made the impact. In words, manner, and attitude, much is communicated as one begins to preach. In this example, it was not the words themselves that indicated the significance of the message to follow, it was simply the way the preacher physically moved to the pulpit. In every way, the preacher needs to communicate that he has something to say. The importance of the task at hand and the significance of the message itself should be evident in the preacher's manner and in his words as he begins speaking. Lengthy, unrelated comments and meanderings can give the impression that the message can wait. The message is the "main thing" and the preacher's purpose, obligation, and passion should be to declare that message.

The preacher also needs to think through how he is going to enter into the message itself. Options abound. Transitional statements and pauses are very helpful and even necessary to indicate movement even within these early parts of a message. Prayer expressing dependence upon God is appropriate and significant, especially within a worship service context. Such prayer is not only important for the preacher, but also for the audience as they recognize afresh that the activity to follow is a spiritual one. One can see the direct relevance of the apostle Paul's thanksgivings and prayers at the beginning of his letters to the content that follows. It is appropriate when praying before a message to pray along the lines of the message to follow. It is important, though, that the prayer be a genuine prayer rather than an introduction to the sermon. Such moments in prayer may be a welcome pause in the worship service, particularly at this critical moment before people are asked to give attention to the exposition of the Word of God. This pre-sermon prayer may be offered at a number of points in time: before the initial comments, after the initial comments, before the Scripture reading, or after the Scripture reading. It is worth taking some time to think through this matter carefully, although it may appear obvious. You may choose not to offer a specific public prayer right before the sermon. Whatever the case, the preacher should be clear and convinced in his own mind as to how he is going to proceed through the earliest part of the preaching event. The preacher should seek to draw people's attention to the task at hand and the truth to be declared. Distractions and detours should be avoided.

The Reading of the Text

The text of Scripture needs to be read. The reference and version of the text being read needs to be stated clearly, and probably repeated, even if written in an order of worship. The preacher may want to give some basic background and contextual information even before reading the text to introduce the text to the audience. We have already addressed the matter of the reading of the text of God's Word in a previous chapter.[11] Here we want to underscore the need to give utmost significance to the reading of the text. Make sure every aspect of the reading of the text—from announcing the text to the statements immediately following the reading—is honoring to the Scriptures and, indeed, honoring to the Lord of the Scriptures. Avoid being too familiar and casual with the Word of God, as if it were just a quotation that leads into what you as the preacher want to say! Pauses before and after you read can help to set apart the reading from other aspects of the preaching event. Appropriate words before and after the reading can draw attention to the nature and significance of the Scriptures: "Please listen carefully as I read the Word of God," "Let us stand together to hear the Word of God," "Hear the Word of the Lord," etc. Appropriate closing statements can serve to give further significance to the reading: "This is the Word of God," "May God grant us clear understanding and appropriate response to the truth of His inerrant Word," "God's Word has been read, let all the people say—amen," etc.

The actual reading itself should be done meaningfully, with appropriate interpretation.[12] Every reading is an interpretation. Thus, time needs to be given to the reading of the text. Common mistakes include reading too quickly and reading with too little expression. Both will cause the reading to lack meaning and "life." If the preacher finds himself reading too quickly, it may be helpful to find good places for "Selah pauses" before moving on. Helpful expression and pauses are especially critical when the reading is long and filled with difficult names, places, or concepts. If read well, though, the text will not only be more understandable, it will be more interesting.

The reading of the text needs to receive its proper importance, whether it is read as part of the preaching event or read earlier in a worship service. We recommend that the preacher read the text for preaching himself, unless he is sure that it will be read meaningfully and carefully by someone else. If time is a concern, then the preacher needs to make sure that he accounts for a careful reading of the text within the time constraints of the preaching situation. If the exegetical text is very long, it may be that the text for reading (the homiletical text) may need to be shorter. In such situations, seek to read that portion of the text that states or points to the dominating theme of the message.

The decision concerning the length of the reading may also be influenced by the context of preaching. A street-corner message may need a brief text that can be expounded simply and within a limited amount of time. In a church worship service, however, the reading of the Scriptures should be given highest priority. If the preacher is tempted to "cut" the reading because of time on a regular basis, then he needs to examine the ordering and timing of the various elements of the worship service. It may be that some other aspect of the worship service may need to be abbreviated or eliminated if the reading of the text of God's Word is consistently rushed or cut short. Certainly some readings can be abbreviated to aid understanding and focus, but the issue should not be time alone.

The Introduction

Now let us consider some practical matters related to the major divisions of the message. The introduction should lead the people right to the text, the truth, and the theme of the message. There should be clarity of focus and purpose right from the start. Generally speaking, this will mean that the subject (dominating theme) of the message will be stated and explained. Watch out for lack of clarity at this point. Multiple titles, multiple subtitles, multiple subjects and issues to be covered can confuse or blur the focus of the message. As we have already suggested, the background of the text and the burden of the message need to be shared so that the preacher can meaningfully enter into the exposition of the text itself. The preacher needs to be "in contact" with the people, especially during the introductory section of the message. The people should sense that this message is for them, that the preacher is deeply concerned that they hear and appropriate the truth being proclaimed. On the practical level, the preacher needs to address the people directly and make every effort to express the theme, background, and especially the burden of the message in terms the people can understand. This is a good time for a lot of eye contact and relational directness with the people. The preacher, generally speaking, should not be tied to notes in such a way that his concern and passion for the truth are hindered or hidden. The audience should not only discern the significance of the message but also the purpose and the passion of the preacher. It should be evident from the very beginning that the message is real and urgent to the preacher, even if the audience doesn't believe or accept it. At the same time, the preacher's manner of delivery should commend the truthfulness of what he is declaring. Directness, humility, honesty, and convictional passion should be aspects of the preacher's manner, and this should be apparent in the introduction of the message.

It is our observation that introductions are more often too long than too short. A lengthy introduction can lack focus and can contain a lot of material that could have been expressed within the flow of the textual-thematic exposition. A lengthy introduction can take time away from the exposition itself, resulting in a sense of rushing through the exposition instead of a more deliberate pace needed to facilitate the understanding of textual insights. Another possible result of a lengthy introduction is a thin piece of exposition that barely scratches the surface of the text. The preacher needs to introduce the message, but then move without needless delay into the textual-thematic exposition.

The Exposition

The main part of the sermon is the proclamation of the textual theme on the basis of textual evidence. The preacher should present this exposition with a sense of movement, but not rush. Under each thought presented there is the careful interweaving of explanation-illustration-application (if all are needed). The creative presentation of the specifics of the text within this context is the challenge of sound textual-thematic exposition. Generally speaking, the preacher needs to maintain a sense of flow and purposeful progression within this part of the message. Maintaining homiletical distinctiveness and harmonious relatedness will help to guard a sense of unity, progression, and purpose. Watch out for detours or exegetical bogs that detract from the clear proclamation of the truth of the text. Seek to discern if the people are with you or not. It is wise to use transition points to review, restate, clarify, and tie together. The more you can help the audience think through the truth with you, the better. The clear, careful, and fearless proclamation of the truth itself will give people the opportunity to think through the message.

At the same time, using questions, constantly applying, carefully illustrating, and repeating key words and truths all help to keep people thinking along with the preacher as the message unfolds. Be careful not to waste words. Every word and phrase ought to be integrally connected to the primary truths being proclaimed. As we have noted,[13] word choices need to be made carefully. Watch out for general words, vague expressions, and dull or technical terms that simply do not clarify or communicate. Clarity should be sought through the most concrete words, precise details, meaningful expressions, and truly helpful explanations. The preacher must recognize that words carry with them many associations. Avoid as much as possible words that you know will unlock worlds of thought or memory that will distract people from the truth being declared. Try not to lose sight of the theme in the details of the message. Such focus on the part of the preacher helps to keep the audience focused. Also, if the preacher maintains his interest and passion for the truth, he is helping the audience to do the same. Encourage the people to move with you through the message so that they will hear and understand each part of the exposition. Most of all, let the truth do the talking! The Word itself along with the work of the Holy Spirit will be effectual according to the will of God.

The Conclusion

As we deal with parts of the proclamation of the message, no part is of greater importance than the conclusion. The preacher must avoid rushing or deadening the conclusion. Regardless of the flow or the apparent impact of the message to that point, in faith the preacher must seek to clarify, exhort, and invite the response that the truth deserves and demands. Here we want to stress that this may be the toughest and most challenging aspect of the actual delivery of the message. The conclusion crystallizes, personalizes, and helps actualize the response called for by the message. In that sense the conclusion is intentionally the most confrontational aspect of the message.

Although application should be taking place throughout the message, it is in the conclusion that the preacher challenges the listeners to respond to the main issue of the message. The whole thrust of the message is now presented in its clearest form on the basis of the exposition that has taken place. The conclusion calls for careful word choice. The preacher needs simplicity and authority as he challenges the audience to embrace and own the truth. The preacher must recognize that spiritual warfare is taking place as people are thinking through the implications of the truth. These closing moments can be intense and all sorts of things can go wrong or distract from the critical nature of what is taking place. Therefore, careful preparation of the conclusion is recommended as well as that special spiritual sensitivity to proceed through the actual delivery of the conclusion. Trust God, pray for clarity and boldness, and make sure that people know what to believe and what to do with the message that has been declared. Avoid preaching another mini-sermon. Avoid trying to add something you forgot to say under the second point of the message. Avoid complicated or cumbersome material that deflects or distracts from the purpose of the conclusion. Even a great story that does not lead into a time of reflection and response needs to be eliminated. Seek to be purposeful, and to communicate that to the audience. You are answering personally and directly the potential question from someone in your audience, "What do I need to do about this message?" Have an accurate, specific, clear, and personal answer for your listeners. In faith, follow through by providing an answer that clarifies, exhorts, and invites response.

The preacher's final words are significant. They not only con-clude the message they also form a transition to what happens next. One final step in the conclusion is to ask people to pray and then to lead them in a prayer of response. These are sacred moments, and the preacher must be sensitive to the Holy Spirit. He is not to manipulate response; he is to exhort, allow for, and guide response. After prayer (if this has taken place), outward response and confession can take many forms, thus the preacher must think this matter through and be ready to adjust to the leading of the Holy Spirit. It is imperative that whatever takes place at the end of the message is in keeping with the truth and is meaningful in the fullest sense. People should not be asked to respond in a specific way without a clear explanation as to why this is appropriate and what it involves. The preacher must seek to make every aspect of the end of the message meaningful. This means that the preacher must plan for the time involved in these moments. They should not be rushed, nor should they be robbed of their significance or meaning.

PRACTICAL ASPECTS OF THE COMMUNICATION OF THE MESSAGE

Our focus for the remainder of this chapter will be practical aspects of the actual delivery of the message. All sorts of personal and practical factors generally impact the *style of delivery*: personality, gifting, training, church tradition, the preaching context, the audience, etc. In preaching workshops at our center we have witnessed a wide range of delivery styles, and there are others as well. Delivery style is ultimately a matter of personal conviction on the part of the preacher as he seeks to communicate the truth clearly and passionately.

We want to encourage preachers to think this matter through in relation to the priority concerns mentioned above. The manner of preaching, the style of delivery, should assist in the clear and passionate proclamation of the truth. The concern of the preacher is the truth. The manner of delivery should serve the truth of the message. The message should so dominate us as we preach that our delivery is impacted by the truth itself. For instance, if we are preaching on the text "Rejoice in the Lord always. Again I will say, rejoice!" (Phil. 4:4), something of that command and commitment to rejoice ought to be evident in the very manner of preaching. If there is no evidence of joy or rejoicing on the part of the preacher in such a message, then his delivery actually contradicts the very message he is seeking to proclaim. The wrath of God is an awesome reality and theme for preaching, and if one presents a textual-thematic exposition dealing with that theme, then something of that awesome reality should be evident in the manner of delivery. This is the practical outworking of truth that has been related to our own lives and is now preached "incarnationally." The priority concern for the preacher should be that the style of delivery promotes the truth and in no way hinders or detracts from it. This is an important point to emphasize within the multiplicity of other factors that often impact style. Should you sit, stand, or walk as you preach? Should you speak, shout, or sing? Should you use visual aids or not? The preacher needs to think such matters through in terms of how he can best communicate the truth clearly and passionately within the particular context anticipated. He is not to compromise the message in the way he preaches. The truth of the message should be enhanced by the choices the preacher makes in terms of delivery style. Sensitivity to the Holy Spirit is needed as one thinks these matters through. As we have been saying throughout, the preacher needs to be guided by the truth and the Spirit.

The truth and the Spirit of God are not against creativity. *Creativity* in presentation can be driven by the truth and by the Spirit of God. Each preacher will be unique in the combination of factors that will impact the particular style of expository preaching he exercises. In this sense, there is an intrinsic uniqueness to the creative potential of each preacher that is sovereignly given by God. This uniqueness comes as a result of God's creative work, His redeeming work, His equipping work, and His continuing work of grace in each of our lives. This should encourage each preacher to faithfulness to the Lord, to the truth, to the task, and to the gifting that God has entrusted to him.

The preacher's gifting may be more of a teaching gift, an evangelistic gift, an exhortatory gift, a "prophetic" gift, or even other categories of speaking gifts that could be identified. Such a gifting and emphasis in a person's ministry can impact the style of presentation, which is certainly appropriate. We want to be careful not to stereotype such gifting into particular styles, but such gifting impacts the burdening and the emphasis in communication that the preacher senses. Categories may be debated, but the point here is that the preacher needs to be sensitive to and indeed accountable for the gifting that he has and is seeking to exercise. Although we learn and rightly pattern aspects of our lives and ministries on others (as they follow Christ), we cannot and should not be exactly like someone else in the way we preach. Fundamental similarities may exist, but the preacher must seek to use his unique spiritual experience, personality, gifting, training, etc., for the Lord. Many questions concerning style must remain unanswered because of the uniqueness of each preacher and the diversity of factors and contexts that might influence aspects of style. Yet, if the priority concerns are correct, the purpose is clear, and the motivations are pure, then matters of style can be viewed appropriately.

We offer the following comments for all preaching, regardless of the specific style of the preacher. First of all, *audibility* is an important concern. The preacher must be heard. There is little point in preaching if people cannot hear the message. Therefore, the preacher must be aware of his audience, the quality of his voice production, and the limits of his projection, aided or unaided by sound systems. The preacher needs to gain a sense of the reach of his voice. Strengthening the voice is certainly advised in the light of the diversity of situations that the preacher will confront.[14] The preacher should be able to preach in situations without any amplification and still be heard. And when we speak of being heard, we are speaking of a sufficient vocal presence so that people are not straining to hear you. More specifically, there needs to be quality voice production and sufficient projection so that people hear you clearly without you shouting continuously.[15] Our concern here is to encourage the preacher to be aware of what he needs to do to be heard in any given situation. You don't want people saying to you after the message, "I'm sure you had something to say, but I couldn't hear you from where I was sitting." The preacher wants to be heard as he preaches.

It is good to get whatever information you can about the sound system you are using, if any, and the acoustics of the building or setting. The need to be heard can impact the volume of the preacher, his posture since he must speak out towards the people, his positioning in relation to a supporting microphone, and movements while preaching. Adaptability is called for as the preacher responds to the particular preaching situation. Once we were in a church building that had a dead spot as far as the sound system was concerned. In fact, the dead spot was right in the center of the church, a few rows in front of the pulpit. In such a situation, the preacher must preach through and over the microphone in order to be clearly heard by those people sitting in that area of the building. We remember another situation in a large church when a guest preacher used a conversational style of preaching. An elderly person sitting nearby heard very little of the message because the sound system at the church did not carry the speaker's voice, and he often walked back and forth without projecting his voice outward. The message that day was not heard by someone who came to hear a message from the Word of God.

The preacher needs to make sure that he is heard as well as possible in every situation, but especially if people are not used to his voice and preaching. Therefore projection is important, posture and positioning can be significant, and familiarity and adaptability with sound systems can impact greatly the size of your "hearing audience." If you are preaching regularly in a specific location, it may be helpful to get input from selected people concerning the reach of your voice and the sound system. It would be very sad if people regularly are having problems hearing the message or are distracted due to some aspect of the sound system.

It is possible for people to hear the sound of your voice without being able to distinguish your words. There is the need for *clear and clean articulation* on the part of the preacher. This is especially the case when people are not used to your voice and when there are potential problems with the acoustics or sound system. More generally, though, there is a tendency to slur words when the rate of speech increases. The preacher needs to be careful not to sacrifice understanding when moving rapidly in delivery. He should also be aware of his own accent and the way in which he pronounces words. Bad pronunciations can result in missing particular words, concepts, and especially names and places. Exercises to strengthen articulation can be suggested.[16] Because of the importance of Scripture reading, it may be especially helpful to practice reading the Scriptures, being careful to articulate every word clearly. Working to pronounce and articulate names and places in the Scriptures is a profitable exercise. Take a genealogy, such as in Luke 3:23–38, and read it clearly and loudly. Make sure every syllable is articulated and vowels and consonants are clear. Another possibility is to work with some tongue twisters to test your articulation of difficult phrases. If the preacher really struggles with articulation, it may be helpful to work with someone trained in speech to give further direction and advice.

The preacher must seek to be understood as he speaks. The choice of words and phrases is critical for understanding. We have discussed this in terms of preparation, but we are speaking here of that awareness of the audience as the preacher speaks. One needs to be careful of trying to read the audience while preaching, but certainly the preacher is helped by an awareness of whether or not the message is being understood. Indeed, sometimes the audience is different than anticipated and the wise preacher adjusts to make sure that the essentials of the message can be understood. Explanations may need to be simplified and certain illustrations changed to help the listeners see the truth. The message may call for more repetition than anticipated because you realize that the truths being expressed are new to this group of listeners. Word choice may need to be adjusted accordingly. Such adjustments are not made to compromise the truth or to manipulate the audience, they help to make the truth clear in the specific setting. In this regard, it is good for the preacher to discern how the message is being processed.

Neutrality or no response at all over a period of time should concern the preacher. We recognize that there are spiritual dimensions to message comprehension, and a whole chapter is devoted to that matter.[17] Here, though, we are saying that it is possible to improve one's preaching by striving for the best ways to make the truth clear to particular audiences. Attention to wording, phrasing, and even speech punctuation is called for to assist in the communication of the message. A key word or phrase may be the most significant "vehicle" of communication within a given message. The preacher needs to work at such words or phrases, especially as they relate to the primary theme and thrust of the message. Many preachers demonstrate a special gifting in this regard, and they are the preachers who are quoted regularly by other preachers. Why? Because they can capture a truth or an application in a word, phrase, or statement that really "communicates." There is nothing wrong with quoting others in this regard, but we should also try to improve our own expressive abilities. Strive for clarity and utmost effectiveness in communication.

There are many options available to the preacher to assist in emphasizing or drawing special attention to key words, concepts, truths, applications, etc., within a given message. The outline of the message itself is a way of emphasizing the main truths of the message. Another effective tool is *repetition*, repetition, repetition! Repetition in oral communication serves as does underlining, boldface, and italics in print. You can use exact repetition or repetition with variation. In either case, the listener is made aware of the importance of what is being said. Repetition can be immediate when you repeat the same word, phrase, etc., successively, or it can be carried throughout a message as a refrain. Repetition can take place strategically at transition points and in the conclusion. Although some people may be bothered by repetition, use it! It is easy for people to miss what you are saying or to not really "get it." How many times have you seen people checking with one another for a hymn number or Scripture reference that was stated but was not repeated or emphasized? Repetition can be exercised by the preacher alone, or he may ask the people in certain situations to repeat what he has said. There is room for creativity and variety in the way repetition is used.

Handing out outlines or a synopsis of the message, or using some type of visual presentation of the wording of the message are all visual ways of repeating and capturing the message. We recommend that regardless of what *visual aids* are used, the preacher continue to repeat orally. Generally speaking, we encourage preachers to preach the same way with or without visual aids. The visual helps should simply reinforce what is being said. Be sure that the visual aids are done well, that they do not detract or distract from the incarnational aspect of the message. Ultimately in preaching, the preacher is the primary visual aid—the truth needs to come through the preacher as directly as possible to the people. Technological advances have created numerous options for audio and visual helps. The wise preacher will discern the proper use of such tools without sacrificing the personal and relational dynamics of preaching.

The sound of the voice and, specifically, variations in the sound of the voice are a significant facet of oral communication. We consider a number of these *vocal variables* here, focusing on their role as a means of emphasizing or stressing the truth being communicated through words.[18]

Pauses are very significant within the flow of oral communication. In the context of preaching, pauses invite attention or reflection, depending on how the preacher uses them. Pausing after a word or statement and then repeating a key word or statement is a meaningful way to stress the importance of what is being said. Pauses can give people time to think about what has just been said, or they help to focus attention on what is about to be said. The preacher does not need to be in a hurry when he preaches. Pauses are one way to avoid rushing through a message without points of meaningful assessment, reflection, and application. Make sure to pause and give people time to think if you have asked them a question or have called for special reflection in some way. Remember, people need to think as they listen! Needless to say, the faster the rate and pace of one's delivery, the more the preacher needs to use pauses carefully and helpfully. He must recognize that he is not only speaking, he is making noise. Constant noise, just plain sound, can be difficult to listen to, and people may choose their own attention pauses if you don't provide them. We are not suggesting that the preacher write the phrase "pause here" on his preaching notes, even though some might be helped by such a practice. We encourage sensitivity to the message, the Spirit, the audience, and the preaching event as a whole so that the preacher is alert to the need to emphasize, draw attention, and help people think and respond at given points in the message. Think of how you would seek to communicate vital information one-on-one. The urgency of the message may cause you to speak quickly, yet at the same time you would want to make sure that the person understands what you are saying. Pauses help people stay with you and think with you.

Volume, specifically change in volume, is another tool for emphasis. This could mean an increase or decrease in volume. Preaching styles and settings impact the use of volume tremendously. Here we simply want to emphasize that change in the use of volume draws attention. Consistent volume at whatever level loses impact as a tool for specific emphasis within the message. As we noted above, the preacher is not only speaking, he is making "noise." Diversifying the level of the noise is helpful for emphasis and understanding. This is just as true for the more "conversational" preacher as it is for the "high-volumed" proclaimer. Let the nature of the content and the types of truths that are being declared impact the volume used. Also, recognize that the setting, size of audience, and acoustics will impact general volume levels used.

The *rate of speech* is another facet of vocalization worthy of comment here. Rate has to do with the actual speed of delivery, words per minute. Preachers will have different regular rates of speaking, and that is understood. The preacher needs to watch out for a "wooden" or almost unnatural continuous rate of speech when preaching. This can take place at the slow or fast ends of the spectrum. Under the pressure of a public speaking situation a rate can develop that has nothing to do with the content of the message.

Generally speaking, there is a natural variety in the rate of speech in regular conversation. This rate is often dictated by the content and the speaker's feelings about the content, as well as how carefully the content needs to be communicated in detail. A faster rate often indicates special excitement over what is being said. Also, a fast rate may be used because of the type of content, one that does not demand detailed retention on the part of the listener. Time and the pressure to communicate quickly can also be a factor in maintaining a fast rate. A slower, deliberate rate is often used when care is needed to get across more important or complicated information. The expositor needs to let the content impact the rate of delivery. For instance, rate can be increased when "lighter" or illustrative material is being presented. But, generally speaking, if the preacher wants to emphasize a truth and he is speaking quickly, he may need to slow down to stress the words he is using. Otherwise, he needs to use repetition or other vocal variables. Enthusiasm born of the truth and the Spirit will often impact the rate, and that is appropriate. At the same time, the preacher must be sure that the truth can be followed by the listeners. Probably the times for the slowest rate are when clarifying key truths or textual meanings, or applying the message directly and personally to the listeners. Clarification, exhortation, and invitation will need moments of careful presentation that often call for a deliberate rate. The rate of speech is, in fact, an important way to emphasize the content being presented. You lose the impact of rate upon content if the rate is always the same. Variety in this regard is extremely helpful. Ask the Lord for boldness, passion, and freedom in delivery so that the rate will be a function of the content and your perspective on the content.

Alongside the natural and helpful variations in rate, it is helpful for the preacher to maintain a purposeful pace to the message. The pace of the message is something you sense and feel rather than quantify. The preacher is not to hurry through the message, nor is he to meander aimlessly along without a sense of progression or purpose. The responsibility and desire to declare the whole message and to call for the appropriate response should keep the preacher moving forward, while helping to pace each aspect of the message.

Pitch has to do with the "tonal qualities produced in vocalization."[19] Changes in pitch intonation and inflection can impact the meaning and expression of the truth. This is something that you can witness every day in regular conversation. The way the speaker elevates or lowers the pitch in words or within phrases or sentences can be vital for the intended emphasis. Therefore, the preacher should avoid patterns of pitch that become difficult to listen to and have little to do with the truth being communicated. You may have heard someone try to sound like a preacher, and they spoke in an affected way with a particular pitch pattern. Drone, whine, snore!

A practical way to maintain a natural variation in pitch patterns is to modulate other vocal variables such as the volume and rate of speech, as well as the meaningful use of pauses. Furthermore, if the other vocal variables are guided by the burden and content of the message, it will be difficult to maintain a predictable and, indeed, boring pattern of pitch if the message content impacts pitch as well. A pitch pattern that is difficult to listen to can actually detract from the message, and even distract the listeners. A routine or predictable pitch pattern can "deaden" the delivery, and the preacher loses another tool for clarity and emphasis. Listen to yourself. Is the meaning, dynamic, and life of the message coming through? The primary need is to let the message impact every facet of delivery. On the practical level, Al Fasol recommends finding

your *"optimum pitch,"* which is "the median level from which higher and lower pitch levels are developed by the speaker."[20] The
preacher can then seek to develop a "wider pitch range, used with
effect to support content."[21]

The sound of the voice is an important aspect of the actual
delivery of the message. The preacher, to great profit, can ask the
question, "What do I sound like?" What is being conveyed through
the sound of the voice? In keeping with our principles, the "sound"
of the voice should be in harmony with the content of the message. Again, it is a valuable exercise to listen to yourself. You may
be surprised! Listen to others, not critically, but to learn from them.
Our desire is not professionalism, it is a delivery that conveys the
truth we preach. A stronger vocal "presence" in tone may be
appropriate for a message affirming or defending basic truths.
More passion in the actual sound of the voice may be in keeping
with the passion of the heart. Compassion or righteous anger may
need to come through depending on the content and thrust of the
message. Certainly, though, one needs to have a sound that
bespeaks our Lord, His gospel, and the Word we proclaim.

The *visual presence and impact* of the preacher are also significant. The appearance and appeal should be governed by the
truth and the Spirit. Gestures, facial expressions, and the whole
ethos of the preacher ought to be Christlike and "messagelike."
The body language and facial expressions of the preacher should
be reflective and expressive of the message itself. An incarnational message should come through the preacher with the honest
appearance of personal ownership, and this should translate into
gestures and expressions in keeping with the message and, of
course, the personality of the preacher. Certainly the preacher
should avoid any inappropriate or distracting gestures. The
preacher in cross-cultural situations and even in cross-subcultural
situations needs to be sensitive to movements, gestures, and facial
expressions that could be misread, causing damage to the message and the cause of Christ. Our sovereign God can gloriously
overrule our mistakes, but that is not an excuse for ignorance or
insensitivity when dealing with people. We need to be aware of
anything that would needlessly cause offense or distraction in the
arena of "appearance" while preaching. It is the subtle uncon-
scious gestures and facial expressions that can communicate volumes, and thus the emphasis on the incarnational approach to
preaching. The preacher needs to pray that the message will come
through in every sense.

Gestures and facial expressions are a great means of framing and extending the meaning of the words spoken. An appropriate gesture can visually drive a word, truth, or concept home in a powerful way. The preacher's facial expressions can affirm and confirm a truth in ways that even argumentation and illustration cannot. Although the preacher should avoid completely forced or false gestures, there is nothing wrong with purposeful gestures in keeping with the words being spoken. The concern of the preacher is to proclaim the truth clearly and passionately, and every facet of the communication will be impacted by this purpose.

There may be certain illustrations or points that are dramatized by the preacher in the flow of the message,[22] but when the preacher is speaking directly and personally to his audience (as the preacher himself), the gestures should not appear in any way "acted" or programmed. The best example of natural and unaffected "visual language" is a little child. Watch a little child seeing bubbles for the first time! Watch the range of movements, expressions, and gestures in different situations. This is not to say that the preacher should become something he is not, but the preacher should be as free and expressive as is helpful to the communicating of the message through his personality.

Coldness, lack of passion, and even lack of love, can be (and we emphasize *can be*) communicated through limited visual movement or expression. Also, limited gestures, facial expressions, etc., obviously limit the supportive role that the physical can have to the verbal. Outward and wide gestures seem to embrace the audience within the concern of the preacher. In a day when so many words come to people indirectly through various media, meaningful, purposeful, natural gestures remind people of the reality of the messenger as well as the message. Therefore, the preacher needs to think this through. Ask trusted people to share with you what they think and "feel" that you say through your appearance as you preach. Watch yourself on video or have someone critique you objectively. The preacher, generally speaking, should demonstrate natural variety and balance in this arena of the visual, all in keeping with who he is, whose he is, what he is doing, and what he is preaching.

We recommend avoiding the following mannerisms:
- swaying (unless everyone is swaying with you)
- grasping the pulpit tightly and never letting go
- using only one hand or arm in gestures if you are able to use both

- always pointing one finger or having clenched fists
- holding the Bible in a flippant or dishonoring way
- putting one hand in a pocket, especially if you have keys or coins
- looking at one section of the audience or one spot on the wall the whole time
- gestures that scold when you are not scolding

In general, avoid patterns and habits of gestures, facial expressions, etc., that do not communicate or enhance the truth.

It is appropriate for the preacher to seek for and even ask for the attention of the hearers. The preacher can say, "Men of Judea and all who dwell in Jerusalem, let this be known to you, and heed my words" (Acts 2:14), or "Men of Israel, and you who fear God, listen" (Acts 13:16). At the same time, the preacher can seek and ask for the attention of the audience throughout the message. Such attention is appropriate because of the source of the message, because of the message itself, and because of the messenger's role.

On the practical level, the preacher should seek to preach in such a way that he deserves the attention of the audience. This is not to say that attention will always be given, but the preacher's message and delivery should call for attention. The preacher ought consistently to affirm and convey the critical importance of the message and the importance of the audience's attention to it. We list here some practical aspects of delivery that are in keeping, we believe, with a message that deserves attention.

Direct address to the audience as a whole or groups within the audience is certainly appropriate and may be necessary. In Romans 12:1–2, when the apostle Paul gives his exhortation based on the gospel, he begins by stating, "I beseech you therefore, *brethren*, by the mercies of God" (v. 1a, emphasis ours). Paul identifies his audience here in a personal and theological way. There are personal and relational designations, and there are designations that have theological and spiritual significance as well. Any designations used should be accurate, appropriate, and purposeful. Such designations should bring people into the arena of the message again, alerting them to the particular importance or relevance of the message to them. Designations can be as simple as "Young people, middle-aged, and older ones here today," or they may be more theologically/spiritually significant, "You may be new to these truths I am presenting today," "You may be a new Christian here today," "You may have walked with the Lord for many years now," or "Elders, deacons, other leaders in the church, Sunday school teachers, church workers, there's a challenge for you today."

Designations indicate not only the importance of the message to the "designee," but such direct address reminds people of the preacher's awareness of the audience. This is important! People need to know that you know that they are there, that you want them to hear the message. "For I speak to you Gentiles; inasmuch as I am an apostle to the Gentiles" (Rom 11:13a). "I have a word for those of you here today who have never honestly claimed Jesus Christ as your Lord and Savior."

As illustrated above, we place within this category of direct address *direct designations* as well as *descriptive terms* for individuals and/or groups within a congregation or audience. The preacher should never be needlessly offensive, and he should avoid names, terms, and descriptive language that have "detour" written all over them. The issue is not fear or compromise; the issue is distraction from the truth. When there is the need for bold direct exhortation or challenge, this must be done with the boldness and the love of Christ. The preacher may need to challenge, renounce, or strongly warn in the course of a given message or ministry. Jesus had some direct words to say to the leaders of His day: "Woe to you, scribes and Pharisees, hypocrites!" (Matt. 23:13, 14, 15, 23, 25, 27, 29). Such words must be stated with conviction and care, even in the midst of boldness and passion. The full weight of Scripture and biblical truth needs to be behind such prophetic declarations, and the preacher should give the specific reasons for such denouncements or declarations at that time.

We have tried to cover a number of options under direct address. Direct address is actually an aspect or logical part of direct communication. *Preaching should be direct communication.* It is proclamation, a specific proclamation to a particular audience on a given occasion. The preacher is not seeking to manipulate the audience, but he does want the audience attentive to the truths being declared.

Interrogatives, both rhetorical and direct, help people to think through the message with you. Such questions help to focus the attention of people on the main truths or issues at stake. A good study for the preacher would be to read through the Book of Romans and make a note of the questions Paul asks and uses to move his presentation of the gospel. Romans 1–11 is aided greatly by the use of penetrating questions.

Questions can be very helpful in isolating and drawing attention to specific truths or insights that might otherwise be missed. "What does this word *living* really mean when Paul speaks of a 'living sacrifice'?" Questions can help to move forward whole sections of a message while drawing attention to the key theme or truth. "What is our Lord's strategy or program for the Great Commission?" Indeed, an interrogative can lead into the body of the entire exposition, relating the theme to the thoughts. "What can we learn from this text about the seriousness of 'Spiritual Heart Disease'?" Each point really answers that question.

Questions can be combined and expressed, one after the other, to focus thoughts on various aspects of a truth or issue. Speaking of the righteousness accounted to Abraham, Paul asks, "How then was it accounted? While he was circumcised, or uncircumcised?" (Rom. 4:10a). The second question is more specific than the first and isolates the key issue for the truth being presented in context. Questions can be asked and answered in a progressive series to teach or proclaim the clear movement from one thought to the other. These questions help to guide people thoughtfully through the truths.

Lastly, interrogatives/questions can be of great help in the application of truth at any point in the message, especially in the conclusion. "Now, what does this mean to you today?" "How can you embrace and experience this marvelous truth we are considering?" "When was the last time you prayed meaningfully about this critical issue? Will you pray right now as we conclude this message?" Such questions help the listener to think of the truth in relation to his/her own life and experience. The issue at stake is made personal and relevant to each member of the audience.

Many practical comments could be shared concerning how to ask questions. We offer a few comments here. Make sure your question can be easily understood. You want people to think about the answer to the question, and not stumble over the question itself. Make sure you give people the time they need to really think about what you have asked. Pauses can be very helpful at such times. Rephrasing questions in a number of ways can assist as well.

Application of the truth—regularly, personally, practically, and specifically—keeps the preacher in touch with his audience and calls for attention. The preacher is not just "throwing out" thoughts; he is proclaiming a relevant, applicable message because it's God's message to the specific audience. We encourage the consistent application of textual truth throughout the message. A commitment to careful and thoughtful application of the truth will "force" the preacher to relate the truth to people's lives today.[23]

Illustrations can help to maintain attention as well. This type of content invites people to *see,* not just to *hear.* Illustrations can bridge beautifully between explanation and application, and they can help to reinforce the application. In our chapter on application we refer to the role of *symbolism,* capturing the truth in a form that helps to represent it.[24] Such forms, pictures, stories, accounts, visual aides, or wordings can strengthen the presentation of truth and, in so doing, call for attention on the part of the audience. We are not talking about gimmicks or audience manipulation; we are speaking about that type of illustrative preaching that is witnessed to in the biblical text itself.

Keeping to the subject, also, helps to maintain attention. Meandering through a message is not only hard to follow, it can give the impression that the subject is not significant and that the preaching event is not critical. Keeping to the theme, and on each thought as you proceed, helps to move the message with a sense of clarity and purpose. Clarity and purpose both help to call for attention because people can understand what is being said, and they sense the critical nature of the preaching event.

Speaking from the heart and *to the heart* are both worthy of mention here. If the preacher is speaking passionately from his own heart, this demands and deserves attention. The importance of the truth *to the preacher* is seen and sensed. Also, the audience senses the concern that the preacher has not only for the truth, but for the audience. The preaching event is not just some objective exercise to fill time and cover material. The heart of the preacher for his God, for the message, and for the audience is exposed. People ought to have a clear answer to the questions: Is the message *real* to you? Is this just religious jargon, or are you speaking about truths that are really true and make a difference? The incarnational approach to preaching calls for and encourages authentic preaching from the heart. Also, incarnational preaching should foster a concern to preach to the hearts of others. We are not dealing with surface or superficial matters. Biblical truths are truths that address the core of man's being, and it is from the heart that men believe (Rom. 10:9) and obey (Rom. 6:17).

Avoid getting petty or superficial. The preacher can be very practical, but such practicality should be tied to deep, personal response to the truth. The heart of man, the core of each individual's being, should be addressed as you preach. If people sense that you have a great concern for them and for the significant impact that the truth can have on their real lives, this calls for attention. The love *of* Christ should come through as well as a love *for* Christ. An intensity of concern for the truth should be a given for the preacher, but an intensity of concern for the person should be a given for the Christian!

Authority calls for attention and maintains it. The preacher—under the anointing of the Holy Spirit and with a divine message to declare—has an authority for the preaching event.[25] His authority should be expressed in a message that clarifies God's will and ways for the people. People are confronted with God's Word for them—its implications and demands. Authority is not the same thing as volume in delivery. Authority has to do with being mastered by the Word and by the Spirit. *Authority* is expressed in clarity and authenticity of presentation along with a boldness and passion for the truth. A person "under authority" has a derived authority from the one he is under. The preacher is under the authority of his Lord. The authority of the preacher should be matched by humility and simplicity (reality). It is then that authority will be expressed without carnality or willful manipulation. True authority in preaching cannot be forced or faked. It is a product of the preacher's calling, gifting, relationship with the Lord, knowledge of the Word, readiness to preach, fullness and anointing of the Spirit, and presence under authority at that moment. You cannot work up authority to gain respect or response. Real authority in preaching ultimately is derived from the Lord, and is developed by the Lord in the context of faithfulness to the Word and dependence on the Holy Spirit. Such authority was a characteristic of the New Testament preacher.

CONCLUSION

We began this chapter by asking the question, How ought we to speak? We searched for guiding priorities and principles that resulted in a concern for the clear and passionate proclamation of the truth. Then, when thinking of specific messages, we stated that the message should dictate the manner of communication. The content of the message should impact the character of the delivery.

As we conclude this section, we want to draw attention to some broader considerations that can and should affect communication. These broader considerations really amount to reflections on preaching as presented and witnessed to in the New Testament.

The preacher should preach with an apocalyptic purpose. The privilege and responsibility of the preacher is to make known what otherwise might remain unknown or hidden. Each message preached is an opportunity for an "apocalyptic moment." Anointed biblical preaching is a glorious activity that opens up truth to people. The preacher should preach with that sense of responsibility, privilege, and dependence, since God must work to reveal what needs to be revealed to each person.

The preacher should preach with a theological position. The New Testament preachers had a sense of the scriptural veracity of what was being declared, and they saw the events and theology of the gospel as part of God's eternal plan. There was a theological framework and biblical support for what God had done in Christ and what must be done in response. This platform provided a solid foundation for authority in proclamation. This authority was—and is—grounded in the very will and way of God as revealed through His authoritative Word. The preacher should always be able to rely upon, and rest in, the authority of the Word of God itself. The preacher can declare the message with authority "according to the Scriptures," and this needs to characterize both the preacher's message and manner.

The preacher should preach with a christological priority. "Him we preach," Paul declared (Col. 1:28a), and certainly declaring Christ should be at the core of the preacher's concern and ministry. The gospel message must center on Jesus Christ, and our preaching to edify the saints must draw people closer to Christ, call people to "walk in Him," to abide in Him, to Christlikeness, etc. This may not impact certain aspects of delivery, but it does impact the central concern of communication. We are not just preaching concepts, reflections, or applications; ultimately we are declaring a Person. The preeminence of Christ in our lives, ministries, and messages should be evident.

The preacher should preach with an eschatological perspective. There must be a sense of urgency in the light of the climactic days in which we live. Christ has come, He is risen and ascended, and He will come again. We minister within that theological, experiential, and chronological reality. We are under a mandate to preach in "these last days." There is a "must" in God's agenda for these days and it involves the preaching of the gospel to the nations (Mark 13:10), and the making of disciples (Matt. 28:18–20). When preaching becomes routine, "institutionalized," and detached from a sense of eschatological mission, it loses its proper ethos and atmosphere. A sense of mandate and mission should surround one's preaching ministry. The divine agenda is set, and it has chronological limits. Things will not always be the same. We minister between the "now" and the "not yet" of God's eschatological-redemptive plan. We need to preach with an eschatological perspective.

The preacher should preach with dependence upon a soteriological power. The atoning work of Christ for our redemption is complete. Yet, God ordained that the message of salvation be preached and believed: "It pleased God through the foolishness of the message preached to save those who believe" (1 Cor. 1:21b). The gospel is "the power of God to salvation" (Rom. 1:16), and this is a gospel that is preached. Soteriological power is God's and God's alone, but such power is marvelously, sovereignly, and specifically demonstrated in relation to the preaching of the gospel. In the context of his declarations concerning Israel and the gospel, Paul speaks of how one is, in fact, "saved" (Rom. 10:1–13). Having supported his soteriological statements with Scripture, Paul then questions, "How then shall they call on Him in whom they have not believed? And how shall they believe in Him of whom they have not heard? And how shall they hear without a preacher? And how shall they preach unless they are sent?" (Rom 10:14–15a). Such questions strongly indicate the significant role of preaching within the matrix of human activities that are associated with divine soteriological power.

We must ever remember that the preacher is involved in saving and sanctifying activities and realities. How this is and can be is a mystery of God's grace beyond our comprehension! But we hold on to the Word of God for our understanding of preaching itself, as well as the preacher. Such truths impact the concern we have for accuracy, clarity, and passion concerning the message we preach. Such truths also guard and guide as we seek to communicate the message. Preaching should be purposeful. Preaching should be authoritative. Preaching should be focused with a sense of priority, characterized by urgency and mission. Preaching should be viewed as a part of God's powerful process of saving and sanctifying His people.

Ultimately *preaching is for the glory of God*, and any genuine fruit will bring glory, honor, and praise to Him who has called, gifted, and sent the messenger. "To Him be glory."

PART THREE

The Word to Proclaim

CHAPTER TWELVE

THE PREACHER AND CONSECRATION

*The Spirit of the Lord is upon Me, because He
has anointed Me to preach the gospel to the poor;
He has sent Me to heal the brokenhearted, to
preach delivereance to the captives and recovery
of sight to the blind, to set at liberty those who
are oppressed, to proclaim the acceptable year of
the Lord.*

—Luke 4:18–19

Study Text: Luke 3:21–22; 4:16–30

We now move from the preparation of an expository sermon to the dynamics of incarnational preaching. Only the Holy Spirit can transform a manuscript into a message. "Rightly dividing the word of truth" (2 Tim. 2:15) can bring together the subject, structure, and substance of the sermon, but it is God alone who can quicken to life our "unashamed workmanship." We are confident that what we dedicate He consecrates! That includes both the servant and his sermon.

214

When Moses finished all the work of the tabernacle, he was instructed to take "the anointing oil, and anoint the tabernacle and all that [was] in it" (Exod. 40:9). As soon as that was done "the glory of the LORD filled the tabernacle" (Exod. 40:34).

Centuries later, the Eternal Word, by the power of the Spirit, "became flesh and [tabernacled] among us, and we beheld His glory . . . full of grace and truth" (John 1:14).

Today, we are the tabernacles of the Holy Spirit "who is in [us]" (1 Cor. 6:19), and if we desire to glorify God in our bodies, by life and by lip, we must earnestly seek what Charles H. Spurgeon dubbed "the sacred anointing."[1]

In Old Testament times, the words *consecration* and *anointing* were interchangeably employed for "setting apart" servants of God like Aaron and his sons. The instructions were clear: "You shall anoint them, consecrate them, and sanctify them, that they may minister to Me" (Exod. 28:41; Lev. 21:10). Indeed, the ceremony of anointing related to *all* important offices and ministries of the servant of Jehovah. The prophet was anointed that he might be the messenger of God to the people (1 Kings 19:16). The priest was anointed that he might be holy unto the Lord (Lev. 8:12). The king was anointed that the Spirit of the Lord might rest upon him in power (1 Sam. 16:13). No servant of the Lord was (or is) considered qualified for ministry without this holy anointing.

How true this was of Jesus in His perfect humanity! Before He began His public ministry He was "anointed" by God His Father (Acts 10:38). This is all the more significant since we know that He was *filled* with the Spirit from His mother's womb and throughout His "silent years" (Luke 1:35; 2:52). Indeed, the plenitude of the Spirit's power was always available to Him. The distinguished exegete and Greek scholar A. T. Robertson suggests that the precise event referred to by Peter in Acts 10:38 concerning the "anointing" of Jesus "could be the Incarnation (Luke 1:35f.), the Baptism (Luke 3:22), [or] the Ministry at Nazareth (Luke 4:14)."[2] Then provokingly he asks, "Why not to the life and work of Jesus as a whole?" After all, the New Testament makes it clear that "he [the Son of God] whom God sent utters the words of God, *so measureless is God's gift of the Spirit*" (John 3:34 REB, emphasis ours). While we acknowledge that God's dealings with His Son are transcendently unique, there are, at the same time, *abiding principles* for us today; for "as He is, so are we in this world" (1 John 4:17).

The point we make here is that there came a crisis in the life of Jesus when He appropriated (by faith and prayer [Luke 3:21–22]) the anointing of the Spirit to fulfill His messianic mission. And, as we shall see in a moment, this anointing was essentially associated with proclamation (Luke 4:18), ministration (Acts 10:38), and opposition (Acts 4:17) as He "went about doing good" (Acts 10:38).

As preachers, we likewise *need* this "sacred anointing." We received this "unction" when we first believed (see Acts 5:32; 1 John 2:24, 27); but for many of us, we have not appropriated what is ours *already* in Christ. Through lack of clear teaching or blatant *neglect* of God's "so great a salvation" (Heb. 2:3), we have failed to recognize that the "God and Father of our Lord Jesus Christ . . . has blessed us [past tense] with every spiritual blessing . . . in Christ" (Eph. 1:3). The word *spiritual* is emphatic, and in Ephesians emphasizes "the work of the divine Spirit upon the human spirit. Not spiritual as distinguished from [the] bodily, but *proceeding from the Holy Spirit*."[3] Among these blessings are three that must be clarified before we proceed:

Baptism. This represents our spiritual *position* in Christ. "By one Spirit we were all baptized into one body . . . and have all been made to drink into one Spirit"; literally, "we were all given the one Spirit to drink" (1 Cor. 12:13). This is a *one-time* experience (Eph. 4:5), and is synonymous with regeneration or new birth.

Filling. This represents our spiritual *condition* in Christ. The filling of the Spirit is not strictly a biblical term, but believers are said to be "filled with the . . . Spirit" (Acts 2:4; 4:8, 31; 9:17; 13:9). The key verse, of course, is Ephesians 5:18, where we are *commanded* to "be filled with the Spirit." Being filled with the Spirit means more than being *indwelt* by Him. It is possible for the Holy Spirit to be *present* in the life without being *president*! To be obedient preachers (and believers generally), we need to be under the *control* of the Spirit. This is why the verb is in the imperative mood, the passive voice, and the present tense. This calls for obedience and allegiance *to* and dependence *on* the Holy Spirit every day of our lives—in the church, in the home, and in the world (Eph. 5:18–6:20). This aspect of the Spirit's work is *inward* and relates primarily to normal Christian living and Christlikeness.

Anointing. This represents our spiritual *vocation* in Christ. As we observed earlier, the anointing of Jesus was related to His proclamation (Luke 4:18), ministration (Acts 10:38), and opposition (Acts 4:17). In a similar way, the anointing for preachers (and believers generally) is for *special* Christian service. It is "the Promise of the Father" (Acts 1:4, 8) and is referred to as *enduement with power* (Luke 24:49). The verb *endued* means to "be clothed upon or with" (see the examples of this outward clothing in passages like Rom. 13:12; 13:14; Eph. 4:24; Col. 3:10, etc.). "Anointing" or "unction" enables us to *appreciate* the Word of God (see 1 John 2:20, 27) and also to *authenticate* the work of God (2 Cor. 1:21–22). This unction (*chrisma*) is God's safeguard against error, in the light of His inerrant Word. The Word is the objective safeguard, while the Spirit is the subjective safeguard. What is important to see and seek is the *ongoing* need for this anointing. We are commanded to "*abide in Him* [the Holy Spirit, the Unction]" (1 John 2:27c). *Abide* is an imperative active verb. Jesus employed it when speaking of Himself (John 15:4). It means to "keep on doing this as a general habit or lifestyle." As the filling suggests an *inward* working of the Spirit, the anointing stresses the *outward* clothing with power.

Another important verse is 2 Corinthians 1:21–22. Here Paul defends his authority in ministry and emphasizes "that God, through the gospel of his Son and through . . . the indwelling [and anointing of the] Spirit, has *authenticated* Paul's ministry . . . [and] his integrity" (emphasis ours).[4]

One more observation is in order. When we read the Acts of the Apostles—and especially key verses like 2:4; 4:8, 31; 9:17; 13:9—the common expression employed for enduement is "filled with the . . . Spirit." This must not confuse us any more than does the comprehensive word *salvation* which includes many aspects of God's redeeming work in our lives (e.g., justification, sanctification, glorification, etc.). "Filled with the . . . Spirit" is an "umbrella" term. We cannot be anointed unless we are filled with the Spirit. This was true in the life of Jesus, and it must be true in our lives as well.

With the foregoing clarification established in our minds, we are now ready to concentrate on the selected text for this chapter. Let us, with reverence, learn what happened to Jesus at His baptism in Jordan, and what the "sacred anointing" is all about.

THE PROMISE OF THE ANOINTING

"The Spirit of the LORD is upon Me, because He has anointed Me to preach the gospel" (Luke 4:18). Isaiah the prophet had already predicted—and therefore promised—this holy anointing upon Jehovah's Servant (see Isa. 61:1–2). Later, in all the power of His resurrection, the Lord Jesus similarly promised the anointing of the Spirit for His disciples. He said, "I send the Promise of My Father upon you; but tarry in the city of Jerusalem until you are *endued with power* from on high" (Luke 24:49, emphasis ours). On the day of Pentecost that promise was gloriously fulfilled.

There are two aspects of this promise of the anointing that we must examine: the secret and the symbol.

The Secret of the Anointing

"While [Jesus] prayed, the heaven was opened. And the Holy Spirit descended in bodily form like a dove upon Him, and a voice came from heaven which said, 'You are My beloved Son; in You I am well pleased'" (Luke 3:21–22). As we have observed already, Jesus was filled with the Holy Spirit from His mother's womb (see Luke 1:35); His birth and His subsequent life were "overshadowed" by the power of the Highest. But His *anointing* took place when He presented Himself to His Father for His life's ministry. The secret of this anointing is best summed up in three words: holiness, yieldedness, and prayerfulness.

The Life of Holiness. God declared from heaven, "You are My beloved Son; in You I am well pleased" (Luke 3:22). Looking back over thirty years of His hidden life, the Father affirmed with the writer to the Hebrews that He was "holy, harmless, undefiled, separate from sinners" (Heb. 7:26). This amazing statement is three-dimensional. In relation to His God, He was—and is—"holy," for all His words and actions reveal the very nature of His heavenly Father. In relation to His fellow man, He was—and is—"harmless," for His life and ministry were totally free from all malice. In relation to Himself. He was—and is—"undefiled," for as Prophet, Priest, and King, He was not stained with any kind of impurity, having no defilement in Himself. Moffatt suggests that the language may be intended to show a contrast between the deep, ethical purity of Jesus and the ritualistic purity of the Levitical high priest who had to take extreme precautions against outward defilement. In this three-dimensional sense He was therefore "separate from sinners." This was true of all of His life; but when God said, "You are My beloved Son; in You I am well pleased" (3:22), He was obviously referring to those first thirty years.

God can only bless with the anointing of His Holy Spirit those who *pursue* a life of holiness. This is what He expects of all of us (see Heb. 12:14; 2 Cor. 7:1). As we face our respective ministries week by week, we must ever hear and heed those words of Jehovah through the prophet Isaiah: "Be clean, you who bear the vessels of the LORD" (Isa. 52:11).

The Life of Yieldedness. Addressing John the Baptist, Jesus insisted, "Permit it to be so now, for thus it is fitting for us to fulfill all righteousness" (Matt. 3:15). Then we read that "Jesus . . . was baptized" (Luke 3:21). In yielding Himself to John the "baptizer," Jesus demonstrated His total obedience to the will of His Father—an attitude and activity that characterized the whole of His life and ministry. In another verse we are reminded that "though He was a Son, yet He learned obedience by the things which He suffered" (Heb 5:8). Obedience does not imply that Jesus was previously rebellious or disobedient—that is unthinkable! At the same time, in His *humanity* He had to evidence obedience to the will of the Father in order to qualify as the Author of eternal salvation (Heb. 5:8–9). Indeed, as God's Servant, Jesus was "obedient to the point of death, even the death of the cross" (Phil 2:8).

We, likewise, must be obedient if we would know the anointing of the Holy Spirit, for God gives "the Holy Spirit . . . to those who *obey* Him" (Acts 5:32, emphasis ours). We must initially obey the gospel to know the gift of the Spirit; but we must *continually* obey to know the fullness and anointing of the Spirit.

Bobby Richardson, former New York Yankees' second baseman, spells out this attitude of obedience. On one occasion he offered a prayer at a meeting of Fellowship of Christian Athletes. It was classic for its brevity and poignancy: "Dear God, Your will—nothing more, nothing less, nothing else, Amen."[5]

The Life of Prayerfulness. Luke records that as Jesus was being baptized He was praying (present tense, see 3:21). Later the Master reminded His disciples that if they were to know the power of the Holy Spirit in their lives, they would have to ask in prayer. He declared, "If you then, being evil, know how to give good gifts to your children, how much more will your heavenly Father give the Holy Spirit to those who ask Him!" (Luke 11:13). Commenting on this verse, G. Campbell Morgan affirms that *"the highest in prayer is that attitude that seeks and obtains from God, His Holy Spirit.* That is initial, but also continuous. This is where we begin, and when we receive the Holy Spirit at first, we are born again; but the prayer-life is the life that is always seeking and always receiving—the filling, the infilling and overflowing of the Spirit" (emphasis ours).[6] That is why the verbs *ask, seek,* and

knock (Luke 11:9) are in the present tense. We are to go on asking for God to go on giving. The reason why we do not know
authority in our preaching is because we do not know *anointing*,
and the reason we do not know anointing is because we do not
go on asking. As Professor Leon Morris points out, "Luke is interested in the work of the Spirit and here he sees the gift of the
Spirit as man's highest good. . . . The reference is . . . to the Spirit's
work in the Christian's life generally, as in Romans 8."

The Symbol of the Anointing

"The Holy Spirit descended in bodily form like a dove upon
Him" (3:22). Without pressing the analogy, it is important that we
understand the symbol of the anointing. The general teaching of
Scripture is that the dove is a symbol of peace, purity, passion,
and power.

The Dove Is a Symbol of Peace. When Noah put forth his hand
from the ark and welcomed the dove with the olive leaf in its beak
(see Gen 8:11), it was a sign that God was declaring peace with
the earth once more. The waters of judgment were subsiding, and
very soon Noah and his family were to step out of the ark onto
dry land. Ever since then, in Hebrew thought and Christian teaching, the dove has been a symbol of peace.

This ministry of peace was supremely characteristic of the life
of our Lord Jesus Christ! He was ever speaking words of peace
to those around Him—especially to His disciples (see John 14:1,
27; 16:33; 20:19, 26). When He commissioned the apostles to go
forth, even as the Father had sent Him, He said, "'Peace be with
you.' . . . And when He had said this, He breathed on them, and
said to them, 'Receive the Holy Spirit'" (John 20:19–22).

In like manner, we must preach peace through the blood of the
cross and be ministers of reconciliation (Eph. 2:17; 2 Cor. 5:18–19).
We need men of peace in our pulpits, our community— and especially in our homes. Oh, to pray daily:

> Drop Thy still dews of quietness,
> Till all our strivings cease;
> Take from our souls the strain and stress,
> And let our ordered lives confess
> The beauty of Thy peace.

—John G. Whittier

The Dove Is a Symbol of Purity. When Jesus exhorted His disciples to be "harmless as doves" (Matt 10:16), His emphasis was on
transparency and purity. *Akeraios* literally means "*pure* [and] is

used metaphorically in the N.T. of what is . . . harmless (Matt. 10:16)."[8] We must ever remember that God can only pour out His Spirit upon lives that are ready and receptive for His dove of purity. This was true of the Lord Jesus, and it must be true of preacher. Remember the words of the Master when He said, "If you love Me, *keep My commandments.* And I will pray the Father, and He will give you another Helper, that He may abide with you forever" (John 14:15–16, emphasis ours). Only as we live in the Word and walk in the light (1 John 1:7) do we qualify for the Spirit of purity in our lives. Would to God that the words of the Shunammite woman could be said of us: "Look now, I know that this is a holy man of God, who passes by us regularly" (2 Kings 4:9). What was it about Elisha that evoked such a commendation?

It is on record that when the saintly Robert Murray M'Cheyne (1813–1843) "entered the pulpit, his spirituality was so evident, his congregation would weep. The Scotsman declared his approach to the ministry in one of the finest lines ever spoken by a pastor: 'My people's greatest need is my personal holiness.'"[9]

The Dove Is a Symbol of Passion. The cooing of the dove is used in Scripture to signify suffering, mourning, and passion (see Ezek. 7:16). We must remember that the dove was used in sacrificial offerings (see Lev. 12:6; 14:4–8). Our Lord's passion sent Him to the cross to give Himself in sacrifice that men and women might be saved. That same passion came through in all His public utterances.

G. Campbell Morgan insists that all authentic preaching must have "Truth, Clarity, and Passion."[10] *Truth* comprehends the totality of our message. Ultimately, truth is the eternal Word, even our Lord Jesus Christ Himself. We are to "preach the word!" (2 Tim. 4:2). *Clarity* means lucidity of statement and utterance in every way. Martin Luther once said: "A preacher ought so to preach, that when the sermon is ended, the congregation shall disperse, saying, 'The preacher said *this*'"[11] (emphasis ours). But *passion* is our focus in this particular context. To quote G. Campbell Morgan again:

> In the true sermon there must always be passion. But the passion must be something that is created by no conscious effort. It must come out of what we are declaring, and out of our consciousness of it. Half the sermons today—may I be forgiven if I am cruel—are failing because they lack . . . passion. . . . I am not arguing for mere excitement. Painted fire never burns; . . . an imitated enthusiasm is the most empty thing that can possibly exist in a preacher. [But] given the preacher with a message from the whole Bible, and seeing its bearing on life at any point, I cannot personally understand that man not being

swept sometimes right out of himself by the fire and the force and the fervor of his work.[12]

All this happens when we know in personal experience the *Spirit of passion* in our lives. Dr. Morgan's successor, Martyn Lloyd-Jones, speaking before a group of theological students, urged: "This 'unction,' this 'anointing,' is the supreme thing. Seek it until you have it; . . . until you can say, 'And my preaching was not with the enticing words of man's wisdom, but in demonstration of the Spirit and of power.'"[13]

The Dove Is a Symbol of Power. We read that the Holy Spirit "descended in bodily form like a dove upon [the Lord Jesus]" (Luke 3:22). In Hebrew thought, the Holy Spirit is always regarded as "the outgoing of God's power" (see Luke 24:49; Acts 1:8; 2:2–3; 1 Peter 1:12). The dove, *because of its gentleness*, is a symbol of power. David could say, "Your gentleness has made me great" (2 Sam. 22:36; Ps. 18:35). These words mean that God "condescends to 'stoop down' in order to make David great."[14] This is the paradox of the Christian life and ministry. When we acknowledge our utter weakness, then—and only then—are we strong (2 Cor. 12:10). The power of the Holy Spirit only comes upon those who acknowledge their inadequacy before God (see 1 Cor. 2:1–5). What an incentive to claim this promise of the Spirit's anointing! Without this anointing there is no power, and without power there is no redemptive authority in our preaching.

THE PURPOSE OF THE ANOINTING

"The Spirit of the Lord is upon Me, because He has anointed Me to preach the gospel to the poor; He has sent Me to heal the brokenhearted, to proclaim liberty to the captives and recovery of sight to the blind, to set at liberty those who are oppressed, to proclaim the acceptable year of the LORD" (Luke 4:18–19). As we analyze this prophetic statement it is clear that the anointing on preachers has a twofold purpose: to reach people and to preach the gospel.

We Are Anointed to Reach the People

"He has anointed Me to preach the gospel to the poor; He has sent Me to heal the brokenhearted, to proclaim liberty to the captives and recovery of sight to the blind, to set at liberty those who are oppressed" (4:18). There are five categories of people who must be reached redemptively, and this can never happen without the anointing. Indeed, more often than not, many preachers drive people away. This is a serious matter and demands careful thought and self-examination. Jesus always drew needy people to Himself: "The common people heard Him gladly" (Mark 12:37). And He declared that if He were lifted up from the earth, He would draw all men unto Himself (John 12:32).

The Bankrupt. "The poor" (4:18). At the outset of His ministry, Jesus made it clear that His aim was to preach the gospel to the poor. Even though He said in another context, "You have the poor with you always" (Mark 14:7), He was always moved with compassion as He contemplated the poor. He understood and appreciated the sacrificial giving of a poor widow (Mark 12:41–44). He recognized the continuing obligation toward the poor, as He taught His disciples. This is why the early church regarded the poor as a solemn responsibility before God (Acts 2:45; 4:32–37; 6:1–6; 2 Cor. 8:2–5, 9–15). The Jerusalem council asked Paul and Barnabas to remember the poor (Gal. 2:10); and James, the brother of our Lord, has some sharp words about the relationships between rich and poor (James 1:9–11; 2:1–13; 5:1–6).

No one can be anointed with the Holy Spirit and be insensitive to the desperate need around us today. Every church should be responsible for its own community. Indeed, were this social concern demonstrated with practical action, we believe that the impact would not only affect the poor themselves, but constrain the rich to become involved. This is what Paul means when he writes, "Command those who are rich in this present age not to be haughty, nor to trust in uncertain riches but in the living God, who gives richly all things to enjoy. Let them do good, that they be rich in good works, ready to give, willing to share, storing up for themselves a good foundation for the time to come, that they may lay hold on eternal life" (1 Tim 6:17–19).

The Burdened. We need the anointing in order to reach "the brokenhearted" (4:18). The very word reminds us of people like Mary and Martha, who were brokenhearted because of the death of their brother Lazarus. So identified was the Master with their sorrow that we read "Jesus wept" (John 11:35). It wasn't long after that that Mary and Martha were rejoicing in a resurrected and reunited brother. The point we are making is that Jesus identified with the brokenhearted. As pastors/preachers, we will find that the most eloquent language in similar situations is our own brokenheartedness and our falling tears. There is a ministry in "anointed tears."

The Bound. "The captives" (4:18). When we think of bondage we recall the demoniac of Gadara (Mark 5:1–20). Here was a man so enslaved by demons that he could not be tamed or tied. But Jesus, with one glorious anointed command, liberated him. This poor demoniac ran from his fellowman, but "when he saw Jesus from afar, *he ran and worshiped Him*" (gave Him obeisance, Mark 5:6, emphasis ours)! Our world today abounds with captives bound by sin, self, and Satan. Oh, for the authority to speak the liberating Word to "the captives" and hear them exclaim:

> My chains fell off, my heart was free;
> I rose, went forth, and followed Thee.

> —Charles Wesley

The Blind. "Recovery of sight to the blind" (4:18). Here we relate at once with blind Bartimaeus, the wayside beggar. The striking thing about this story (mentioned in all three of the Synoptics) is the attempt of people to silence his cry for mercy and virtually block his way to Jesus. But Mark tells us that "he [cast] away his garment, rose, and came to Jesus" (Mark 10:50 KJV). He was blind; he was threatened, and even encumbered with a dangling garment; but "he rose and came to Jesus" (Mark 10:46–52). There was a magnetic authority in Jesus to draw the needy to Himself. Of course, Bartimaeus received his sight! Preacher, you never deliver a sermon without spiritually blind people sitting in your congregation. Do they leave seeing?

The Bruised. "To set at liberty those who are oppressed" (4:18). The word *oppressed* is used only here in the New Testament. The verb form means "to break in pieces." Jesus had a mission to mend broken hearts. He loved to serve people that society considered beyond repair. Think of the woman of John 8,[15] taken in adultery. Jesus redressed the tragedy of her life and then restored the dignity of her life. Likewise, the Samaritan woman of John 4. How we need *anointed compassion* to reach the burdened, the bound, the blind, and the bruised!

We Are Anointed to Preach the Gospel

"To proclaim the acceptable year of the Lord" (4:19). The expression "the acceptable year of the Lord" has a direct reference to the Year of Jubilee, celebrated in Old Testament times. On the first day of the Year of Jubilee the priest, with the sound of trumpets, proclaimed the blessings of that year (see Lev. 25:8–17). This great passage portrays Jesus as the proclaimer of liberty and victory. In the Year of Jubilee, Israel had to put their house in order: relationships had to be put right, restitutions had to be made, and slaves had to be released.

In New Testament terms, the preaching of the gospel affirms that Jesus Christ is *Lord*, and that under that lordship men and women have to get right with God and with one another. It was when Peter preached the lordship of Christ in his Pentecostal sermon that conviction fell upon the assembled crowd, and they cried out, "Men and brethren, what shall we do?" Peter's response was, "Repent, and let every one of you be baptized . . . and you shall receive the gift of the Holy Spirit" (Acts 2:37–38). We have not truly preached with anointing if we do not declare the lordship of Christ. After all, *biblical* preaching is about God—and Jesus as Lord. "If one must distinguish, God is the term of pure exaltation, while Lord carries with it more expressly the idea of sovereign rulership in actual exercise, evoking obedient service."[16]

THE POWER OF THE ANOINTING

"So all bore witness to Him, and marveled at the gracious words which proceeded out of His mouth. . . . So all those in the synagogue, when they heard these things, were filled with wrath" (4:22, 28). Preaching with the unction of the Holy Spirit never neutralizes an individual, a group, or a congregation. On the contrary, Holy Spirit-anointed preaching always precipitates a decision. Read through the Gospel of John and note the occasions where the preaching of the Savior brought division among the people (John 7:43; 9:16; 10:19). They either believed on Him or took up stones to stone Him.

This is precisely what we find in the text before us. There was a twofold reaction: wonder and wrath.

There Was the Reaction of Wonder

"All bore witness to Him, and marveled at the gracious words which proceeded out of His mouth" (4:22). There are always those who welcome the message of God and accept God's offer of mercy. All through His ministry people came to put their trust in the Savior.

And this has been true of preachers throughout the centuries. Every truly anointed pastor sees this happen Sunday by Sunday. And what shall we say of evangelists like Dr. Billy Graham and other lesser known preachers who, preaching in the power of the Holy Spirit, have won multitudes to Christ?

A convention once met in Indianapolis to discuss "How to Reach the Masses." One day during that convention a young man stood on a box on a corner and began to preach. A crowd gathered, mostly working men going home to their suppers. They were electrified by the sermon. They forgot that they were tired. They forgot that they were hungry. The crowd became so dense that it had to move. The preacher announced that he would preach again at the Academy of Music. They followed him down the street, singing as they went, and they filled the main floor of the building, sitting with their dinner buckets while he preached again with such power that they were to moved to tears. But he had only a few minutes to preach because the convention on "How to Reach the Masses" was gathering in the same auditorium. While the convention was discussing how to reach the masses, D. L. Moody was *doing* it! He was preaching the kingdom of God and every man was pressing violently into it![17]

There Was the Reaction of Wrath

"So all those in the synagogue, when they heard these things, were filled with wrath, and rose up and thrust Him out of the city; and they led Him to the brow of the hill . . . that they might throw Him down over the cliff" (4:28–29). The fact is—they rejected Him and would have stoned Him to death there and then, but it is recorded that "passing through the midst of them, He went His way" (4:28–30). A preacher is immortal until his task is done. We must remember that the gospel is "the aroma of death leading to death, and to [others] the aroma of life leading to life" (2 Cor. 2:16). The very apostle who wrote these words preached on Mars' Hill. On that occasion, some mocked the Savior, some missed the Savior, but some met the Savior (see Acts 17:32–34)! This will always be true as long as we know the power of the anointing.

Adrian Rogers said at a Congress on the Bible in San Diego, California, some years ago (1982): "There was a time when preachers would stand in the pulpit and thunder, 'The Bible says . . .' Then they said, 'The church says . . .' Now most say, as they scratch their heads, 'It seems to me . . .'" Whatever happened to biblical authority?

What we need today is a fresh anointing of the Holy Spirit if our ministry is to penetrate the hearts of saint and sinner alike. Where there is an anointing there is the *authority*. Concerning the Lord Jesus, it is recorded that when He had finished speaking "the people were astonished at His teaching, for He taught them as *o n e having authority*, and not as the scribes" (Matt. 7:28–29, emphasis ours). Martyn Lloyd-Jones always emphasized the necessity of the Spirit's anointing. He called it the greatest essential in connection with preaching. He insisted, "Careful preparation and the unction of the Holy Spirit must never be regarded as alternatives, but as complementary to each other." He then asked, "Do you always look for and seek this unction, this anointing, before preaching? Has this been your greatest concern? There is no more thorough and revealing test to apply to the preacher."[18]

Consider this story concerning the great American evangelist Dwight L. Moody:

> [He] had already been greatly used by God in Chicago. Two humble Free Methodist women prayed faithfully for him during his Sunday services. At the close of the service they would say to him, "We have been praying for you." "Why don't you pray for the people?" Mr. Moody would ask. "Because you need the power of the Spirit," was the reply. "I need the power! Why," he said in relating the incident afterwards, "I thought I had power. I had the largest congregation in Chicago, and there were many conversions!"
>
> One day Moody said to them, "I wish you would tell me what you mean." And they told him about the definite [anointing] of the Holy Spirit. So he asked them to pray with him and not merely for him. Shortly thereafter their prayers were suddenly answered on Wall Street in New York. Moody's co-worker R.A. Torrey described what happened. "The power of God fell upon him as he walked up the street and he had to hurry off to the house of a friend and ask that he might have a room by himself, and in that room he stayed alone for hours; and the Holy Ghost came upon him, filling his soul with such joy that at last he had to ask God to withhold His hand, lest he die on the spot from very joy. He went out from that place with the power of the Holy Ghost upon him."
>
> Moody's own words were: "I was crying all the time that God would [anoint] me with His Spirit. Well, one day, in the city of New York—oh, what a day!—I cannot describe it . . . I can only say that God revealed Himself to me, and I had such an experience of His love that I had to ask Him to stay His hand. I went to preaching again. The sermons were not different; I did not present any new truths; and yet hundreds were converted. I would not now be placed back where I

was before that blessed experience if you should give me all the world—it would be as the small dust of the balance."[19]

We, the authors, can testify to the reality of Moody's experience of the anointing. The difference it makes is the difference between night and day. Fellow preacher, we urge you to proceed no further in your work for the Lord until you have believed the promise (Acts 1:4) and received the power (Acts 1:8), both as an initial act of faith and then as a continual appropriation of faith. Face every opportunity for ministry with this prayer:

> Anoint me with Your Spirit, Lord,
> For this strategic hour;
> That I may preach Your holy Word,
> With consecrated power.

> —Stephen F. Olford

CHAPTER THIRTEEN

THE PREACHER AND PROCLAMATION

*And I, brethren, when I came to you, did not come
with excellence of speech or of wisdom declaring
to you the [mystery[1]] of God. For I determined
not to know anything among you except Jesus
Christ and Him crucified. I was with you in
weakness, in fear, and in much trembling. And my
speech and my preaching were not with persuasive words of human wisdom, but in demonstration of the Spirit and of power, that your faith
should not be in the wisdom of men but in the
power of God.*

—1 Corinthians 2:1–5

Preaching is God's ordained means of communicating His
redeeming truth (1 Cor. 1:21). The *kerygma* is the preached
message, "the message of the cross" (1 Cor. 1:18). Preaching
is rooted in God's self-revelation. The patriarchs preached. They

communicated the commandments and promises of God (Gen. 18:19; Deut. 11:19). The prophets preached. They went from city to city reading and expounding the law (2 Chron. 15:3; 17:7–9; 35:3; Neh. 8:1–12; note v. 8). John the Baptist preached "repentance for the remission of sins" (Mark 1:4). Finally, Jesus came "preaching the gospel . . . saying, 'The time is fulfilled, and the kingdom of God is at hand. Repent, and believe . . . the gospel'" (Mark 1:14–15).

It is this uniqueness of "Christian preaching" that the apostle Paul addresses in our text. In the previous chapters he has argued that any other kind of preaching, such as "wisdom of words," neutralizes the power of the cross (1 Cor. 1:17). His reference, of course, is to the rhetorical display and philosophical style of the popular preachers of the day. Both the method and message of those pundits drew the admiration of the Greeks, but it had no redemptive value whatsoever. This repudiation of the "wisdom words" does not impugn the careful choice of suitable phraseology or "homiletical structure"; but it does point up the fundamental difference between preaching the "wisdom of the world" and the "wisdom of God."

Paul sets in contrast "the [word] of the cross" (1 Cor. 1:18) and the "wisdom of words" (1 Cor. 1:17). The "word" here stands for the preaching of the cross. "The word of the cross," to the Jews was a stumbling block, and to the Greeks, foolishness; but to the called [of God], both Jews and Greeks, it was the power of God and the wisdom of God. "The order 'power' and 'wisdom' is significant. Bengal remarks that we recognize God's power before we recognize His wisdom. They are set in contrast to the human *weakness* and *ignorance* consequent upon the Fall. God's grace allows the discovery of each to those who, acknowledging their sin, accept His conditions in Christ. Christ then provides the remedy."[2]

True biblical preaching is "power" and "wisdom" in the Holy Spirit, and Paul was cognizant of this as he stormed the city of Corinth to capture it for Christ. His dependence was *not* the "persuasive words of human wisdom, but in demonstration of the Spirit and of power" (v. 4). He "determined not to know anything among [them] except Jesus Christ and Him *crucified*" (v. 2, emphasis ours). He knew that a preacher cannot preach a crucified Christ without a crucified life (Gal. 2:20). Only identification with the cross by the power of the Holy Spirit releases both the power and wisdom of God (see 2 Cor. 4:7–12).

This quality of proclamation has three essential ingredients: the motivation, the incarnation, and the presentation of truth.

THE MOTIVATION OF TRUTH

Paul says, "I came to you . . . not . . . with excellence of speech or of wisdom declaring to you the [mystery] of God" (v. 1). His motivation was to share the truth concerning Christ, and Him crucified (v. 2).

A Conscious Call to Preach the Truth

He recalls, "I came to you" (v. 1). While this primarily relates to his historical visit to Corinth, it also implies his sense of call to preach. He could say, "It pleased God. . . . to reveal His Son in me, that I might preach Him [the Truth] among the Gentiles" (Gal. 1:15–16). In another place he exclaims, "Woe is me if I do not preach the gospel!" (1 Cor. 9:16). Preaching, for Paul, found its motivation in a compelling desire to impart the truth of God as revealed in Jesus Christ and Him crucified.

As preachers we need a fresh passion for *truth*. In a pluralistic world and a pessimistic church we must return to the *absolutism* of God's truth as it is in Jesus Christ. The Oxford scholar Alister McGrath, in his recent book *A Passion for Truth: The Intellectual Coherence of Evangelicalism*, states that the two major evangelical intellectual foundations are the centrality of Jesus Christ and the authority of Scripture. He adds that "Evangelical Christianity is . . . unashamedly Christ-centered."[3] Paul, likewise, unashamedly could say: "I *resolved* that while I was with you I would not claim to know anything but Jesus Christ—Christ nailed to the cross" (v. 2 REB). Immediately before the cross, Jesus made this stupendous claim. Looking into the faces of His disciples He declared, "I am . . . the truth" (John 14:6). One of Paul's favorite characterizations of the Christian message is "the truth of the gospel" (Gal. 2:5, 14; Eph. 1:13). No wonder he affirms, "We can do nothing against the truth, but for the truth" (2 Cor. 13:8).

A Consecrated Gift to Preach the Truth

"My speech and my preaching were not with persuasive words of human wisdom, but in demonstration of the Spirit and of power" (v. 4). While Paul sensed his own human weakness, he was nonetheless aware of his God-given gift. Underscore those two words "my *speech* and my *preaching*." *Speech*, most frequently translated *word* (*logos*), signifies discourse—referring to the manner of his setting forth of the gospel; *preaching* points to the contents of his message. The two might be rendered "my preaching and my message" (W. E. Vine).

(*Note:* It is not without significance that the preaching gift is described by the use of some *thirty* different terms in the New Testament!)

The apostle exhorts Timothy—and every preacher since—to do three things in regard to the preaching gift: first, *recognize* the gift—"the gift of God which is in you" (2 Tim. 1:6). For Timothy, this God-given talent was so evident that it was confirmed by the laying on of hands by the elders of the church.

Secondly, *maximize* the gift—"Do not neglect the gift that is in you" (1 Tim. 4:14). The word *neglect* means "to make light of." It occurs in Matthew 22:5 where those invited to the celebration dinner of the king's son "made light" of the royal occasion. It is a serious sin to "make light" of God's gifts. We are all originals, for God never makes duplicates! So we need to drop on our knees and thank Him for our gifting. This forever cures us from the paralysis of envy! Instead, we rejoice in the gifts of others, as well as our own.

Thirdly, *utilize* the gift—"Stir up the gift of God which is in you" (2 Tim. 1:6). For Timothy—and for some of us—the flame (of gifting) can flicker and burn low. By the power of the Holy Spirit we must stir up the gift of God in us day by day.

A Compelling Aim to Preach the Truth

"I determined not to know anything among you except Jesus Christ and Him crucified" (v. 2). Paul had no doubt as to why God had given him the preaching gift. Within the immediate context, Paul spells this out. It was to glorify the Son of God (1 Cor. 1:29, 31), magnify the Word of God (1 Cor. 1:18), edify the church of God (1 Cor. 1:30), and satisfy the heart of God (1 Cor. 1:21). The Lord Jesus and Him crucified *must be* the compelling aim of all our preaching to the world and in the church.

THE INCARNATION OF TRUTH

Paul tells us that he came to Corinth "not . . . with excellence of speech or of wisdom declaring . . . the [testimony] of God" (v. 1). Other versions read "the *mystery* of God," and that does not alter the essential meaning of the apostle's mission or message; but it does change the emphasis. True preaching is an incarnational mystery. That is why it is "foolishness" (1 Cor. 1:23) to the natural mind. Both the incarnation and the crucifixion of Jesus make no sense to those who are perishing. The Greeks had difficulty conceiving how a god, being spirit, could become incarnate and thus provide a God/man atonement for sin. But for us who are saved, and for us who are preachers, the mystery is resolved. In most cases in the New Testament, the word *mystery* refers to the preaching of the gospel and its apprehension (1 Cor. 2:7; 4:1; Eph. 6:19; Col. 4:3). Preaching is best defined in John's Gospel by the majestic statement "the Word became flesh" (1:14). The God who "no one has seen . . . at any time" contracted to the measure of a woman's womb and was born to "flesh out" deity clothed with humanity. This "fleshing out" of the Father is characterized by John as "exegesis"—"He has declared Him" (John 1:18). George R. Beasley-Murray observes that "this 'exegesis' is authoritative by virtue of the unity of the Son with God," expressed in the phrase, 'who is in the bosom of the Father,' in closest fellowship with Him (see John 1:13–23). . . . *The finality of the revelation of God through the Logos-Son could hardly be more strongly expressed*"[4] (emphasis ours). This incarnational revelation is the essence of *redemptive* preaching. What is not incarnational is not redemptive, and what is not redemptive is not life-transforming.

No one has developed this aspect of preaching like the famous preacher Phillips Brooks. In his book *The Joy of Preaching* he spends an entire chapter developing the concept that *preaching is truth through personality*. He maintains that no one can transmit saving truth unless these two elements of truth and personality become incarnational both in preparation and preaching.[5] "Dr. Lloyd-Jones believed preaching involved communication through personality. He remembered Demosthenes, whom he reckoned to be one of the great orators of all time. When the Greek was asked what was the first rule of great oratory, he gave a fulsome answer, 'the first great rule of oratory is action: and the second great rule of oratory is—action: and the third great rule of oratory is—action.'"[6] While Demosthenes was no Christian preacher, he recognized that if a message is to be effectively communicated, it must be *felt* inside and *fleshed* outside! In a word, it must be incarnational. When God chose to reveal Himself redemptively to a sinful world He took *action*; He became flesh.

J. C. Macaulay, writing on this same theme, says: "I have heard ministers say, with a fine air of piety, . . . 'Forget me but remember the truth I am declaring to you.' For one thing, [this] is bad psychology; for another, it is bad divinity, and besides, there is a little hypocrisy in it! When the Word of God is doing its utmost to assure our being kept in remembrance, it is false modesty on our part, to invite our hearers to forget us. Rather, let us give them something vital, something precious, by which to remember us."[7] You cannot detach the messenger from his message if preaching is going to be redemptive and, therefore, life-changing.

We Must Master the Word We Have to Preach

Paul says, "Declaring to you the [mystery] of God" (v. 1). That is quite a phrase! It involves living in the Word of God and in the will of God until we can "open [our mouths] boldly to make known the mystery of the gospel" (Eph. 6:19). This calls for all the demands of preparation that we have delineated in part 2 of this book. The Word of God cannot be mastered until *we are mastered* by the Word of God. Read through the prophets and see how these flaming preachers regarded the Word of the Lord as a *burden*. We read of "the burden which Habakkuk the prophet did see" (Hab. 1:1 KJV); and again: "The burden of the word of the LORD" which came to Zechariah (Zech. 12:1); and once again, "The burden of the word of the LORD" came to Malachi (Mal. 1:1; see also Jer. 23:33–40). These men were so weighed down with the message from Jehovah that they could not keep their peace; they had to declare what God had said to them. Their preaching was a literal unburdening of their souls. Here were prophet/preachers who were not detached from the truth they were seeking to communicate.

We Must Master the Way We "Have to" Preach

"My speech . . . [was] . . . in demonstration of the Spirit and of power" (v. 4). Only the Holy Spirit can take truth and incarnate it in the soul of a preacher. This is a supernatural phenomenon which is beyond human understanding or undertaking. Just as we cannot explain the Virgin Birth, so we cannot explain the incarnational encounter that takes place between the Word and the preacher or between the preacher and the congregation. There is a divine fusion that makes "the Word [become] flesh" (John 1:14). This is what separates preaching from all other forms of human speech or utterance.

When the Virgin Mary became the chosen and willing vessel for the delivery of God's Son (Luke 1:35, 37–38), there was a threefold process that took place. First, there was the *impartation* of the Word—"that which is conceived in her is of the Holy Spirit" (Matt. 1:20). This must take place in every preacher's heart. The manuscript must become the message. Every detail of the structured sermon must be consciously *applied* and *obeyed* until "conception" takes place. Our fervent prayer must be, "Lord, make this alive *to* me and *in* me."

Secondly, there was the *maturation* of the Word—"the days were completed for her to be delivered" (Luke 2:6). This is where so often we fail as preachers. Because we do not "give ourselves continually [exclusively] to prayer and to the ministry of the word" (Acts 6:4) the message is not "mixed with faith" and, therefore, does not "profit" us (Heb. 4:2). We need time for meditation and maturation.

Thirdly, there was the *presentation* of the Word—"She brought forth her . . . Son" (Luke 2:7). We talk about "delivering" a sermon—and we are right. This is incarnational preaching. Our task every time we preach is to "deliver Jesus"!

Of course, it is possible for anyone to get up and recite a memorized sermon or even to parrot verses from the Bible, but this is not preaching. Preaching is an incarnational action that transmits truth through personality to men and women by the power of the Holy Spirit, challenging them for a verdict. We do not understand divine proclamation unless we appreciate this incarnational fact and force. Of all the things we could say about preaching we regard this as of *ultimate* importance. Let us never stand in the pulpit until we can honestly say "the Word has become flesh."

THE PRESENTATION OF TRUTH

"And my speech and my preaching were not with persuasive words of human wisdom, but in demonstration of the Spirit and of power" (v. 4). As we analyze this statement, it becomes apparent that the redemptive event of proclamation requires a vital, vocal, and visual presentation of truth. Let us consider these in turn.

The Vital Aspect of Proclamation
It must be "in demonstration of the Spirit and of power" (v. 4). We must not pass over this statement without an important comment. In

the previous chapter we dealt fully with "the sacred anointing"; but Paul, as he expounds God's Word, adds something else here that every preacher should prayerfully seek. He speaks of his *preaching*, rather than his *person*, and he emphasizes three aspects of divine communication that we desperately need in our pulpits today.

The first is *clarity*. The word *demonstration* indicates a clearness which is produced in the hearer's mind "as by a sudden lifting of a veil" (Godet). It is the Christ-centered conviction impacting the listener with the sovereign force of moral evidence (see 14:24–25).

The second aspect is *mastery*. The genitive "of the Spirit" suggests the control of the Holy Spirit in the act of preaching. This control is the supreme function of the Spirit in the Christian's life (see Eph. 5:18). There is nothing more comforting and compelling than to know that the Lord the Spirit is directing and dominating every word that proceeds out of our mouths. As Martyn Lloyd-Jones puts it: "There is all the difference in the world between preaching merely from human understanding and energy, and preaching [with] *the conscious smile of God*" (emphasis ours).[8] How important it is, therefore, to make sure that we do not "grieve the Holy Spirit of God" (Eph. 4:30) or "quench the Spirit" (1 Thess. 5:19), but rather yield to the Spirit for His control and mastery (Eph. 5:18).

The third aspect of divine communication is *energy*. Once again, we have the genitive "of power." The word here is the familiar *dunamis*, which A. T. Robertson characterizes as "moral power rather than intellectual acuteness" (cf. 1:18). We can justifiably extend this thought, however, to include mental and physical energy. Preaching is strenuous at best; but it is exhausting if not undergirded by the quickening power of the Holy Spirit (Rom. 8:11). As a preacher, Paul could testify, "To this end I am toiling strenuously with all the *energy* and power of Christ at work in me" (Col. 1:29, REB).

The Vocal Aspect of Proclamation

"My *speech* and my *preaching* were not with persuasive words of human wisdom, but in demonstration of the Spirit and of power" (v. 4, emphasis ours). We must not be misled by the modesty with which Paul describes his preaching. The apostle is not seeking to give the impression that he was not careful about what he said and how he said it. His reference, rather, is to what was known as "the Corinthian words" of orators and philosophers in that pagan city. Hours, and even days, were spent listening to speeches and orations, both in stadiums and in auditoriums. Paul is thinking of this as he talks about the presentation of the gospel. Paul found his strength in the anointed authority, simplicity, and humility of Christ and Him crucified, made *real* in Him by the Holy Spirit.

At the same time, it is important to give attention to *vocal* proclamation. The average preacher or evangelist does injustice to the vocal art of preaching. If teaching and training are not available in college or seminary, then we recommend that every preacher should take lessons from those qualified to educate him in the principles of voice production, breath control, and clear articulation.

We have proved the value of professional coaching. Without it we would have paid a severe penalty in later years. Here are some of the exercises we recommend.

The Practice of Building the Voice. Breathe deeply from the diaphragm, and inhale and exhale with measured control. Then vocalize by using musical scales or repeating the alphabet A-Z with exaggerated *accentuation*! Do this daily.

The Practice of Training the Voice. Visualize your congregation and read the Scriptures aloud with careful attention to articulation, pronunciation, and enunciation. Remember what we said in chapter 2 on this subject. In addition to the Scriptures, read at "preaching" speed and vocal variables one of C. H. Spurgeon's sermons, some contemporary ones, and, of course, your own. Do this often.

The Practice of Testing the Voice. Three key words are projection, production, and protection. *Projection* is the ability to "throw" the voice by using the diaphragm correctly to propel air through the vocal chords, off the palate of the mouth, and out to your target congregation. Sound must not come from the throat! *Production* is the art of breath-control. This is vital for sustaining and maintaining the quality of voice and the constancy of sound. *Protection* is the power of restraint. Every preacher must know his strength and limitations if he is to preserve his voice. The secret is one word: control.

The Practice of Resting the Voice. Like every part of the human body, rest is a must! Learn how to rest your voice by disciplined periods of silence, relaxation of muscles—especially at night— with correct head rest or pillow, and minimal use of the phone— the enemy of the voice!

The Practice of Healing the Voice. Here are three tips you will find helpful. Gargle with warm and mild salt water and *not* with astringents. Use throat lozenges or something similar immediately before preaching. Lubrication is essential, especially when the atmosphere is dry or when you are nervous and your saliva glands seem to quit on you. Then rest, rest, rest the voice!

The Practice of Guarding the Voice. Never speak or preach into the flow or draft of an air-conditioner or an outdoor wind. The normal physical reaction to such a situation is the tightening of the muscles of the neck, throat, and larynx with consequent spasms. Never speak or preach with a tight collar and tie. Vigorous preaching can expand your neck by one-quarter of an inch. Never speak or preach by "forcing" your voice beyond your known limits.

The Practice of Using the Voice. When on vacation or traveling, vocalize daily. You will find that the chances of being hoarse or strained will follow a time of inactivity.

Finally, practice speaking correctly and commendably at all times! Our modern TV talk shows and political speeches are a travesty of the English language, and we need to get back to the purity and power of public speech.

Ed Newman, the illustrious reporter and commentator, has written two helpful books on the use of the English language. The first is *Strictly Speaking*[9] and the second is *A Civil Tongue*.[10] We believe that both these works are mandatory reading for the preacher.

One of the reasons why men of the pulpit are not more articulate in their diction is because they are not accurate in their use of language. When a person is tentative in what he says, the net result is that of garbled speech. Think of those words that introduce the Sermon on the Mount. It is recorded that when the Lord Jesus "went up on a mountain, and . . . was seated . . . He *opened* His mouth and taught them" (Matt. 5:1–2). In the Greek, the phrase, "He opened His mouth," has a double significance. It implies "dignified utterance." It also means "opening the heart and pouring out the mind" (William Barclay). Most preachers try to speak through their teeth either because they are unsure of what they are saying or haven't been trained on how to say it.

The Visual Aspect of Proclamation

Paul admits: "I was with you in weakness, in fear, and in much trembling" (v. 3). Phillips' translation reads, "In myself I was feeling far from strong, I was nervous and rather shaky. What I said and preached had none of the attractiveness of the clever mind, but it was a demonstration of the power of the Spirit of God!"

All of us can testify to this sense of weakness and nervousness. G. Campbell Morgan once said that as he made his way to the pulpit each Sunday, Isaiah 53:7 repeatedly came to mind: "He was led as a lamb to the slaughter"!

This nervousness and shakiness of which Paul speaks were undoubtedly subjective and inward, rather than anything he projected outwardly. We cannot read this epistle or any of his other writings without sensing the authority with which Paul wrote. Indeed, in chapter 9, as well as in chapters 11 and 12 of the second letter, Paul defends his authority with competence and confidence. Surely, how he wrote was but a literary expression of how he spoke. When people listened to the great apostle they were aware of this anointed authority.

So it must be with preachers today. While the man of God prays to be eclipsed by the glory of the outshining Christ, he cannot avoid projecting what is his God-given personality. For this reason he must study to eliminate anything calculated to distract from the message he has to deliver. This applies to his *physical appearance*, as well as *personal appeal*. The rule of thumb is what we call the two *Ms*—modesty and mastery. In regard to his physical appearance, the preacher must strive to be modest in dress, looks, and poise. In regard to his personal appeal, he must equally strive, by the power of the Holy Spirit, to master the lust of the flesh, the lust of the eyes, and the pride of life (1 John 2:16). Even behind the sacred desk, the threefold enemy can intrude with devastating results. A preacher who does not know the anointing of the Holy Spirit can be controlled by *carnal domination*—"the lust of the flesh"; *carnal satisfaction*—"the lust of the eyes"; and *carnal reputation*—"the pride of life" (1 John 2:16). This is where we need the application of the cross to our self-life (Rom. 8:13). So we repeat, we cannot preach a crucified Savior without a crucified self-life.

In relation to this visual aspect of proclamation there is such a thing as body language—the look in the eyes, the expression on the face and, especially, the gesture of the hands. These are all part of visual communication. Even the involvement of the body—how a man stands or moves—is part of preaching. This is especially evident in the exertions of a vigorous preacher. Of course, physically and dispositionally men differ in this regard, and therefore every preacher must be himself. As we have said before, God never makes duplicates; He only makes originals. Because of this we deprecate any attempt of a preacher to copy another man's stance, style, or speech. In protecting our God-given identity and Spirit-anointed authority, however, we must remember that our bodies are not our own; they are bought with a price for *the purpose of glorifying God alone* (1 Cor. 6:19–20). Like the Lord Jesus, the Incarnate Word, the glory of God should radiate from our bodies with "grace and truth" (John 1:14).

Thus far we have examined what we mean by Christian proclamation. It calls for the motivation of truth, the incarnation of truth, and the presentation of truth. Once again, we need to be reminded that it is a high and holy calling, and that when we preach we are doing nothing less than declaring "the mystery of God" (v. 1). May Jesus Christ, the Head of the church, open our mouths boldly "to make known the mystery of the gospel" with clarity and confidence (Eph. 6:19–20) "in living color"!

CHAPTER FOURTEEN

THE PREACHER AND COMPREHENSION

It is written: "Eye has not seen, nor ear heard,
nor have entered into the heart of man the things
which God has prepared for those who love
Him." But God has revealed them to us through
His Spirit.

—1 Corinthians 2:9, 10

Study Text: 1 Corinthians 2:6–16

Many people to whom we minister in churches, conferences, or even crusades are religious, but not regenerate. This explains why our united Christian witness lacks the salt of influence and the light of radiance in our English-speaking world. What is more, preachers and pastors are frustrated. They seem to be making no lasting impact upon their congregations. They go through the routines and rituals of weekly services without *spiritual* results. Of course there are the notable exceptions—to the glory of God; but it is the general rule that concerns us.

Anyone who doubts this state of affairs needs to read Eddie Gibbs' book *In Name Only: Tackling the Problem of Nominal Christianity*. He asks:

> Can there be such a person as a "nominal" Christian? Are such people masquerading as believers? Do nominal Christians lack spiritual vitality because they are spiritually malnourished? Or is nominality a fluid state? The normally exemplary believer is not immune from spiritual lethargy. But why are so many who profess Christianity believers "in name only"?
>
> Any assessment of nominality will be influenced by one's theology of the church. Are those on the fringes "fragile" Christians, primarily in need of pastoral care, or *are they unbelievers, eternally lost and in need of the Savior?*[1] (emphasis ours).

Questions like these drive us to examine what we mean by spiritual comprehension. The word *comprehension* means "the act of or capacity for understanding"; and the issue that we have to face in our studies, as well as our pulpits, is one of spiritual comprehension. Do our people have the capacity to understand our message? If not, why not? In essence this is what the apostle Paul was grappling with as he came to Corinth, known for its "persuasive words of human wisdom" (v. 4). "The wise" (the Grecian philosophers) and "the scribe" (the Hebrew scholars) expected Paul to preach in the worldly terms of scholastic learning, convincing logic, forensic reasoning, and cultured eloquence (1 Cor. 1:20). But the apostle refused. He knew that "the natural man does not receive the things of the Spirit of God, for they are foolishness to him; nor can he know them, because they are spiritually discerned" (v. 14). Spiritual comprehension could only occur through preaching "Jesus Christ and Him crucified. . . . in demonstration of the Spirit and of power" (vv. 2, 4). Only such preaching would effect the moral result of the new birth—and consequent spiritual comprehension.

Because of the seeming "foolishness of the message [he] preached" (1 Cor. 1:21), Paul anticipated those who might infer from his argumentation that there is no place in the economy of God for *wisdom* and that Christian truth is wholly outside the realm of the intellect. The apostle meets this objection by pointing out that the gospel *does* contain a wisdom, but that this wisdom is *spiritual* and therefore is only comprehended by spiritual means. He then proceeds to expound the crisis and process by which a person, and hopefully a congregation, can experience spiritual comprehension.

SPIRITUAL INITIATION

"However, we speak wisdom among those who are mature, yet not the wisdom of this age, nor of the rulers of this age, who are coming to nothing. But we speak the wisdom of God in a mystery, the hidden wisdom which God ordained before the ages for our glory" (vv. 6–7). Paul is saying, "Do not imagine that Christianity is devoid of philosophy or wisdom; that it is something outside the realm of the [renewed] intellect; it is not. It has its own wisdom, its own philosophy. Indeed, Christian philosophy is the ultimate philosophy! It is not to be tested by other philosophies; they are to be tried by it. 'We speak wisdom,' he states with absolute finality."[2]

It is clear, therefore, that Paul draws a clear distinction between "the wisdom of this world" and "the wisdom of God" (vv. 21–22). The wisdom of the world is limited by its *age*. This is the word Paul uses. Literally this sentence reads: "However, we speak wisdom among those who are mature [or perfect], yet not the wisdom of this age" (v. 6). The supreme characteristic of human philosophy is that it is always bounded by the age in which it evolves. Men are circumscribed in their reasoning by the period in which they live.

It is not so with divine philosophy. The wisdom of God is timeless and, therefore, changeless. Paul describes this wisdom as a mystery, even "the hidden wisdom which God ordained before the ages for our glory" (v. 7). It is a wisdom that comes out of eternity, invades time, and lives on throughout the ages. *To know such wisdom, men and women must be spiritually initiated.* That is why Paul uses this term "mystery" (v. 7). The Greek word signifies "something whose meaning is hidden from those who have not been initiated, but which is crystal clear to those who have."[3]

Now the question arises as to how men and women can be initiated into this wisdom of God, which is nothing less than the revelation of God in Christ and Him crucified. The answer is implicit in the little word *mature,* which occurs in verse 6—"We speak wisdom among those who are mature." A careful exegesis of the passage makes it plain that Paul equates those who are mature with those who are spiritual (see v. 15). This means that spiritual initiation can only take place where there is a spiritual birth.

A Spiritual Birth

"We speak wisdom among those who are mature" (v. 6). The actual word *mature* denotes the full grown in contrast to the babe. Before there can be spiritual development and maturity there must be a spiritual birth. This was the whole thrust of our Savior's approach to one of the most intellectual and religious men of His day named Nicodemus. Although steeped in theology, he was not born again. To him, the Savior said, "Most assuredly, I say to you, unless one is born again, he cannot *see* the kingdom of God" (John 3:3, emphasis ours). There is only one realm in which the revelation of God can be understood and that is the kingdom of God. That realm can never be entered except by a spiritual initiation—a new birth. So the Master added, "Most assuredly, I say to you, unless one is born of water and the Spirit, he cannot *enter* the kingdom of God" (John 3:5, emphasis ours).

It is of historical significance that this emphasis on the new birth was the overriding burden on the heart of the great evangelist and revivalist George Whitefield (1714–1770) when he came to America. Religious nominalism abounded on every hand. He recognized this at once and started preaching. "Whitefield's essential message to all mankind was 'Ye must be born again!' This brought upon him the wrath of many, but he met their opposition only with kindness."[4] Such preaching transformed Britain and was the chief contribution to the Great Awakening in America. "He preached so as to be understood by the poor and unlearned, but he also ministered to audiences composed of the aristocracy of England and was gladly heard by many great ones in America."[5]

Is it not time we preached in like manner? How can we expect our people to comprehend spiritual things until they "see" and "enter" the kingdom of God by means of the new birth?

Yet spiritual birth is only the beginning.

A Spiritual Growth

"However, we speak wisdom among those who are mature" (v. 6). William Barclay contends that the word *mature* or *perfect* describes "an animal or a person who is full grown and who has reached the height of his physical development."[6] He goes on to say that Paul uses this word to indicate the spiritual and mental growth of those who can appreciate the deep things of God.

Pythagoras divided his disciples into those who were babes and those who were mature—people who had gotten beyond the rudimentary instruction in the elements of any subject. This is the sense in which Paul employs the word.

"Out in the streets, and to those who have just newly come into the Church, we talk about the basic elements of Christianity; but when people are a little more mature we give them deeper teaching about what these basic facts mean."[7] It is in this respect that Paul shuts up the understanding of the wisdom of God to the "initiates." The wisdom of this age passes away or comes to nothing (v. 6), but the eternal wisdom of God, ordained before the world, is designed to bring men and women into the full purpose of God's glory by a crisis and a process of initiation that we call spiritual birth and spiritual growth.

SPIRITUAL ILLUMINATION

"But it is written: 'Eye has not seen, nor ear heard, nor have entered into the heart of man the things which God has prepared for those who love Him.' But God has revealed them to us through His Spirit" (vv. 9–10). One of the hardest lessons men and women have to learn is that human observation, inculcation, and contemplation can never penetrate or discover the deep things of God. The philosophical approach and the scientific method are limited by time and sense and can only bring us to the end of human reasoning. But where human investigation fails, spiritual illumination prevails.

The Revelation of the Spirit

"But God has revealed them to us through His Spirit" (v. 10). To illustrate his point, the apostle says, "For what man knows the things of a man except the spirit of the man which is in him? Even so no one knows the things of God except the Spirit of God" (v. 11). What he is saying is that there are certain things that only a man's spirit can know. Every one of us is aware of this. No one can really see into our hearts and know what is there except our own spirits.

The same thing is true of God. There are deep and intimate things about God that only God's Spirit knows; therefore, only the Holy Spirit can lead us to understand the mind of God. To put it in another form, there are areas of truth that the unaided power of thought can never find out. The Holy Spirit alone must reveal them to us. This is why the Lord Jesus, when leaving His disciples, promised them the Holy Spirit who would teach them all things, and bring all things to their remembrance (John 14:26).

The Exploration of the Spirit

"For the Spirit searches all things, yes, the deep things of God" (v. 10). The function of the Holy Spirit is not only to reveal truth as it is in Christ but also to explore truth. The verb *searches* in our text is a most interesting one. It occurs in the Moulton and Milligan's vocabulary "for a professional searcher's report, and for the search of customs officials."[8] Just as an experienced customs official brings to light the hidden articles from a traveler's suitcase, so the Holy Spirit, in a more transcendent sense, explores the deep and hidden things of God and makes them understandable and available to the humblest Christian who is prepared to trust Him.

The apostle John teaches the same truth when he informs his children in the faith, "You have an anointing from the Holy One, and you know all things" (1 John 2:20). This amazing phenomenon is what baffles the intellectuals of every age. The philosophers and scientists have never been able to understand how it is that even the unlettered mind can appreciate and discuss truths that are totally unknown to the world at large. The answer, of course, is that there is such a thing as spiritual illumination.

The Lord Jesus rejoiced in this fact when He exclaimed, "I thank You, Father, Lord of heaven and earth, that You have hidden these things from the wise and prudent and revealed them to babes. Even so, Father, for so it seemed good in Your sight" (Luke 10:21). When Peter made his great confession concerning the deity and messiahship of Jesus Christ, the Master commended him with these significant words, "Simon Bar-Jonah, . . . flesh and blood has not revealed this to you, but My Father who is in heaven" (Matt. 16:17).

There is nothing more sublime than to share in the revelation and exploration of the Spirit of God. Anyone who has reached this point can say with the apostle Paul: "Now we have received, not the spirit of the world, but the Spirit who is from God, that we might know the things that have been freely given to us by God" (v. 12).

Thus far we have seen that complete comprehension of the Christian message, requires not only spiritual initiation but also spiritual illumination. Yet there is a third necessity we must discuss.

SPIRITUAL INTERPRETATION

"These things we also speak, not in words which man's wisdom teaches but which the Holy Spirit teaches, comparing spiritual things with spiritual" (v. 13). We now reach a point in Paul's argument where we need to follow him very closely. Verse 13 is often used as a proof text by proponents of verbal inspiration—a doctrine that is biblical. But Paul says here, "we . . . speak" not "we . . . write." Thus he is referring to interpretation rather than inspiration. He is teaching us that a knowledge of truth can be arrived at by an understanding of two necessary essentials: the Spirit's use of language and the Spirit's terms of reference.

The Spirit's Use of Language

"These things we also speak, not in words which man's wisdom teaches but which the Holy Spirit teaches" (v. 13). It cannot be emphasized enough that he who knows the mind of God also chooses the words of God to interpret divine truth. This is essentially the ministry of the Holy Spirit. What an importance this places on expository preaching throughout this church age. The preacher's task by the power of the Holy Spirit is to interpret the Bible to men and women who know the experience of spiritual initiation and illumination.

Let it be emphasized, however, that the Holy Spirit never speaks outside of the context of the divine revelation we call the Holy Bible. That is why we need to give special attention to the Spirit's use of language. Not one jot or tittle is inconsequential. This is why Jesus said, "Till heaven and earth pass away, one jot or one tittle will by no means pass from the law till all is fulfilled" (Matt. 5:18). He also added, "When He, the Spirit of truth, has come, He will guide you into all truth" (John 16:13). This is the secret of interpretation: the Spirit using His own words to make known the mind of God.

The Spirit's Terms of Reference

"The Holy Spirit . . . comparing spiritual things with spiritual" (v. 13). Commentators have differed in their interpretation of this sentence. Some say it means "matching spiritual things with spiritual words." Others maintain that it reads "interpreting spiritual things by spiritual men." In either case, the point the apostle Paul is making is that "no prophecy of Scripture is of any *private* [isolated] interpretation" (2 Pet. 1:20 emphasis ours). The Holy Spirit has His terms of reference, and through the body of truth—the Bible—here is sufficient support for every cardinal doctrine we hold dear.

What is more, we have what is known as the Christian tradition which is made up of the contributions of spiritual men throughout the centuries. Therefore we are not left in the dark about divine revelation. There is no truth vital to Christian life and practice that does not have the support of both divine revelation and Christian tradition. When Paul writes to Timothy concerning the communication and comprehension of divine truth, he says, "And the things that you have heard from me among many witnesses, commit these to faithful men who will be able to teach others also" (2 Tim. 2:2).

Paul concludes this amazing paragraph by pointing out that "the natural man does not receive the things of the Spirit of God, for they are foolishness to him; nor can he know them, because they are spiritually discerned" (v. 14). The plain fact is that without spiritual initiation, illumination, and interpretation, *truth is nothing more than foolishness to the unregenerate*-the man of the world. He looks upon revelation as an absurdity. Once we have understood this we have an explanation of the attitude that is adopted by the non-Christian to spiritual things. We must, therefore, be patient with him and pray that he may submit to the terms of divine revelation.

On the other hand, states the apostle, "He who is spiritual judges all things, yet he himself is rightly judged by no one" (v. 15). The person who knows spiritual initiation, illumination, and interpretation possesses a God-imparted ability to "read, learn and inwardly digest" the things that are divinely revealed.

At the same time, the Christian cannot be subject to the examination or judgment of the one who is destitute of the Spirit. No unregenerate person has the right to criticize or judge a believer regarding his personal faith in Christ. He is without the faculty of spiritual discernment and, therefore, cannot understand the nature of the miracle that has taken place. Just as he cannot judge the Christian, so he cannot instruct the Lord (v. 16). It is human impertinence for the natural man to raise his voice against the God he is unwilling to accept.

By way of contrast, however, the Christian has *the mind of Christ*. The whole passage closes with this astounding conclusion. The wisdom of God is nothing less than the mind of Christ. The word *mind* here means "intellect" or "consciousness." We have the consciousness of Christ, the mind of Christ, the outlook of Christ. This is not the same word that Paul uses in the Epistle to the Philippians (chap. 2). There it "implies moral interest or 'reflection,'" (W. E. Vine); here it is the intelligent understanding or wisdom of God.

How awesome is the realization that we, as preachers, can know the very mind of the Son of God! (v. 16). The wonder of it all is that throughout time and eternity we are going to continue to explore that mind, and so become more and more like Jesus. What a vast universe of knowledge, life, and blessing stretches out before us! Just to contemplate it makes us feel like Sir Isaac Newton when he remarked, "I am like a little child standing by the seashore, picking up a pebble here and a pebble there and admiring them while the great sea rolls in front of me."

Paul climaxes this critical subject with the loftiest of concepts. He tells these Corinthians, and those of us living today, that when we have experienced the initiation, illumination and interpretation of the Holy Spirit, we qualify to comprehend *the mind of Christ.* This is the ultimate comprehension!

Our solemn responsibility, as preachers, is "to make known" the mind of Christ (Eph. 6:19). The word *mind* comprehends "the thoughts and counsels of God" (W. E. Vine) as revealed in Christ. Paul has already spelled these out in 1 Corinthians 1:30. Four doctrinal terms are used to unveil the mind of Christ:

Wisdom. Those who are in Christ Jesus have the mind of Christ. Through the indwelling ministry of the Holy Spirit, they are able to perceive and comprehend the plans and purposes of God which are hidden from the rest of the world.

Righteousness. That which is so elusive to us that we can never apprehend it is made available to us in Christ. Our sinfulness is transferred to Him on the cross. We in turn are accorded His righteousness.

Sanctification. The term righteousness *(dikaiosune)* is forensic in nature, having to do with our legal standing before God. If our salvation, however, were limited to a right standing before God, then the effects of salvation would be primarily eschatological and of only relative consequence for the present. Such is not the case, since Christ is also made our sanctification. Those who are in Christ are thus set apart to God, becoming partakers of His holiness (Heb. 12:10).

Redemption. The word redemption *(apolutrosis)* means "to loose or to free by means of payment." There is a sense in which we are slaves to sin and desire (Titus 3:3). The cross of Jesus Christ not only provided for us the mind of Christ, right standing before God, and position in the holiness of God, but it also released us from the slavery and the penalty of our sin.[9]

No wonder the apostle exclaims, "He who glories, let him glory in the LORD" (1 Cor. 1:31).

May the mind of Christ, my Saviour,
Live in me from day to day,
By His love and pow'r controlling
All I do and say.

May the Word of God dwell richly
In my heart from hour to hour,
So that all may see I triumph
Only through His pow'r.

May the peace of God, my Father,
Rule my life in everything,
That I may be calm to comfort
Sick and sorrowing.

May the love of Jesus fill me,
As the waters fill the sea;
Him exalting, self abasing,
This is victory.

May I run the race before me,
Strong and brave to face the foe,
Looking only unto Jesus
As I onward go.

May His beauty rest upon me
As I seek the lost to win,
And may they forget the channel,
Seeing only Him.

—Kate B. Wilkinson

CHAPTER FIFTEEN

THE PREACHER AND APPLICATION

God be thanked that though you were slaves of sin, yet you obeyed from the heart that form of doctrine to which you were delivered.
—***Romans 6:17***

Study Text: Romans 6:1–23

Webster's New World Dictionary defines *application* as "relevance." While relevance is an overused term in religious jargon, it is an indispensable component of biblical preaching. That which is relevant is germane and apposite. It would be safe to say that there is no part of Scripture that is unrelated to some aspect of faith and life. C. H. Spurgeon used to tell his students that "Where application begins, there the sermon begins!"

251

In an interview in *Preaching* magazine, John R. W. Stott had this to say: "In my early days I used to think that my business was to expound and exegete the text; I am afraid I left the application to the Holy Spirit. It is amazing how you can conceal your laziness with a little pious phraseology! The Holy Spirit certainly can and does apply the Word for the people. But it is wrong to deny our own responsibility in the application of the Word. All great preachers understand this. They focus on the conclusion, on the application of the text. This is what the Puritans called 'preaching through to the heart.' This is how my own preaching has changed. I have learned to add application to exposition."[1]

Haddon W. Robinson states with characteristic candor: "Application is not incidental to effective expository preaching, it is crucial! In relating the Bible to experience, however, the expositor dare not twist the Scriptures to fit men's lives. Instead, he calls men to bring themselves into subjection to the standards of the Bible. Christians must conform to the age to come, not this present age. The application moves both ways. Biblical truth must be related to men's lives; but on the other hand, men's lives must be changed to be relevant to biblical faith."[2]

One of the key verses in Scripture on the use of biblical application is Romans 6:17. Before we consider it in context, let us suggest three laws that are inherent in the art of biblical application: the law of content, the law of intent, and the law of movement. Let us examine each of these laws in the light of our text.

THE LAW OF CONTENT IN THE APPLICATION OF SCRIPTURE

"God be thanked that . . . you obeyed from the heart that form of doctrine to which you were delivered" (v. 17). The operative word here is *doctrine* or "teaching." In preaching, it is impossible—leave alone irresponsible—to apply supracultural principles without the content of truth. Therefore we must examine the context to discover the content.

Paul's theme throughout this chapter is "newness of life" (v. 4), which comes through union with Christ and freedom from sin (vv. 5–7). For doctrine to be applied, there has to be syllogism and symbolism in our exposition of a given passage.

Biblical Application Demands Doctrinal Syllogism

"God be thanked that . . . you obeyed from the heart that form of doctrine to which you were delivered" (v. 17). Simply stated, syllogism is deductive logic. It means reasoning from the general to the particular. What confuses most people in our congregations is the preaching of generalities. Indeed, it is a well-nigh hopeless task to apply generalities. The man or women in the pew is saying: "Be specific; be logical; give me an example."

So we find Paul in these verses arguing from the general fact of sin in the believer's life to the specific force of Christ in the believer's life. By union with Christ in death, burial, and resurrection, we can know victory; and even more than this, deliverance! Paul exclaims, "Sin shall not have dominion over you, for you are not under law but under grace. . . . Shall we sin because we are not under law but under grace? Certainly not!" (vv. 14–15). Having reached that conclusion, he bursts forth with the words of our text, "God be thanked that . . . you obeyed from the heart that form of doctrine to which you were delivered" (v. 17).

God has made men and women to understand logic, even though they may not be schooled in this discipline. This is what distinguishes us from brute creation; hence the need for reason, argumentation, and homiletics in our preaching.

The average listener wants to know your dominating theme, your integrating thoughts, and your motivating thrust. If he cannot follow you from 1 to 2 then it is very unlikely that he will reach number 3. The very use of syllogism, which is an essential part of exposition, is a form of application. Every member in the congregation must be able to say, "I can hear you"; "I am with you"; "That makes sense!"

Biblical Application Demands Doctrinal Symbolism

"God be thanked that . . . you obeyed from the heart that *form* of doctrine to which you were delivered" (v. 17, emphasis ours). Symbolism is the *form* with which God frames His word pictures. In this case, as the passage shows, the form is baptism. Paul says,

> Therefore we were buried with Him through baptism into death, that just as Christ was raised from the dead by the glory of the Father, even so we also should walk in newness of life. For if we have been united together in the likeness of His death, certainly we also shall be in the likeness of His resurrection, knowing this, that our old man was crucified with Him, that the body of sin might be done away with, that we should no longer be slaves of sin. For he who has died has been

freed from sin. Now if we died with Christ, we believe that we shall also live with Him, knowing that Christ, having been raised from the dead, dies no more. Death no longer has dominion over Him. For the death that He died, He died to sin once for all; but the life that He lives, He lives to God. Likewise you also, reckon yourselves to be dead indeed to sin, but alive to God in Christ Jesus our Lord (vv. 4–11).

Nothing could be clearer than the three aspects of baptism to illustrate and apply the doctrine of deliverance from sin. The very practice of baptism involves immersion, submersion, and emergence, and this symbolizes death, burial, and resurrection. Paul says, "[We] were baptized into His *death*" (v. 3, emphasis ours). The Lord Jesus spoke of His death as a baptism. He declared, "I have a baptism to be baptized with, and how distressed I am till it is accomplished!" (Luke 12:50). That baptism took place when the holy Son of God was immersed in the waves and billows of divine wrath against sin (see Ps. 69:1–2).

Now the amazing fact is that in that death *w e* also died. In that awful judgment *w e* were also judged. In the sight of God, therefore, our standing in Adam came to an end there and then. This means that we who were, in Adam, dead *in* sin are now, in Christ, dead *to* sin.

But more than this, baptism is union with Christ in His *burial*. "Therefore we were buried with Him through baptism into death, that just as Christ was raised from the dead by the glory of the Father, even so we also should walk in newness of life" (v. 4). To leave a dead body unburied was, to both Jew and Greek, the greatest possible indignity. So for the Christian, nothing could be more shameful than to dig up the past. When a man is buried, he is out of sight and soon beyond all possibility of recognition or identification.

Praying Hyde of India observed: "It is not enough to have the self-life crucified. It must be buried, for the stench of it will drive souls away from Jesus."

But once again, baptism is union with Christ in His *resurrection*—"That just as Christ was raised from the dead by the glory of the Father, even so we also should walk in newness of life. For if we have been united together in the likeness of His death, certainly we also shall be in the likeness of His resurrection" (vv. 4–5). Resurrection can only follow where death has taken place. The old life must die before the new life can emerge. This new life is wholly from God. This is why the apostle declares, "Therefore, if anyone is in Christ, he is a new creation; old things have passed away; behold, all things have become new" (2 Cor. 5:17).

So we see how biblical application is dramatized by doctrinal symbolism; and when we speak of symbolism, we use it in the broadest sense. Symbolism might be a choice quotation, a pertinent observation, or a suitable illustration (like the ordinance of baptism cited in our text). The point is that the preacher is applying doctrine by means of syllogism and symbolism.

THE LAW OF INTENT IN THE APPLICATION OF SCRIPTURE

Once again, "God be thanked that . . . you obeyed from the heart that form of doctrine to which you were delivered" (v. 17). Here we pick up on the word *delivere d*. The verb means "to be handed over," "to commit," or "to surrender." As we have seen, baptism symbolizes our union with Christ. Therefore, to be handed over to the "form" or "mold" of the teaching of the gospel is to bring the listener into conformity with our Lord and Savior Jesus Christ. This "handing over" or commitment takes place in the act of preaching. Here, once again, is applied theology. This calls for *conscious intent* in preaching.

We Must Be Personal in Our Application

Paul says, "*Yo u* were delivered" (v. 17, emphasis ours). That personal pronoun occurs some thirty-three times in twenty-three verses in this one chapter! Paul is pressing home the fact that his readers were slaves of sin, to whom they surrendered obedience. The Roman Christians, to whom Paul wrote, had been slaves to sin, but now they had "obeyed from the heart that form of doctrine to which [they] were delivered" (v. 17). They had heard God's Word and had allowed it to influence their lives. Like a "form" or "mold," it had shaped them into the image of holiness. They had been made free from sin and had, instead, become slaves of righteousness (vv. 17–18). God's will for them (v. 19) is God's will for you and me. Instead of presenting the members of their bodies to sin, they were now to present themselves to God. Throughout this entire treatment of sin versus righteousness, the emphasis is on you . . . you . . . you. *We* must be personal in our application.

We Must Be Practical in Our Application

"You obeyed from the heart that form of doctrine to which you were delivered" (v. 17). Implicit in that word *delivere d* is a call to practical action. As we preach, we must keep in mind that we have a target, and we must aim to hit it. There are practical steps that we must clearly set forth in reaching our goal. So many people hear the *what* of our message but never hear the *how* of our message.

A distinguished medical doctor who had been led to Christ was asked why he had never made a decision until that particular point in time. His answer was astonishing. He simply said, "Nobody ever told me *how* to be saved." He had heard many gospel messages but had never learned how to yield to the claims of Christ. To put it bluntly, there was no practical application in the preaching!

There are three practical applications that should be included in every sermon.

There Must Be the Call to Biblical Repentance. In our overreactions against Reformation preaching on works versus faith, and in our rejection of Arminian activism, we have fallen into the philosophical habit of thinking, "How can I preach man's responsibility to repent when I know he has no ability to do this?" Apparently this problem did not bother the apostle Paul. No one spoke more clearly than he of man's utter inability to do anything to save himself, and yet he preached man's responsibility to repent. Addressing the Ephesian elders, he declared, "I . . . taught you publicly and from house to house, testifying to Jews, and also to Greeks, repentance toward God and faith toward our Lord Jesus Christ" (Acts 20:20–21). Later in Damascus and throughout Judea he proclaimed that men "should repent, turn to God, and do works befitting repentance" (Acts 26:20).

When we speak of repentance we are not thinking of the sinner only, but also of the saint. Four of the seven churches addressed by our risen Lord in the Book of Revelation are told to repent. We have lost the sense of sin; so we have ceased to preach repentance. This must change—fast!

There Must Be the Call to Biblical Renewal. Our preaching is weak in application when we fail to present the whole Christ to the whole man. For the sinner, the call will be for regeneration; for the saint, the call will be for revival—which is a return to normal Christian living. This will involve being daily filled with the Holy Spirit and walking in unquestioned *obedience* to the Word of God under the lordship of Christ.

There Must Be the Call to Biblical Reality. We live in a day of nominal Christianity, rather than biblical Christianity. Paul never hesitated to challenge Christians to "examine [themselves] as to whether [they were] in the faith" (2 Cor. 13:5). We must not hesitate to proclaim from the pulpit: "Brethren, . . . make your call and election sure" (2 Pet. 1:10). Al Martin puts it this way:

> I have found that such preaching never harms the true child of God. The most searching applicatory preaching in this area will serve to bring the true child of God to a more solid assurance. The only thing that stands to be harmed by a close scrutiny is the counterfeit. Suppose I were to go to my local bank to deposit two $20 bills. If the teller were to take them and say to me, "Just a minute, . . . I think there might be a counterfeit here." If those bills are genuine, they stand to lose nothing by the close scrutiny which the bank teller gives them. In fact, they gain something.[3]

We Must Be Purposeful in Our Application

"God be thanked that . . . you obeyed from the heart that form of doctrine" (v. 17). In the final analysis, that word *form* implies conformity to Christ. Paul always had this goal in his ministry to the church. He could say, "Christ in you, the hope of glory. Him we preach, warning every man and teaching every man in all wisdom, that we may present every man perfect in Christ Jesus. To this end I also labor, striving according to His working which works in me mightily" (Col. 1:27–29). He again reminds the believers at Corinth that "we all, with unveiled face, beholding as in a mirror the glory of the Lord, are being transformed into the same image from glory to glory, just as by the Spirit of the Lord" (2 Cor. 3:18).

In the last analysis, the whole purpose of preaching the Word is to bring people into conformity to Christ. Referring to the Old Testament, the apostle declares, "All Scripture is given by inspiration of God, and is profitable for doctrine, for reproof, for correction, for instruction in righteousness, that the man of God may be *complete*, thoroughly equipped for every good work" (2 Tim. 3:16–17, emphasis ours). "Power without a purpose is piffle." Those words were the motto of a British college, but they are relevant right here. One of our greatest failures in preparation and proclamation is carelessness about the intent (purpose) of our preaching.

THE LAW OF MOVEMENT IN THE APPLICATION OF SCRIPTURE

"You obeyed from the *heart* that form of doctrine to which you were delivered" (6:17, emphasis ours). W. E. Vine, in his *Expository Dictionary of Biblical Words*, defines what Paul means by the word *heart*. It is the Greek *kardia* from which we get our word "cardiac" or "cardiology." It is "the chief organ of physical life ('for the life of the flesh is in the blood,' Lev. 17:11), [and] occupies the most important place in the human system. By an easy transition the word came to stand for man's entire mental and moral activity, both the rational and the emotional elements. In other words, the heart is used figuratively for the hidden springs of the personal life."[4] Peter calls the heart "the hidden man" (1 Pet. 3:4)— literally "the inmost self" (REB).

So we see that the heart includes the mind, the heart, and the will. Given that frame of reference, we must recognize that if preaching is going to be applied with any degree of effectiveness there must be *movement* in the application of truth. We must move from the mind to the heart and from the heart to the will.

The Mind Must Be Educated by Our Preaching

To obey from the heart (v. 17) involves this educative process. The emphasis here must be on the exercise of discernment. The writer to the Hebrews underscores this need for discernment when he says, "For everyone who partakes only of milk is unskilled in the word of righteousness, for he is a babe. But solid food belongs to those who are of full age [those who have reached maturity], that is, those who by reason of use have their senses exercised to discern both good and evil" (Heb. 5:13–14). The problem with so much preaching today is that the average communicator is "unskilled in the word [or standard] of righteousness" (Heb. 5:13). As a consequence, our people have no discernment between good and evil. Shallow preaching will produce nothing more than shallow Christians. We must apply truth to the mind if we are going to have an educated church.

The Heart Must Be Motivated by Our Preaching

Motive refers to any impulse, emotion, or desire that moves someone to action. For example, we read in the newspaper that a certain individual's only motive for stealing was greed. The emphasis here is not so much on discernment, but *desire*.

We have never finished preaching until we have lit the fires of desire that motivate members of our congregation to seek after God or to hunger after righteousness or to pray for missionaries or to help the poor—and the list could go on.

The Will Must Be Activated by Our Preaching

Here the emphasis is on *decision*. We have to learn that surrender is the conquest of the will. If the rest of the life is not right, the reason is that the will has not been surrendered. The great crisis is when we surrender the will. God never crushes a man's will into surrender. He beseeches him, as Paul says in Romans 12:1–2. He waits until the man thoroughly yields his will up to Him. Jesus said, "If any man *will* come after me, let him deny himself" (Luke 9:23 KJV). The surrender here involves the handing over of our selfhood to Jesus. "If you would be My disciple," said Jesus, "then give Me the rights to yourself." Once the full surrender of the will has taken place, the consequences are in God's hands. The crisis of surrender is all that God wants from you and me. This involves a Gethsemane, but when a Gethsemane is truly experienced, it never needs to be repeated. These are hard-hitting words, but they are a paraphrase of Oswald Chambers' treatment of the battlefield of the will.

So we see that there must be *movement* in the application of Scripture. There are three essential elements in a sermon: unity, movement, and purpose. First, there is *unity*, which is the theme of the sermon. That theme must never be lost in the delivery of the sermon. It is what integrates the line of thinking. Secondly, there is *movement*. That movement must educate the mind, motivate the heart, and activate the will. Such movement is the accumulative application of truth until the whole man bows to the claims of Jesus as Lord. Thirdly, there is *purpose*. The ultimate goal of all teaching or preaching is conformity to Christ.

Here, then, are the three laws of biblical application. There must be content. Without doctrine there can be no application of truth. Secondly, there must be intent. The preacher must know where he is going. Therefore, his application must be personal, practical, and purposeful. Finally, there must be movement. It is not sufficient to satisfy the mind; that only produces the intellectual convert. It is not sufficient to win the heart; that only produces the emotional convert. It is not sufficient to strengthen the will; that only produces the volitional convert. The movement in preaching must affect the whole personality—mind, heart, and will. To do this, as we have observed, we must educate the mind, motivate the heart, and activate the will. Failure to fulfill these laws of biblical application is failure to fulfill what is 50 percent of our preaching responsibility.

As John Stott has put it: "It is wrong to deny our own responsibility in the application of the Word. All great preachers understand this. They focus on the conclusion, on the application of the
text. This is what the Puritans called 'preaching through to the
heart.'"[5] Paul said it best: "God be thanked that . . . you obeyed
from the heart that form of doctrine to which you were delivered"
(v. 17). God make us preachers who can send our congregations
away, Sunday by Sunday, *shaped* in the mold of Christ through
the Spirit-anointed application of truth!

CHAPTER SIXTEEN

THE PREACHER AND INVITATION

We are ambassadors for Christ, as though God were pleading through us: we implore you on Christ's behalf, be reconciled to God. For He made Him who knew no sin to be sin for us, that we might become the righteousness of God in Him.

—2 Corinthians 5:20–21

Study Text: 2 Corinthians 5:14–6:4

John Stott, in his book *The Preacher's Portrait*, rightly points out that *"we must never issue an appeal [invitation] without first making the proclamation*. Much harm has been done to the souls of men, and much dishonor brought to the name of Christ, through neglect of this simple rule. . . . The gospel is not fundamentally an invitation to men to do anything. It is a declaration of what God has done in Christ on the cross for their salvation. The invitation cannot properly be given before the declaration has been made. Men must grasp the truth before they are asked to respond to it." On the other hand, *"we must never make the proclamation without then issuing an appeal [invitation]. . . .* It is not enough to teach the gospel; we must urge men to embrace it"[1] (emphasis ours).

In spite of a clear statement such as this, we would venture to say that there is much confusion among preachers over this matter of the invitation.[2] It is important, therefore, that the preacher should carefully think through this question of the invitation in the light of Scripture, and then fulfill the injunction of the apostle Paul who commands in categorical terms, "Preach the word! . . . *do the work* [aorist imperative] of an evangelist" (2 Tim. 4:2, 5, emphasis ours). Let us remember that by definition the "evangelist" possesses the God-given ability to preach and invite people (saints and sinners alike) to respond to the Word of God. It is true that some preachers are better sowers, while others are better reapers; but whether sowers or reapers, every proclaimer behind the pulpit *must* "Preach the word! . . . [and] *do the work of an evangelist."* With the Scripture reading before us, let us now learn some of the basic principles that determine the legitimate use of the invitation in the preaching event.

A careful reading of Paul's second epistle to the Corinthians makes it abundantly clear that chapters 5 and 6 contain the central theme of his letter. In essence, it is a clarion call to proclaim the *word* of reconciliation (5:19) and to perform the *work* of reconciliation (6:1). As R. V. G. Tasker succinctly states it: "In Chapter 5 and verse 20 Paul has spoken of the *appeal* [emphasis ours] that God makes to men through the preaching of His apostles. The work of evangelism is therefore a work in which man cooperates with God (see 1 Cor. 3:9); so Paul can and must appeal to his readers to receive the salvation God offers."[3] To follow through the apostle's close argumentation is to trace not only the preacher's responsibility in the proclamation, but also the *preacher's responsibility in the invitation*. Let us then follow this theme and consider the pattern, the purpose, the power, and even the peril of the gospel invitation. In doing this, we are principalizing the applications to demonstrate how to preach for a verdict.

THE PATTERN OF THE INVITATION

"We are ambassadors for Christ, as though God were pleading through us: we implore you on Christ's behalf, be reconciled to

God. For He made Him who knew no sin to be sin for us, that we might become the righteousness of God in Him" (5:20–21). These verses help us to understand the relationship of proclamation to the invitation. God is revealed to us here as the Preacher, and therefore as the supreme Pattern for those of us who would rise to this holy calling of inviting—yes, and imploring—men and women to be reconciled to God.

Two remarkable disclosures of God are seen here.

We See God Becoming Man

"For He made Him who knew no sin to be sin for us, that we might become the righteousness of God in Him" (5:21). Before God could take upon Himself the sin of the world *He had to become man*; and in that sinless body He endured the full penalty of sin in dying upon the cross. He assumed our total sinfulness in order that we might accept IIis total righteousness. In this paradox of all paradoxes, we discover a solemn but significant principle. It is simply this: before we can issue an invitation to men and women to be reconciled to God, we must identify with humanity's predicament. This does not in any way imply compromise. To identify with human need does not, and must not, involve actual sinning. On the other hand, in our preaching we must declare our message as dying men to dying men; or to put it another way, as saved sinners we must relate to lost sinners. In short, there must be a "humanness" about our invitation.

After years of preaching, we have learned from Scripture and from our own experience that there can exist a gulf between the preacher and the needy soul out in the audience. The very nature of preaching can make a person feel so removed and alienated from the proclaimer that the power of appeal is nullified.

In order to reconcile us to Himself, God actually became sin for us, even though He knew no sin, in order that "we might become the righteousness of God in Him" (5:21). Therefore *we see God becoming man*; and this must be our pattern when issuing the invitation.

We See God Beseeching Man

"We are ambassadors for Christ, as though God were pleading through us" (5:20). How can anyone understand these words without tears? Here is the Almighty Creator, Preserver, Redeemer, and Judge of all men pictured on His knees, entreating sinners to be reconciled to Himself. In the words of Alexander Maclaren, we see "Love upon the Throne [bending] down to ask of the rebel that lies powerless and sullen at His feet . . . [to] put away all . . . bitterness . . . and come back to the love and the grace which are ready to pour over him."[4] This is a staggering thought, to be sure, but nonetheless true. In fact, this is the strongest argument for persuading men to come to terms with the claims of Jesus Christ. If God beseeches men by us, how can we dodge the responsibility of issuing an invitation once we have proclaimed the gospel of a reconciling God?

We once lectured on the subject of the invitation using the above quote from a sermon by Alexander Maclaren. A young seminarian jumped up from his seat and yelled: "How dare you reduce God to a beggar on His knees, pleading with sinners!" After a quiet pause we replied, "Young man, go *beyond* Maclaren's characterization. See God in Christ not only on His knees, but on a wooden cross, bleeding from head, hands, and feet, with outstretched arms pleading with sinners to be reconciled to Himself!"

This, then, is the pattern of invitation, revealed in God who is our Savior and Teacher. By becoming man and beseeching man, He spells out the true nature of the preacher's invitation; and we can do no other than accept this pattern.

THE PURPOSE OF THE INVITATION

Our text informs us that God has committed to us "the ministry of reconciliation" (5:18). As ambassadors, we are to go out and call men to decision, confession, and instruction. No one understands the nature of the gospel invitation without appreciating these three elements in the evangelistic appeal.

There Must Be Decision

"Be reconciled to God" (5:20). For a true evangelistic decision to be made, the mind must be satisfied, the heart must be stirred, and the will must be strengthened to respond to Christ. This is beautifully illustrated in one of the great invitation texts of the Bible. Jesus positions Himself at the door of the human heart and appeals, "Behold, I stand at the door and knock. If anyone hears My voice and opens the door, I will come in and dine with him, and he with Me" (Rev. 3:20). While these words are primarily addressed to a lukewarm church, they serve to illustrate the kind of response that the Lord Jesus expects from saint and sinner alike. Leon Morris says it best: "Christ is there now standing at the door. He is knocking, where the present tense signifies not a perfunctory rap, but a knocking continued *in the hope of response*"5 (emphasis ours).

Let us notice first of all, that the appeal is to the faculty of *perception*—"*Behold*, I stand at the door and knock" (Rev. 3:20). Men and women are invited to focus on Christ and to see in Him, and in Him alone, their Savior and Lord.

Then there is the faculty of *emotion*—"*If anyone hears* my voice." There is no power on earth calculated to stir the heart like the voice of Christ. "Faith comes from hearing the message, and the message is heard *through the word of Christ*" (Rom. 10:17 NIV, emphasis ours). God's final message to a sin-cursed race is, "This is My beloved Son, in whom I am well pleased. *Hear Him!*" (Matt. 17:5, emphasis ours). How often we have witnessed hard-hearted men and women *melt* when quoting the words of Jesus!

This leads to the faculty of *volition*—"If anyone . . . *opens the door*, I will come in to him and dine with him, and he with Me." In His inscrutable wisdom and sovereignty, God has given us the freedom to choose. We can open the door, or we can shut the door of our lives to Him. And what is true of the lukewarm Christian is equally true of the lost sinner.

So in calling for a decision, we must remember these three essential elements of perception, emotion, and volition (or mind, heart, and will). This only emphasizes again the importance of proclamation and invitation.

There Must Be Confession

"The love of Christ compels us, because we judge thus: that if One died for all, then all died; and He died for all, *that those who live should live no longer for themselves, but for Him who died for them and rose again*" (5:14–15, emphasis ours). If the sinner (or saint) has truly understood the nature of God's love in Christ revealed at Calvary, then there is only one option he can justifiably follow, and that is to live unto Him who died and rose again. This calls for open confession. In grateful response to the One who died upon a cross before the gaze of a mocking world, the saved sinner will want to identify with Jesus before the same mocking world.

We cannot read the Gospels without observing that Jesus seldom permitted people who sought blessing from Him to leave without confessing Him. According to Kendell Easley, professor of New Testament and Greek at Mid-America Baptist Theological Seminary, Memphis, Tennessee: "The Gospels should be understood as *kerygma* (preaching) which originated in first-century churches. The first preachers, of course, were the apostles. What did they preach, except what they remembered of their beloved Master? In many ways the Gospels are simply the collective memories, the preaching material, of one or more of the apostles *and . . . each of them contains a serious call to commitment*"[6] (emphasis ours).

The man with the withered hand had to stand publicly before his critics before the healing miracle took place. So we read that Jesus said to him, "Step forward," *then* added, "Stretch out your hand" (Mark 3:3, 5).

The woman with the issue of blood touched the hem of His garment and was healed instantly, but before she could leave Jesus announced, "Somebody touched Me." And the record reveals that when she saw that she could not be hid, "she declared to Him *in the presence of all the people* the reason she had touched Him and how she was healed immediately." Only then did Jesus say, "Your faith has made you well. Go in peace" (Luke 8:43–48, emphasis ours).

Zaccheus thought he could get what he wanted by hiding in a sycamore tree, or more correctly, a combination of a fig and mulberry tree. But when Jesus looked up and saw Zaccheus, He made him declare himself before every eye, and commanded him to "come down" and receive full and free salvation (Luke 19:1–10).

The rich young ruler was told to "sell all . . . and distribute to the poor" and follow Jesus (Luke 18:18–23). To quote Dr. Easley again: "If that's not a call to serious commitment I don't know what is. So if we are looking for material to preach from, with a call to commitment, there's no better place to start than the Gospels."[7]

When we read the Acts of the Apostles, the story is just the same: public baptism had to follow personal commitment to Christ. There was no such thing as "secret discipleship." It was our Lord Himself who declared: "Whoever confesses Me before men, him the Son of Man also will confess before the angels of God. But he who denies Me before men will be denied before the angels of God" (Luke 12:8–9).

There Must Be Instruction

"If anyone is in Christ, he is a new creation; old things have passed away; behold, all things have become new" (5:17). It is our task as preachers to instruct the newly-committed convert (or, in some cases, believers who respond to an invitation) in the "all things [which] have become new."

In this regard, we follow a simple, but effective, procedure, both in the local church situation as well as the citywide crusade. Briefly, the steps are as follows. After the moment of commitment and the act of confession, we invite those who responded to remain behind. Then we lead in three phases of aftercare instruction:

First phase of instruction. When the occasion calls for it, we employ *the aftermeeting method.*[8] We rarely hold an evangelistic service in the local church or in a crusade (or, indeed, in a convention for the deepening of spiritual life) without the aftermeeting. In the moments that follow the dismissal of the main congregation, we invite those who have openly confessed Christ, together with other seekers who may wish to remain, to listen to words of instruction that make clear the way of salvation—we virtually dot the *i*'s and cross the *t*'s of the sermon to which they have already responded. We also give helpful advice on how to grow in the Christian life and become associated with the local church.

Second phase of instruction. For those who require personal help, there must be a season of counseling, following the public instruction, when seeking souls are linked with those who are trained to minister to specific needs of the seeker or new convert. Needless to say, this necessitates a team of men and women who are always ready and alert to be called upon to assist the pastor and his associates. It is imperative that spiritually mature men, women, and young people be skilled in soul-winning and *discipling* procedures and be on hand for *every* preaching service in the church, open-air meeting, or other ministry opportunities (see 2 Tim. 4:2a). We might add that "one-on-one" discipling should continue until the convert or the believer seeking spiritual help is integrated into the life of the church.

Third phase of instruction. This includes literature follow-up which is done by mail; personal follow-up by individual counselors or the office staff of the church; and then pastoral follow-up, which involves discipleship classes once or twice a week, where consecutive lessons are taught on such subjects as Christian certainty, daily devotions, believers' baptism, church fellowship, consecrated living, systematic giving, dedicated serving, and then a closing talk on the covenant of membership. Attendance at these sessions must be mandatory. This discipline, as well as the instruction, always pay off. In church life, we have never recommended anyone for membership who has not "graduated" from these classes of instruction.

After membership, we have always emphasized *involvement in church life*, according to the respective gifts of the people concerned. This is where it is important to exercise discernment in detecting gifts, then developing them, and finally deploying them. To facilitate this procedure it is wise to use a talent survey which can be completed during the weeks of instruction. The "talent survey" is the breakdown of the New Testament gifts listed in such passages as Romans 12:6–8; 1 Corinthians 12:4–30; Ephesians 4:7–16; and 1 Peter 4:7–11. Every pastor should work out, in terms of his local church, the roster of ministry needs. He must not forget the area of "helps!"[9]

These, then, are suggested means by which the work of evangelism and discipleship can be conserved in the life of the local church. It is one thing to press for *decision*, it is quite another matter to push for *discipleship*. If there is a weakness in preaching for a verdict, it is in this aspect of conservation. It is alarming to learn of the turnover in churches across the land, and even worse, to see defection from church membership because of lack of aftercare and spiritual shepherding.

According to British demographer David B. Barrett, editor of *World Christian Encyclopedia: A Comparative Study of Churches and Religion in the Modern World A.D. 1900–2000*, "more than 53,000 people leave church every week and never come back."[10] Disillusioned with programs and structures, they search for spirituality outside organized religion. Dean M. Kelley, author of the book *Why Conservative Churches Are Growing*, contends that, "conservative churches are 'growing' all right—but not through conversion growth. Most of it [comes through] babies and transfers."[11] Instead of preaching the message of a living, reigning, and caring Lord who is totally adequate for every human need, many men behind our pulpits have watered down the truth of the grace of God, thus giving reign to licentiousness and antinomianism.

THE POWER OF THE INVITATION

"We then, as workers together with Him also plead with you not to receive the grace of God in vain. For He says: 'In an acceptable time I have heard you, And in the day of salvation I have helped you.' Behold, now is the accepted time; behold, now is the day of salvation" (6:1–2). Inherent in this whole concept of the invitation are aspects of truth that need to be recalled and renewed in the ministry of preaching and evangelism.

There Is the Necessity of God's Call

"We . . . as workers . . . with [God]. . . plead with you not to receive the grace of God in vain" (6:1). If we are doing our task in the fear of God, then we have to cry with the apostle, "Necessity is laid upon me; yes, woe is me if I do not preach the gospel!" (1 Cor. 9:16). This means that we have to plead with men "not to receive the grace of God in vain" (6:1).

In our understanding of God's sovereign work in the human heart, we must remember two aspects of the Holy Spirit's activity. There is, first of all, the *prevenient* work of grace. Jesus affirmed: "No one can come to Me unless the Father who sent Me draws him; and I will raise him up at the last day" (John 6:44). In ways that *we can never fathom*, God has His own process for preparing hearts for the act of commitment and subsequent Christian living.

Gordon D. Fee makes the following observations in his scholarly and monumental book *God's Empowering Presence*:

> The relationship of the Spirit to faith is one of the more complex issues in the corpus: indeed, its very complexity bears mute witness against our attempt to fit all of Paul's words about the Spirit into our own prior categories. On the one hand, in Gal. 3:2–5 Paul is adamant that the gift of the Spirit is the result of "faith in Christ Jesus." According to any "systematic" presentation that should demand that faith itself precedes the reception of the Spirit. On the other hand, in 1 Cor. 12:8 and 13:2, "faith" is considered one of the manifestations of the Spirit. If those passages can be dismissed as referring (correctly so) to that unusual gift of faith that accompanies the miraculous, the same can scarcely be said of the "faith" that is the fruit of the Spirit (Gal. 5:22), which refers to "saving faith" in its continuing expression, or of 2 Cor. 4:13, where Paul refers to "having the same Spirit who effects faith as the Psalmist had," who leads us "to believe."
>
> This prompts us to suggest, therefore, that faith itself, as a work of the Spirit, leads to the experienced reception of the Spirit that also comes through that same faith. Although it does not fit our logical schemes well, the Spirit is thus both the cause and the effect of faith. This same close relationship of the Spirit to faith is also presupposed in Gal. 5:5, where Paul urges that we, in contrast to them (the Jewish Christian agitators), "by the Spirit, on the basis of faith, await the

final righteousness for which we hope." The object of faith, as always, is Christ; the Spirit is the means whereby such faith is sustained.

What all of this means, then, is that for Paul both the understanding of the gospel and the event of preaching, including the hearing that leads to faith, are the work of the Spirit (2 Cor. 4:13).[12]

Second, there is the *persistent* work of grace. The Scriptures speak of God's patient, yet persistent, dealings with people. He declares: "My Spirit shall not *strive* with man forever" (Gen. 6:3, emphasis ours); but, until the divine point of termination, God strives, and that word (Hebrew, *diyn*) means *contends* and *pleads* (Gen. 6:3). At the same time, the Lord Jesus is pictured as One who knocks, and goes on knocking, at the door of the human heart until His saving purpose is fulfilled.

There Is the Immediacy of God's Call

"He says: 'In an acceptable time I have heard you, and in the day of salvation I have helped you.' Behold, now is the accepted time; behold, now is the day of salvation" (6:2). We have to remind those to whom we preach that we cannot "boast about tomorrow, for [we] do not know what a day may bring forth" (Prov. 27:1). So our message must ever be: "Now is the accepted time; now is the day of salvation."

There is no contradiction between the necessity of God's call and the immediacy of God's call; they are complementary truths. Even though God is patient in His attitude toward us, He is also prudent. There does come a time when He has to lament, "How often I wanted to gather your children together, as a hen gathers her chicks under her wings, but you were not willing! See! Your house is left to you desolate" (Matt. 23:37–38).

So we see that the necessity and immediacy of God's call are the power behind our proclamation and invitation.

THE PERIL OF THE INVITATION

"We give no offense in anything, that our ministry may not be blamed. But in all things we commend ourselves as ministers of God" (6:3–4). As stated at the beginning of this chapter, there is a great deal of confusion regarding the preacher and the invitation.

And while the verses before us are not directly related to the peril involved, they certainly serve as a corrective to the harm and hurt that so many preachers inflict upon their congregations. Let us then "principalize" the cautionary words of the apostle.

Misleading the Seeker

"We give no offense in anything, that our ministry may not be blamed" (6:3). God alone knows how many people are put off about coming to church or listening to the gospel because of high-pressure appeals, evangelistic tricks, or the misuse of mass psychology. We are justly criticized for insulting the intelligence and playing on the emotions of men and women, in the name of evangelistic preaching. This is nothing less than giving offense and causing the ministry to be blamed.

Gary Collins, in his book *Search for Reality*, observes that "decisions can be influenced by a speaker, but the preacher should permit a decision contrary to his views. For a person to make a decision without real alternatives freely considered is manipulation, not real commitment. . . . Even in the spiritual realm the end (the appearance of conversion by coming forward) does not justify the means [of] manipulative high-pressure preaching. . . . Some [people] are changed and truly converted under high pressure, but many others soon lose their beliefs, or even lose respect for Christianity because of the manipulation involved."[13]

Donald Ratcliff, in the *Journal of the American Scientific Affiliation* (March 1982), makes a similar comment. He writes that if the original commitment to Christ is made in a highly emotional context, "the person may come to associate emotions with spirituality. . . . Eventually the person may come to believe himself or herself less spiritual or even not a Christian because of lags in emotional feelings."[14]

The danger in misleading the seeker in our invitation is largely due to the employment of *worldly* methods. In his epistle, the apostle John defines *worldliness* as the lust of the flesh, the lust of the eyes, and the pride of life (1 John 2:16). It is quite amazing how this spirit of the world can motivate and activate even when giving the invitation!

After years of careful observation, we have come to see that, very often, high pressure appeals are made for one or all of the following reasons:

The lust for the "stats" of publicity. This represents "the lust of the eyes" (1 John 2:16). There is something extremely intriguing and appealing about numbers, both in the size of congregations as well as the strength of response. Like the world in which we live, nothing counts like numbers. Just listen to clerical chitchat or ministerial reports!

The lust for the skills of psychology. This represents "the lust of the flesh" (1 John 2:16). Equally attractive is the acquired ability to manipulate people until the intended objective is achieved. No one has argued this point more brilliantly than William Sargent in his book *The Battle for the Mind*,[15] which is a psychology of conversion and brainwashing. While we do not agree with most of his conclusions, or the fact that he does not make room for the work of the Holy Spirit, his warning is well taken.

The lust for the signs of prosperity. This represents "the pride of life" (1 John 2:16). This emphasis and technique are perilously in vogue today. It is an appeal to the need in all of us to *prosper* by responding to the gospel. It goes without saying that everyone who responds and believes the gospel will come into blessing. But that should never be the *motive* for response—especially if there is the added suggestion that respondees will become materially rich or physically healed by turning to God through Jesus Christ. The Master never promised "a bed of roses"; on the contrary, He told us to *deny* ourselves, take up our cross, and follow Him (Luke 9:23).

> As many Jews in Jesus' day thought the coming of Messiah would bring them political peace and material prosperity, so today many in the Church think that Jesus' presence will bring them a kind of tranquility. But Jesus insisted that His mission entailed strife and division [see Matt. 10:32–39]. Prince of Peace though He is (see Matt. 5:9), the world will so violently reject Him and His reign that men and women will divide over Him. Before the consummation of the Kingdom, even the peace that Jesus bequeaths his disciples will have its setting in the midst of a hostile world (John 14:27; 16:33; cf. James 4:4).[16]

Misrepresenting the Savior

"In all things we commend ourselves as ministers of God" (6:4). We must remember, as we have observed earlier, that "we are ambassadors for Christ" (5:20). "An 'ambassador,' as Hodge pertinently remarks, 'is at once a messenger and a representative. He does not speak in his own name. He does not act on his own authority. What he communicates is not his own opinions or demands, but simply what he has been told or commanded to say. But at the same time, he speaks with authority; in this case, the authority of Christ Himself.'"[17] Therefore, in the most solemn sense, we are the representatives of our Lord and Savior Jesus Christ, and the worst thing we can ever do is to preach or perform in such a fashion that we disqualify ourselves as ministers of God. This can be said, alas, of local pastors as well as itinerant evangelists, and we need to be warned before God judges us.

The apostle Paul sensed this concern so keenly that he says, "I discipline my body and bring it into subjection, lest, when I have preached to others, I myself should become disqualified" (1 Cor. 9:27). In sharing this, he was referring to his ministry as a gospel preacher. Paul's fear was not that he might lose his salvation, but that he might lose his crown through failing to satisfy his Lord. So in this athletic language he speaks of the manner in which he disciplined the flesh. He talks about keeping under his body. He borrows a verb from the world of boxing which literally means "to give one's self a black eye" or "bruising one's body." He further speaks of bringing fleshly desires under control. Needless to say, he could never do this in his own strength. So the same apostle affirms, "I can do all things through Christ who strengthens me" (Phil. 4:13).

We know what critics have to say about preaching for a verdict. Much of this prejudice, however, is unfounded and unjustified. On the other hand, we have to admit that a good deal of it is only too true of those who have caused the ministry to be blamed and, therefore, have brought preaching and the invitation into disrepute.

Before we bring this chapter to a conclusion, a further important consideration is in order. As we think of the invitation, we tend to restrict this essential aspect of preaching to "the evangelistic meeting." This is a big mistake, and it effects serious consequences in church life and conference ministry.

Every preaching event requires an invitation. And in asserting this, we are not referring to the raising of hands, the walking of the aisles, the signing of cards, or the use of counseling rooms. These invitation methods when not abused are legitimate procedures for *follow-up purposes.* Even some of our "truly Reformed" colleagues use their vestries or studies for seekers who desire counseling; and that is right and proper—even though it is an "invitation method" nonetheless!

What burdens us is not the methodology but the theology of the invitation. If a church as a whole, or a Christian as an individual, is to progress in spiritual growth, then every message, sermon, or truth declared, *must* elicit a total response on the part of those who hear us. The apostle Paul verbalizes this when he exclaims, "God be thanked that . . . *you obeyed from the heart* that form of doctrine to which you were delivered" (Rom. 6:17, emphasis ours; see also James 1:22–25). The following couplet is so true:

> Light obeyed bringeth light;
> Light rejected bringeth night.

Revelation and obedience move in parallel lines. As people obey so God reveals; when people refuse to obey God withholds further *light* on truth. Secondhand information may be acquired— yes, even notebooks of sermon outlines—but there will be no progress in spiritual maturity.

So whether or not *outward* evidence is called for in any given service, *inward response* is a critical part of the preaching event. And, alas, this is where most preachers fail miserably! You can have a church objectively instructed in biblical doctrine and yet be *dead* in practical results. Only obedience to truth brings life through the power of the Spirit (see John 7:17 and 2 Cor. 3:6b). Carl Henry has observed with keen perception that "the greatest sin in evangelicalism today is unapplied orthodoxy."

Many times we have seen an invitation given that only impacts a small minority of the congregation, while the rest of the attendees, by their own admission, have left the church *uncommitted* to the motivating truth and thrust of the pastor's sermon! In this connection, we urge a careful study chapter 15.

We have now considered the role of the preacher and the invitation. We do well to return to the passage of Scripture that we have taken as our lesson and read it and reread it until the pattern, purpose, power, and peril of the invitation are incarnated and then implemented in our ministries. Only then shall we fulfill God's imperative to, "*Preach* the word!. . . [and] *do the work* of an evangelist" (2 Tim. 4:2, 5, emphasis ours)

CHAPTER SEVENTEEN

THE PREACHER AND CONSERVATION

"Let all the house of Israel know assuredly that God has made this Jesus, whom you crucified, both Lord and Christ." Now when they heard this, they were cut to the heart, and said to Peter and the rest of the apostles, "Men and brethren, what shall we do?" Then Peter said to them, "Repent, and let every one of you be baptized in the name of Jesus Christ for the remission of sins; and you shall receive the gift of the Holy Spirit." . . . Then those who gladly received his word were baptized; and that day about three thousand souls were added to them.

—Acts 2:36–38,41

Study Text: Acts 2:36–41

I t is generally conceded that the fatal weakness in the work of evangelism today is the lack of follow-up—or what we are calling evangelistic conservation. No one can fault the preparation that goes into citywide crusades, local church missions, or the normal weekly evangelistic ministries of *live* congregations; but most experts on the subject would question whether or not the same care and planning go into the work of conserving the gains.

By definition, the primary meaning of *conservation* is "the protection from loss and waste." As we reflect upon these words we have to acknowledge with shame that "loss and waste" characterize much of what is done in the name of evangelism. We only have to think of defection from our own churches, or the disappointing results of follow-up attempts after major evangelistic efforts. As we pointed out in our last chapter, "more than 53,000 people leave the church every week and never come back."[1]

If there is one emphasis in this book that needs precedence, it is that of evangelistic conservation. With this in mind, we can do no better than turn to the early chapters of the Acts of the Apostles. Here in the record left for us are principles that should direct and determine all evangelistic enterprise throughout the age of grace. What happened on the day of Pentecost is a good place to start. Peter had just delivered the Pentecostal sermon. It was God-conceived, Christ-centered, and Spirit-controlled. And like all good biblical preaching, it concluded with the claims of Jesus Christ as Lord. All Scripture and all history converge at this point. The message of the Bible is that Jesus Christ is Lord, and the meaning of life is that Jesus Christ is Lord. And such was the impact of Peter's sermon that men and women were transformed and became members of the new church in Jerusalem. What must engage our attention is the process, the pattern, and the product of evangelistic conservation following the preaching of Peter.

THE PROCESS OF EVANGELISTIC CONSERVATION

"That day about three thousand souls were added to them" (v. 41). Before we go further we need to examine the process by which three thousand souls became members of the local church in Jerusalem. In a day of "easy believism" it is important to understand what qualifies people to receive the right hand of fellowship.

The Conviction of Sin

"They were cut to the heart, and said to Peter and the rest of the apostles, 'Men and brethren, what shall we do?'" (v. 37). This is what happens when there is true anointed preaching. And from this passage we learn that *the issue of conviction* is the lordship of Christ. Peter had declared that even though men had crucified Jesus, *God had made Him both Lord and Christ* (v. 36). How can any hell-deserving sinner do anything else but be convicted of their sin? Paul reminds us that "no one can say that Jesus is Lord except by the Holy Spirit" (1 Cor. 12:3). The issue is plain: either people crucify Christ or crown Him; there is no other alternative (see Acts 16:31; Rom. 10:9–10).

The instrument of conviction was the Holy Spirit. The Lord Jesus had already predicted this when He promised, "When He [the Holy Spirit] has come, He will convict the world of sin, . . . because they do not believe in Me" (John 16:8, 9). When the Holy Spirit anoints the preaching, people can never dodge the fact of sin or the claims of Christ. He must be received or rejected, and only those who receive the Lord Jesus can be members of His church.

The Conversion of Life

"Then Peter said to them, 'Repent, and let every one of you be baptized in the name of Jesus Christ for the remission of sins; and you shall receive the gift of the Holy Spirit'" (v. 38). These words reveal that the conversion of life involves repentance, remission, and regeneration. *Repentance* is a change of mind—an intellectual revolution—that leads to a change of life. It involves turning *from* sin, self, and Satan *to* God, His Son Jesus Christ, and to a life of obedience and holiness.

We once taught the Bible to a group of soldiers and came to the word *repentance*. We paused to ask if anyone knew what the word meant. Instantly a hand was raised, and a young private offered to give his definition. He came forward and started marching from right to left across the room, shouting in a loud voice: "My back is turned to God; I am on my way to a life of self-seeking and destruction. Then I hear a voice from heaven saying, 'Halt! Right about turn. Forward march.'" The private stopped, grinned, and said, "That is repentance, sir"—and he was right! Nothing less than this is true repentance. This radical change in direction is what is so lacking today. Repentance is both a crisis of decision and a process of direction.

Then there is *remission* or the forgiveness of sins. This comes through a personal faith in the Lord Jesus Christ who shed His precious blood for us men and our salvation. Baptism is the outward and visible sign of this inner cleansing power of the blood of Christ.

Simultaneous with this is *regeneration,* or the receiving of the Holy Spirit. No one can truly be converted without the incoming and indwelling of the Holy Spirit, for as Paul reminds us, "If anyone does not have the Spirit of Christ, he is not His" (Rom. 8:9). By the same token, however, when He does enter a person's life, He, the Holy Spirit, bears "witness with our spirit that we are children of God" (Rom. 8:16).

So we see that the entitlement to church membership is not only the conviction of sin, but the conversion of life—which leads to confession.

The Confession of Faith

"Those who gladly received his word were baptized; and that day about three thousand souls were added to them" (v. 41). For many of the Jewish converts that day this confession of faith was the most costly aspect of their response to the claims of Christ. For them—and for you and me today—it involves obedience to the Son of God—"Those who gladly received his word were baptized" (v. 41). Jesus not only commissioned His disciples to baptize all nations (Matt. 28:19), but He gave us an example by His own baptism in Jordan. He had no sins to repent of, but in order to be identified with the death, burial, and resurrection that He was about to accomplish, He obeyed the will of His Father and was baptized by John the Baptist. He could say, "Permit it to be so now, for thus it is fitting for us to fulfill all righteousness" (Matt. 3:15). In being baptized He openly declared His obedience to the redemptive will of His Father. And that is the meaning of baptism for every true believer today. We must publicly identify with Jesus Christ in the meaning of His death, burial, and resurrection.

With obedience to the Son of God there was allegiance to the church of God—"about three thousand souls were added to them" (v. 41). The word *added* means "to place beside," or "to join to." The imperfect verb *added* suggests a process that was followed in receiving the new converts into the fellowship of the church. Then Luke tells us, without further qualification, that they "continued steadfastly in the apostle' doctrine and fellowship, in the breaking of bread, and in prayers" (v. 42). God's conditions for membership have not changed. To share in the community of a local church there must be the conviction of sin, the conversion of life, and the confession of faith. This is basically the process of evangelistic conservation.

THE PATTERN OF EVANGELISTIC CONSERVATION

"And they continued steadfastly in the apostles' doctrine and fellowship, in the breaking of bread, and in prayers" (v. 42). In the Greek, these means of grace are introduced with the article *the* to distinguish and to emphasize the importance of each of these means of grace.[2] Until the Lord Jesus comes back again, we have here all that is necessary for the maintenance of the church on earth. Let us briefly examine this apostolic pattern of conservation. If we are to establish those who respond to the preaching of the gospel, we must do everything in our power to encourage them to continue "steadfastly in the apostles' doctrine and fellowship, in breaking of bread, and in prayers." If they are going to grow in grace and in the knowledge of the Lord Jesus Christ, they must diligently attend upon four means of grace: The exposition of the Scriptures, the congregation of the saints, the celebration of the Lord's Supper, and the adoration of the Savior.

The Exposition of the Scriptures

"They continued steadfastly in the apostles' doctrine [or teaching]" (v. 42). Quite obviously, this was the oral teaching of the apostles, for they had no New Testament at that time, though it was obvious that they drew heavily from the Old Testament Scriptures.

Today, however, we have the completed canon of Scripture which is sufficient for all matters of faith and practice. It follows, therefore, that the exposition of the Scriptures in a local church is of first and fundamental importance. If we truly believe this, we shall see to it that converts, as well as mature members of our congregation, sit under the teaching of God's Word whenever the opportunity affords itself. There is no greater need in our churches today than a return to expository preaching. When Harold Ockenga, former pastor of the famous Park Street Church in Boston, Massachusetts, was asked what he considered to be the most important thing in the life of the church he replied in one word: "Preaching." Everything else flows from this.

That is why Luke puts it first in the pattern of evangelistic conservation. Needless to say, pulpit preaching must be augmented by smaller classes, such as are available in normal Sunday school work, as well as special sessions of instruction for those who are young in the faith.

The Congregation of the Saints

"And they continued steadfastly in the . . . fellowship" (v. 42). The word *fellowship* is a precious one. It is used again and again for participation in living, loving, giving, and serving in the church. However, in this immediate context its reference is primarily to that of the assembling of God's people. Without the congregation of the saints there is no purpose in the exposition of the Scriptures. This is why the writer to the Hebrews exhorts believers of all time to forsake not "the assembling of ourselves together, as is the manner of some, but exhorting one another, and so much the more as [we] see the Day approaching" (Heb. 10:25). There is something God does in our lives when we gather together that cannot be achieved in any other way. This is why the electronic church is no substitute for the congregation of the saints.

The Celebration of the Supper

"And they continued steadfastly in the . . . breaking of bread" (v. 42). In the early days of the church the breaking of bread was part of a regular meal. Since then it has come to be known as the ordinance of the Lord's Supper. The importance of this "sacrament" can never be overestimated. It is the one service of the church that demonstrates and declares our core beliefs about Christ and His church. It is not only a service of celebration, but of consecration. We not only celebrate the life, death, resurrection, and return of the Savior, but we dedicate ourselves afresh as we identify with the body He gave and the blood He shed—symbolized by the bread and the wine.

The Adoration of the Savior

"And they continued steadfastly in . . . prayers" (v. 42). Archbishop Trench points out that of the several words that are used for prayer, Luke uses the most exclusive and inclusive one in our text. It is exclusive because it is used of prayer to God alone, but it is inclusive in that it embraces *all* the exercises and disciplines of a worshipping congregation. It means adoration, confession, petition, and thanksgiving. For practical purposes, the emphasis here is on the prayer meeting, which is the spiritual barometer of every local church and which, more often than not, registers "very dry." Hence it is the least attended service—to our eternal shame. For this very reason the prayer meeting demands not only the attention, but also the attendance of everyone who is a church member. Here is where God's face is sought; here is where Satan's powers are thwarted; here is where men's souls are blessed; and most importantly, here is where the Savior is adored and worshiped. We must never forget that "the church marches on its knees."

Put these four means of grace together and you have the secret of a church that is nourished and strengthened to meet the continuing challenge of contemporary life.

THE PRODUCT OF EVANGELISTIC CONSERVATION

"Then fear came upon every soul. . . . And the Lord added to the church daily those who were being saved" (vv. 43, 47). While these concluding verses of the chapter record certain phenomena that were singularly unique to those early days of the church, we *must not* overlook the abiding principles that determine and direct the activities of every local fellowship.

The Ministry of Daring Action

"Many wonders and signs were done through the apostles" (v. 43). The church is a supernatural community with a supernatural ministry. The day we cease to believe this is the day the church ceases to exist as God intended. In every congregation where the Word of God is being preached in the power of the Holy Spirit there should be miracles of salvation, sanctification, and service that cannot be explained in human terms. There is an awesomeness and attractiveness when God is at work. This is why Luke tells us that "fear came upon every soul"; and again, the believers had "favor with all the people" (vv. 43, 47).

The Ministry of Caring Action

"Now all who believed were together, and had all things in common, and sold their possessions and goods, and divided them among all, as anyone had need. So continuing daily with one accord in the temple, and breaking bread from house to house, they ate their food with gladness and simplicity of heart" (vv. 44–46). Great needs were precipitated by the growing pains of those early days of the church in Jerusalem, but the new community rose to the occasion with a ministry of caring action. These new believers were concerned with *people*, first of all: "All who believed were together, and had all things in common." How we need this in our local fellowships today! People mattered, even though there were thousands of them.

They were concerned with *possessions*. Where there was need, these possessions were shared with a spirit of liberality and hospitality. No New Testament church should have to depend on government handouts for its members or the needs of the immediate community! This should be part of the witness of a "live" church.

They were concerned with *programs*:"[They continued] with one accord in the temple, and . . . from house to house praising God and having favor with all the people." Clearly they had a program of ministry for the *temple*, for the *home*, and for the *world*; and this was executed with steadfastness—"[They continued] daily." One of the true evidences of a church in revival is its caring ministry for the Body.

The Ministry of Sharing Action

The believers had "favor with all the people. And the Lord added to the church daily those who were being saved" (v. 47). In a fellowship of such joy and singleness of heart, believers could have succumbed to self-satisfaction and complacency—*but that did not happen*; the church was on the march. Christian worship and Christian welfare issued in Christian *witness*.

It was *an excited witness*. These Christians had "favor with all the people" because they were a praising community. Nothing attracts people like wholesome excitement and enthusiasm. There was no room for apologies or reticence in their witness; they had something to share and they did it with exuberance and hilarity.

A. T. Pierson has pointed out that "witnessing is the whole work of the whole church for the whole age." This is because witnessing is not a gift ministry, but rather an anointed lifestyle. "A light that does not shine, a germ that does not grow, a spring that does not flow, is no more of a [contradiction] than a Christian who does not witness."

It was also *an expectant witness*. Something happened "daily," or day by day. This fact should shame us for our lethargy and unbelief in our witness today. Since when have we seen people saved on a daily basis? And yet this is what these early Christians expected and, therefore, experienced.

Finally, it was *an effective witness.* "The Lord added to the church daily those who were being saved." Three thousand had just been saved, and many more were to be saved on the basis of individual witness happening daily in the temple, in the home, and in the world. People were getting converted, *and being added to the new community.* This was church *growth* in the highest sense of the word.

It has been our experience and that of many of our fellow pastors and evangelists that often the keenest members of a witnessing church are the newly converted people! The salvation of one man or woman, boy or girl, leads to a chain reaction that affects whole families, school friends, college communities, and especially fellow workers in the market place. *Nothing conserves the work of evangelism like evangelism itself.* It is impossible to be an effective soul-winner without living daily in the Word, knowing daily the fullness of the Holy Spirit, and enjoying daily the presence of Christ.

In this chapter you have seen what we mean by evangelistic conservation. The process involves the conviction of sin, the conversion of life, and the confession of faith. The pattern calls for steadfast continuance in the apostles' doctrine, fellowship, the breaking of bread, and prayers. And the product issues in a threefold ministry of daring, caring, and sharing outreach. These are eternal principles that God has laid down for the conservation of His work so they transcend time; they are effective, so they must not be ignored. Indeed, it is because we have turned from these principles and sought our own ways of doing things that we have lost the vision, the passion, and the mission of the church. May God give us the grace to return to the exposition of His Word, the power of His Spirit, and the purpose of His Church—before it is too late. Only then shall we be able to sing, "Like a mighty army moves the Church of God."

CHAPTER EIGHTEEN

THE PREACHER AND INCULCATION

*I want you to know what a great conflict I have for
you and those in Laodicea, and for as many as have
not seen my face in the flesh, that their hearts may
be encouraged, being knit together in love, and
attaining to all riches of the full assurance of understanding, to the knowledge of the mystery of God,
both of the Father and of Christ, in whom are hidden
all the treasures of wisdom and knowledge. Now this
I say lest anyone should deceive you with persuasive
words. For though I am absent in the flesh, yet I am
with you in spirit, rejoicing to see your good order
and the steadfastness of your faith in Christ. As you
have therefore received Christ Jesus the Lord, so
walk in Him, rooted and built up in Him and established in the faith, as you have been taught, abounding in it with thanksgiving. Beware lest anyone cheat
you through philosophy and empty deceit, according
to the tradition of men, according to the basic principles of the world, and not according to Christ. For in
Him dwells all the fullness of the Godhead bodily;
and you are complete in Him, who is the head of all
principality and power.*

—Colossians 2:1–10

I n our last chapter, "The Preacher and Conservation," we stressed the need for follow-up and discipleship to accompany our preaching ministry. The defection of so-called "members" from our churches today is an eloquent testimony to the urgency of this task. But an equally urgent issue that faces us, as preachers, is the *reason* for this defection. Is it failure on our part to teach core doctrines that ensure convictional commitment to Christ and His church? What, in fact, is the essential message that grips the heart and guards the life of the young believer—and, indeed, the mature Christian, as well?

Paul's letter to the Colossians was written with this very real problem in mind. There is no evidence that the apostle had ever visited the church at Colosse. Notwithstanding this, he was personally interested in their gospel testimony, and not a little concerned with the report that he had heard of false teachers who were seeking to influence the believers by mixing Jewish legalism, Oriental mysticism, and Greek rationalism with a veneer of Christianity. So he writes to them with the express intention of preventing them from being carried away from the simplicity that is in Christ Jesus (2 Cor. 11:3). In simple terms, he shows them how to live the life and keep the faith. One of the key passages in the whole of the epistle is the one now before us (vv. 1–10). Summed up in a sentence, his basic message is: "As you have therefore received Christ Jesus the Lord, so walk in Him" (v. 6). Here he spells out what we are electing to call "the preacher and inculcation." In our preaching and teaching, we must emphasize the three leading principles that determine such inculcation.

THE INITIAL ACCEPTANCE OF CHRIST

"[Receive] Christ Jesus the Lord" (v. 6). No one can live the Christian life without believing and receiving Christ Jesus as Lord. There are people who think that they can live the Christian life by attempting to imitate the Christ of history, but it cannot be done. There is only one Person in the universe who ever lived the Christian life to the pleasure and approval of God: that was Christ Himself. The genius of the Christian gospel is that this same Christ can live His life again in us!

Capt. Reginald Wallis (an honored Bible teacher in the United Kingdom) used to put it this way: "You cannot live the Christian life without the Christian life to live the Christian life." By this he meant that no one can live the Christian life without the *Christ-life* to live the Christian life. If this is clearly understood, then it remains for us to understand what we mean by an initial acceptance of Christ.

Commentators are agreed that the name "Jesus" and "Lord" are modifiers of the basic title "Christ." Therefore, to receive Christ involves the acceptance of Him as Jesus and Lord.

The Acceptance of Christ as Savior

"[Receive] Christ *Jesus*" (v. 6 NIV, emphasis ours). No one can live the Christian life without being saved from sin; and what is equally true is that no one can be saved from sin without knowing Christ as Savior. The advent of the Lord Jesus into this world was announced with these words: "You shall call His name Jesus, for He will save His people from their sins" (Matt. 1:21). Later on, the apostle Paul declared, "This is a faithful saying and worthy of all acceptance, that Christ Jesus came into the world to save sinners" (1 Tim. 1:15). The reason why we need a Savior is that we "all have sinned and fall short of the glory of God" (Rom. 3:23). God's standard of glory is His own Son, Jesus Christ. Because we have miserably failed, we need His saving grace and power before we can begin to live the Christian life.

It is important, therefore, to underscore the saviorhood of Jesus. "Jesus" is the God-man embodied in humanity through the incarnation in time and space. *Jesus* is the Greek for the Hebrew name which means "the Lord is salvation." So men and women must receive Him as the Captain of their salvation. To qualify as "the author of eternal salvation," He "learned obedience by the things which He suffered" (Heb. 5:8–9). That obedience led Him to "the death of the cross" (Phil. 2:8). With that in mind, Paul summarizes the gospel in these famous words: "I delivered to you first of all that which I also received: that Christ died for our sins according to the Scriptures, and that He was buried, and that He rose again the third day according to the Scriptures" (1 Cor. 15:3–4). That is why Peter and John could confront "the priests, the captain of the temple, and the Sadducees" (Acts 4:1) with those powerful words, "There is no other name under heaven given among men by which we must be saved" (Acts 4:12). Yet our acceptance of Christ will not be complete until we do more than accept Him as our Savior; we must accept Himas Lord and King.

The Acceptance of Christ as Sovereign

"[Receive] Christ Jesus *as Lord*" (v. 6, NIV, emphasis ours). Jesus and Lord are one Person, but so often we are prepared to accept His saviorhood without acknowledging His sovereignty. Indeed, perhaps this is one of our greatest failures, both in the preaching of the gospel and in the acceptance of the Christian message. Everybody wants to know his sins are forgiven and have an assurance of heaven, but it does not necessarily follow that this "easy believism" prepares us to bow to the demands of Christ as *Lord* of all life. To accept Christ as Lord means:

> Lord of every thought and action,
> Lord to send and Lord to stay,
> Lord in speaking, writing, giving,
> Lord in all things to obey;
> Lord of all there is of me,
> Now and evermore to be.

> —E. H. Swinstead

C. H. Spurgeon's comment on our text is both insightful and appropriate. He writes: It is interesting to notice that the apostles preached the lordship of Christ. The word *Savior* only occurs twice in the Acts of the Apostles (5:31; 13:23). On the other hand, it is amazing to [observe] that the title *Lord* is mentioned ninety-two times; Lord Jesus thirteen times; and *the Lord Jesus Christ* six times in the same book. The gospel is "Believe on the Lord Jesus Christ, and you will be saved." (Acts 16:31).[1]

Like Spurgeon, Hudson Taylor was accustomed to saying: "Christ must be Lord of all or not Lord at all" at every stage of our Christian life. It is a contradiction in terms to name Jesus "Lord" over *part* of life. He can only be Lord of the *whole* of life. Christ must sway the scepter of sovereign rule over our entire personalities. In our preaching, we must ask: "Have you accepted Christ as Savior?" and "Have you accepted Christ as Lord?"

The debate on "lordship salvation" fails to recognize that you cannot separate saviorhood from sovereignty. As John Stott has put it, "When you come as a sinner, you open your hand to receive forgiveness and eternal life, but you come *on bended knee*."

In our preaching of the gospel, then, it is important to inculcate the initial acceptance of Christ as Savior and Lord.

However we must not stop there. Our second emphasis is equally important.

THE CONTINUAL OBEDIENCE TO CHRIST

"As you therefore have received Christ Jesus the Lord, so walk in Him, rooted and built up in Him and established in the faith, as you have been taught, abounding in it with thanksgiving" (vv. 6–7). This *imperative* statement, "walk in Him," is our clue to understanding this second aspect of inculcation. Especially is this so in a time when we have cheapened the grace of God and toned down the obligations of Christian obedience. When the apostle Paul commands us to "walk in Him," he is describing the kind of obedience that is both demanded and then defended. Let us examine this more closely.

There Is Obedience That Is Demanded

"Walk in Him" (v. 6). As you will see from the text, this "demanded obedience" is qualified by the words "rooted and built up in Him and established in the faith, as you have been taught, abounding in it with thanksgiving" (v. 7). Paul is not using hyperbole here or merely adding words for the sake of literary finesse. On the contrary, he is describing the quality of obedience that is demanded of anyone who has accepted Christ as Savior and Sovereign.

It Is a Growing Obedience. "Rooted and built up in Him" (v. 7). The verbs *rooted* and *built up* suggest two distinct metaphors— and yet they are related. *Rooted* is in the perfect tense, suggesting a once-for-all experience of being permanently rooted. The word only occurs here and in Ephesians 3:17–18. The doctrine of *eternal security* is implied here, because when God plants a tree He never uproots it. The apostle could well have had the opening words of Psalm 1 in mind, where David speaks of "a tree planted by the rivers of water" (Ps. 1:3). A rooted tree has the prerequisites of life. It has security as well as sufficiency. By its roots it is established and strengthened against the blasts of the wind and the reversals of nature. By its roots it is also supplied with nourishment from the minerals of the moist soil.

The other metaphor is just as colorful. Paul talks about being "built up," which is in the present tense, indicating a continual process. Here the idea is development and progress. Buildings are not completed in an instant, nor do buildings build themselves; they are constructed by conscious planning and work. It is stone upon stone or brick upon brick. Buildings require an architect, a plan, material, and a builder. In the case of the Christian, Jesus

Christ is the Master Architect and Builder, and therefore we are to count on Him in *total obedience* if we are going to grow tall and strong in the Christian life. We must have a growing obedience.

It Is a Learning Obedience. "Established in the faith, as you have been taught" (v. 7). This third participle is also in the present tense. "In the faith" speaks of faith as a body of truth (the faith system) and, therefore, the sphere within which the Christian is strengthened. Some versions read "your faith," suggesting trust in or reliance on Christ. The whole appeal here, however, is that faith should be exercised in accordance with what has been taught. In the case of the Colossians, it represented the great tradition of the gospel, as preached by the church planters in Colosse.

It is important to emphasize here the necessity of clear teaching through *the anointed expository preaching of the Word.* There is *no* substitute for the faithful, *fearless*, and fervent exposition of the Scriptures at *every* service of the church. This was the secret of the early disciples, for we read that "they continued *steadfastly in the apostles' doctrine* and fellowship, in the breaking of bread, and in prayers" (Acts 2:42).

It Is a Praising Obedience. "Abounding in it with thanksgiving" (v. 7). This final phrase reads "overflowing with thankfulness." It is a favorite expression that Paul uses more than twenty-six times. It means "overflowing"—like a river overflowing its banks. Once again, the tense is present and suggests that the believer's thanksgiving is to be a continual, habitual thing. It is gratitude that Lightfoot calls "the end of all conduct." Implicit in the language is the idea of worship. If a man or a woman is truly born again, obedience is not irksome or burdensome, but rather a discipline that brings joy and thanksgiving. The following little chorus puts it well:

> Trust and obey, for there's no other way
> To be happy in Jesus, but to trust and obey.
>
> —John H. Sammis

But with the obedience that is demanded:

There Is Obedience that Is Defended

"Beware lest anyone cheat you through philosophy and empty deceit, according to the tradition of men, according to the basic principles of the world, and not according to Christ" (v. 8). Paul was well aware of the errors that were attacking the Colossian church. They were a constant threat to the young believers.

This has never changed in the history of the Christian church. As evangelists, pastors, and teachers, we must be always on the lookout—for the enemy of our souls seeks to lead astray those who are not taught in the doctrines of Holy Scripture. So the apostle warns "Beware!" and then proceeds to talk about *philosophy.* In using that term, the apostle was not putting down the concept of philosophy, which simply means "love of wisdom." Everything that has to do with theories about God, the world, and the meaning of life was (and is) called philosophy—both in the pagan and Jewish schools of his day and ours. Paul had no problem with philosophy, as such. What he was warning against was a dangerous philosophy made up of elements of Hebrew Judaism and Greek Gnosticism. Without going into the history of these philosophies, it is only necessary for us to point out three important aspects of philosophy that are rooted in human error. Paul defines them in terms of what is "not according to Christ" (v. 8).

Deceptive Philosophy. "Now this I say lest anyone should deceive you with persuasive words. . . . Beware lest anyone cheat you through philosophy and empty deceit" (vv. 4, 8). The singular "anyone" (v. 8) has led interpreters to suggest that Paul had in mind a particular person—perhaps the leader among the heretical teachers. These enemies of the cross were brilliant orators who used fine-sounding arguments known as "persuasive rhetoric" that fascinated the unsuspecting listener. In our day we would call such teachers "fast talkers." These characters not only invaded the church, but often called on people in their homes.

These same enemies are just as real in our contemporary scene as they were in Paul's day. They may wear different clothes, but they have the same evil hearts. It is both curious and serious how winsome "champions of error" can be. They catch the simple minded. We must all remember how this verse concludes. Such people do not measure up to the plumbline of truth as it is in Christ—"*not according to Christ*" (v. 8). It was Jesus who said, "I am the . . . truth" (John 14:6).

Discursive Philosophy. "The tradition of men" (v. 8). The reference here is undoubtedly to the rabbinical theology with its almost endless regulations of life and ceremonies of religion. The term "tradition of men" may also refer to "various pagan theories current in that day."[2] Paul warned Timothy of these false teachers who engage in "fables and endless genealogies, which cause disputes rather than godly edification which is in faith" (1 Tim. 1:4).

Modern examples of this would be the ties of tradition, the chains of contemporary culture—and even the forms of worship and the exaggerated importance of methodology. It is amazing how the enemy stirs up what Paul calls "the war of words" which ultimately deflects Christians from "rightly dividing the word of truth" (2 Tim. 2:15).

Destructive Philosophy. "The basic principles of the world" (v. 8). This could refer to elementary teaching that never moves beyond the ABCs of the gospel. Nothing dwarfs and deadens a congregation like preaching that never completes the alphabet! However in this context the reference is probably related to "elemental spirits." Paul had already referred to the worship of angels (see 2:18), which was one of the heresies in the Colossian church. In our day we would call it Satanism and aspects of the New Age movement, etc. Nothing is more destructive in the life of any church or, indeed, in the life of any believer. The devil is a destroyer by nature and goes about "like a roaring lion, seeking whom he may devour" (1 Pet. 5:8). He is also by nature a deceiver who, as "an angel of light" (2 Cor. 11:14), leads astray the weak and gullible. So Paul warns against destructive philosophy. The phrase "take you captive" means "to carry off as prisoners those who are captured by a victorious army."

No one can be aware of events that are taking place in our country today without observing the serious relevance of this warning to the church of Jesus Christ. Every day, numerous cults evolve, and many of them grow at an incredible pace, engulfing literally thousands of those who have no inculcation of doctrine rooted in our Lord Jesus Christ.

We see, then, that continual obedience to Christ is not only vital but urgent in our task of inculcating the truth. Every preacher should study carefully and prayerfully Acts 20:17–38 and observe *Paul's personal testimony* (vv. 18–20, 33–35), *Paul's pivotal teaching* (vv. 21, 25, 27), and *Paul's pastoral training* (vv. 28–32) in the Ephesian church. In this farewell address, Paul mentions all three as he prepares the leaders to *take over* as he leaves them for good. They would "see his face no more" (v. 38). What a challenge this is to those of us who are preachers/pastors! Have we inculcated our people—and especially our leaders—to "stand and withstand" in the evil day?

But there is a third emphasis in our "core" teaching that is indispensable.

THE ESSENTIAL DEPENDENCE ON CHRIST

"In whom are hidden all the treasures of wisdom and knowledge"; and again: "In Him dwells all the fullness of the Godhead bodily; and you are complete in Him, who is the head of all principality and power" (vv. 3, 9–10). It is comforting to know that there is no demand made upon our lives for which there are not adequate resources in our Lord Jesus Christ. What is called for from us is a moment-by-moment dependence upon Him. Thus the apostle spells out, in this passage, what we have in Christ. Look at the list.

We Have Knowledge in Christ

"In whom are hidden all the treasures of . . . knowledge" (v. 3). Knowledge is the perception of objects and the acquisition of information concerning those objects. Everything we need to know can be learned by what Jesus Christ can teach us. Writing to young believers, John says, "You have an anointing from the Holy One, and you know all things. . . . But the anointing which you have received from Him abides in you, and you do not need that anyone teach you; but as the same anointing teaches you concerning all things, and is true, and is not a lie, and just as it has taught you, you will abide in Him" (1 John 2:20, 27).

There is no knowledge that has ever been investigated or ascertained which is not already comprehended in the knowledge that is in Christ. We certainly live in a wonderful age of knowledge. Time would fail to tell of the advances that have been made in innumerable fields of research. But in the last analysis, when we have gathered up all the treasures of knowledge, we find that we are only "thinking God's thoughts after Him." All knowledge is in the One who declared, "I am . . . the truth" (John 14:6).

We Have Wisdom in Christ

"In whom are hidden all the treasures of wisdom" (v. 3). Wisdom is the right application of knowledge. It is reasoning out and applying knowledge already acquired. A little boy may have the knowledge to put a plug in a socket, but his knowledge without wisdom could lead him into danger or harm. In Christ, however, both the knowledge and the wisdom are available.

The word *hidden* does not mean that knowledge and wisdom are concealed, but rather that they are stored away as a treasure for us to appropriate. The Gnostics taught that wisdom and knowledge were only available to a very exclusive elite; but thank God, this is not true when it comes to Christian experience! The simplest believer can claim *all* that there is in Christ for his daily need.

So Christ is our knowledge and wisdom. But even these two treasures require the divine dynamic to translate them into action and life. Paul has already anticipated this. He lists a third treasure.

We Have Fullness in Christ

"For in Him dwells all the fullness of the Godhead bodily" (v. 9). Everything else is included in that word *fullness*. There is power, patience, purpose, and every other conceivable resource for Christian living. As we count upon the indwelling Christ, He becomes to us all that we need for life and service. Charles Wesley put it perfectly when he wrote:

> Thou, O Christ, art all I want;
> More than all in Thee I find

This concept of Christ's fullness is the heart of the Christian gospel. If we do not grasp this, it is utterly impossible to meet the demands of obedience or to master the dynamics of allegiance to Christ. It was Christ Himself who said, "Without Me you can do nothing" (John 15:5).

The greatest danger today is the false teaching we hear from pulpits all across the land. We are being told that we need *something more* than Christ! These misguided teachers insist that there is "a gospel"—plus something else! That was the error that threatened to curse the church at Colosse. The fact of the matter is: *the gospel is Jesus only, and Jesus fully.* Right from the beginning we, as preachers, must inculcate these glorious "core" truths—then everything else in the Christian life makes sense.

So we have seen what we mean by "biblical inculcation." In the first place, it means an initial acceptance of Christ as Savior and Sovereign. Then it involves a continual obedience to Christ, both demanded and defended. Best of all, it calls for that essential dependence on Christ who is our knowledge, our wisdom, and our fullness!

THE PREACHER AND MOTIVATION

For our light affliction . . . is working for us a far more exceeding and eternal weight of glory. . . . Knowing, therefore, the terror of the Lord, we persuade men. . . . For the love of Christ compels us.

—2 Corinthians 4:17; 5:11, 14

Study Text: 2 Corinthians 4:7, 16–5:15

In this final chapter, we may well ask, with the apostle Paul: "Who is sufficient for these things?" (2 Cor. 2:16). Thank God, there is an answer to that question, and once again, it is Paul who verbalizes it: "Our sufficiency is from God" (2 Cor. 3:5). But given that sufficiency for our ministry, we, as preachers, are pressed to ask yet another question: Where do we derive our motivation, and how do we maintain it?

Motivation is that inner drive, impulse, intention, or desire that causes a person to do something or act in a certain way. Gordon W. Allport contends that "in the course of development relatively stable units of personality gradually emerge. Such units are always the products of the two central and vital functions of mental life: motivation and organization. Motivation refers to the 'go' of mental life, organization to its patterning. . . . Organized motive . . . is a system of readiness, a mainspring of conduct, preparing the person for adaptive behavior whenever the appropriate stimulus or associations are presented."[1] Charles Kingsley wrote: "I go at what I have to do as if there were nothing else in the world for me to do"; and George Whitefield summed up motivation with these words: "God give me a deep humility, a well-guided zeal, a burning love and a single eye, and then let men or devils do their worst."[2]

When we turn to the Scriptures, there are few passages that deal with the subject of motivation like 2 Corinthians, chapters 4 and 5. Already we have drawn from this well of truth when we expounded on "the preacher and invitation."

This time our focus is on "the preacher and motivation." As Paul dilates on "the gospel of the glory of Christ" (4:4), he reminds us that God has ordained that this treasure—the light of the gospel—should be incarnate "in earthen vessels, that the excellence of the power may be of God and not of us" (4:7). Or, as he states it in an earlier verse, "We do not preach ourselves, *but Christ*" (4:5, emphasis ours). Then he instructs us on what motivates us for this quality of ministry that God expects of us. Three words sum it up: *hope, fear,* and *love.* Let us look at each in turn.

THE MOTIVATION OF HOPE

Paul defines this hope as an "eternal weight of glory" (4:17). From the context, and other relevant passages, he tells us that his belief in the eschatological hope motivated his everyday ministry, both as a Christian and a preacher. It gave him perspective.

The Right Perspective for the Ministry

"For our light affliction, which is but for a moment, is working for us a far more exceeding and eternal weight of glory, while we do not look at the things which are seen, but at the things which are not seen. For the things which are seen are temporary, but the things which are not seen are eternal" (4:17–18). The apostle discovered, as all mature Christians do, that life and service in *time* only derive their full significance when viewed from the perspective of *eternity*. With magnificent phrasing, he shows us that it is only from heaven's standpoint that we will be able to understand the following three truths.

Human Weakness in Our Ministry Is Outmatched by Divine Strength. "Therefore we do not lose heart. Even though our outward man is perishing, yet the inward man is being renewed day by day" (4:16). Paul is not thinking of two distinct entities—"the body" and "the soul"; he is rather describing his total existence from two different viewpoints. His "outer man" is his "creaturely mortality." His "inner man" is his whole person as a new creation (5:17). This daily "inward" renewal is the blessed compensation which only the Christian can experience. As his earthly faculties weaken and decay, the things of the Spirit become increasingly real to him. In the words of James Denney: "The decay of the outward man in the godless [person] is a melancholy spectacle, for it is the decay of everything; in the Christian [however], it does not touch the life which is hidden with Christ in God, and which is in the soul itself a well of water springing up to life eternal."[3]

Present Suffering in Our Ministry Is Outweighed by Future Glory. "For our light affliction, which is but for a moment, is working for us a far more exceeding and eternal weight of glory" (4:17). Because of this daily renewal, the hope of glory transfigured the apostle's afflictions and made them appear relatively light and of brief duration. As Hodge remarks, "It was only by bringing these sufferings into comparison with eternal glory that they dwindled into insignificance."[4] Paul writes in the same vein in his epistle to the Romans: "If indeed we suffer with [Christ], that we may also be glorified together. For I consider that the sufferings of this present time are not worthy to be compared with the glory which shall be revealed in us" (Rom. 8:17–18).

Temporal Things in Our Ministry are Outclassed by Eternal Things. "For the things which are seen are temporary, but the things which are not seen are eternal" (4:18). No one can study the life of the apostle without being impressed with the fact that oftentimes he could have been overwhelmed by outward problems and inward pressures; but such was his eschatological view of the ministry that temporal things were outclassed by eternal things.

You will remember that the secret which kept the Old Testament saints steady, secure, and true to God, amid the trials and temptations of everyday life, was the perspective of a heaven-born hope. Abraham *looked* for a city that had foundations, "whose builder and maker is God." Moses "endured as *seeing* Him who is invisible." The rest "all died in faith, not having received the promises, but having *seen* them . . . were assured of them" (Heb. 11:10, 27, 13, emphasis ours).

So we are exhorted *not* to "look at the things which are seen, but at the things which are not seen" (4:18). With this "upward look," afflictions, ultimately, will pass; the night of sorrow will end; and victory will characterize our ministry in time—and certainly in eternity.

The hope of glory not only provided the apostle with this heavenly perspective on his ministry, it also helped him determine his objectives.

The Right Objective for the Ministry

"For we know that if our earthly house, this tent, is destroyed, we have a building from God, a house not made with hands, eternal in the heavens" (5:1). Paul's objective for the ministry was determined by two aspects of the motivating hope.

The Realization of a Glorified Life. "For in this we groan, earnestly desiring to be clothed with our habitation which is from heaven, if indeed, having been clothed, we shall not be found naked" (5:2–3). No passage in 2 Corinthians has prompted more discussion and division than this. As a result, the diversity of scholarly interpretation is bewildering, to say the least. For our purpose, however, we affirm the balanced position of R.V.G. Tasker, who writes: "Paul is here underlining his certainty that a heavenly shelter awaits him immediately after death, . . . making it clear that that certainty is in no way diminished by the thought that his departure to be with Christ may precede the Lord's return in glory and his own assumption of the resurrection body."[5] Paul knew that at the Rapture or, alternatively, at the Resurrection, he would be transformed into the likeness of his Lord. He tells us about this in his letter to the Philippians (3:20–21). But the apostle was also aware of the fact that life and service here on earth can determine the measure in which we will reflect the resplendent glory of our Lord in a day to come. The solemn fact is that there can be a "nakedness" which is the consequence of an unfaithfulness on earth. G. Campbell Morgan, commenting on these verses (5:2–3), gives this searching interpretation: "It is possible to enter into the heavenly condition with no results accruing from our earthly testimony; *we may be found naked*" (emphasis ours).[6]

What is comforting to know, however, is that the realization of the glorified life can begin right now, through the liberating work of the Holy Spirit in and through our ministry. The apostle affirms, "The Lord is the Spirit; and where the Spirit of the Lord is, there is liberty. But we all, with unveiled face, beholding as in a mirror the glory of the Lord, are being transformed into the same image from glory to glory, just as by the Spirit of the Lord" (2 Cor. 3:17–18). As we daily look into the face of our Lord, mirrored in the Holy Scriptures through the power of the Holy Spirit, we are transfigured into His image, from one degree of glory to another. This metamorphosis should be evident in our lives as preachers. If this change is not taking place, then we are not achieving the true objective of the ministry: "Can others see Jesus in us?"

The Satisfaction of a Glorified Lord. "Therefore we make it our aim, whether present or absent, to be well pleasing to Him" (5:9). Only a life lived with this objective can ensure the unashamed joy of being fully "at home" with the Lord, after the folding of the earthly tent. This "at-homeness" with the Lord is strikingly illustrated by the words of John Wesley when asked, "Supposing you knew you were to die at 12 o'clock tomorrow night, how would you spend the intervening time?" "Why, just as I intend to spend it now. I should preach this evening at Gloucester and again at 5 tomorrow morning. After that I should ride to Shaftesbury, preach in the afternoon and meet the societies in the evening. I should then repair to Martin's house, converse and pray with the family, as usual retire to my room at 10 o'clock, commend myself to my heavenly Father, lie down to rest and wake up in glory."[7]

This is what the motivation of hope calls for in our ministry! But lest we should lose heart, Paul reminds us that the secret of fulfilling this heaven-born hope is the work of God in our hearts by the indwelling of the Holy Spirit. He states, "Now He who has prepared us for this very thing is God, who also has given us the Spirit as a guarantee" (5:5). The presence of the Holy Spirit is not only the source of our unshakable confidence, but also of our sustained courage as we face our duties now, or death if Jesus calls us home.

THE MOTIVATION OF FEAR

"Knowing, therefore, the terror of the Lord, we persuade men" (5:11). The Revised Version renders these words as follows:

"Knowing therefore the fear of the Lord." Nearer the mark is the translation of Conybeare and Howson: "Knowing therefore the fearfulness of the Lord's judgment." Quite plainly, what Paul has in view here is the believer's life and service, as seen in the light of the judgment seat of Christ. Such a prospect should fill every preacher (indeed, every believer) with a healthy and holy fear. There are two reasons for this.

Our Daily Accountability to God

"We must all appear before the judgment seat of Christ, that each one may receive the things done in the body, according to what he has done, whether good or bad" (5:10). The purpose of this review of life and service is that all of us will have to give an account of "the things done in the body" while here on earth. If our motives and ministry are judged as being "good," there will be rewards; on the other hand, if the motives and ministry are judged as being "bad," there will be the loss of reward.

The apostle is even more explicit in his first letter to the Corinthians:

> According to the grace of God which was given to me, as a wise master builder I have laid the foundation, and another builds on it. But let each one take heed how he builds on it. For no other foundation can anyone lay than that which is laid, which is Jesus Christ. Now if anyone builds on this foundation with gold, silver, precious stones, wood, hay, straw, each one's work will become [clear]; for the Day will declare it, because it will be revealed by fire; and the fire will test each one's work, of what sort it is. If anyone's work which he has built on it endures, he will receive a reward. If anyone's work is burned, he will suffer loss; but he himself will be saved, yet so as through fire (1 Cor. 3:10–15).

If our ministries have been dominated by the power of the Holy Spirit, the result will be "gold, silver, [and] precious stones" in the day of judgment; on the other hand, if dominated by the energy of the flesh, our work will represent "wood, hay, [and] straw." A sobering truth indeed—and yet a mighty motivation to not live after the flesh, but after the Spirit!

Our Daily Responsibility to Men

"Knowing . . . the terror of the Lord," says the apostle, "we persuade men" (5:11). His knowledge of the fearful day of judgment not only prevented him from flagging in his work, but provided him with a motivation to persuade men to believe the gospel. For Paul, "the open statement and defense of 'the truth of the gospel' [included] both [the] exposition of the Scriptures about Jesus and the kingdom of God (Acts 17:2–4; 18:4; 19:8; 28:23) and disputation concerning the practical implications of the gospel (Gal. 2:14)."[8] His sense of responsibility was expressed with such authority and exercised with such enthusiasm that the Corinthians, in their blindness, had to conclude that he was mad. So Paul says, "If we are beside ourselves, it is for God; or if we are of sound mind, it is for you" (5:13). We cannot discharge our solemn responsibilities, in the light of eternity, and not be criticized for "excessive emotion" or "sheer lunacy" (Murray J. Harris). Jibes like this were aimed at our Lord (Mark 3:21; John 10:20) and have been leveled at faithful servants of the gospel throughout the centuries.

The famous British preacher, Rowland Hill, addressing the people of Wootton during one of his pastorates, exclaimed: "Because I am earnest in my preaching men call me an enthusiast, a fanatic. When I first came to this part of the country I was walking on yonder hill and saw a gravel pit fall in and bury three human beings alive. I lifted up my voice for help so loudly that I was heard in the town below at a distance of nearly a mile. Help came, and two of the sufferers were rescued. No one called me an enthusiast that day; yet when I see eternal destruction ready to fall on poor sinners, and I call upon them to escape, men dare to call me an enthusiast and a fanatic. How little they know of the fearfulness of my responsibility to men!"

It is well to remember what God said through the prophet Ezekiel, "[If] you do not speak to warn the wicked from his way . . . his blood I will require at your hand" (Ezek. 33:8).

THE MOTIVATION OF LOVE

"For the love of Christ constrains us" (5:14). Of the three aspects of our motivation in Christian service, the greatest of these is love. Paul calls it the *constraining* love of Christ. That word *constraining* is a most interesting one. It occurs twelve times in the New Testament and nine times out of that number it is employed by Luke. Paul uses it here to indicate the twofold manner in which the love of Christ should motivate our ministry.

The Love of Christ Compels Us

"The love of Christ constrains us" (5:14). The concept of "being compelled" is the first idea behind the word. Luke illustrates this powerfully when he describes how Paul, arriving in Corinth, "was *constrained* by the Spirit, and testified to the Jews that Jesus is the Christ" (Acts 18:5, emphasis ours). The Revised Version reads that "Paul was constrained by the word, testifying to the Jews that Jesus was the Christ." Paul was so motivated that he was compelled to testify to the Jews that Jesus was the Christ by the sheer pressure of the Word upon his spirit. As he viewed that great heathen metropolis and saw men and women, for whom Christ died, so beaten by sin and bound by Satan, "necessity [was] laid upon [him to] . . . preach the gospel" (1 Cor. 9:16).

In like manner, we should be compelled by the love of Christ. If our reading of Scripture, as illumined and applied by the Spirit, does not release the compelling love of Christ in us and through us, then our hearts are not right with God, and our service constitutes nothing more than ashes upon a rusty altar! For it is *not our love to Christ* that is in view here, but rather it is *the love of Christ working in us*—mastering, driving, and compelling us. It is the love of God "poured out in our hearts by the Holy Spirit who was given to us" (Rom. 5:5). Such compelling love never flags, never falters, never fails. It is "the expulsive power of a new affection."

The Love of Christ Confines Us

"The love of Christ constrains us" (5:14). "Being confined" is the second idea implicit in our word. When the Lord Jesus disclosed His set purpose to go through with the work which His Father had given Him to do, He said, "I have a baptism to be baptized with; and how am I *straitened* till it be accomplished!" (Luke 12:50 RV). Straitened! That is our word. It denotes being confined within the limits of a certain course of action. It is a straitening that never allows us to deviate from the one set purpose.

This is how the love of God motivated and activated the life of the Lord Jesus; and this is how the love of Christ must motivate and activate our lives. For Him it meant the path of the cross, even unto death, that He might be raised to the glory of God the Father, and so fulfill heaven's redemptive purpose. For us also it must mean the path of the cross unto death, that we might die indeed unto sin and live unto God alone.

Paul declares that the only reasonable interpretation of the love of Christ, as seen at Calvary, is that when He died at Calvary we also died with Him unto sin—once and for all; and that when He rose from the dead, we also rose to live only unto Him. This is the pathway to which the love of Christ confines us (5:14–15).

What an impact such a motivation of love should have on our daily ministry! It should *compel* us to do nothing but the *work* of God, and *confine* us to do nothing but the *will* of God. To be driven by this motivation we need a new vision of Calvary, a deeper understanding of the cross, and a holy baptism of redemptive love.

After Henry Martyn had completed a brilliant education as a student, the Lord called him to serve abroad. "Though several attractive, lucrative vocations were open to him, he said, 'Here I am, Lord: send me to the ends of the earth. Send me even to death itself if it but be in Thy service and in Thy kingdom!' When he fell deeply in love with a girl named Lydia, he told her of his call from God to live and minister in India. Was this agreeable to her? he asked, and pleaded that it might be. But it was not. If he would stay in England, he could have her as his bride; if he went to India, he must do without her. The question came like a drumbeat in his brain—India or Lydia? Lydia or India? Henry Martyn was a mastered man, . . . constrained by the love of Christ. The mastery was his in a crisis involving a crucial choice. 'My dear Lydia and my duty call me different ways, yet God has not forsaken me. I am born for God only, and Christ is nearer to me than father or mother or sister.' So he went to India to 'burn out for God.'"[9]

Here then is the threefold motivation for our ministry: the hope of glory, the fear of judgment, the love of Christ. It only remains for us to ask ourselves whether or not this motivation is real in *personal experience*. Do we know anything of the pull of the unseen, "the powers of the world to come," (Heb. 6:5 KJV) and the pressure of eternal love upon our spirits? If our answer is negative, let us ask God to motivate our lives and service with the hope of glory, the fear of judgment, and the love of Christ. Soon—perhaps sooner than we think—we shall stand before the Bema, the judgment seat of Christ, to give an account of what we have done in the body, whether good or bad. What is our Lord going to say to us? Will it be "Well done, good and faithful servant" or "Shame on you, slothful servant!" A lot depends on our motivation for the ministry. God give every preacher the grace to be activated by the same hope, fear, and love that enabled the apostle to exclaim: "I am compelled to preach!" (1 Cor. 9:16).[10]

"A great philosopher said, 'I have spent my life laboriously doing nothing.' A great emperor said, 'I have tried everything and nothing is of any profit.' Goethe, the great German poet, said, 'My life has been a continual rolling of a stone uphill, which has continually rolled back.'"[11]

But Paul, the preacher, at the end of his life could say, "I have fought the good fight, I have finished the race, I have kept the faith. Finally, there is laid up for me the crown of righteousness, which the Lord, the righteous Judge, will give to me on that Day, and not to me only but also to all who have loved His appearing" (2 Tim. 4:7–8, emphasis ours).

So, preacher friend, our final word to you is:

> Preach the "whole" Word, O man of God,
> Cost what it will, don't compromise;
> Walk in the path the Master trod,
> Then, in "pure faith," expect the prize!

—Stephen F. Olford

CONCLUSION

I charge you therefore before God and the Lord Jesus Christ, who will judge the living and the dead at His appearing and His kingdom: Preach the word! Be ready in season and out of season. Convince, rebuke, exhort, with all longsuffering and teaching. For the time will come when they will not endure sound doctrine, but according to their own desires, because they have itching ears, they will heap up for themselves teachers; and they will turn their ears away from the truth, and be turned aside to fables. But you be watchful in all things, endure afflictions, do the work of an evangelist, fulfill your ministry.

—2 Timothy 4:1–5

A s we conclude these expanded lectures and lessons on the walk, the work, and the word of the preacher "under God," some final thoughts of explanation and exhortation are in order.

First, our *explanation*. As we stated in our introduction, the chapters of this book contain nothing *new*, but they do offer "fresh insights" that we have derived from intensive teaching and training at the Stephen Olford Center for Biblical Preaching. We might add that this material is also backed by over seventy years of combined pastoral and pulpit ministry, both at home and abroad.

Our "tandem teaching" has been designed to complement and supplement each other so as to ensure full coverage of the subjects taught. This will explain the presence and purpose of repetition and amplification in some related chapters.

The most difficult task has been to eliminate *so much* that would be profitable to young preachers and even to older ones! But, in the very nature of things, there has had to be a cutoff point.

Our prayers throughout the whole writing project are best expressed by a "preacher in prison"—even the great apostle—whose only concern was that utterance might be given to him; that he might open his mouth boldly to make known the mystery of the gospel for which he was an ambassador in chains; that he might speak boldly, as he ought to speak (Eph. 6:19–20). That apostolic request of long ago underscores what preaching is all about!

Secondly, our *exhortation*. The ultimate exhortation to any preacher is encapsulated in the words quoted above (vv. 1–5). The imperative urgency of this divine exhortation must be the final challenge to every preacher who reads this book. This is why all attendees at the Stephen Olford Center for Biblical Preaching are handed a copy of *Preaching the Word of God*.[1] The following excerpt summarizes the essence of our view on this topic.

PREACH THE WORD CONSCIENTIOUSLY

"I charge you therefore before God and the Lord Jesus Christ, who will judge the living and the dead at His appearing and His kingdom: Preach the word!" (vv. 1–2). The Greek word rendered "*I charge you*" more accurately reads "*I solemnly charge you.*" Paul employs this language to bring home to Timothy the seriousness of the calling of a preacher. He directs the young man's attention to God and the Lord Jesus Christ, in whose presence the charge is issued and received. He reminds him that he is to preach the Word conscientiously because of *the eternal accountability of the preacher:* "I charge you therefore before God and the Lord Jesus Christ, who will judge the living and the dead at *His appearing. . . .*" The appearing refers, of course, to the Lord's second coming when every believer will have to give account of himself before the judgment seat of Christ (2 Cor. 5:10). Nothing will be hidden before the glorious brightness of the Savior's presence in that day. Paul says, "Each one's work will become manifest; for the Day will declare it, because it will be revealed by fire; and the fire will test each one's work, of what sort it is. If anyone's work which he has built on it endures, he will receive a reward. If anyone's work is burned, he will suffer loss; but he himself will be saved, yet so as through fire" (1 Cor. 3:13–15).

When a servant of God preaches, he cannot afford to be influenced by the reaction of his congregation, or the opposition of his critics: he is accountable to his Lord alone, before whom he will stand or fall in that coming day. No one can preach with eternal values in view and be anything less than conscientious.

Paul takes this thought even further when he warns his son in the faith to remember *the eternal responsibility of the preacher—* "I charge you therefore before God and the Lord Jesus Christ, who will judge the living and the dead at His appearing *and His kingdom.*" Commenting on the phrase *and His kingdom,* the eminent scholar Charles John Ellicott wrote, "Timothy was conjured [charged] by the 'appearing' of Christ when he would have to stand before Him and be judged; he was conjured, too, by 'His kingdom' in which glorious state Timothy hoped to share, for was it not promised that His own should reign with Him?"

Paul has already reminded Timothy that "if we endure, we shall also reign with Him. If we deny Him, He also will deny us" (2 Tim. 2:12). In that coming kingdom, faithful servants of the Master are going to be given places of lasting responsibility. These positions will be determined by the way they have served the Lord here upon earth. Dr. Donald Guthrie points out that "there are many passages in which Paul expounds his idea of rewards for believers," and that this whole concept of eternal responsibility "leaves room for degrees of rewards" (Rom. 14:12; 1 Cor. 3:8; 2 Cor. 4:17; Gal. 6:7; Col. 1:5; 2 Tim. 4:8).

How can any preacher of the Word contemplate such solemn facts and be less than conscientious and transparent in his accountability and responsibility as a preacher?

PREACH THE WORD CONTINUOUSLY

"Preach the word! Be ready in season, out of season" (v. 2). While some differences of opinion exist among commentators on the meaning of this clause, the general idea is plain. Paul is saying literally, "Stand by, be ready at hand." The force of the exhortation must be found not in the verb itself alone, but by coupling it with the word *season*. Essentially, he is saying, "Be at your work, attend to it, always; . . . let nothing stop you; be *always* ready, *always* at hand." Chrysostom, in one of his writings, breaks down the exhortation into two imperatives: take opportunities and make opportunities to preach the Word.

If we are to preach the Word continuously we must *take* opportunities to preach the Word—"Preach the word! Be ready in season." Every opportunity that is planned or programmed for the ministry of the Word should be redeemed to the very best advantage. Our highly-organized religious life affords wide-open doors for an effectual witness. Not only are there the regular church services, but the many other scheduled opportunities which come through the normal channels of Christian work. Within the judicious limits of time and strength, therefore, we should preach the Word *in season*.

To go a step further, we must *make* opportunities to preach the Word—"Preach the Word . . . out of season." So often this statement is misquoted by prefacing the phrase *out of season* with the conjunction *and*. But there is no such word in our text. The reading is "Be ready in season, out of season." *In season* suggests the traditional and prearranged opportunities that come along in the normal program of the church. A preacher can be so conformed to and bound by the great machinery of Christendom that he can lose his inspiration and vision, his sense of freedom and anointing. The minister is to save himself from that. He is not only to take the opportunities given him, but also to make opportunities.

In exhorting Timothy in such a manner, the apostle was practicing what he preached. You have only to study his missionary journeys, as recorded in the Acts of the Apostles, to see how Paul took opportunities to preach the Word, and also made opportunities in city after city (e.g., Acts 16:16–34; 19:9). This was likewise true of our Lord. He not only took advantage of the opportunities to preach the truth in the recognized centers of religious life on the Sabbath day, but He also made opportunities for communicating the message of life. He transformed a mountainside into a Bible conference; a fishing boat into an evangelistic platform; a well-side into a counseling room, and the shadows of evening into an opportunity to lead Nicodemus into the experience of the new birth. He preached the Word continuously—and so must we. Before moving on, we must underscore that the continuous preaching of the Word must *never* be influenced by *changing times* or *clashing trends*. The apostle warns that "the time will come when they [including church members] will not endure sound doctrine" (2 Tim. 4:2). Preachers who say what "itching ears" want to hear will be more popular than the expositor of God's Word. Even more disheartening is the fact that, after years of faithful preaching, people will "turn . . . away from the truth" preferring "myths," rather than solid doctrine! (vv. 3, 4). But come what may, we are to obey the eternal mandate to "preach the word!" (v. 2).

PREACH THE WORD COMPREHENSIVELY

"Preach the word! . . . Convince, rebuke, exhort with all long-suffering and teaching." An examination of these words makes it evident that Paul is here covering the whole range of the preacher's responsibility. Whenever he declares the truth of God he is to make sure that his preaching contains three essential ingredients.

First, there must be *the convictive word*. "Preach the word! . . . Convince [or 'convict']." The word *convict* is the same one which was employed by our Savior when He spoke of the ministry of the Holy Spirit. He announced that "when He has come, He will convict the world of sin, and of righteousness, and of judgment" (John 16:8). Sin must be brought home to the consciousness of the saint, as well as the sinner, in order that he may repent.

It is quite well known how the congregation was deeply moved as Jonathan Edwards preached his sermon "Sinners in the Hands of an Angry God." He had the manuscript held up so close to his eyes that they could not see his face. He went on and on until the people in that crowded church were moved almost beyond control. One man sprang up, rushed down the aisle, and cried, "Mr. Edwards, have mercy!" Others caught hold of the backs of pews lest they should slip into the pit. Most thought that the day of judgment had dawned on them. The power of that sermon is still felt in the United States today. However, the secret of that sermon's power is known to few Christians. Some believers in that vicinity of Enfield, Massachusetts, had become alarmed that, while God was blessing other places, He s ould in anger pass them by. And so they met on the evening before the sermon—and spent that whole night in agonizing prayer. The rest is history. Is it any wonder that conviction of sin followed by repentance and revival swept New England?

Second, there must be *the corrective word*. "Preach the word! . . . rebuke" (v. 2). This is a sharper word than the preceding one. It was used by the archangel Michael when he addressed the devil and said, "The Lord rebuke you" (Jude, v. 9). The term frequently occurs in the Gospels where we read of the Lord Jesus rebuking winds and waves, demons and fevers (see Matt. 8:26; 17:18; Luke 4:39). It is the aspect of preaching which reprimands the sinner (or saint) and seeks to correct his ways. When necessary, the preacher must *chide* or *censure* the backsliders or impenitent people in his congregation. G. Campbell Morgan used to say that the task of the minister was "never to catch, but . . . correct the spirit of the age." In preaching, as well as in our personal witness, God's servants are to be salt in the earth and the light of the world.

Every week affords the opportunity to address moral, social, political, and ecological issues that hit the national and international headlines. But, as we shall see in a moment, our treatment of these *burning issues* should derive its final *authority from the Bible*. If the Word of God has nothing to say on these matters, then our preaching is no better than any other voice outside the pulpit. On the other hand, if we believe that the Bible is God's revelation to man on all matters of faith and practice, then we must also believe that this same Bible relates to all cultures, all countries, and all centuries.

Third, there must be *the constructive word*. "Preach the word! . . . exhort, with all longsuffering and teaching" (v. 2). Having brought his hearers to the place of correction, the servant of God is to build them up. The word *exhort* conveys the thought of encouragement, edification and instruction. While a constructive ministry will be exercized with all gentleness and patience, there must ever be present the solid content of biblical truth.

Expository preaching puts content, power, substance and authority into preaching. The expositor pulls up his chair to where the inspired authors sat as he deals with an explanation of Scripture, focusing the listener's attention on the Bible. He realizes that *the authority behind preaching resides not in the preacher but in the biblical text.* Being conscious and aware of his own inadequacy and weakness, he discovers the power of God in the Word he preaches, which is "living and active, and sharper than any two-edged sword" (Heb. 4:12).

How important, therefore, that all who minister the truth of God should preach the Word comprehensively!

PREACH THE WORD COURAGEOUSLY

"Be watchful in all things, endure afflictions, do the work of an evangelist, fulfill your ministry" (v. 5). The apostle leaves us in no doubt as to what he means by courageous preaching. With well-chosen language he makes it plain that every true preacher of the Word must be *realistic*—"Be watchful in all things" (v. 5). Paul is saying here, "Keep your coolness and presence of mind so as not to be entrapped in forgetfulness or carelessness. Be ever wakeful and ready; be on the watch." The apostle is summing up the warnings and directions that he has given already from chapter 2:14 onward. He is concerned that Timothy should not entangle himself with senseless arguments or subtle allurements, but confine himself to the simple word of truth and steadily tread the old paths in which the apostle walked. This called for realistic courage in Timothy's day, and it calls for similar courage in our times.

The servant of God must be *altruistic:* "Endure afflictions." The context suggests that the afflictions which Timothy was going to face would result from courageous preaching. What was true of Timothy is basically typical of the servant of God today. However, since "we can do nothing against the truth, but for the truth" (2 Cor. 13:8), an altruistic person becomes one who is disinterested in anything save that which is absolute. He is not concerned about his reputation or his preservation so long as he lives and preaches the eternal truth of God.

The courageous preacher must be *evangelistic*: "Do the work of an evangelist" (v. 5). A. T. Robertson suggests that the word *evangelist* here means *the gospelizer* or *the messenger of good news.* As an evangelist, the preacher has the twofold responsibility of proclamation and invitation. As John R. W. Stott aptly puts it:

"We must never issue an appeal without first making the proclamation. Much harm has been done to the souls of men, and much dishonor to the Name of Christ, through neglect of this simple rule. . . . The gospel is not fundamentally an invitation to anything. It is a declaration of what God has done in Christ on the cross for our salvation. The invitation cannot properly be given before the declaration has been given. Men must grasp the truth before they are asked to respond to it." [On the other hand], 'we must never make the proclamation without then issuing an appeal. . . . It is not enough to teach the gospel; we must urge men to embrace it."

The servant of God must be *optimistic*: "Fulfill your ministry" (v. 5) or "see your way through to a completed ministry." There will be times when a minister asks himself, "Can I go any further? This is too much for me!" But he is to remember that God is on the throne. His purposes will never be thwarted. Therefore, the preacher of the Word must never be a defeatist. On the contrary, he must follow in the triumphant train of the Prince of preachers Who steadfastly set His face to do His Father's will until He could exclaim, "It is *finished*" (John 19:30).

Later the great apostle exclaimed in a similar vein: "I have fought the good fight, I have *finished* the race, I have kept the faith. Finally, there is laid up for me the crown of righteousness, which the Lord, the righteous Judge, will give to me on that Day, and not to me only but also to all who have loved His appearing" (2 Tim. 4:7–8, emphasis ours).

What does that mean for you as a preacher of the gospel? In poetic terms, let us state it this way:

> Finish the course, O man of God,
> Follow the path the Master trod.
> Fight the good fight, in Jesus' name,
> Preach the pure Word, with heart aflame.
> Then, in good faith and patient love,
> Wait for your "crown" reserved above!

—Stephen F. Olford

THE PREACHER AND WORSHIP

Joseph M. Stowell, president of Moody Bible Institute, recalls how a friend told him that he was attending a new church. "The services were especially meaningful and fulfilling," he said, "*because they consisted almost entirely of worship*" (emphasis ours). "Doesn't the pastor preach?" asked Stowell. The answer was revealing. The friend replied, "There's a ten-minute message, and it's helpful, but the real focus of the service is worship."[1] This is by no means an isolated practice. In many churches in the U.S.A., the U.K., and in many other parts of the world, it is the "norm."

In our judgment, this mindset not only exposes a fundamental weakness in the local church, but an erroneous understanding of the nature of worship as taught in the Word of God.

THE NATURE OF WORSHIP

As preachers, we need to think through this matter of the nature of worship with great care and much prayer. In the final analysis, *worship* is the very heart of our lives, our *preaching*, and our ministry.

Worship Is Demanded by God

"You shall worship the Lord your God, and Him only you shall serve" (Matt. 4:10; see also Deut. 6:13; 10:20). Worship is not optional, it is obligatory. Our Lord backed this imperative with all the force of divine authority. For any of us to seek worship would be presumption of the highest order, but when the Father seeks worshipers (John 4:23), He is requiring only what is His due. Moreover, if we expect to join the heavenly host of angelic worshipers, we should be practicing here!

Worship Is Directed by God

"God is Spirit, and those who worship Him must worship in spirit and truth" (John 4:24). "The essence of true worship must be on God's terms and in accord with His nature."[2] The point we are stressing here is the fact that *worship is not worship when detached from the Word of God and the Spirit of God.* We cannot substitute preaching for worship or vice versa.

Worship Is Dedicated by God

"We are the circumcision, who worship God in the Spirit, rejoice in Christ Jesus, and have no confidence in the flesh" (Phil. 3:3). This statement gives us a rare insight into God's estimate of true Christian worship. While "the worship of God" is nowhere defined in Scripture (W. E. Vine),[3] it is nonetheless described as "the most momentous, most urgent, and the most glorious action that can take place in human life."[4] In three descriptive clauses Paul elevates "worship" to an "otherworldly" level. Worship is *Spirit-controlled*: "We . . . worship God in the Spirit" (Phil. 3:3). We are not prompted or hampered by human traditions, external rites, or cultural changes. Worship is *Christ-centered*—we worship and "rejoice in Christ Jesus" (Phil. 3:3). Our holy satisfaction comes from recognizing that our help and hope are found in Christ alone. Free from the demands of the law, we rejoice in the liberating grace of Christ. Worship is *God-conceived:*—we worship without "confidence in the flesh" (Phil. 3:3). "Flesh" (*sarx*) refers to what man is outside of Christ. The true believer in Christ has no grounds whatsoever for human pride or boasting. *All true worship is God-conceived and God-received.* Man was created to render worship, while God eternally exists to receive worship!

With these preliminary observations we now want to underscore what we mean by "the preacher and worship." Preaching is *not* a solo effort! It is part of worship; indeed, it is the very heart of worship. Few preachers/writers have expressed this more clearly and convincingly than Paul S. Rees in the material reproduced here from his article "The Art of Preaching as an Act of Worship."[5]

> No sermon, however homiletically artistic, is ever complete if considered solely as an individual effort by the preacher. It is the congregational context, as well as the sermonic content, that must be taken into account.
>
> The subject is worship. The issue is homiletics versus liturgics. While some Protestant groups have been far out on the rim of this debate, others have been fervently involved. Shall we revive liturgy in order to enrich worship? Or, as some would prefer to put it, shall we enrich liturgy in order to enhance worship? This is not the place to explore the ramifications of the debate. It is the place, however, to point out—and to protest against—a false antithesis. Granted that in evangelical Protestantism, particularly of the "free church" variety, the tendency has been to misconstrue and undervalue those forms of congregational prayer and praise which precede the sermon. In this distorted perspective we tend to look upon these exercises and offerings as "preliminaries." The word should be an offense to us. The abandonment of its absurdity cannot be too swift.
>
> But now an opposite peril threatens. Protestants, we are told, have become a sermon-tasting breed who, whether fascinated by a pulpit star or bored by a homiletical hack, are strangers to the art, the beauty, the dignity, the sacramental mysticism of worship. On the whole, those who exalt ritual denigrate preaching. Whether by accident or design, it is generally true that the heavily liturgical service is the service of the ten-to-twelve-minute sermon. Again, the numerous facts and facets of the present discussion are beyond the range of our purpose. The extremists in both camps can ill afford to be unteachable. What one deplores is fallacy of fancying the sermon as something apart from worship. It is implied—and occasionally declared—that in the liturgy God is acting, while in the preaching it is man.
>
> This is dangerously opaque thinking, the corrective answer to which is the following series of insights:

PREACHING IS A REDEMPTIVE EVENT

True preaching, says Dr. Donald G. Miller in *Fire in Thy Mouth,* "is an extension of the Incarnation into the contemporary moment, the transfiguration of the Cross and the Resurrection from ancient facts of a remote past into living realities of the present." What we have in authentic preaching is not a repetition of Calvary (since that is unrepeatable) but a contemporizing of it. The Scriptures having dependably recorded it, the Holy Spirit now dynamically affirms it; and in the preacher, if he be the man of God he should be, both the record and the affirmation find a claiming voice. This makes the sermon vastly more than something said; it is something *done*. It is the saving, healing, strengthening God in action through his servant for the people. To separate this from a church's worship experience is perilous nonsense [emphasis ours].

PREACHING, MOREOVER, IS ACTUALLY A CONGREGATIONAL FUNCTION

In an essay entitled "Preaching as Worship" the scintillating theologian of a generation ago, Peter T. Forsyth, observes that "true preaching presupposes a church, and not merely a public." Reading this, my own mind leaped back to Peter's sermon on the day of Pentecost. The account begins with the revealing statement, "But Peter, standing up with the eleven, said . . ." (Acts 2:14). The proclamation of the gospel to an unbelieving "public" was made in the context of a believing "church."

Furthermore, it will be seen that in Peter's preaching that day the church was preaching. A New Testament sermon, far from being a parade of the opinions of a man with a clerical title, should be in effect the congregation witnessing to its faith—both for its own edification and for the persuasion of those who were without faith. It is the congregation "hearing their one hope," not with "an empty wonder" but with illuminated adoration, not 'sadly contented with a show of things' but discontented with anything through which the eternal is failing to show.

To say that such preaching does not have in it the dimension of worship is to be under a strange illusion.

PREACHING, WE SHOULD NOT HESITATE TO SAY, HAS A SACRAMENTAL CHARACTER

Not sacerdotal, mind you, but sacramental! A sermon is not a communication of grace in which the transmission is guaranteed by the insignia of the office of preacher. On the other hand, the sermon is indeed the visible and audible sign of the grace that is given when, to borrow the language of the epistle to the Hebrews, "the word preached" is "mixed with faith" on the part of those who hear (Heb. 4:2). The pulpit should be seen as a sign of the grace of God standing within the divinely created community of faith—the church.

When I was a young preacher I read something by the Archbishop of Canterbury, William Temple, that has lived with me across these several decades: "For worship is the submission of all our nature to God. It is the quickening of conscience by His holiness; the nourishment of mind with His truth; the purifying of imagination by His beauty; the opening of the heart to His love; the surrender of will to His purpose; and all of this gathered up in adoration, the most selfless emotion of which our nature is capable, and therefore, the chief remedy for that self-centeredness which is our original sin and the source of all actual sin."

Surely that person holds too low a view of preaching who doubts that it can contribute magnificently to the worthy ends so eloquently described by Archbishop Temple.

A further insight is this: Preaching is an oblation. My Webster gives, as one definition of oblation, "something offered in worship." So be it! An authentic sermon qualifies.

An authentic sermon is an offering of prayer. The preacher's? Yes. And the congregation's too. A sermon not steeped in prayer is unworthy of the name.

It is an offering of the intellect. Read Paul in 1 Corinthians 14 on the relation between prophesying and intelligibility. As John Stott says tersely, "The mind matters." Preaching is seriously flawed if it consists of little more than an entertaining engagement of the emotions.

It is an offering of the will—first the preacher's and then the congregation's. Whether the sermon is about the gift of eternal life, the summons to holy living, the practice of stewardship, the life of prayer, or the lordship of Christ over our attitudes on race, money, sex, and war, it brings the hearers to some "valley of decision" in which the response is Yes or No or, at least, Not yet.

A lecture may feed the mind or titillate the emotions; a sermon, while doing both, is distinctively a call to action. It confronts the will.

A sermon is, in Forsythe's unforgettable phrase, "the organized Hallelujah" of the church, joyously confessing its faith in the gospel, obediently submitting to its claims.

If such an offering is not worship, then nothing is!

PRAYERFULLY DETERMINE THE ORDER OF WORSHIP

With the foregoing material from Paul S. Rees as a backdrop, we now want to offer some suggestions.

With a weighed balance between *form* and *freedom*, determine that you have a *purpose*, as well as a procedure for the worship service. Here we are not talking about an evangelistic effort; that will be dealt with in appendix C. Needless to say, in the normal course of events, "unsaved" people will come to a worship service, and if it is *truly* a "worship service"—alive with the awesome presence of God and the authentic message of God—such an "unbeliever" will be "convinced by all, ... and . . . falling down on his face, he will worship God and report that God is truly among you" (1 Cor. 14:24–25).

But here we are talking about a *worship* service for those who "worship the Father in spirit and truth; for the Father is seeking such to worship Him" (John 4:23). Here are some specifics.

The Contemplation of Worship

Preparation is our key word here. Although preparation should be a way of life from one Sunday to another, Saturday night—and Sunday morning in particular—should be devoted to getting ready to meet God in corporate worship. As A. W. Tozer used to put it: In worship, "our spirits . . . stand silent and breathless . . . in the presence of that awful Wonder, that Mystery, that unspeakable Majesty, before whom the prophets used to fall, and before whom Peter and John and the rest of them fell down as if dead."[6] We cannot view worship in these terms and not be serious about personal and family preparation. This was a "family discipline" in our home, and it paid off then, and now!

The Celebration of Worship

With "unhurried punctuality" worship should begin with a sense of reverence and relevance. It should include a call to worship, an invocation, an appropriate choral or choir number, or a well-chosen hymn. What is important is the pastor/preacher's conscious attempt to *draw* the whole congregation into *the attitude, activity, and atmosphere of worship*. This will include praising, praying, and preaching.

The Celebration of Praising. All that takes place under this heading should be a symphony of sequence and significance. Whether it is the anthem by the choir, the song by the soloist, or the hymns/choruses by the congregation, all *must* prepare for the sermon. The importance of sequential thrust cannot be overstressed. C. S. Lewis used to say, "Cut the trough and the water will flow!" The impact and importance of the exposition of God's Word are hindered or helped by this aspect of the worship service. Great care should be given to the *timing* of this praise period. In no way should any activity of a worship service cramp or curtail the reading and preaching of God's Word.

The Celebration of Praying. Congregational involvement should be carried over to this vital aspect of worship. The apostle Paul exhorts that "*first of all* . . . supplications, prayers, intercessions, and giving of thanks be made for all men" (1 Tim. 2:1, emphasis ours). When did you last hear a *genuine pastoral prayer* that lifted you into the very throne room of heaven? However prayers are offered, the congregation should be invited, involved, and impacted by the celebration of praying. Sometimes it is a good practice to have those who have needs or who desire to pour out their hearts before God to quietly move to the altar or some assigned section of the church to pray and praise. This, of course, can be done in the pews as well; but for some people the very fact of coming forward is an open confession of their need and purpose. The pastor should prepare his prayers as well as his sermons! Read C. H. Spurgeon's prayers, as well those of other great men of the pulpit. You will be ashamed—if not convicted—of your own shallow, self-centered, and sporadic public prayers.

The Celebration of Preaching. This is the *heart* of worship. As we have observed from the words of Dr. Rees, "The art of preaching is the act of worship." This is where the anointed expositor, through incarnational commitment and involvement, becomes part of his congregation. The whole redemptive event should be interactional and invitational from beginning to end. It is not without significance that most of the personal pronouns found in the applicatory portions of the Epistles are in the *plural* rather than the singular form. *You cannot separate the reading of Scripture from the preaching of Scripture.* So make much of the public reading of God's Holy Word. There is a very real sense in which the reading of Scripture is the most important part of a worship service. For this reason, it is a good practice to ask your people to *stand* for the reading of God's Word (see Neh. 8). Encourage participation by inviting everyone to bring his or her Bible and to read along—*some portions in unison.* In your preaching, use *all* the "arts of proclamation" to keep your listeners involved: the rhetorical questions, the repeated applications, the personal invitations, the interest builders, the human interactions, and above all, the anointed authority of true biblical preaching.

The Consummation of Worship

There are two aspects of the consummation of a worship service that require comment.

The Invitation. The whole purpose of proclamation is to invoke an appropriate response from the worshiping community. If that does not occur, the congregation has *not* worshiped! So often we think of "invitations" in terms of evangelistic appeals alone. But this is a big mistake. As we have pointed out elsewhere,[7] without obedience on the part of the Christian to imparted truth (the sermon), there follows stunted growth and immaturity in the church. Scattered manna (by the preacher) without corresponding appropriation and assimilation breeds worms! (Exod. 16:20). The apostle Paul puts it this way: "Knowledge puffs up, but love edifies. And if anyone thinks that he knows anything, he knows nothing yet as he ought to know. But if anyone loves God, this one is known by Him" (1 Cor. 8:1–3).

How the invitation is given and *followed up* is a matter of first importance for every preacher/pastor. This must be thought through with great care within the context of your particular church tradition and practice; but it cannot be ignored without dire consequences.

J. C. Macauley summarizes the importance of calling people to worship:

> If worship is an activity of the mind, it will call for meditation upon the transcendent being of God—His power, His glory, His holiness, His love, and all His other attributes. To put it in one comprehensive phrase, His infinite worth.
>
> If worship is an activity of the heart, it will involve emotion, as some of the Hebrew and Greek terms imply: such as *yare,* which conveys the thought of godly fear; or *sebomai* with its sense of veneration.

> If worship is an activity of the will, it will call for deliberate full sub-mission to the divine will. Again the Hebrew and Greek terms help us: *sabah,* signifying a bowing down in token of submission; or *prosku-neo,* a picture word suggesting a kissing of the hand of the one to whom you give allegiance.
>
> From this it is evident that worship is a moving out of the whole being to God, not some sensual feeling mistaken for blessing.[8]

What is this "moving out of the whole being to God"? The answer to that question is summed up in our New Testament word *sacrifice.* Response to God's truth is worshipful sacrifice. W. E. Vine has researched this for us, so let us give heed to his findings:

1. "The body of the believer [is] presented to God as a living 'sacrifice,' Rom. 12:1." This is the *personal response.* It could be the initial response of someone newly come to faith, but it *must* be the affirmed response of every Christian if he or she is to know the transforming power of the Word to renew the mind in order to appreciate more deeply "the good and acceptable and perfect will of God" (Rom. 12:2).

2. "Material assistance rendered to servants of God, Phil. 4:18." This is the *possessional response.* The receiving of the sacrificial offerings of God's people is an act of worship. Once again, the appropriate response to proclaimed truth is sacrifice in kind. The offering is not an insignificant "appendage" to a religious service!

3. The "praise" of God's people, Hebrews 13:15. This is the *praiseful response.* This is a serious deficiency in our worship ser-vices. After great preaching under the anointing of the Holy Spirit, why not let God's people confess their faith, hope, and love in praiseful response? "Out of the abundance of the heart the mouth speaks" (Matt. 12:34b). This is a universal principle, and we ignore it in our worship services. If singing has to be curtailed in the ear-lier part of the service, so be it! Even the invitation to confess Christ publicly or the invitation for baptism and church membership can be appropriately included in this time of *praiseful response.*

4. "Doing good to others and communicating with their needs, Heb. 13:16." This is the *practical response.* Included in this aspect of worshipful response we could add such references as Philippians 2:17 and 1 Peter 2:5.[9]

All this and more are implicitly and explicitly involved in the giving of a Spirit-guided and guarded invitation. This is worship!

The Benediction. Whether you employ the New Testament benediction (1 Cor. 16:23; 2 Cor. 13:14) or the Old Testament benediction (Num. 6:24–26), make this act of worship both meaningful and *memorable*. In the Old Testament version you are invoking the blessing of *divine security*—"The LORD . . . keep you"; the blessing of *divine sufficiency*—"The LORD . . . be gracious to you"; and the blessing of *divine serenity*—"The LORD . . . give you peace." That is dynamite! Your people must leave with the sense of God *upon* them and *in* them!

CAREFULLY DELETE THE OBSTRUCTIONS TO WORSHIP

Every pastor/preacher should study the dynamics of a worship service and determine what constitutes potential or actual obstructions to worship. This exercise should be carried out on a regular basis. Churches differ in practice and tradition, so to generalize would be out of place; but we all know how a Sunday morning can be virtually ruined because precautions or preparations were not in place. Among the "legion" of obstructions that could be named, let us give you a sample of three.

Introductions
Whether this refers to a person or an event in the worship service is not our concern. Lengthy and flowery introductions distract and divert from the purpose and *flow* of worship. What is more, it *wastes* the precious time that should be given to God in worship. Worship is not a "spectator sport." The platform is not a performance stage; and more importantly is the Word of the Lord which says, "'Let not the wise man glory in his wisdom, let not the mighty man glory in his might, nor let the rich man glory in his riches; but let him who glories glory in this, that he understands and knows Me, that I am the LORD, exercising lovingkindness, judgment, and righteousness in the earth. For in these I delight,' says the Lord" (Jer. 9:23–24). It is not without significance that when Paul writes his most definitive statement on preaching (1 Cor. 2:1–5), he quotes Jeremiah and declares, "He who glories, let him glory in the LORD" (1 Cor. 1:31).

Intimations
If you attend worship in Scotland, you will hear the word *intimations* when the notices are given! *Webster's New World Dictionary* defines it as "a formal announcement or notice or declaration."

There is a famous church in London where *three* minutes, and *no more*, are allowed for the "intimations." Notices should be given before the call to worship or at the end of the service. Depending on the information, announcements can steal time and stifle truth. Imagine a long statement being read about a church meeting upcoming that has to do with some *emotional issue!* That is tough to block out before God's man approaches "the sacred desk" to expound the Scriptures! How such an obstruction is handled is not our purpose here; but you must devise the right and effective way to deal with the problem of intimations.

Interruptions

Every church will have these; but how can they be minimized? Here is where ushers, deacons, elders, and even staff have to be trained for such emergencies. At our church in New York, *anything* could happen on a given Sunday: a person could faint or have a heart attack; a baby could cry (even though provision for all infants was available); a heckler could challenge the preacher; or a latecomer could march right down to the front of a packed church and then not find a seat! We trained our leaders to handle every eventuality—and rarely was worship interrupted. If and when there was a crisis, our procedure was to pause, ask people to bow in prayer, and request God's overruling; during this time the crisis was taken care of.

Much more could be added to underscore the need to delete potential or actual obstructions to worship; but this must suffice.

In conclusion, let us remember the inspired words of David: "Give to the LORD the glory due His name; bring an offering, and come before Him. Oh, worship the LORD in the beauty of holiness!" (1 Chron. 16:29).

THE PREACHER AND MUSIC

W e cannot read church history without observing the great influence music has had on the evangelization of the world and the edification of the church. Hostile and barbarous tribes that had never heard of the name of Jesus were converted through the singing of the early Christian fathers. The hymns of Martin Luther did much to fire the Reformation, and so it has been with all evangelistic endeavors in every age of the church. But music, which is the language of the soul, has found its greatest expression in *the ministry of worship and teaching of the local congregation.* In Old Testament times, the form of praise was more organized and dramatized than what we find in the early days of the church. Then, singing seems to have been characterized more by spontaneity, simplicity, and sincerity.

Having said this, however, there is ample evidence that clear principles are laid down for us in the New Testament concerning the substance, standard, and secret of music in the church. Let us examine these principles in greater detail.

THE SUBSTANCE OF MUSIC IN THE CHURCH

Writing on the subject, Paul exhorts: "And do not be drunk with wine, in which is dissipation; but be filled with the Spirit, speaking to one another in psalms and hymns and spiritual songs, singing and making melody in your heart to the Lord" (Eph. 5:18–19).

We have here not only an interesting portrayal of worship as it was conducted in the early church but also an apostolic directive for Christian worship for all time. The context draws a sharp contrast between the pure and simple observances of the Christian assembly at Ephesus and the riotous extravagances that characterized the heathen festivities. In those pagan ceremonies, intoxication and licentiousness were recognized accompaniments. In the local church, however, Christians were to be filled with the Holy Spirit, thus abandoning carnal practices and giving themselves to corporate worship by singing and making melody to the Lord. The pagans separated morality from religion, while believers saw neither possible without the other. Thus worship to God was rendered "in the beauty of holiness" (Ps. 29:2).

William Barclay points out that "the early church was a singing church. Its characteristics were psalms, hymns, and spiritual songs. The early church had a happiness that made men sing."[1]

Let us, therefore, examine the substance of church music in God's plan throughout this age of grace.

The Psalms

The "psalms" primarily denoted music with instrumental accompaniment; "a sacred song, sung to musical accompaniment" (W. E. Vine). Psalms refer, of course, to the Old Testament Psalter which has provided a perennial source of Christian praise from the earliest time. They were familiar in Jewish worship and, as we know, used in apostolic worship (Acts 4:24; 1 Cor. 14:26; James 5:13). These psalms constitute the greatest songbook known to man. Born out of rich experience and inspired by the Holy Spirit, the Hebrew hymnbook contains every form of worshipful expression. Would to God that something of the substance of these wonderful psalms could be heard more often in our congregational singing today!

The Hymns

The "hymns" are distinguished by most scholars as being mainly vocal music rendered by the congregation and directed to God in devotion as well as petition (Matt. 26:30; Acts 16:25). Examples of these hymns are found both in the Gospels and in the Epistles. We can think, for instance, of the Christmas music of Mary (Luke 1:45–55); of Zacharias (Luke 1:67–79); and Simeon (Luke 2:25–32, 34–35), and then of such a lofty expression of hymnody as Paul's words concerning the incarnation, where he exclaims: "Great is the mystery of godliness: God was manifested in the flesh, justified in the Spirit, seen by angels, preached among the Gentiles, believed on in the world, received up in glory" (1 Tim. 3:16). Since then there has been a wealth of good and great hymns that have come down to us from one generation to another. But whether ancient or modern, the hymn should be the vehicle for expressing what might be termed "musical theology."

The Songs

The "songs" were the lyrical effusions of the early church. Dr. Lightfoot includes in this concept of "spiritual songs"—solos, instrumental music, and spiritual utterances. Songs were often rendered spontaneously, like the genuine "spirituals" of more modern times; and it is interesting to observe that Paul qualifies this kind of song with the word "spiritual." Only those who know what it is to be consciously filled with the Holy Spirit can truly sing "spiritual songs."

This brings us to examine, in the next place:

THE STANDARD OF MUSIC IN THE CHURCH

Writing again on this theme, Paul says: "Let the word of Christ dwell in you richly in all wisdom, teaching and admonishing one another in psalms and hymns and spiritual songs, singing with grace in your hearts to the Lord. . . . Be filled with the Spirit. . . . Whatever you do, do all to the glory of God" (Col. 3:16; Eph. 5:18; 1 Cor. 10:31).

Taking these three exhortations into consideration puts the standard of music on a high level indeed. Let us remember that "holiness adorns [God's] house" (Ps. 93:5), and that in all our acts of worship we are ever to observe the apostolic injunction that "all things be done decently and in order" (1 Cor. 14:40).

All Music in the Church Must Be Biblically Edifying

"Let the word of Christ dwell in you richly in all wisdom, teaching and admonishing one another in psalms and hymns and spiritual songs, singing with grace in your hearts to the Lord" (Col. 3:16).

The worship of the church is here viewed from the standpoint of the edification of the believers. Singing is never intended to be an exercise in emotional release, or even intellectual entertainment, but rather a ministry of biblical instruction. This instruction is to be understood as representing positive and negative truth.

Teaching refers to the positive impartation of truth, while *admonishing* introduces the negative element in doctrine. So we see that all singing must be rooted in God's Word. This is why you cannot ever separate singing from preaching (see appendix A).

While there is such a thing as "absolute music," with its own distinctive place and function in the life of the church, it fails if it does not convey the Word of Christ.

> Absolute music may carry the worshiper to the border of revelation, but cannot in its wordless state have any part in revelation. At its very best, it is part of creation, praising its Creator, but never a carrier of the Gospel of salvation. There is . . . a certain relationship between the wordless instrumental music and speaking in tongues, in the early church. The speaking in tongues had no power to edify or bring the unsaved to repentance and salvation. Interpretation, through the Word, was always necessary.
>
> Music is the ideal means for communicating inward and subjective concepts. No power on earth is more potent than good church music for inspiring the faithful to higher motives and nobler resolves (emphasis ours).[2]

It is on record that when sinful men, who were bent on murder, could not be tamed by the austere utterances of John Wesley or the powerful oratory of George Whitefield, the singing of spiritual songs by Charles Wesley humbled them.

So it has been with all gospel endeavors in every age of the Christian church. No wonder Paul says: "Singing with grace in your hearts to the Lord" (Col. 3:16). John Calvin interprets this as singing "graciously" or "acceptably." Handley Moule renders it as "gratefully singing." Thus as we sing, it should be with grace, gratitude, and glory; *for all music is unto the Lord.* And we can never engage in this exercise without being edified.

All Music in the Church Must Be Spiritually Unifying

"And do not be drunk with wine, in which is dissipation; but be filled with the Spirit, speaking to one another in psalms and hymns and spiritual songs, singing and making melody in your heart to the Lord, giving thanks always for all things to God the Father in the name of our Lord Jesus Christ, *submitting to one another* in the fear of God" (Eph. 5:18–21, emphasis ours).

Even in life outside of the church there is a unifying power in music. This is why countries have their national anthems; this is why armies have their bands; this is why halls of learning have their school songs; and so on. But what is true outside is even more significantly real inside the church.

In the Old Testament we read that "it came to pass, when the trumpeters and singers were as one, to make one sound to be heard in praising and thanking the LORD, and [that] when they lifted up their voice with the trumpets and cymbals and instruments of music, and praised the LORD, saying, 'For He is good, for His mercy endures forever,' that the house, the house of the LORD, was filled with a cloud, so that the priests could not continue ministering because of the cloud; for the glory of the LORD filled the house of God" (2 Chron. 5:13–14).

"Music thus serves as a catalyst to unify the atoms of human individuality. This is especially true of congregational singing. St. Basil, one of the church fathers, once said, 'Singing is a mighty bond of union, linking people together in a symphony of one song.'

"This unique power of music stems from the fact that it instills in us a sense of well-being, spiritually, physically and emotionally. We respond to sounds unconsciously. This natural reaction to sound underlies all our music experience."[3]

Even more important is the theological aspect of this phenomenon. Paul says: "And do not be drunk with wine, in which is dissipation; but be filled with the Spirit; speaking . . . singing and . . . submitting" (Eph. 5:18–21). And we must remember that the Agent of unity in the church is the Holy Spirit. In this epistle to the Ephesians, Paul has already exhorted his readers to "keep the unity of the Spirit in the bond of peace" (4:3). Thus the church that sings together stays together. Just as it is necessary to come together for prayer, so it is imperative that the church gather for psalms, hymns, and spiritual songs. How important, then, is that exhortation not to forsake "the assembling of ourselves together" (Heb. 10:25).

A further word here is in order. In appendix A, we pointed out the importance of celebrating *singing with preaching*. With that in mind, let us add that singing only contributes to preaching when it prepares or undergirds the congregation with the theme and thrust of the sermon. Spiritually insensitive and biblically uninformed ministers of music or choir directors can virtually nullify the impact of a sermon with irrelevant and irreverent music. This could be a solo, a choir number, or an inappropriate hymn (plus deadening remarks). We have just observed from Scripture that *all music in the church must be spiritually unifying*. Ministers of music should work closely and prayerfully with the pastor/preacher for EVERY service in the church, convention/conference ministry, and even evangelistic crusades.

All Music in the Church Must Be Personally Purifying

"Whatever you do, do all to the glory of God" (1 Cor. 10:31). Since glory is the outshining of God's character, it follows that only music calculated to reflect God's Person, reveal God's presence, and release God's power in any given service is music performed to the glory of God.

Few theologians have ever valued music higher than did Martin Luther. In a preface to a songbook published in 1538, he wrote: "Experience testifies that, after the Word of God, only music deserves to be praised as the mistress and the governess of the emotions of the human heart, by which emotions human beings are ruled and often torn asunder as if by their masters. A greater praise of music than this we cannot imagine. . . . It is out of consideration for this power of music that the fathers and the prophets willed, and not in vain, that nothing be more closely bound up with the Word of God than music."[4]

Such a statement as this leads us inevitably to the question as to what constitutes *good* music. Surely the supreme answer is the effect that it has upon our spirits, our minds, our hearts, our wills, our total behavior. If music leads us to know, love, praise, and serve God, then it is good music. On the other hand, if music lowers the high concepts of worship and merely stirs our baser natures, then it is bad music.

> It becomes our duty as Christians to learn how to discern between that which is musically fitting and that which is not. Especially is this so today when church music suffers from certain chronic ills, such as sentimentalism, theatricalism and virtuosity. We must be alert to prevent these ills from developing through weak melodies or harmonizations.

The melody is a carrier of sensual energies and may open the portals to the highest as well as the lowest regions of our souls. Weak and effeminate melodies may move people emotionally but have little or no effect on the will. Many will insist that this is "useful" music, but . . . the church would be better off by cultivating a sense of abstract beauty and give this so-called usefulness a good rest!

Music must be listened to seriously. The more one learns to appreciate the beautiful, the more he will avoid and despise the ugly. Frank Roscoe has truly said, "Education is more a matter of infection than injection." If we expose ourselves to the infection of great church music we are bound to catch it. This is true concerning all the arts as vehicles for worship.

Music may have the power to move the soul of man for good or ill, but let us not forget that it cannot add anything to God's Word—nor can . . . architecture or painting. But no art communicates more directly to the heart of man than music; [thus] in the words of Ulrich Zwingli, the great Swiss scholar and reformer, "No teaching, no injunctions, sink so deeply into the heart of man as does music." Music has power to intensify the word sung and to prepare the way for the Holy Spirit to edify the believer or to transform the unbeliever.[5]

So we see that the standard of music in the church should be biblically edifying, spiritually unifying, and personally purifying. This brings us to our closing consideration.

THE SECRET OF MUSIC IN THE CHURCH

"I will sing with the spirit, and I will also sing with the understanding" (1 Cor. 14:15). In these words lie the secret of all good church music. To help us understand what the apostle is saying, let me state the secret in this form. For music to be all that God intended it to be in the life of the church, it must be rendered with fervent participation and faithful interpretation.

Fervent Participation

"I will sing with the spirit" (1 Cor. 14:15). The New Testament speaks of "worship in [the] spirit" (John 4:24), "pray[ing] with the spirit" (1 Cor. 14:15), "sing[ing] with the spirit" (1 Cor. 14:15), "serv[ing] with my spirit" (Rom. 1:9), etc. The spirit realm is always associated with fervency. For example, we read of Apollos who "being fervent in spirit . . . spoke and taught accurately the things of the Lord" (Acts 18:25). Then again, Paul exhorts his readers in Rome to be "fervent in spirit, serving the Lord" (Rom. 12:11).

Fervency characterized the life and ministry of our Lord. Indeed, His fervency speaks of spiritual warmth, passion, action, intensity, and feeling. There is nothing static about fervency. Add to this the word *participation* and you have what it means to "sing with the spirit."

We remember Martyn Lloyd-Jones remarking on one occasion that he could always discern the spiritual state of any congregation by the spirit of their singing. This was a great encouragement at the time, because he was commenting on the congregational singing of Calvary Baptist Church in New York City! He had traveled widely throughout the States and was disturbed by what he found elsewhere. Indeed, he gave us one of the greatest compliments by stating publicly that he had not heard such singing since he left Wales!

Along with this fervent participation, there is another element in the secret of music in the church.

Faithful Interpretation

"I will also sing with the understanding" (1 Cor. 14:15). You will remember that Paul has been speaking about tongues, and then he adds: "Yet in the church I would rather speak five words with my understanding, that I may teach others also, than ten thousand words in a tongue" (1 Cor. 14:19). Earlier in this passage, Paul has declared that to *fail* to communicate is to be *unfruitful in understanding* (v. 14). Thus, the proof of faithful interpretation in music is fruitfulness. If sinners are not saved and saints are never sanctified by the music of the church, then that music does not justify its place in the house of God. The Bible teaches that when sinners are converted, God puts "a new song in [their] mouth[s]—praise to our God; many will see it and fear, and will trust in the Lord" (Ps. 40:3). It is clear also that saints would be sanctified by singing as they teach and admonish "one another in psalms and hymns and spiritual songs" (Col. 3:16). For this very reason, music is described in Scripture as a "sacrifice of praise" (Heb. 13:15).

Thus for music to fulfill its true function in the church, it must *interpret* the being and nature and purpose of God as revealed in the Lord Jesus Christ. Our primary attention will be on that which is *divine*, rather than that which is merely human. Today, alas, the attitude of most congregations is that of passivity. They are not *involved* in the worship service. This may be due, in many instances, to faulty interpretation, rather than faithful interpretation of music.

It is evident, then, that music requires the best and highest that is possible to produce with the material and talents at our disposal. It may be brilliant, but it must not be showy; it may be expressive, but it must not be sentimental; it may be solemn, but it must never be dull; it may even display a measure of excitement, but there must be no taint of sensualism. Entertainment has never been, and must never be, the function of music in the church. Faithful interpretation must always lead us to God the Father, God the Son, and God the Holy Spirit—through the performed combination of melody, harmony, poetry, and theology that evokes a worshipful response.

So we have seen what the New Testament has to say about the preacher and music in the church. God has not left us in the dark as to our holy privilege and high responsibility in the art of "making melody . . . to the Lord." In the words of Robert Shaw: "Let us see to it that music shall be as worthy an act of worship as the spoken word." God has married *preaching* and *praising*; and what God has joined together, let not man put asunder!

To ensure that the divine principles discussed above are implemented in the music program of the church, we suggest a choir covenant that we have tested and proved to the glory of God and the blessing of the church.

CHOIR COVENANT

In applying for membership in our Church Choir, we wish you to be fully acquainted with the spiritual and practical implications of such an important share in the worship of God. Experience has proved that the influence of a Choir can never be neutral, and that the whole spiritual life of the church is affected by the condition of the Choir. We want you, therefore, to give prayerful consideration to the terms of this "Covenant of Membership," and then append your signature and return it to the Pastor before being received into the membership of the Choir.

1. I hereby give witness to the fact that I have received the Lord Jesus Christ as my personal Saviour, and acknowledge His authority to rule my life by the power of the Holy Spirit.

2. I appreciate the importance and significance of my membership in the Church Choir and will therefore endeavor to relate my interest and work in the Choir to the rest of the life of the church.

3. I recognize that failure to comply with the terms of this covenant will call for such discipline as may be deemed necessary by action of the church.

4. I agree to submit my voice to such evaluation as the Music Director may require, and to accept his decision as to my suitability for the Choir as final.

5. I promise to be regular in attendance at Choir rehearsal, and to give loyal support to the Music Director and to all the ministry of the Choir.

6. I acknowledge that the testimony of my lips should be the outward expression of my Christian experience and that, therefore, holiness of character and conduct should characterize my life at all times.

7. I understand that although I am leading the worship of the church in song, I must be inconspicuous in so doing and that my whole aim must not be to attract attention to myself, but rather by my Christian behavior and humility seek to point people to the Lord Jesus Christ. My ambition must be to sing every anthem, solo, or hymn with the definite object of magnifying my Lord and bringing blessing to those who watch and listen.

8. I realize that every service in the church constitutes a spiritual conflict between the forces of heaven and hell, and that the enemy of souls will always seek to oppose the work of conversion and blessing. Knowing this, I shall endeavor by a constant spirit of prayerfulness and expectancy to share the burden of the ministry with the Pastor.

Having carefully and prayerfully read the conditions and implications of Choir membership, I gladly assent to them and trust by the power of the Holy Spirit to adhere to them.

Signature _____

Date _____

THE PREACHER AND EVANGELISM

Our focus in this appendix is on expounding the Word of God from the pulpit with a view to reaching the unsaved. The problem the average preacher/pastor faces is that of addressing an audience that does not constitute an *evangelistic target!* So before we can move on to the main burden of evangelistic preaching from the pulpit, we must think in terms of *preparation*—not so much of the sermon material, but of the human material—the people who fill the pews every Lord's Day, morning or evening.

Let us begin by stating a general principle. In church ministry, *we gather for worship, and we scatter for witness.* The primary purpose of expository preaching is to warn every man and teach "every man in all wisdom, that we may present every man perfect in Christ Jesus" (Col. 1:28). Only as the saints are edified will they effectively impact society as "salt" and "light" (Matt. 5:13–16), for every Christian is a witness by virtue of the indwelling and enabling Spirit (Acts 1:8). Therefore witnessing is a Spirit-empowered *lifestyle*. By the same token, *not every* Christian is a gifted evangelist. The New Testament method was every-member evangelism (Acts 1:8). Bearing that in mind, every pastor/preacher must decide how to tackle the work of evangelism. Even if he does not have the *gift* of the evangelist, he is mandated to "do the work of an evangelist" (2 Tim. 4:5), remembering that in his congregation he has 12 to 15 percent of his people who *do* have the evangelistic gift. His job, therefore, is to "harness" this potential for reaching the lost.

The pastor/preacher must equip "the saints for the work of service," including evangelism (Eph. 4:11–12 NASB). Failure to do this leads inevitably to preaching without a target and praying without a vision.

At Calvary Baptist Church in New York it was our practice to conduct schools of evangelism using a home study Bible course entitled *Successful Soul-Winning*, supplied by Moody Bible Institute of Chicago.[1] Students were expected to enroll, study, and complete the examinations in preparation for the evangelistic work of the church. The value of such methodical training was that it produced and preserved an evangelistic awareness and accountability in the life of the church. Alongside of this was the careful instruction in the ministry of evangelistic praying.

While it is assumed that all church services will draw some outsiders, and that the way of salvation will be presented in the course of preaching, the disturbing fact remains that the percentage of lost people is very small. The exception to this reality check is the megachurch where "crowds draw crowds," and because of the high-tech programs and good preaching lost people do attend, and God sovereignly saves by grace!

It is our judgment, however, that the average church should be *selective* and *specialized* in its evangelistic methodology. At Calvary Baptist Church in New York City, the Sunday A.M. service was called "Morning *Worship*," while the P.M. service was known as the "Evening *Witness*." All our people knew that on Sunday mornings it would be *all* edification, and Sunday evenings would be *all* evangelism! With that as a settled methodology, we could concentrate on our respective responsibilities in relation to the total ministry.

Assuming that a clear purpose and a consuming passion to reach the lost have been conveyed to the "core" membership of your church, you can begin to think of ways to *bring* souls under the sound of the gospel. Here are some simple suggestions:

• *Telephone Calls.* Invite members to make a list of people they have thought and prayed about, and telephone them each weekend to accompany them to the "selected service" of the church. Where calls prove unfruitful, members may substitute new names and work on them prayerfully and continuously until they become regular attenders.

• *Car Service.* Invite members who own cars to bring their neighbors to church. A meal before, or refreshments afterward, may be an added incentive.

• *Bus Parties.* Invite members to join with other friends to charter a minibus and fill it with interested people. Here, again, refreshments or a meal can be planned to make the occasion a pleasant and attractive one.

• *Every-Member Evangelism.* Invite members to pray and talk with fellow believers regarding ways and means of bringing at least one individual to faith in Christ—and to church for discipling (Acts 2:47b).

• *Street Fishing.* Invite members who are happy to engage in such work to "fish for souls." It is good to have a permanent group of people who are ready for this form of evangelism. Such a team of "fishers" should be given a short course of instruction on the techniques of street-fishing. This method of evangelism can only apply to downtown churches where crowds of people walk up and down immediately outside of the church. With an attractive publicity piece, and alert and courteous soul-winners under the control of the Holy Spirit, it is quite astonishing how many people gladly respond. We found this method both workable and fruitful.

• *Prayer List.* Invite members to prepare a notebook in which they enter names of people they want to see converted, e.g., mother, father, brother, sister, office colleagues, etc. As they pray regularly for these individuals they will find that God will give them ingenious options on how to bring them under the sound of the gospel.

• *Hospitality Evangelism.* Invite members to use their homes for God. This is a splendid way to contact and influence unconverted friends. The idea is to invite them for a time of refreshment and friendly informality and then tactfully tell them about the church's program. If the church has a video ministry, a sample clip of one of the services could be played at an appropriate point in the proceedings. This helps to whet the appetite of those who have never had a true initiation into church life.

- *Tract Distribution.* Invite members to engage in street or house-to-house tract distribution. (All materials should have full details of church location and phone number). The material to be used and the areas to be covered should be organized by the pastor and staff after simple instructions have been given on the right methods of approach and evangelistic presentation.

- *Radio and/or TV Ministry.* Invite members to employ gospel broadcasts or telecasts as a means of evangelism. By calling friends and neighbors and inviting them to tune in, miracles can take place within the confines of many a home! Such mass media exposure can prepare the way for further discussion on the things of God.

- *Pre-Service Open-Air Meetings.* Invite and train your members to attend a pre-service open-air meeting at a strategic location near the church. When properly conducted—with special music, testimonies, and a brief message—a gathering of this kind can attract many outsiders. It is relatively simple, then, to invite interested people to proceed to the main church service.

- *Guest Service Once a Month.* The whole format and freedom of such a service should be planned and programmed for the "unchurched" person. Well-known singers, sport personalities, other Christian celebrities, compelling sermon topics, and meticulous handling of the flow and final moments of "the evangelistic rally" must be drenched with prayer and then driven by the conscious leading of the Holy Spirit.

We could go on with numerous methods that have been tried and proven to work in the cause of evangelism, but the above must suffice. Our purpose in naming a few is to encourage the pastor/preacher to make a clear distinction between *worship* and *witness.* Remember, "we gather for worship, we scatter for witness."

It is now assumed that the church or neutral venue is well filled with those who need the message of God's saving grace. This is where proclamation has its place. To help us understand what we mean by proclamation, we have selected the first five verses of 1 Corinthians 2.

No one can read the New Testament without being impressed by the effectiveness of the preaching of the early church. The apostles preached with supernatural power. As F. D. Coggan puts it: "The infant church was multiplied out of all recognition by a single sermon. By preaching, a fellowship was formed which astounded the world by its demonstration of love, which held together in community men and women of different backgrounds.

The modern preacher is compelled to question his own heart, as he faces the astounding success of the apostolic preaching."[2]

In simple and succinct terms, the apostle Paul here reveals that the power of evangelistic preaching is related to the message of the preacher, the manner of the preacher, and the motive of the preacher. Let us consider these three aspects of our subject, with the prayer that God will inspire us—as well as instruct us—in the art of evangelistic preaching with power.

EVANGELISTIC PREACHING IS RELATED TO THE MESSAGE OF THE PREACHER

"And I, brethren, when I came to you, did not come with excellence of speech or of wisdom declaring to you the testimony of God. For I determined not to know anything among you except Jesus Christ and Him crucified" (1 Cor. 2:1–2). We cannot examine these words in their context without discovering that the power of evangelistic preaching was and is inherent in the very message Paul proclaimed. It is not difficult to arrive at what was the content of his message: the person and passion of Christ.

The Message of Evangelistic Preaching Is the Person of Christ

"For I determined not to know anything among you except Jesus Christ" (v. 2).

In 1936, C. H. Dodd wrote a book entitled *The Apostolic Preaching and Its Developments.* According to A. M. Hunter, Dodd's book is "one of the most important and positive contributions to New Testament science in our generation."[3] And I may add that it will more than repay the prayerful and careful perusal of preachers of the gospel. In this work Dodd points out that the central message of apostolic preaching was the person and work of the Lord Jesus Christ. He amplifies this by showing that there were five main emphases in the "kerygma." The first emphasis was on "the fulfillment of the Old Testament proclamation of the Messiah. . . . The second emphasis [was] on the earthly life of Jesus. . . . The third emphasis [was] on the death of Christ. . . . The fourth emphasis [was] on the resurrection and exaltation of Christ [and] the fifth emphasis [was] on repentance."[4]

Coggan has made a similar study in his book *The Ministry of the Word*, where he reveals that each of the four main words employed in the Acts of the Apostles to describe the activity of Christian preaching has as its object "Jesus," "Jesus Christ," "the Lord Jesus," "Jesus and the resurrection," "peace through Jesus Christ," "the word of the Lord,"[5] and so on. It is clear, therefore, that the central message of apostolic preaching was the person of our Lord Jesus Christ.

This was not only true of the apostles but also of the Lord Jesus Christ Himself. As one German theologian has phrased it, "Jesus Christ the Son of God knew no greater task than to point men and women to Himself." To support this, we might quote R. V. G. Tasker who says, "The prime duty of the Christian preacher is not to bid men to undertake the impossible task of solving their social and economic problems in the light of the Sermon on the Mount, but to call them to repent and to submit to the rule of God. . . . Jesus . . . was not an expounder of a noble system of ethics, nor a reformer of society, but a proclaimer of God's will, in obedience to which He Himself lived, spoke, suffered and died."[6]

Now the point in stressing the *centrality of Christ* in our preaching is simply that Jesus Himself is "the power of God and the wisdom of God," as Paul makes plain in this very epistle (1:24). Only as we make Christ our message does preaching become powerful and evangelistic. There is little to encourage us to believe that God will bless our sermons, our homiletics, or our oratory. But we can be sure that when we preach Christ, the Spirit of power will overshadow us.

In our judgment, this is precisely what Paul means when he says, "I determined not to know anything among you except Jesus Christ and Him crucified" (v. 2). God make us like John Wesley, who could say again and again as he traveled across England: "I offered Christ to the people."[7]

The Message of Evangelistic Preaching Is the Passion of Christ

"For I determined not to know anything among you except Jesus Christ and Him crucified" (v. 2).

As one commentator puts it: "We can scarcely realise [in our day] the stumbling block which the preaching of a crucified Christ must have been to Jews and Greeks, the enormous temptation to keep the cross in the background which the early teachers would naturally have felt, and the sublime and confident faith which must have nerved

St. Paul to make it the central fact of all his teaching."[8] And yet the apostle knew from the Scriptures, as well as from personal experience, that the preaching of the cross constituted "the power of God" (1:18). It is the cross of Christ that expresses the divine mind, reveals the divine estimate of human sin, exhibits the divine righteousness, demonstrates the divine love, and does all this on a human platform so that we are enabled to appreciate the mystery of the heavenly counsels. Although the cross is a stumbling block to the religionist and a laughing stock to the rationalist, it is nonetheless the power of God to those who are saved. Only in the cross of Christ is man's greatest need dealt with and God's greatest answer displayed and offered.

There is something irresistibly attractive about the message of the cross. Jesus said, "And I, if I am lifted up from the earth, will draw all peoples to Myself" (John 12:32). What is more, there can never be a Pentecost in our preaching before there is a Calvary in our preaching. As the Moravians used to put it, "The Spirit always answers to the blood."

Billy Graham often tells the story of how he preached in one of our great outdoor stadiums on one occasion and sensed a deadness, not only in his message, but in the whole meeting. On his way back to the hotel that night, he was accompanied by a well-known layman. As they talked together, Billy Graham shared his experience with this businessman, who immediately responded with this remark: "I agree with you, there was no power in that service tonight, and apparently little blessing, and I think I know the reason," added the gentleman, "You did not preach the cross." The evangelist thoroughly concurred and made a resolution there and then that he would never preach again without specifically lifting up Christ and Him crucified. Let us never forget the words of the apostle: "For the message of the cross is foolishness to those who are perishing, but to us who are being saved *it is the power of God*" (1:18, emphasis ours).

So we have seen that evangelistic preaching is related to the message of the preacher. But in the second place, observe that the manner of the preacher is also crucial to evangelistic success.

EVANGELISTIC PREACHING IS RELATED TO THE MANNER OF THE PREACHER

"I was with you in weakness, in fear, and in much trembling. And my speech and my preaching were not with persuasive words of human wisdom, but in demonstration of the Spirit and of power" (vv. 3–4). In His inscrutable wisdom, God has chosen people like us to be preachers of the gospel. The awesomeness of this calling is well-nigh overwhelming when we realize that "God had only one Son, and He made Him a preacher."[9] It follows, therefore, that the nearer we conform to the character of our Lord, the more effective we shall be as preachers. Paul underscores this in the text before us when he describes what should be the manner of the preacher. Three characteristics are clearly evident: humility, simplicity, and authority.

The Humility of Christ

"I was with you in weakness, in fear, and in much trembling" (v. 3). Commentators are not all agreed as to what Paul means by these words. Some suggest that the apostle was referring here to physical weakness (see 2 Cor. 12:7), and particularly to his "bodily presence" and "speech contemptible" (2 Cor. 10:10). Others maintain that this great preacher was acutely conscious of the shocking wickedness and the bitter antagonism that confronted him in Corinth. But over and above this was surely the self-distrust which his sensitive spirit experienced as he contemplated the exalted mission of preaching the cross. William Barclay renders it as "the trembling anxiety to perform a duty." This sense of helplessness in the work of God is the evidence of true humility. To quote Barclay again: "It is not the man who approaches a great task without a tremor who does it really well. The actor who is really great is the actor who is wrought up before the performance; the preacher who is really effective is the preacher whose heart beats faster while he waits to speak. The man who has no fear, no hesitancy, no tension in any task, may give an efficient and competent performance; but it is the man . . . who has that intensity which is the essence of real greatness, *who can produce an effect which artistry alone [cannot] achieve*"[10] (emphasis ours).

In this connection, it is well to remember Paul's words in his second letter to the Corinthians where he says, "Most gladly I will rather boast in my infirmities, that the power of Christ may rest upon me" (2 Cor. 12:9). Paul had long discovered that only *when he was weak could he be strong*. And so it is today. The power of the Spirit can only rest upon those who know the humility of Christ. It is the broken life that God blesses, and it is the empty vessel that God fills. So Jesus says to us: "Learn from Me, for I am gentle and lowly in heart" (Matt. 11:29).

The Simplicity of Christ

"And my speech and my preaching were not with persuasive words of human wisdom" (v. 4). Already Paul has said in the opening verses of this section, "And I, brethren, when I came to you, did not come with excellence of speech or of wisdom declaring to you the testimony of God" (v. 1). The reference here, of course, is to what was known as "the Corinthian words." The philosophers and orators of Corinth were known for their Corinthian words of human eloquence and brilliant rhetoric. They were masters of "crowd psychology," as we would call it today. But such "speechifying" lacked the quality of real instruction or authoritative power.

The Bible teaches—and experience has proved—that one of the secrets of effectiveness in preaching is simplicity. This simplicity, of course, characterized our Savior's utterances. Read through His sermons and stories and you will be impressed all over again by the sheer simplicity and directness of His language. No wonder Paul exhorts the Corinthians to beware lest the devil, through his subtlety, should corrupt their minds from the simplicity that is in Christ (2 Cor. 11:3). Today, our danger is that of preaching over the heads of people. The philosopher has a jargon of his own, the scientist has his, and, alas, the preacher has his own brand as well! If God is to own the message, then it has to be delivered in language understood by the people and in words dictated by the Spirit. This is implicit in that statement of the apostle where he says, "These things we also speak, not in the words which man's wisdom teaches but which the Holy Spirit teaches, comparing spiritual things with spiritual" (v. 13).

The Authority of Christ

"My speech and my preaching were . . . in demonstration of the Spirit and of power" (v. 4). This particular word rendered *demonstration* is used only here in the New Testament. Literally, it signifies "a showing forth" and has the force of *that which carries conviction through the power of the Holy Spirit.* What a definition of the authority of Christ!

When the Lord Jesus Christ preached in the days of His flesh, we read that "the people were astonished at His teaching, for He taught them as one having authority, and not as the scribes"

(Matt. 7:28–29). He spoke not only as One who imparted truth, but as One who was the living demonstration and embodiment of truth. This is why preaching has been described as "truth through personality." In the words of John's majestic prologue, preaching is "the Word [becoming] flesh." Only when a man wields "the sword of the Spirit, which is the word of God" (Eph. 6:17) is preaching authoritative. When Jesus spoke, people had to make a decision: they either believed on Him or picked up stones to stone Him; He never neutralized either individuals or congregations. His utterances were both incisive and decisive, and this is the evidence of the authority of heaven.

The secret of this humility, simplicity, and authority is found in the words of our Savior who said, "You shall receive power when the Holy Spirit has come upon you" (Acts 1:8). This is the anointing of the Spirit. It is more than the filling, even though it includes the filling. It is an anointing which gives, first of all, *the ability to appreciate the Word of God.* John says, "You have an anointing from the Holy One, and you know all things. . . . and you do not need that anyone teach you" (1 John 2:20, 27). And secondly, it is an anointing that gives *the power to authenticate the Word of God.* This is undoubtedly Paul's thought in 2 Corinthians 1, where he reminds his readers that his preaching of Christ was not sometimes "yes" and other times "no," but rather an unwavering *yes,* since God had established him in Christ and also anointed him (vv. 20–21).

So we have seen that the manner of the preacher has a great deal to do with either the evidence of power or the absence of it. Oh to know the mighty filling and anointing of the Spirit which brings the humility, simplicity, and authority of apostolic preaching!

In the third place, we must look at the preacher's motives.

EVANGELISTIC PREACHING IS RELATED TO THE MOTIVE OF THE PREACHER

"That your faith should not be in the wisdom of men but in the power of God" (v. 5).

Richard Roberts, in his book *The Preacher as a Man of Letters,* says: "It is our calling to persuade, and, if it may be, to convince. That is not preaching which is not preaching for a verdict."[11]

With the proclamation there is the declaration of that which God has done and is doing in Christ and His cross; then the invitation calls men and women to respond to this Good News. If this is not our motive, then our preaching will be powerless and fruitless. God never releases His power for personal aggrandizement or carnal objectives; on the contrary, He only sends His Holy Spirit to seal unto the day of redemption that which fulfills His redemptive purposes. Therefore, the motive of the preacher must be to lead men and women into an experience of a sound, saving, and steadfast faith in Christ. Let us take a few moments to amplify this further. No preacher of the gospel fulfills what God has designed unless men and women come to repose their faith in the power of God, which is Jesus Christ and Him crucified.

A Sound Faith

"That your faith should not be in the wisdom of men" (v. 5). In the preceding verses of this epistle, Paul has demolished the notion that faith can be sound when reposed in the wisdom of men. In the language of the apostle James, such wisdom is "earthly, sensual, demonic" (3:15). On the other hand, to be sound, faith must be exercised in the Savior Himself without dependence upon this human wisdom. Paul develops this point when he writes later concerning the death and resurrection of the Lord Jesus. He declares: "If Christ is not risen, your faith is futile; you are still in your sins!" (1 Cor. 15:17). If Christ were not alive from the dead, then sin was not put away, the gospel was not true, the Christians had believed a lie, the apostles were false witnesses, and the loved ones who had fallen asleep were lost forever. So to be sound in the faith, men and women must believe in the Son of God who literally and physically rose from the dead. All other tenets of the evangelical faith are both included and implied in the great doctrine of the death and resurrection of Jesus Christ.

Yet a sound faith must also be a saving faith.

A Saving Faith

"That your faith should not be in the wisdom of men but *in the power of God*" (v. 5, emphasis ours). Paul has already interpreted to us the meaning of the power of God in the previous chapter. You remember how he says that "the message of the cross is foolishness to those who are perishing, but to us who are being saved it is the power of God" (1:18). Saving faith, to Paul, was a faith which had and was effecting a mighty transformation in the believing soul. It meant knowing the Lord Jesus as Savior and Master in every sense of the word.

Finally, our motive, as preachers, is to bring our listeners to a sound, saving, and *steadfast* faith.

A Steadfast Faith

"That your faith should not *be* in the wisdom of men but in the power of God" (v. 5). It has been well said that "what depends upon a clever argument is at the mercy of a more clever argument." This is not so, however, when faith is centered in the unchanging Son of God. This is what Paul means by a faith which stands "in the power of God." His words convey the idea of steadfastness. Twice over in this epistle he exhorts the believers to be steadfast in the faith. The first mention follows the glorious treatment of the unalterable facts of the death and resurrection of our Lord and Savior Jesus Christ in chapter 15. Having declared the Son of God as the triumphant One, he says, "Be steadfast, immovable, always abounding in the work of the Lord, knowing that your labor is not in vain in the Lord" (15:58).

The second occurrence coincides with the conclusion of the epistle where the apostle expresses his parting word to the believers at Corinth in these terms: "Watch, stand fast in the faith, be brave, be strong" (16:13).

Here, then, we have the supreme motive of the preacher: that the faith of his hearers should not stand in the wisdom of men but in the power of God. So we see that to be pure in our motives is to be powerful in our preaching. When the purpose of God is fulfilled, the Spirit of God confirms the Word with "accompanying signs" (Mark 16:20). It is not without significance that Paul describes the object of preaching in terms of settling men and women "in the power of God." It follows, therefore, that only when this "power" is manifest is preaching authentic and effective.

Thus we have seen what we mean by evangelistic preaching. No greater task has ever been entrusted to the sons of men. And in these days of what J. I. Packer calls "the lost word,"[12] we need to recapture not only the glory of preaching but also the power of preaching. As preachers and pastors, we must ever remember the eternal link which God has forged between preaching and evangelism. The imperatives ring out throughout the centuries to this very hour: "Preach the word! . . . *Do* the work of an evangelist" (2 Tim. 4:2, 5).

THE PREACHER
AND
ROMANS

Preaching can become superficial and tangential if the preacher loses sight of his God-given ministry (his designated role) or loses sight of what he seeks to accomplish through the preaching ministry (his desired result). One could appeal to many places in the Scriptures in this regard, and indeed one should! Here we briefly use the apostle Paul as our example, viewing his designated role in ministry and his desired result in ministry as he presents them in Romans.

THE DESIGNATED ROLE OF PAUL THE PREACHER

A Sacred Ministry

Paul, the apostle, was set apart by God for gospel ministry (Rom. 1:1). This ministry was divinely given and confirmed

(1:1, 5; 12:3; 15:15–21). In short, Paul was "graced" with what can be called, first of all, a sacred ministry. It was a ministry from God and confirmed by God. It was the divine bestowal and confirmation of Paul's ministry that gave him the authority to write to the saints in Rome in the manner he did (15:15; 12:3).

A Sacrificial Ministry

Paul describes this ministry in "priestly" terms as he fulfills a sacrificial service resulting in an acceptable offering, an offering that consisted of the obedient lives of the Gentiles themselves (15:16). Thus, we speak of Paul's designated role, secondly, as a sacrificial ministry.

Paul's sacred and sacrificial service was apostolic gospel proclamation (1:1–5, 14–17), specifically to the unreached nations (15:19–21). Paul was obligated by virtue of his apostleship and grace to preach to the Gentiles (1:14), and this obligation placed even those in Rome within the sphere of his ministerial grace (1:11–15). It may be, in fact, that Paul's letter to Rome was foundational for the spiritual gift that he wanted to impart in Rome (1:11–12) before he was to be sent by the faithful in Rome to minister in Spain (15:24, 28). In Rome and Spain, as in other places, Paul was called of God to bring about obedience to the gospel on the part of the Gentiles (15:18). This was the acceptable offering that God had ordained Paul to bring, presenting the obedient lives of the Gentiles (compare with Col. 1:24–29).

This sacred and sacrificial picture of the calling of the apostle, his designated role, is one that preachers can learn from and meditate upon. In a very real sense, the preacher is a chosen priestly servant who enables and ensures sacrifices pleasing to God. The astounding thing is that this sacred and sacrificial service deals with human lives. Expanding Paul's picture slightly (but legitimately, we trust) the preacher presents divine grace to people through gospel proclamation, and he calls forth the obedience of faith that ultimately brings pleasure to God. What a ministry! Certainly this offering is based upon justification by grace alone, through faith alone, in Christ alone. However, the ultimate fruit of such justification and salvation are lives offered to God, sanctified by the Holy Spirit.

THE DESIRED RESULT OF PAUL THE PREACHER

It is this kind of preacher with this understanding of his designated role who exhorts his readers in Romans 12:1–2. Because this exhortation comes at such a crucial point in the letter—after Paul has presented his gospel—we view it as a picture of the obedience (15:18) of faith (1:5) that Paul, the sacred and sacrificial minister, calls for (note 15:16) on the basis of his gospel. As we have indicated, this response in Romans 12:1–2 is based upon the justification and salvation expounded upon in chapters 1–11. Romans 12:1–2 may reveal for us, then, in summary form, the ultimate desired result of Paul's gospel proclamation.

Life That Is Totally Dedicated to God

Paul, the preacher, calls for life that is totally dedicated to God (12:1). Paul uses the language of sacrifice and worship, possibly language appropriate to a baptismal setting, to graphically portray his challenge. The sacrificial self-presentation of the community, "brothers", is to be corporeal (involving concrete bodily existence), corporate (involving the bodies [pl.] of the community members), and complete (as any holy and pleasing sacrifice had to be). Both the sacrificial image and whatever baptismal connotations there may be make this call a decisive one; there can be no partial sacrifice or baptism. Each believer and every aspect of the life of each believer is subject to this call. Total dedication is demanded, a total giving or yielding of the self to God in a manner that pleases Him, as a living and holy sacrifice.

Looking back at an earlier part of Romans, it seems reasonable to suggest that this total dedication involves the logical reckoning, the active yielding of each aspect of the believer's existence to God in Christ Jesus (6:11–13). The Christian has died with Christ, and is called upon to live a new life to God in Christ Jesus (6:11). Life now involves righteous choices, sanctification (6:19, 22), and ends in eternal life (6:22). This new life of righteousness in Christ by faith is possible because the Christian has been freed from the bondage, control, and slavery of sin through the death, burial, and resurrection of Christ. This transfer from sin to righteousness in the life of the believer takes place experientially as the Christian responds rightly (reckons) to the cross and resurrection of Christ. This is the appropriate and desired ultimate response to Paul's gospel: the obedience of faith (1:5; 15:18; 16:26).

It is no surprise that Paul speaks of the Christian sacrifice as "your reasonable [or logical] worship" in 12:1 (compare with 6:11). Such a sacrifice is the appropriate and authentic response of the believer to the gospel that the priestly preacher desires.

Life That Is Totally Transformed Because of God

If the first aspect of Paul's exhortation calls for life that is totally dedicated to God, the second calls for life that is totally transformed because of God (Rom. 12:2). Here Paul moves away from the sacrificial image. The radical call for different thinking and living because of the gospel, however, is very clear. Paul's language is unusual for him, but it seems to express the same truth that is found in Ephesians 4:17–24 (also Rom. 13:11–14). The Christian is called to a mental renewal based upon truth (Rom. 6:17), a renewal that separates one from the thinking and living of the age, and enables one to put on Christ (Rom. 11:14) (putting off the old man and putting on the new—Eph. 4:22–24). The result is that the Christian is to discern and prove the will of God (Rom. 12:2; note Eph. 5:10).

This renewal ultimately, we suggest, looks like Christ Himself in the life of the Christian and the church (Rom. 13:14; 15:3, 7; 8:29; note Phil. 2:5ff). On the practical and concrete level, this renewal based on the gospel is reflected in Paul's community ethics in 12:3 and following. Paul speaks of a sober self-appraisal (humility) and then speaks of an appreciation of the body-nature of the community and the use of different gifts (unity and service, 12:3–8). The following directives are too numerous to spell out, but service, love, submission, liberty, tolerance, and pleasing others in likeness to Christ (15:1–7) are emphasized. Ultimately it is the glorifying of God by the nations that is to take place (15:8–13).

Paul does not discuss the process of this renewal in such a short space, but undoubtedly it involves adherence to the teaching received (6:17; 16:17–19) and walking in it (13:13–14). Furthermore, the role of the Spirit should be remembered since Paul has already discussed the setting of the mind on the things of the Spirit and not the flesh (8:5–11), and the need for the Spirit in the process of putting to death the deeds of the body (8:13). Although the Spirit is not mentioned in this text, it is not inappropriate to note the Spirit's role in transformation elsewhere (2 Cor. 3:18). Also, it is the Spirit who sanctifies the offering of the Gentiles (15:16), and surely the Spirit is involved in the transformation that is fundamental to gospel living.

Such a dedication and transformation is what the preacher is looking for in the lives of his listeners. What an exciting prospect; what a worthy desire to have as one ministers! Thus, the desired result of the preaching ministry is not simply decisions for Christ; it is disciples committed to Christ and conformed to Him (Col. 1:28–29).

CONCLUSION

Paul begins in Romans by declaring that man is under God's wrath (1:18) and that God has given man over to vile passions (1:24) and to a debased mind (1:28).

In the midst of this picture of depravity, Paul states that the worship of man has been false because man worshiped the creature rather than the Creator (1:25). In Romans 12:1–2 there is a transformation of this situation. On the basis of the mercy of God (not wrath), man is given the opportunity for bodily obedience (not dishonor) and mental transformation (not debasement). Furthermore, rather than man exchanging the truth for a lie and worshiping falsely, Paul now speaks of the worship that is "truthful" or reasonable before the God of the gospel.

Each preacher calls men who deserve wrath and are subject to depravity into a right relationship with the Creator by faith on the basis of the redeeming death of His Son. This enables men to worship God "truly," living obediently in body and being renewed in mind. To minister in this way, each preacher in a very real sense is set apart and graced of God to be involved in a sacred and sacrificial service. This service brings much pleasure to our God as He accepts the lives of those who respond obediently in faith to the gospel. This is the picture that Paul presents and within which he sees the Lord at work.

What greater joy can we have in life than to bring pleasure to our God! May this be the case with those involved in the ministry of the gospel as we, like Paul, fulfill a biblically designated role and seek the appropriate desired result in our ministries.[1]

NOTES

Introduction, pages 1–5

1. Taken from *The Expositor's Bible Commentary*, vol. 5 edited by Frank E. Gaebelein, 1196. Copyright © 1991 by The Zondervan Corporation. Used by permission of Zondervan Publishing House.

2. James Daane, *Preaching with Confidence: A Theological Essay on the Power of the Pulpit* (Grand Rapids: Wm. B. Eerdmans Publishing Co., 1980), 6.

3. Ibid., 11.

4. We contend that if preaching is biblical, then the Bible is the final source of information on preaching.

5. Daane, *Preaching with Confidence,* 5–6.

6. David S. Dockery, *Holman Bible Dictionary* (Nashville: Holman Bible Publishers, 1991), 1183.

7. Tony Sargent, *The Sacred Anointing: The Preaching of Dr. Martyn Lloyd-Jones* (Wheaton, Ill.: Crossway Books, 1994), 189.

8. John R. Stott, *Between Two Worlds* (Grand Rapids: Wm. B. Eerdmans Publishing Co., 1982), 125–126.

9. Arthur S. Hoyt, *The Work of Preaching* (London: The Macmillan Co., 1909), 12.

10. Bishop Carl J. Sanders, "A Vision for the Church," *The United Methodist Reporter* (Dallas: UMR Communications, 11 January 1974), 2.

Chapter 1: The Preacher and the Call of God, pages 7-18

1. Thomas D. Lea, *1, 2 Timothy, The New American Commentary* (Nashville: Broadman Press, 1992), 34:108.

2. Tony Sargent, *The Sacred Anointing: The Preaching of Dr. Martyn Lloyd-Jones* (Wheaton, Ill.: Crossway Books, 1994), 24–25.

3. Lea, *The New American Commentary*, 77.

4. Ibid., 73.

5. Warren W. Wiersbe, *With the Word* (Nashville: Oliver-Nelson Books, 1991), 496.

6. William Barclay, *The Letters to the Galatians and Ephesians, The Daily Study Bible* (Edinburgh: Saint Andrew Press, 1954), 13.

7. W. Graham Scroggie, "Counsels to Young Pastors," *The All Nations Missionary Review* (winter 1951–52): 5.

9. Richard N. Longenecker, *Galatians, Word Biblical Commentary*, ed. Ralph P. Martin (Dallas: Word, 1990), 41:31.

10. *Apostello* "suggests official or authoritative send" (Thayer) *Pempo* is a more general term. Both of these verbs are found in John 20:21.

11. Sargent, *The Sacred Anointing*, 29.

12. Adapted from the biography of Stephen F. Olford, *Only One Life*, by John Phillips (Neptune, N.J.: Loizeaux Brothers, Inc. 1995), 285. Used by permission.

13. C. I. Scofield, *The Scofield Reference Bible* (New York: Oxford University Press, 1967), 1264.

14. R. W. DeHaan, 1980 *Radio Bible Class*, Grand Rapids, Michigan 49555 [May 9].

15. Herbert Lockyer, *Last Words of Saints and Sinners* (Grand Rapids: Kregel Publications, 1969), 167.

16. Quoted in Archibald Naismith, *2400 Outlines, Notes, Quotes, and Anecdotes for Sermons* (Grand Rapids: Baker Book House, 1967), 184.

Chapter 2: The Preacher and the Word of God, pages 19–28

1. W. C. G. Proctor, "Infallibility," in *Baker's Dictionary of Theology* (Grand Rapids: Baker Book House, 1960), 284.

2. James S. Stewart, *A Man in Christ* (London: Hodder & Stoughton, 1935), 39.

3. Roy McCloughry, "Basic Stott," *Christianity Today,* 8 January 1996, 28.

4. George Müller, *Soul Nourishment First* (Bristol, England: Müller Homes for Children, n.d.), 1.

5. *The Expositor's Bible Commentary*, vol. 11, edited by Frank E. Gaebelein, 357. Copyright © 1978 by The Zondervan Corporation. Used by permission of Zondervan Publishing House.

6. Fred Kerr, "Meet Daily with Jesus," *The Alliance Witness,* 14 March 1984, 6.

7. "Someone to teach you," stands over against "teachers" and points up the contrast. Their knowledge of the faith is minimal when it ought to have been advanced. "The elementary truths" (NIV) render an expression that is equivalent to our "ABCs." (Taken from *The Expositor's Bible Commentary*, vol. 12, edited by Frank E. Gaebelein, 51. Copyright © 1981 by the Zondervan Corporation. Used by permission of Zondervan Publishing House.)

8. Ibid., 12:52.

Chapter 3: The Preacher and the Life of God, pages 29–37

1. Handley C. G. Moule, *Veni Creator* (London: Pickering & Inglis, n.d.), 3.
2. W. E. Vine, *Expository Dictionary of Biblical Words* (Nashville: Thomas Nelson Publishers, Inc., 1985), 664.
3. Charles Colson, *The Body* (Waco, Tex.: Word, 1992), 304.
4. John Stott, *Only One Way: The Message of Galatians* (Downer's Grove, Ill.: InterVarsity Press, 1973), 148.

Chapter 4: The Preacher and the Man of God, pages 38–49

1. William Barclay, *The Letters to Timothy, Titus and Philemon* (Edinburgh: Saint Andrew Press, 1960), 143.
2. William Hendriksen, *Exposition of I & II Timothy and Titus* (Grand Rapids: Baker Book House, 1955), 200.
3. Ibid., 200–201, adapted.
4. James Mann, "Why Churches Get into Money Muddles," *U.S. News and World Report*, 16 August 1982, 36.
5. Taken from *We Prepare and Preach: The Practice of Sermon Construction and Delivery* by Clarence Stonelynn Roddy, ed., 30. Copyright © 1959 by Moody Press. Used by permission.
6. Henry G. Bosch, "The Beauty of Holiness," *Our Daily Bread* (Grand Rapids: RBC Ministries, July 29, 1972).
7. Austin L. Sorenson, "Preparing the Pastor's Heart," quoted in *Pulpit Helps,* (April 1979), 1.
8. The word *godliness* "refers to a respect for God which profoundly alters behavior." See Thomas D. Lea and Hayne P. Griffin Jr., on 1 Timothy 6:11, *op. cit.* 172.
9. Austin L. Sorenson, "What Is A Minister?" quoted in *Pulpit Helps*, (July 1983), 20.
10. Lea and Griffin Jr., *New American Commentary*, 172.
11. Archibald Naismith, *2400 Outlines, Notes, Quotes and Anecdotes for Sermons* (Grand Rapids: Baker Book House, 1967), 194.
12. While "the washing of water by the word" is generally interpreted as "the washing of rebirth" (Titus 3:5), the cleansing ministry of the word *(rhema)* by the husband is still a valid application of the term in the context of the home.
13. Hendriksen, *Exposition of I & II Timothy and Titus*, 205.

Chapter 5: The Preacher and the Work of God, pages 50–65

1. Taken from *Zinger* by Paul Azinger with Ken Abraham. Copyright © 1995 by Paul Azinger. Used by permission of Zondervan Publishing House.
2. Donald Guthrie, *Pastoral Epistles, Tyndale New Testament Commentaries* (Grand Rapids: Wm. B. Eerdmans Publishing Co., 1976), 141.
3. Ibid., 99.
4. Ralph Earle, *The Expositor's Bible Commentary*, vol. 11, edited by Frank E. Gaebelein, 373. Copyright © 1978 by The Zondervan Corporation. Used by permission of Zondervan Publishing House.
5. Stephen F. Olford, *Christianity and You* (Grand Rapids: Wm. B. Eerdmans Publishing Co., 1958), 45.
6. John R. W. Stott, *I Believe in Preaching* (London: Hodder & Stoughton, 1982), book jacket.

7. The judgment of Jonathan M. Olford, clinical psychologist with Link Care Center, Fresno, California.

8. Heard by Stephen F. Olford during a pastors' conference.

9. This could be called a "deacon board" in embryonic form, as described in 1 Tim. 3:8–13.

10. Taken from *The Expositor's Bible Commentary,* vol. 9, edited by Frank E. Gaebelein, 331. Copyright © 1981 by The Zondervan Corporation. Used by permission of Zondervan Publishing House.

11. John R. W. Stott, *Between Two Worlds: The Art of Preaching in the 20th Century* (Grand Rapids: Wm. B. Eerdmans Publishing Co., 1982), 181–182.

12. Walter C. Kaiser Jr. *Preaching* 11, no. 2 (September/October, 1995), 4.

Chapter 6: The Preacher and Exposition, pages 67–79

1. John R. W. Stott, "Creating the Bridge," taken from Michael Duduit, ed., *Communicate with Power: Insights from America's Top Communicators* (Grand Rapids: Baker Books, 1996), 187–188.

2. J. I. Packer, "The Lost Word," in *God Has Spoken* (Downers Grove, Ill.: InterVarsity Press, 1979), 28.

3. See Walter C. Kaiser Jr., *Toward an Exegetical Theology: Biblical Exegesis for Preaching and Teaching* (Grand Rapids: Baker Book House, 1981), 52–53.

4. "Read" means "to read aloud" (Exod. 24:7; Deut. 17:19; 2 Kings 5:7).

5. See comments on this in chap. 13, "The Preacher and Proclamation."

6. Ernest W. Bacon, *Spurgeon: Heir of the Puritans* (Grand Rapids: Wm. B. Eerdmans Publishing Co., 1968), 59–60.

7. Walter C. Kaiser Jr., *Toward an Exegetical Theology: Biblical Exegesis for Preaching and Teaching* (Grand Rapids: Baker Book House, 1981), 19.

8. Ibid., 19.

9. See Bibliography.

10. The three questions that follow are "the golden key" that help to open up the text we are studying. In the chapters that follow this will be demonstrated and illustrated more fully.

11. C. H. Spurgeon, *Lectures to My Students* (London: Marshall, Morgan & Scott, 1960), 353.

12. See chap. 13, "The Preacher and Proclamation."

Chapter 7: The Preacher and Preparation: Selection, pages 80–98

1. Walter Bauer, William F. Arndt, F. Wilbur Gingrich, *A Greek-English Lexicon of the New Testament and Other Early Christian Literature* (Chicago: University of Chicago Press, 1957), 145. This work is Arndt and Gingrich's translation and adaptation of Walter Bauer's *Griechisch-Deutsches Wörterbuch zu den Schriften des Neuen Testaments und der übrigen urchristlichen Literatur* (4th rev. and augmented ed., 1952).

2. *Acts: An Introduction and Commentary, Tyndale New Testament Commentaries* (Leicester, England: InterVarsity Press, 1980), 333.

3. Duane Litfin, *St. Paul's Theology of Proclamation,* (Cambridge: Cambridge University Press, 1994), 247–252.

4. Ibid., 244–252. Dr. Litfin affirms Paul's commitment to the message of the cross and his conviction concerning the work of the Spirit (pp. 247–252). Dr. Litfin also argues that Paul did not depend on "the dynamic of rhetorical adaptation" to get results (p. 245).

5. D. Martyn Lloyd-Jones, *Preaching and Preachers* (Grand Rapids. Zondervan Publishing House, 1971), 188 189. Used by permission. We, the authors, hold the position that, generally, planning is helpful, but that our planning must be done prayerfully, and there must be continued submission to the sovereignty of God and continued sensitivity to the Holy Spirit. God can always change our plans! We will discuss this further later in this text.

6. John R. W. Stott, *Between Two Worlds: The Art of Preaching in the Twentieth Century* (Grand Rapids: William B. Eerdmans Publishing Company, 1982), 214–220.

7. Sinclair B. Ferguson, "Exegesis" in *The Preacher and Preaching: Reviving the Art in the Twentieth Century*, Samuel T. Logan Jr., ed., (Phillipsburg, N.J.: Presbyterian and Reformed Publishing Company, 1986), 197.

8. Sidney Greidanus, *The Modern Preacher and the Ancient Text: Interpreting and Preaching Biblical Literature* (Grand Rapids: William B. Eerdmans Publishing, 1988), 16–17.

9. This approach is presented rather than a topical approach where numerous texts are used without a primary text.

10. The preacher could devote one message to all seven things, or a message for each one as it is stated in context.

Chapter 8: The Preacher and Preparation: Investigation, pages 101–138

1. Sidney Greidanus, *The Modern Preacher and the Ancient Text* (Grand Rapids: William B. Eerdmans Publishing Company, 1988), 122.

2. Ibid., p. 131.

3. See chapters 12 and 14..

4. John Stott, *Between Two Worlds: The Art of Preaching in the Twentieth Century* (Grand Rapids: William B. Eerdmans Publishing Company, 1982), 259. Dr. Stott also says that a beginner needs to allow ten to twelve hours per sermon for study.

5. Steve Brown, Haddon Robinson, William Willimon, *A Voice in the Wilderness* (Sisters, Oreg.: Multnomah Press Books/Christianity Today, Inc., 1993), 125–126.

6. Commentaries, generally speaking, can be divided into four categories: critical, exegetical-expositional, homiletical, and devotional. Critical commentaries focus on the original language and meaning of the text. Exegetical-expositional commentaries refer to the original language, but are often based on English translation. Homiletical commentaries present *messages* on the text that have homiletical structure. Devotional commentaries offer insights and reflections on the text. All of the above can be helpful. Use them accordingly, with an awareness of the perspective and purpose of the author.

7. Exactly *when* this contextual study is done is not as important as seeing *that* it is done. The preacher is greatly helped by having a sense of the setting of the text, both in terms of history and literature.

8. If the message is part of an expository series through a biblical book, aspects of this contextual study will only need to be done once. This study may even take place as you prepare to do the whole series.

9. For much helpful information on genre, especially in relation to preaching, see: Sidney Greidanus, *The Modern Preacher and the Ancient Text: Interpreting and Preaching Biblical Literature* (Grand Rapids: William B. Eerdmans Publishing Company, 1988); *Handbook of Contemporary Preaching*, ed. Michael Duduit (Nashville: Broadman Press, 1992), esp. 245–389; Walter C. Kaiser Jr., *Toward an*

Exegetical Theology: Biblical Exegesis for Preaching and Teaching (Grand Rapids: Baker Book House, 1981), especially 185–231 on prophecy, narrative, and poetry; and Gordon D. Fee and Douglas Stuart, *How to Read the Bible for All Its Worth: A Guide to Understanding the Bible* (Grand Rapids: Zondervan Publishing House, 1982).

10. See Genesis 2:4; 5:1; 6:9; 10:1; 11:10; 11:27; 25:12; 25:19; 36:1; 36:9; 37:2; also R. K. Harrison, *Introduction to the Old Testament* (Grand Rapids: William B. Eerdmans Publishing Company, 1969), 542.

11. See Judges 2:10–23; 3:7–11, and key phrases in 3:12; 4:1; 6:1; 8:33; 10:6; 13:1; 17:6; 18:1; 19:1; 21:25.

12. *Webster's 7th New Collegiate Dictionary* (Springfield, Mass.: G & C Merriam Company, 1965), 894.

13. See Walter Kaiser, *Towards an Exegetical Theology* (Grand Rapids: Baker Book House, 1981), 165–181; George Zemek, "Grammatical Analysis and Expository Preaching," in *Rediscovering Expository Preaching: Balancing the Science and Art of Biblical Exposition,* John MacArthur Jr. and the Master's Seminary Faculty (Dallas: Word Publishing, 1992), 154–176; Gordon D. Fee, *New Testament Exegesis: A Handbook for Students and Pastors* (Philadelphia: Westminster Press, 1983), 60–82.

14. Textbooks and special studies covering grammatical analysis and exegesis will offer methods of outlining and diagramming. Such procedures force the student to consider every word, describe every word grammatically, and relate every word to the flow of words within the sentence(s). One must be careful, at the same time, not to lose the feel and "flow" of the text and its cumulative impact as a whole. The following helps in diagramming were provided by Dr. Donald A. Hagner in a Greek exegesis class too many years ago, 1976!

15. We use ten hours as a starting figure for preparation time.

16. Concerning basic issues in hermeneutics, see E. D. Hirsch Jr., *Validity in Interpretation* (New Haven and London: Yale University Press, 1967); for basic issues in biblical hermeneutics, see Bernard Ramm, *Protestant Biblical Interpretation* (Grand Rapids: Baker Book House, 1970); Henry A. Virkler, *Hermeneutics: Principles and Processes of Biblical Interpretation* (Grand Rapids: Baker Book House, 1981); Gordon D. Fee and Douglas Stuart, *How to Read the Bible for All Its Worth: A Guide to Understanding the Bible* (Grand Rapids: Zondervan Publishing House, 1982); J. Robertson McQuilkin, *Understanding and Applying the Bible* (Chicago: Moody Press, 1983); Earl D. Radmacher and Robert D. Preus, eds., *Hermeneutics, Inerrancy, and the Bible* (Grand Rapids: Zondervan Publishing House, 1984); Duane A. Garrett and Richard R. Melick Jr., eds., *Authority and Interpretation: A Baptist Perspective* (Grand Rapids: Baker Book House, 1987). Two books that cover recent scholarship in the areas of hermeneutical discussion, theory, and practice are by Anthony C. Thiselton, *The Two Horizons: New Testament Hermeneutics and Philosophical Description with Special Reference to Heidegger, Bultmann, Gadamer and Wittgenstein* (Grand Rapids: William B. Eerdmans Publishing Company, 1980), and *New Horizons in Hermeneutics: The Theory and Practice of Transforming Biblical Reading* (Grand Rapids: Zondervan Publishing House, 1992). A study of common problems in the exegetical process is provided by D. A. Carson, *Exegetical Fallacies* (Grand Rapids: Baker Book House, 1996). A work that relates genre interpretation to preaching is Sidney Greidanus, *The Modern Preacher and the Ancient Text: Interpreting and Preaching Biblical Literature* (Grand Rapids: William B. Eerdmans Publishing Company, 1988).

17. *Toward an Exegetical Theology* (Grand Rapids: Baker Book House, 1981), 134–140.

18. We borrow these helpful descriptive words from V. Phillips Long and his lecture material presented at The Stephen Olford Center for Biblical Preaching. Dr. Long is professor of Old Testament at Covenant Theological Seminary in St. Louis, Missouri. Dr. Long has pointed out key features of Hebrew narrative in *The Reign and Rejection of King Saul: A Case for Literary and Theological Coherence* (Atlanta, Ga.: Scholars Press, 1989), SBLDS 118. See also, George L. Klein, ed., *Reclaiming the Prophetic Mantle: Preaching the Old Testament Faithfully* (Nashville: Broadman Press, 1992), and Thomas G. Long, *Preaching and the Literary Forms of the Bible* (Philadelphia: Fortress Press, 1989).

19. See also the diagram on page 234. The essential truths or principles will become the basis of the message to be preached. Later, they will receive homiletical "shaping."

20. For example, consider the directives concerning sacrificial activities and offerings in Leviticus. As New Testament believers, we are not called to practice these sacrifices, but a study of these Scriptures teaches us much about the character of God, God's provision for cleansing and holiness, the need for holiness, and they point to the sacrifice of Christ.

21. For example, a text like John 15:1–17 indicates God's desire and design for fruitfulness as disciples abide in Christ. An aspect of this abiding is the role of Christ's words and obedience to His commands.

22. See Bryan Chapell, *Christ-Centered Preaching: Redeeming the Expository Sermon* (Grand Rapids: Baker Book House, 1994), 267-286.

23. Ibid., 267–269, 280–286.

24. Ibid., 280–286.

25. Ibid., 280.

26. For expository treatments of this text, see: Stephen Olford, *The Grace of Giving* (Memphis, Tenn.: Encounter Ministries, Inc., 1990), 37–78.

27. *Toward an Exegetical Theology* (Grand Rapids: Baker Book House, 1981), 152.

28. Ibid., 161.

29. Ibid.

30. Ibid.

31. We see this approach to principlization as different from what Ramesh Richard warns against in his appendix "The Perils of Principlization" in *Scripture Sculpture: A Do-It-Yourself Manual for Biblical Preaching.* (Grand Rapids: Baker Books, 1995), 163-168. Dr. Richard is concerned with that abstraction of principles that reduces the text to a source for moralism and "truths." In essence, the "factual character" of the text is lost, and the preacher does not really let the text dictate the message to be preached. Richard mentions a number of problems with this method. He uses the term *contemporization* in his helpful book/manual, rather than *principlization.*

Chapter 9: The Preacher and Preparation: Organization, pages 139–155

1. See chap. 6, "The Preacher and Exposition," for previous development of these organizational questions. We have already used these categories to help us shape the meaning and teaching of the text. Here we use them to make the transition into the shape of the message itself.

2. See the helpful chapter, "Central Ideas, Outlines and Titles" by Donald G. McDougall in *Rediscovering Expository Preaching: Balancing the Science and Art*

of Biblical Exposition by John MacArthur Jr. and the Master's Seminary Faculty (Dallas: Word Publishing, 1992), 225–241. See also, H. C. Brown Jr., H. Gordon Clinard, Jesse J. Northcutt, Al Fasol, *Steps to the Sermon: An Eight-Step Plan for Preaching with Confidence,* rev. ed., (Nashville: Broadman & Holman Publishers, 1996), 64–76.

3. Haddon W. Robinson, *Biblical Preaching: The Development and Delivery of Expository Messages* (Grand Rapids: Baker Book House, 1980), 31–44.

4. G. Campbell Morgan, *Preaching* (London: Marshall, Morgan & Scott, Ltd., 1937), 18.

5. Bryan Chapell, *Christ-Centered Preaching: Redeeming the Expository Sermon* (Grand Rapids: Baker Book House, 1994), 35–48.

6. McDougall, *Rediscovering Expository Preaching,* 229.

7. Ibid., 232.

8. Ibid., 231.

9. Jerry Vines, *A Practical Guide to Sermon Preparation* (Chicago: Moody Press, 1985), 114.

10. Farris Whitesell, *Power in Expository Preaching* (Old Tappan, N.J.: Revell, 1963), 60, quoted in Vines, *A Practical Guide to Sermon Preparation,* 116–117.

11. Ramesh Richard defines expository preaching as "the contemporization of the central proposition of a biblical text that is derived from proper methods of interpretation and declared through effective means of communication to inform minds, instruct hearts, and influence behavior toward godliness." *Scripture Sculpture: A Do-It-Yourself Manual for Biblical Preaching* (Grand Rapids: Baker Book House, 1995), 17. The task of "contemporization" involves taking "what was written centuries ago and [contemporizing] it for present-day audiences" (p. 18).

12. Jerry Vines, *A Practical Guide to Sermon Preparation,* 114–115. Note reference to Walter C. Kaiser Jr., *Toward an Exegetical Theology* (Grand Rapids: Baker Book House, 1982), 152.

13. We prefer using numeral rather than letters for homiletical outlines. Numerical sequence is easy to express in oral delivery.

14. *Webster's New World Dictionary of the American Language 2nd College Edition,* David B. Guralnik, ed. (New York: World Publishing, 1970, 1972), s. v. "memorable."

15. Charles W. Koller, *Expository Preaching Without Notes* (Grand Rapids: Baker Book House, 1962), 93. Dr. Koller also encourages 1) *the use of visual aids in outlining,* 2) *brevity of statement,* 3) *statement of parallel points in parallel form,* 4) *observance of the natural laws of memory,* pp. 91–96. The fourth point includes limiting the points of a message to five or less.

16. Warren W. Wiersbe, *Preaching and Teaching with Imagination: The Quest for Biblical Ministry* (Wheaton, Ill.: Victor Books/SP Publications, Inc., 1994). The whole book addresses this matter.

Chapter 10: The Preacher and Preparation: Finalization, pages 156–182

1. Haddon W. Robinson, *Biblical Preaching: The Development and Delivery of Expository Messages* (Grand Rapids: Baker Book House, 1980), 115–132.

2. For help in this area, consult Warren W. Wiersbe's *Preaching and Teaching with Imagination: The Quest for Biblical Ministry* (Wheaton, Ill.: Victor Books, 1994).

3. For a helpful discussion of illustrations within the context of expository preaching, see Bryan Chapell's *Christ-Centered Preaching: Redeeming the Expository Sermon,* (Grand Rapids: Baker Book House, 1994), especially chap. 7,

"The Pattern of Illustration," 162–197.

4. Dr. Chapell's discussion of application in *Christ-Centered Preaching* is very helpful. See his chapter, "The Practice of Application," pp. 198–225. Quotation above from p. 220.

5. Jay E. Adams, *Preaching with Purpose: The Urgent Task of Homiletics* (Grand Rapids: Zondervan Publishing House, 1982), 111.

6. Ibid., p. 112.

7. Chapell, *Christ-Centered Preaching*, 16–33.

8. We have devoted chapters 12 and 14 to the work of the Holy Spirit in relation to preaching.

Chapter 11: The Preacher and Communication, pages 183–212

1. Duane Litfin, *St. Paul's Theology of Proclamation: 1 Corinthians 1–4 and Greco-Roman Rhetoric* (Cambridge: Cambridge University Press, 1994).

2. Ibid., 247.

3. Ibid., 248.

4. Ibid.

5. Walter Bauer, William Arndt, F. Wilbur Gingrich, *A Greek-English Lexicon of the New Testament and other Early Christian Literature* (Chicago: University of Chicago Press, 1957), 860.

6. Bauer, Arndt, Gingrich, *Greek-English Lexicon*, 635–636.

7. Ephesians 6:10ff.

8. We focus on these two aspects of the prayer requests, recognizing that Paul expressed other concerns as well.

9. See Dr. Litfin's work (cited in note 1) for a full discussion of Paul's perspective on his preaching as set forth in 1 Corinthians.

10. G. Campbell Morgan, *Preaching* (London: Marshall, Morgan, & Scott, Ltd., 1937), 18.

11. See chap. 6, "The Preacher and Exposition."

12. For helpful instruction concerning the public reading of Scripture, see Thomas Edward McComiskey's *Reading Scripture in Public: A Guide for Preachers and Lay Readers* (Grand Rapids: Baker Book House, 1991).

13. See chap. 10, "The Preacher and Preparation: Finalization."

14. This will be discussed in chap. 13, "The Preacher and Proclamation."

15. For an explanation of "Full Vocal Production" see Al Fasol, *A Guide to Self-Improvement in Sermon Delivery* (Grand Rapids: Baker Book House, 1983), 25–39; also Jerry Vines, *A Guide to Effective Sermon Delivery* (Chicago: Moody Press, 1986), 1–57.

16. See Fasol, *Guide to Self-Improvement,* 41–56, and Vines, *Guide to Effective Sermon Delivery,* 23–30.

17. See chap. 14, "The Preacher and Comprehension."

18. Fasol, *Guide to Self-Improvement,* 58–72.

19. Fasol, *Guide to Self-Improvement,* 58.

20. Ibid.

21. Ibid., 58–59. Dr. Fasol's book gives further advice concerning this aspect of vocal presentation.

22. We are not referring here to full dramatic presentations. That is another subject and is really outside the focus of this book.

23. We have devoted chapter 15 to this matter of application.

24. See page 251.

25. See chap. 12, "The Preacher and Consecration."

Chapter 12: The Preacher and Consecration, pages 214–228

1. Tony Sargent, *The Sacred Anointing* (Wheaton, Ill.: Crossway Books, 1994), 29.

2. A. T. Robertson, *Word Pictures in the New Testament,* vol. 3 (New York: Harper & Brothers), 145.

3. Marvin R. Vincent, *Word Studies in the New Testament,* vol. 3 (Grand Rapids: William B. Eerdmans Publishing Co., 1946, 1957), 364.

4. Gordon D. Fee, *God's Empowering Presence: The Holy Spirit in the Letters of Paul* (Peabody, Mass.: Hendrickson Publishers, Inc., 1994), 294.

5. Paul Lee Tan, *Encyclopedia of 7,700 Illustrations* (Rockville, Md.: Assurance Publishers, 1979), 1368.

6. G. Campbell Morgan, *The Gospel According to Luke* (New York: Fleming H. Revell Co., 1931), 144.

7. Leon Morris, *The Gospel According to St. Luke, Tyndale New Testament Commentaries* (Grand Rapids: William B. Eerdmans Publishing Co., 1974), 196.

8. W. E. Vine, *Expository Dictionary of Biblical Words* (Nashville: Thomas Nelson Publishers, Inc.), 291. Used by permission.

9. Andrew Bonar, *Robert Murray M'Cheyne* (London: The Banner of Truth Trust, 1960); quoted in Tony Sargent, *The Sacred Anointing* (Wheaton: Crossway Books, 1994), 128.

10. G. Campbell Morgan, *Preaching* (London: Marshall Morgan & Scott, Ltd., 1937), 18.

11. Ibid., 49.

12. Ibid., 53–56.

13. D. Martyn Lloyd-Jones, *Preaching and Preachers* (Grand Rapids: Zondervan Publishing House, 1971), 325. Used by permission.

14. Taken from *The Expositor's Bible Commentary,* vol. 3 edited by Frank E. Gaebelein, 1074. Copyright © 1992 by The Zondervan Corporation. Used by permission of Zondervan Publishing House.

15. While the earliest and most reliable manuscripts and other ancient witnesses do not have John 7:53–8:11, the story told is typical of our Lord's dealing with broken lives.

16. William C. Robinson, *Baker's Dictionary of Theology* (Grand Rapids: Baker Book House, 1960), 329.

17. Vance Havner in *Moody Monthly.* Quoted in *Knight's Master Book of New Illustrations,* Walter B. Knight, comp. (Grand Rapids: William B. Eerdmans Publishing Co., 1956), 504–505.

18. D. Martyn Lloyd-Jones, *Preaching and Preachers* (Grand Rapids: Zondervan Publishing House, 1971), 305. Used by permission.

19. Taken from *Ablaze for God* by Wesley L. Duewel. Copyright © 1989 by Wesley L. Duewel. Used by permission of Zondervan Publishing House, 302-303.

Chapter 13: The Preacher and Proclamation, pages 229–240

1. NU-Text, 26th ed.

2. W. E. Vine, *I Corinthians* (London: Oliphants Limited, 1951), 27–28.

3. Roger E. Olson, "Scandalous No More?" review of *A Passion for Truth, Christianity Today* 40, no. 7, (17 June 1996): 47.

4. George R. Beasley-Murray, *Word Biblical Commentary* [John], vol. 36 (Dallas: Word Books, 1987), 16.

5. Phillips Brooks, *The Joy of Preaching* (Grand Rapids: Kregel Publications, 1989).

6. *Preaching and Preachers*, p. 82, where Dr. Lloyd-Jones also mentions the way one of his predecessors J. A. Hutton "believed that a preacher should preach with the whole of his body"; cf. *The Puritans*, p. 117, where he quotes Demosthenes and comments on the preaching style of Whitefield. Quoted by Tony Sargent in his book *The Sacred Anointing: The Preaching of Dr. Martyn Lloyd-Jones* (Wheaton, Ill.: Crossway Books, 1994), 187.

7. J. C. Macaulay, *Expository Commentary on Hebrews* (Chicago: Moody Press, 1978), 253.

8. Martyn Lloyd-Jones, *Revival*, 295. Quoted in Tony Sargent, *The Sacred Anointing* (Wheaton, Ill.: Crossway Books, 1994), 79. Used by permission.

9. Edwin Newman, *Strictly Speaking: Will America Be the Death of English?* (Indianapolis: Bobbs-Merrill Company, 1974).

10. Edwin Newman, *A Civil Tongue* (Indianapolis: Bobbs-Merrill Company, 1975).

Chapter 14: The Preacher and Comprehension, pages 241–250

1. Eddie Gibbs, *In Name Only: Tackling the Problem of Nominal Christianity* (Wheaton, Ill.: Victor Books, Bridge Point, 1994), dust jacket.

2. G. Campbell Morgan, *The Corinthian Letters of Paul* (Westwood, N.J.: Fleming H. Revell Co., 1946), 46.

3. William Barclay, *The Letters to the Corinthians* (Edinburgh: St. Andrew Press, 1958), 29.

4. Arnold A. Dallimore, "George Whitefield, English Evangelist." Taken from John D. Woodbridge, ed., *Great Leaders of the Churstian Church* (Chicago: Moody Press, 1988), 295.

5. Ibid.

6. Barclay, *Corinthians*, 29.

7. Ibid.

8. James Hope Moulton and George Milligan, *The Vocabulary of the Greek New Testament* (Grand Rapids: Wm B. Eerdmans Publishing Col, 1930), 252.

9. Paige Patterson, *The Troubled Triumphant Church* (Nashville: Thomas Nelson, 1983), 38–39. Used by permission.

Chapter 15: The Preacher and Application, pages 251–260

1. John R. W. Stott, "Creating the Bridge: An Interview with John R. W. Stott," interview by R. Albert Mohler Jr., *Preaching* 4, no. 5 (March-April 1989): 4–5.

2. Haddon W. Robinson, *We Believe in Biblical Preaching* (Dallas: Dallas Theological Seminary, 1972), 13.

3. Al Martin, *What's Wrong with Preaching Today?* (Grand Rapids: Reformed Fellowship, n.d.), 20.

4. W. E. Vine, et al., *Vine's Expository Dictionary of Biblical Words* (Nashville: Thomas Nelson, 1985), 297. Used by permission.

5. Stott, *Preaching*, 4–5.

Chapter 16: The Preacher and Invitation, pages 261–274

1. John R. W. Stott, *The Preacher's Portrait: Some New Testament Word Studies* (London: The Tyndale Press, 1961), 48, 50.

2. See Iain H. Murray, *The Invitation System* (Edinburgh: Banner of Truth Trust, 1984).

3. R. V. G. Tasker, *The Second Epistle of Paul to the Corinthians, Tyndale New Testament Commentaries* (The Tyndale Press; reprinted ed., Grand Rapids: William B. Eerdmans Publishing Co., 1977), 91.

4. Alexander Maclaren, *Expositions of Holy Scripture on 2 Corinthians*, vol. 9 (Grand Rapids: William B. Eerdmans Publishing Co., 1959), 382.

5. Leon Morris, *The Revelation of St. John, Tyndale New Testament Commentaries* (The Tyndale Press; reprint ed., Grand Rapids: William B. Eerdmans Publishing Co., 1976), 84.

6. Quoted by Dr. Kendell Easley in a lecture on "Preaching Gospel Literature" delivered July 18, 1995, at the Stephen Olford Center for Biblical Preaching, Memphis, Tenn.

7. Ibid.

8. For a "blueprint" of the aftermeeting, study with "anointed eyes" Peter's: Proclamation (Acts 2:1–14); Invitation (Acts 2:36); Explanation (Acts 2:37–39). The Explanation was his aftermeeting in response to the heart-cry—"What shall we do?" (Acts 2:37).

9. A careful study of Peter's invitation on the day of Pentecost reveals the three essential elements we have discussed above: 1) decision (Acts 2:28–40), 2) confession (Acts 2:41), and 3) instruction (Acts 2:42).

10. David B. Barrett, ed., *World Christian Encyclopedia: A Comparative Study of Churches and Religion in the Modern World A.D. 1900–2000* (Nairobi, Kenya: Oxford University Press, 1982), p.v.

11. Dean M. Kelley, *Why Conservative Churches Are Growing* (New York: Harper & Row, 1972), 1.

12. Gordon D. Fee, "The Soteriological Spirit," *God's Empowering Presence: The Holy Spirit in the Letters of Paul* (Peabody, Mass.: Hendrickson Publishers, Inc, 1994), 853.

13. Quoted from *Evangelical Newsletter* 9, no. 10 (Philadelphia: May 14, 1982).

14. Ibid.

15. William Sargent, *The Battle for the Mind* (London: William Heinemann Ltd., 1957).

16. Taken from *The Expositor's Bible Commentary*, vol. 8, edited by Frank E. Gaebelein. Copyright © 1984 by the Zondervan Corporation. Used by permission of Zondervan Publishing House.

17. Tasker, *Second Corinthians*, 89.

Chapter 17: The Preacher and Conservation, pages 275–283

1. David B. Barrett, ed. *World Christian Encyclopedia: A Comparative Study of Churches and Religion in the Modern World A.D. 1900–2000* (Nairobi, Kenya: Oxford University Press, 1982), v.

2. J. C. Macaulay, *A Devotional Commentary on the Acts of the Apostles* (Grand Rapids: William B. Eerdmans Publishing Co., 1946), 37–40.

Chapter 18: The Preacher and Inculcation, pages 284–293

1. Kent Hughes, *Preach the Word [Colossians]* (Wheaton: Crossway Books, 1989), 61.

2. Taken from *The Expositor's Bible Commentary*, vol. 11, edited by Frank E.

Gaebelein, 198. Copyright © 1978 by The Zondervan Corporation. Used by permission of Zondervan Publishing House.

Chapter 19: The Preacher and Motivation, pages 294–303

1. Quoted in *Living Quotations for Christians*, Copyright © 1974 by Sherwood E. Wirt and Kersten Beckstrom (New York: Harper & Row, Publishers), 160. Used by permission.
2. Ibid., 161.
3. James Denney, *The Second Epistle to the Corinthians* (*The Expositor's Bible*), 1894. Quoted in *Tyndale New Testament Commentaries* (*2 Corinthians*) by R.V.G. Tasker, ed. (Grand Rapids: William B. Eerdmans Publishing Co.), 76.
4. Ibid., 77.
5. Ibid., 80.
6. G. Campbell Morgan, *The Corinthians Letters* (London: Charles Higham & Son, Ltd., 1947), 157.
7. Archibald Naismith, *2400 Outlines, Notes, Quotes & Anecdotes for Sermons*, vol. 2 (Grand Rapids: Baker Book House, 1975), 234.
8. Murray J. Harris, *The Expositor's Bible Commentary*, vol. 10, edited by Frank E. Gaebelein, 350. Copyright © 1976 by The Zondervan Corporation. Used by permission of Zondervan Publishing House.
9. Naismith, *2400 Outlines*, 47.
10. Translation by W. Harold Mare, *The Expositor's Bible Commentary*, vol. 10, 243.
11. Samuel Harris, quoted in Naismith, *2400 Outlines*, 243.

Conclusion, pages 304–311

1. *Preaching the Word of God* by Stephen F. Olford, copyright © 1984, revised 1989. Available from Encounter Ministries, Inc., P. O. Box 757800, Memphis, TN 38175-7800. A call for biblical preaching and an anointed tongue, it challenges pastors to restore expository preaching to its proper place in the church.

Appendix A: The Preacher and Worship, pages 312–322

1. Joseph M. Stowell, "In Spirit and in Truth," *Moody*, April 1994, 4.
2. Taken from *The Expositor's Bible Commentary*, vol. 9 edited by Frank E. Gaebelein, 57. Copyright © 1991 by The Zondervan Corporation. Used by permission of Zondervan Publishing House.
3. W. E. Vine, *Expository Dictionary of Biblical Words* (Nashville: Thomas Nelson Publishers, Inc., 1985), 686.
4. Kent Hughes, *Behold the Lamb* (Wheaton, Ill.: Victor Books, 1984), 72.
5. Paul S. Rees, "The Art of Preaching as an Act of Worship," from the book *A Passion for Preaching* by David L. Olford, comp. (Nadshville: Thomas Nelson Publishers, 1989), 111–113.
6. A. W. Tozer, "Worship: The Missing Jewel" booklet (Camp Hill, Pa.: Christian Publications, 1992), 6.
7. See chap. 16, "The Preacher and Invitation."
8. From a precis on worship entitled "The Forgotten Priority" by J. C. Macaulay in *The Calvary Messenger*, the Sunday bulletin for January 16, 1977, Calvary Baptist Church, New York City.

9. Taken from *Vine's Expository Dictionary of Biblical Words* by W. E. Vine, Merrill F. Unger, and William White, Jr., eds. Copyright © 1961, 1985 by Thomas Nelson, Inc. Publishers, 543.

Appendix B: The Preacher and Music, pages 323–332

1. William Barclay, *Letters to the Galatians and Ephesians* (Edinburgh: Saint Andrew Press, 1954), 197.
2. Lee G. Olson, "Music in the Worship Service," *The Alliance Witness,* 3 June 1968, 8.
3. Ibid.
4. Ibid.
5. Ibid., 8, 21.

Appendix C: The Preacher and Evangelism, pages 333–344

1. For further information concerning Stephen Olford's practical course (#2120), contact Moody Bible Institute Center for External Studies, 820 North LaSalle Blvd., Chicago, IL 60610. This course consists of twelve lessons and four exams and can be used by individuals, Sunday school classes, or Bible study groups. Special discount rate for groups of eight or more individuals. Students receive certificate from MBI upon completion of the course.

Another course is Evangelism Explosion. For additional information write to Dr. D. James Kennedy, Coral Ridge Presbyterian Church, 5555 N. Federal Highway, Fort Lauderdale, FL 33308.
2. F. D. Coggan, *The Ministry of the Word* (London: The Canterbury Press, 1945), 11.
3. Quoted in Coggan, *The Ministry of the Word,* 19.
4. Ibid., 66–67.
5. Ibid., 62–63.
6. Ibid., 33.
7. Ibid., 61.
8. Charles John Ellicott, *Ellicott's Commentary on the Whole Bible,* vol. 7 (Grand Rapids: Zondervan Publishing House, n.d), 292.
9. Thomas Goodwin. Quoted in Coggan, *The Ministry of the Word,* 19.
10. William Barclay, *The Letters to the Corinthians* (Philadelphia: The Westminster Press, 1956), 27.
11. Quoted in Coggan, *The Ministry of the Word,* 19.
12. J. I. Packer, "The Lost Word," in *God Has Spoken* (Downers Grove: InterVarsity Press, 1979), 20.

Appendix D: The Preacher and Romas, pages 345–349

1. This is an edited version of an article that first appeared in *The Preacher* newsletter/magazine, vol. 4 no. 1, published by The Institute for Biblical Preaching, Memphis, Tenn., 1985. Printed with permission. For a fuller treatment of Romans 12:1–2 from this perspective see David Olford's "Romans 12:1–2: The Gospel and Renewal" in *Faces of Renewal: Studies in Honor of Stanley M. Horton,* Paul Elbert, ed. (Peabody, Mass.: Hendrickson, 1988), 20–47.

SELECTIVE BIBLIOGRAPHY

Adams, J. E. *Preaching with Purpose: The Urgent Task of Homiletics.* Grand Rapids: Zondervan Publishing House, 1982.

Arthur, Kay. *How to Study Your Bible.* Chattanooga, Tenn.: Precept Ministries of Reach Out, Inc., 1985, 1986, 1987.

Bennett, Bill. *Thirty Minutes to Raise The Dead.* Nashville: Thomas Nelson Publishers, 1991.

Blackwood, Andrew W. *Expository Preaching for Today.* New York: Abingdon Press, 1953.

_____. *The Preparation of Sermons.* New York: Abingdon Press, 1948.

Bodey, Richard Allen. *If I Had Only One Sermon to Preach.* Grand Rapids: Baker Books, 1994.

_____. *Inside the Sermon.* Grand Rapids: Baker Book House, 1990.

Braga, James. *How to Prepare Bible Messages.* Portland, Oreg.: Multnomah Press, 1981.

Broadus, John A. *On the Preparation and Delivery of Sermons,* 1926. Rev. ed. by Jesse Burton Weatherspoon. New York: Harper and Row, 1943.

Brooks, Phillips. *The Joy of Preaching.* Grand Rapids: Kregel Publications, 1989.

Brown, H. C., Jr., H. Gordon Clinard, Jesse J. Northcutt, and Al Fasol. *Steps to the Sermon.* Nashville: Broadman & Holman Publishers, 1996.

Brown, Steve, Haddon Robinson, and William Willimon. *A Voice in the Wilderness.* Sisters, Oreg.: Multnomah Books, 1993.

Bryson, Harold T. *Expository Preaching.* Nashville: Broadman & Holman Publishers, 1995.

Bugg, Charles B. *Preaching from the Inside Out.* Nashville: Broadman Press, 1992.

Carson, Don. *Exegetical Fallacies.* 2d ed. Grand Rapids: Baker Book House, 1996.

Chapell, Bryan. *Christ-Centered Preaching: Redeeming the Expository Sermon.* Grand Rapids: Baker Book House, 1994.

Craddock, Fred B. *Preaching.* Nashville: Abingdon Press, 1985.

Duduit, Michael, ed. *Handbook of Contemporary Preaching.* Nashville: Broadman Press, 1992.

Evans, William. *How to Prepare Sermons.* Chicago: Moody Press, 1964.

Farra, Harry. *The Sermon Doctor: Prescriptions for Successful Preaching.* Grand Rapids: Baker Book House, 1989.

Fasol, Al. *Essentials for Biblical Preaching: An Introduction to Basic Sermon Preparation.* Grand Rapids: Baker Book House, 1989.

_____. *A Guide to Self-Improvement in Sermon Delivery.* Grand Rapids: Baker Book House, 1983.

Fee, Gordon. *New Testament Exegesis: A Handbook for Students and Pastors.* Philadelphia: The Westminster Press, 1983.

Fee, Gordon, and Douglas Stuart. *How to Read the Bible for All Its Worth: A Guide to Understanding the Bible.* Grand Rapids: Zondervan Publishing House, 1982.

Forbes, James. *The Holy Spirit and Preaching.* Nashville: Abingdon Press, 1989.

Green, Christopher, and David Jackman, eds. *When God's Voice Is Heard.* Leicester, England: Inter-Varsity Press, 1995.

Green, Michael P., ed. *Illustrations for Biblical Preaching.* Grand Rapids: Baker Book House, 1982, 1985, 1989.

Greidanus, Sidney. *The Modern Preacher and the Ancient Text: Interpreting and Preaching Biblical Literature.* Grand Rapids: Wm. B. Eerdmans, 1988.

Hirsch, E. D., Jr. *Validity in Interpretation.* New Haven, Conn. and London: Yale University Press, 1967.

Hybels, Bill, Stuart Briscoe, and Haddon Robinson. *Mastering Contemporary Preaching.* Portland, Oreg.: Multnomah Press and Christianity Today, Inc., 1989.

Jowett, John H. *The Preacher: His Life and Work.* Grand Rapids: Baker Book House, 1968.

Kaiser, Walter C., Jr. *Toward an Exegetical Theology: Biblical Exegesis for Preaching and Teaching.* Grand Rapids: Baker Book House, 1981.

Kinlaw, Dennis F. *Preaching in the Spirit.* Grand Rapids: Zondervan Publishing House, 1985.

Klein, George L. *Reclaiming the Prophetic Mantle.* Nashville: Broadman Press, 1992.

Knox, John. *Contemporary Preaching.* Nashville: Abingdon Press, n.d.

Koller, Charles W. *Expository Preaching Without Notes*. Grand Rapids: Baker Book House, 1962.

Lewis, Ralph L. *Persuasive Preaching Today*. Wilmore, Ky.: Asbury Theological Seminary, 1977.

Lewis, Ralph L., with Gregg Lewis. *Inductive Preaching: Helping People to Listen*. Westchester, Ill.: Crossway Good News Pub., 1983.

Liefeld, Walter L. *New Testament Exposition: From Text to Sermon*. Grand Rapids: Zondervan Publishing House, 1984.

Litfin, A. Duane. *Public Speaking*. Grand Rapids: Baker Book House, 1981.

_____. *St. Paul's Theology of Proclamation*. Cambridge, Mass.: Cambridge University Press, 1994. Society for New Testament Studies Monograph Series 79.

Litfin, A. Duane, and Haddon W. Robinson, eds. *Recent Homiletical Thought: An Annotated Bibliography, Vol. 2, 1966–1979*. Grand Rapids: Baker Book House, 1983.

Lloyd-Jones, D. Martyn. *Preaching and Preachers*. Grand Rapids: Zondervan Publishing House, 1971.

Logan, Samuel T., Jr., ed. *The Preacher and Preaching: Reviving the Art in the Twentieth Century*. Phillipsburg, N.J.: Presbyterian and Reformed Pub. Co., 1986.

Long, Thomas G. *Preaching and the Literary Forms of the Bible*. Philadelphia: Fortress Press, 1985.

MacArthur, John, Jr. and the Master's Seminary Faculty. *Rediscovering Expository Preaching: Balancing the Science and the Art of Biblical Exposition*. Dallas: Word Publishing, 1992.

Marshall, I. Howard, ed. *New Testament Interpretation: Essays on Principles and Methods*. Grand Rapids: William B. Eerdmans Publishing Co., 1977.

McComiskey, Thomas Edward. *Reading Scripture in Public*. Grand Rapids: Baker Book House, 1991.

McDill, Wayne. *The Twelve Essential Skills for Great Preaching*. Nashville: Broadman & Holman Publishers, 1994.

McQuilkin, J. Robertson. *Understanding and Applying the Bible*. Chicago: Moody Press, 1983.

Miller, Calvin. *The Empowered Communicator*. Nashville: Broadman & Holman Publishers, 1994.

Miller, Donald G. *The Way to Biblical Preaching*. New York: Abingdon Press, 1957.

Morgan, G. Campbell. *Preaching*. Old Tappan, N.J.: Fleming H. Revell, Co., 1937.

Naismith, Archibald. *2400 Outlines, Notes, Quotes, and Anecdotes for Sermons*. Grand Rapids: Baker Book House, 1967.

Olford, David L., compiler. *A Passion for Preaching: Reflections on the Art of Preaching* (Various Contributors). Nashville: Thomas Nelson Publishers, 1989.

Olford, Stephen F. *Preaching the Word of God*. Memphis, Tenn.: Encounter Ministries, Inc., 1989.

Perry, Lloyd M. *Biblical Preaching for Today's World*. Chicago: Moody Press, 1980.

_____. *A Manual for Biblical Preaching*. Grand Rapids: Baker Book House, 1965.

Perry, Lloyd M., and Faris D. Whitesell. *Variety in Your Preaching*. Westwood, N.J.: Fleming H. Revell Co., 1954.

Perry, Lloyd M., and Warren W. Wiersbe. *The Wycliffe Handbook of Preaching and Preachers*. Chicago: Moody Press, 1984.

Phillips, John. *Bible Explorer's Guide*. Neptune, N.J.: Loizeaux Brothers, Inc., 1987.

Piper, John. *The Supremacy of God in Preaching*. Grand Rapids: Baker Book House, 1989.

Pitt-Watson, Ian. *A Primer for Preachers*. Grand Rapids: Baker Book House, 1986.

Radmacher, Earl D., and Robert D. Preus, eds. *Hermeneutics, Inerrancy, and the Bible: Papers from ICBI Summit II*. Grand Rapids: Zondervan Publishing House, 1984.

Ramm, Bernard. *Protestant Biblical Interpretation: A Textbook on Hermeneutics*. Grand Rapids: Baker Book House, 1970.

Richard, Ramesh. *Scripture Sculpture*. Grand Rapids: Baker Books, 1995.

Robinson, Haddon W. *Biblical Preaching: The Development and Delivery of Expository Messages*. Grand Rapids: Baker Book House, 1980.

_____. *Biblical Sermons: How Twelve Preachers Apply the Principles of "Biblical Preaching."* Grand Rapids: Baker Book House, 1989.

Sangster, W. E. *The Craft of the Sermon: Its Construction and Illustration*. Grand Rapids: Baker Book House, 1981.

Skinner, Craig. *The Teaching Ministry of the Pulpit*. Grand Rapids: Baker Book House, 1973.

Spurgeon, C. H. *Great Pulpit Masters*. Old Tappan, N.J.: Fleming H. Revell Co., 1949.

_____. *Lectures to My Students*. Grand Rapids: Zondervan Publishing House, 1954.

Stewart, James S. *Heralds of God*. London: Hodder & Stoughton, 1946.

Stott, John R. W. *Between Two Worlds: The Art of Preaching in the Twentieth Century*. Grand Rapids: William B. Eerdmans Publishing Co., 1982.

_____. *The Preacher's Portrait*. London: Tyndale Press, 1961.

Streett, R. Alan. *The Effective Invitation*. Grand Rapids: Kregel Publications, 1984.

Stuart, Douglas. *Old Testament Exegesis: A Primer for Students and Pastors*. 2nd edition. Philadelphia: The Westminster Press, 1984.

Thompson, William D. *Preaching Biblically: Exegesis and Interpretation*. Nashville: Abingdon, 1981.

Unger, Merrill F. *Principles of Expository Preaching*. Grand Rapids: Zondervan Publishing House, 1955.

Vines, Jerry. *A Guide to Effective Sermon Delivery*. Chicago: Moody Press, 1986.

_____. *A Practical Guide to Sermon Preparation*. Chicago: Moody Press, 1985.

Virkler, Henry A. *Hermeneutics: Principles and Processes of Biblical Interpretation*. Grand Rapids: Baker Book House, 1981.

Webber, F. R. *A History of Preaching in Britain and America*. 3 vols. Milwaukee, Wis.: Northwestern Publishing House, 1952–1957.

White, Douglas M. *The Excellence of Exposition*. Neptune, N.J.: Loizeaux Brothers, Inc., 1977.

White, R. E. O. *A Guide to Preaching*. London: Marshall-Pickering, n.d.

Whitesell, Faris D. *Great Expository Sermons*. Old Tappan, N.J.: Fleming H. Revell Co., n.d.

_____. *Power in Expository Preaching*. Westwood, N.J.: Fleming H. Revell Co., 1963.

Wiersbe, Warren W. *Listening to the Giants: A Guide to Good Reading and Preaching*. Grand Rapids: Baker Book House, 1980.

_____. *Preaching and Teaching with Imagination: The Quest for Biblical Ministry*. Wheaton, Ill.: Victor Books, 1994.

Wiersbe, Warren, and David Wiersbe. *The Elements of Preaching: The Art of Biblical Preaching—Clearly and Simply Presented*. Wheaton, Ill.: Tyndale House Pub., 1986.

Wood, A. Skevington. *The Art of Preaching: Message, Method and Motive in Preaching*. Grand Rapids: Zondervan Publishing House, 1964.

BIOGRAPHICAL SKETCHES

D **r. Stephen F. Olford** is founder of the Stephen Olford Center for Biblical Preaching in Memphis, Tennessee, where he is senior lecturer. Born in Africa of missionary parents, he received his formal education in England. In 1953 he became the pastor of Duke Street Baptist Church, Richmond, Surrey. From 1959–1973 he was the senior minister of the famed Calvary Baptist Church of New York City.

He has traveled the world preaching the Word in crusades, at conventions, and at centers of learning. He holds a doctorate in theology and has been awarded a number of honorary degrees. Olford is also the author of numerous books and booklets and has contributed to leading Christian periodicals on both sides of the Atlantic. He and his wife have two sons, Jonathan and David.

D **r. David L. Olford** is president of Encounter Ministries, Inc., and director of studies at the Stephen Olford Center for Biblical Preaching. Dr. Olford has a B.A. and M.A. from Wheaton College (Illinois) and a Ph.D. in Biblical Studies from Sheffield University, Sheffield, England. He is editor of the publication, *The Preacher*, and compiler of the book, *A Passion for Preaching*. Besides his responsibilities of leading and teaching at all institute events, Dr. Olford has taught and preached in numerous countries as well as in the united states. Dr. Olford and his wife, Ellen, have two daughters—Lindsay and Stephanie.

251
OL45

93497

LINCOLN CHRISTIAN COLLEGE AND SEMINARY

3 4711 00094 6014